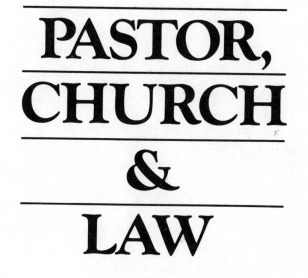

# PASTOR,
# CHURCH
# &
# LAW

# PASTOR,
# CHURCH
# &
# LAW

## Richard R. Hammar

GOSPEL PUBLISHING HOUSE
SPRINGFIELD, MISSOURI

02-0580

This publication is designed to provide accurate and authoritative information in regard to the subject matter covered. It is sold with the understanding that the publisher is not engaged in rendering legal, accounting, or other professional service. If legal advice or other expert assistance is required, the services of a competent professional person should be sought. *From a Declaration of Principles jointly adopted by a Committee of the American Bar Association and a Committee of Publishers and Associations.*

*For my family,*
*Christine, Rachel, and Abe*

# PREFACE

A few years ago I was asked to teach a course on church law at a local seminary. It was not until after I had accepted this invitation that I made an unexpected discovery—no comprehensive book on church law had been written in over fifty years. In retrospect, this discovery should not have been surprising. Churches and clergymen have long enjoyed a privileged position throughout our nation's history. In part, this status derived from the constitutional guarantee of religious freedom. But it derived as well from public deference.

In the latter half of the twentieth century, however, a profound change has occurred. Nearly every privilege enjoyed by churches and clergymen under federal, state, and local law has been challenged in the courts under the First Amendment's nonestablishment of religion clause. Many challenges have been successful. Churches and clergymen suddenly find themselves subject to many laws and regulations that formerly had not applied. The applicability of several other laws is an increasing possibility.

Predictably, much confusion and uncertainty surrounds the application of many of these laws. My objective in writing this book is to help reduce this confusion and uncertainty by providing seminary students, clergymen, attorneys, and accountants with a comprehensive yet readable analysis of the major laws affecting churches and clergymen. My intended audience is diverse. Yet, I have endeavored to present the materials in a manner that will be easily comprehended by those having no familiarity with the law. Technical materials and citations of authority are presented in footnotes, which will assist the attorney and accountant in further understanding and pursuing many of the subjects considered.

Although I have attempted to present the law as it is rather than confuse the reader with a dissertation on how it should be, I have not hesitated to express my opinion when I considered it appropriate. And although I have attempted to confine myself to a strictly legal analysis, I readily confess that I experienced a certain ambivalence in the presentation of some subjects, such as wrongful discharge of clergymen, defamation, or church property disputes, that are as much moral as legal problems.

I am indebted to many colleagues and students whose comments and suggestions led to valuable improvements in this text. Further suggestions and comments are invited. I am especially grateful for the contributions of Clyde L. Hawkins, CPA, who reviewed all of the chapters dealing with taxation, and whose comments were most instructive.

Finally, and most important, I express thanks to my beloved wife, Christine, for her patience and understanding.

RICHARD R. HAMMAR

Springfield, Missouri
May 1983

# CONTENTS

# Part Two—Law and the Church

# Part Three—Church and State

# Part One

## Law and the Pastor

# 1

# DEFINITIONS AND STATUS

## §A. Definitions

The terms *pastor, clergyman,* and *minister* often are used interchangeably. Such usage is perfectly appropriate in most instances. Occasionally, however, it is important to distinguish among these terms, since many state and federal laws apply to only one or some of them. For example, the Military Selective Service Act provides that "[r]egular or duly ordained ministers of religion . . . shall be exempt from training and service."[1] Whether a representative of an organized religion may validly solemnize a marriage depends, in most states, upon his being characterized as a "clergyman,"[2] a "minister,"[3] or a "priest."[4] Confidential communications made to "clergymen,"[5] "ministers,"[6] and "priests"[7] are considered privileged from disclosure in many states.

"Clergymen"[8] and "ministers of the gospel"[9] are excused from jury duty in many states. The exemption is often conditioned upon the timely filing of an

---

[1]50 U.S.C. App. § 456(g).

[2]*See, e.g.,* KAN. STAT. § 23-104(a); MO. REV. STAT. § 451.100.

[3]*See, e.g.,* ARK. STAT. ANN. § 55-216; KY. REV. STAT. § 402.050; OKLA. STAT. title 43, § 7; TENN. CODE ANN. § 36-415; TEX. FAMILY CODE ANN. title 1, § 1.83.

[4]*See, e.g.,* ARK. STAT. ANN. § 55-216; KY. REV. STAT. § 402.050; OKLA. STAT. title 43, § 7; TEX. FAMILY CODE ANN. title 1, § 1.83.

[5]*See, e.g.,* ARK. STAT. ANN. § 28-1001, Rule 505; ILL. REV. STAT. ch. 110, para. 8-803; OKLA. STAT. title 12, § 2505.

[6]*See, e.g.,* KY. REV. STAT. 421.210; MO. REV. STAT. § 491.060; TENN. CODE ANN. § 24-1-206; TEX. STAT. ANN. art. 3715a.

[7]*See, e.g.,* KY. REV. STAT. § 421.210; MO. REV. STAT. § 491.060; TENN. CODE ANN. § 24-1-206; TEX. STAT. ANN. art. 3715a.

[8]*See, e.g.,* ARK. STAT. ANN. § 39-108; MO. REV. STAT. § 494.031; TENN. CODE ANN. § 22-1-103.

[9]*See, e.g.,* ILL. REV. STAT. ch. 78, § 4.

application for exemption.[10] The Internal Revenue Code excludes "housing allowances" from the gross income of "ministers of the gospel."[11] Federal statutes allow common carriers to grant reduced rates to "ministers of religion";[12] exempt the wages of "ministers of a church" from income tax withholding;[13] and impose a tax upon the self-employment income of every "ordained, commissioned, or licensed minister of a church."[14]

The IRS has defined the term *minister* as "one who is authorized to administer sacraments, preach, and conduct services of worship."[15]

One court, in interpreting a state law exempting "buildings . . . actually occupied as a parsonage by the officiating clergymen of any religious corporation," held that an unordained youth minister was not a "clergyman" and thus was not entitled to have his residence exempted from state property taxation.[16] The court concluded that the term *clergyman* implies ordination and accordingly does not include an unordained youth minister.

Another court drew a distinction between the terms *pastor* and *minister:*

> [T]here is a difference between a minister and a pastor. Pastor is defined in Webster's New International Dictionary, second edition,—"the minister or priest in charge of a church or parish"; in Black's Law Dictionary, 4th Edition,—"applied to a minister of the Christian religion who has charge of a congregation or parish."
> . . . .
> Ecclesiastically, all pastors are ministers or priests, but all ministers or priests are not pastors. A minister has no authority to speak or act authoritatively for any local church, but its pastor does because he is the designated leader and top official of the local church.[17]

Other courts and some legislatures have given the terms *clergyman, minister,* and *pastor* a broader interpretation, and have usually thereby obliterated any distinctions among such terms. Rule 505 of the Uniform Rules of Evidence, for example, deals with confidential communications and has been adopted by several states. Its definition of *clergyman* includes "a minister, priest, rabbi, accredited Christian Science Practitioner, or other similar functionary of a religious organization." Similarly, a New York law pertaining to solemnization

---

[10]*See, e.g.,* ARK. STAT. ANN. § 39-108; MO. REV. STAT. § 494.031.

[11]I.R.C § 107.

[12]49 U.S.C. § 22.

[13]I.R.C. § 3401(a)(9).

[14]I.R.C. § 1402(a)(8).

[15]Rev. Rul. 78-301, 1978-2 C.B. 103.

[16]Borough of Cresskill v. Northern Valley Evangelical Free Church, 312 A.2d 641 (N.J. 1973).

[17]Johnson v. State, 173 So.2d 824, 825-26 (Ala. 1964).

of marriages defined the phrase *clergyman or minister of any religion* to include pastors, rectors, priests, and rabbis.[18] And the United States Tax Court, in interpreting the phrase *minister of the gospel* as contained in Section 107[19] of the Internal Revenue Code, concluded that the term must be construed to include a full-time cantor of the Jewish faith.[20]

It is likely that there will continue to be a blurring of the distinctions among the various terms that have been employed in describing ministers.

## §B. Status—Employee or Self-Employed

It is often necessary to determine whether a minister is an employee or self-employed. The following paragraphs will illustrate the importance of this distinction.

### 1. SOCIAL SECURITY

Social security taxes are collected under two separate tax systems. Under the Federal Insurance Contributions Act (FICA)[21] half the tax is paid by the employee and the other half is paid by the employer. Under the Self-Employment Contributions Act[22] the total tax is paid by the self-employed person. Which method applies to a minister who is not exempt from social security?[23]

The Self-Employment Contributions Act provides that a "duly ordained, commissioned, or licensed minister of a church in the exercise of his ministry" is to be treated as self-employed for purposes of social security[24] even if he is considered to be an employee for income tax or other purposes.

[18]Ravenal v. Ravenal, 338 N.Y.S.2d 324 (1972); *see also* In re Silverstein's Estate, 75 N.Y.S.2d 144 (1947).

[19]Section 107 contains the housing allowance exclusion.

[20]Silverman v. Commissioner, 57 T.C. 727 (1972). *See also* Rev. Rul. 58-221, 1958-1 C.B. 53.

[21]I.R.C. §§ 3101 *et seq.*

[22]I.R.C. §§ 1401 *et seq.*

[23]For a complete discussion of social security and the minister, see chapter 5, *infra.*

[24]I.R.C. § 1402(c). *See also* Treas. Reg. § 1.1402(c)-5(a)(2), which provides that "a duly ordained, commissioned, or licensed minister of a church . . . is engaged in carrying on a trade or business with respect to service performed by him in the exercise of his ministry . . . unless an exemption under section 1402(e) . . . is effective . . . ." Similarly, IRS Publication 517 provides that "members of the clergy are treated as self-employed individuals . . . in the performance of their ministerial services." *See also* IRS Publication 560. Regulation 1.1402(c)-5(b)(2) provides that "service performed by a minister in the exercise of his ministry includes the ministration of sacerdotal functions and the conduct of religious worship, and the control, conduct, and maintenance of religious organizations (including the religious boards, societies, and other integral agencies of such organizations), under the authority of a religious body constituting a church or church denomination."

The Federal Insurance Contributions Act provides that the term *employment* does not include "service performed by a duly ordained, commissioned, or licensed minister of a church in the exercise of his ministry."[25]

In summary, ministers who perform services on behalf of a church are treated as self-employed individuals under the social security laws, though the Self-Employment Contributions Act suggests that in other contexts it may be more appropriate to characterize them as employees.

## 2. INCOME TAX

It is important to determine whether a minister is to be treated as an employee or as a self-employed person for income tax purposes. If a minister is treated as self-employed, then he may deduct all of his business expenses in computing adjusted gross income by claiming them on Schedule C of Form 1040 and reporting only net business income on Form 1040. As a result, a self-employed minister can deduct his business expenses even though he does not itemize his deductions. If a minister is treated as an employee, then he ordinarily may deduct only business-related travel and transportation expenses in computing adjusted gross income and thus must itemize his deductions in order to deduct other business expenses.

The distinction is important for other reasons, including the following: (1) if a minister is an employee, then his employing church may be required to issue him a W-2 Form; (2) percentage limitations applicable to charitable contribution deductions are tied to adjusted gross income; (3) the available medical expense deduction is based on adjusted gross income; (4) the disability pay exclusion generally is available only to employees; and (5) certain tax-deferred annuities are available only to employees of religious and other charitable organizations. The IRS has stated:

> Generally the relationship of employer and employee exists when the person for whom services are performed has the right to control and direct the individual who performs the services, not only as to the result to be accomplished by the work but also as to the details and means by which that result is accomplished. That is, an employee is subject to the will and control of the employer not only as to what shall be done but how it shall be done. In this connection, it is not necessary that the employer actually direct or control the manner in which the services are performed; it is sufficient if he has the right to do so. The right to discharge is also an important factor indicating that the person possessing that right is an employer. Other factors characteristic of an employer, but not necessarily present in every case, are the furnishing of tools and the furnishing of a place to work to the individual who performs the services. In general, if an

[25]I.R.C. § 3121(b)(8).

individual is subject to the control or direction of another merely as to the result to be accomplished by the work and not as to the means and methods for accomplishing the result, he is not an employee.[26]

It is clear under this test that most full-time evangelists are self-employed and that most ministers who work for national or regional offices of religious denominations or conferences or associations of churches are employees.

The status of a minister serving full time at a local church is the cause of considerable confusion. Traditionally, such ministers have been considered self-employed for income tax purposes. Although many ministers serving in local churches would meet the IRS definition of *employee* listed above, others would not. As the IRS has noted, whether the relationship of employer and employee exists will in doubtful cases be determined upon an examination of the particular facts of each case.[27]

In 1980 the IRS issued Revenue Ruling 80-110. It held that a minister who is "an employee of a church" may not deduct unreimbursed business expenses on Schedule C but rather must use Schedule A. In Publication 517, the IRS lists a comprehensive example demonstrating how a minister who "is an employee of the church" should report his income and business deductions. In general, the minister is to report his business expenses on Schedule A and Form 2106 rather than on Schedule C. Revenue Ruling 80-110 and Publication 517 have led some commentators to conclude that the IRS now views all ministers serving in local churches as employees rather than as self-employed.[28]

Other commentators contend that neither Revenue Ruling 80-110 nor Publication 517 held that all ministers are to be treated as employees but rather stated only the appropriate manner of reporting income and deductions if employee status was assumed. The latter view would appear to be the correct one, since the IRS did not in fact hold in either Revenue Ruling 80-110 or Publication 517 that all ministers are to be treated as employees. As was noted previously, many ministers serving local churches cannot be considered employees under the IRS test. Treating such ministers as employees for income tax purposes cannot be justified on the basis of either Revenue Ruling 80-110 or Publication 517.

The IRS has recognized in Publication 517 that it is possible for ministers who are employees of their churches to be self-employed in their performance

---

[26]Treas. Reg. § 31.3401(c)-1(b). *See also* IRS Publication 517.

[27]Treas. Reg. § 31.3401(c)-1(d).

[28]One commentator quotes *Tax News,* 1981-11, February 6, 1981, which contains the following IRS directive to its agents: "A duly ordained, commissioned, or licensed minister, who is employed by a congregation on a salaried basis, is a common-law employee and not a self-employed individual for income tax purposes."

of services outside their activities as employees. For example, a minister may receive amounts directly from members of the church (such as fees for performing marriages, baptisms, or other personal services) that are earnings from self-employment for all tax purposes.

In summary, if a minister does not meet the IRS test for an employee quoted above, he logically should continue to be treated as self-employed for income tax purposes. Revenue Ruling 80-110 and Publication 517 would not appear to affect this result since in both cases the IRS simply made an assumption that a particular minister was an employee rather than self-employed. In neither case did the IRS make a substantive determination that all ministers are to be treated as employees. Whether a particular minister is to be treated as an employee or as self-employed is a determination that must be made on a case-by-case basis based upon an examination of all the facts.

Ministers who have a question about their status may get a ruling from the IRS by filing a Form SS-8.

### 3. RETIREMENT PLANS

Federal law permits an employer who establishes an employee retirement plan to obtain significant tax advantages for both itself and its employees by qualifying the plan.[29] In general, these advantages include a tax deduction for the employer for all contributions it makes to the plan, deferral of tax on the employee's interest income, and the exclusion of contributions from the employee's income.[30]

In 1962, Congress enacted the Self-Employed Individuals' Retirement Act (also known as the Keogh Act of H.R. 10). The Act was designed to provide self-employed persons with the substantial tax benefits enjoyed by employees enrolled in qualified pension plans. This was accomplished by expanding the term *employee* for purposes of qualified employee pension plans to include most self-employed individuals.[31] However, the IRS has determined that the expanded class of employees eligible for participation in qualified pension plans does not include those ministers who are common law employees.[32]

In general, the discussion contained in the preceding subsection dealing with income taxes is relevant in determining whether a particular minister is an employee or self-employed. Thus, a minister who satisfies the IRS definition of a common law employee is not eligible for participation in a self-employed individual's retirement plan (Keogh plan) with respect to income received from

[29]I.R.C. §§ 401-409.
[30]I.R.C. §§ 62(7), 404.
[31]I.R.C. § 401(c).
[32]Treas. Reg. § 1.401-10(b)(3)(i). *See also* I.R.C. § 401 (c)(2)(A)(ii).

the church for such services. However, the IRS has determined[33] that even those ministers who meet the definition of *employee* will be treated as self-employed with respect to income received directly from church members. As a result, a minister may create a Keogh plan and fund it with income received for performing marriages, baptisms, funerals, and other personal services.

In 1974 Congress enacted the Employee Retirement Income Security Act (ERISA). This law was intended to extend the tax benefits of qualified pension plans and Keogh plans to the many employees who were not covered by a qualified plan. Under ERISA, most employees not covered by a qualified plan are permitted to establish "individual retirement accounts" (IRAs). Ministers who satisfy the definition of a common law employee discussed in the preceding subsection dealing with income taxes may create individual retirement accounts and fund them with compensation received directly from a church.

### 4. LEGAL LIABILITY

The characterization of a minister as an employee or self-employed is sometimes important in assessing legal liability. It is a well-established principle of law that an employer is generally responsible for the civil wrongs committed by an employee in the course of employment. If the minister is considered to be self-employed, however, then the church is shielded from liability for his wrongs. As an example, if while driving recklessly on church business a minister injures a pedestrian, his church will be vicariously liable for the injury if an employer-employee relationship exists. If the minister is not an employee of his church, then the church will not be liable. The courts have come to both conclusions.[34]

The characterization of a particular minister as an employee or self-employed should be determined in each case upon the basis of the same criteria employed by the courts in determining the status of other kinds of workers. This was the approach taken by the Supreme Court of California in the leading case of *Malloy v. Fong*.[35] The court had been asked to determine whether an ecclesiastical body could be sued on account of the negligence of one of its ministers acting in the course of his employment. Noting that there was "no compelling reason" why a religious organization should not be liable for the negligence of its employees, the court proceeded to determine whether a minister could be characterized as an employee. In reaching its decision that a minister could be

---

[33]IRS Publication 517.

[34]*See, e.g.,* Bass v. Aetna Insurance Co., 370 So.2d 511 (La. 1979); Allen v. College Street Church of God, 217 S.E.2d 196 (Ga. 1975).

[35]Malloy v. Fong, 232 P.2d 241 (Cal. 1951). *See* chapter 4, *infra.*

deemed an employee, the court relied on well-established criteria employed by the courts in determining the status of other workers:

> Whether a person performing work for another is an employee or self-employed depends primarily upon whether the one for whom the work is done has the legal right to control the activities of the alleged employee. The power of the employer to terminate the services of the employee gives him the means of controlling the employee's activities. "The right to immediately discharge involves the right of control." It is not essential that the right of control be exercised or that there be active supervision of the work of the employee. The existence of the right of control and supervision establishes the existence of an employment relationship.[36]

The court also found that a minister could be deemed a church employee under the criteria set forth in the Restatement of Agency:

> (1) An employee is a person employed to perform service for another in his affairs and who, with respect to his physical conduct in the performance of the service, is subject to the other's control or right to control.
> (2) In determining whether one acting for another is an employee or self-employed, the following matters of fact, among others, are considered:
>     (a) the extent of control which, by the agreement, the employer may exercise over the details of the work;
>     (b) whether or not the one employed is engaged in a distinct occupation or business;
>     (c) the kind of occupation, with reference to whether, in the locality, the work is usually done under the direction of the employer or by a specialist without supervision;
>     (d) the skill required in the particular occupation;
>     (e) whether the employer or the workman supplies the instrumentalities, tools, and the place of work for the person doing the work;
>     (f) the length of time for which the person is employed;
>     (g) the method of payment, whether by the time or by the job;
>     (h) whether or not the work is a part of the regular business of the employer; and
>     (i) whether or not the parties believe they are creating the relationship of employer and employee.[37]

In another leading case,[38] a church was sued for injuries and damages caused

---

[36]*Id.* at 249 (citations omitted). The terms *employer* and *employee* have been used instead of the terms *principal* and *agent*.

[37]RESTATEMENT OF AGENCY § 220 (1933). The terms *employer* and *employee* have been used instead of the terms *principal* and *agent*. Compare the current RESTATEMENT (SECOND) OF AGENCY § 220 (1958) which is identical to the quoted provision except that it adds a further factor: "(j) whether the [employer] is or is not in business."

[38]Vind v. Asamblea Apostolica De La Feen Christo Jesus, 307 P.2d 85 (Cal. 1957).

by the reckless driving of its pastor. The injured victim alleged that the pastor was an employee of his church, and thus the employer-church was vicariously liable for the consequences of the pastor's negligence committed in the course of employment. The church denied liability on the ground that its pastor was self-employed and not an employee, and accordingly his negligence could not be imputed to the church.

The court concluded that the pastor was an employee of his church and that his negligence was imputable to the church. In reaching this decision, the court employed the same criteria used by the California Supreme Court in the *Malloy* case.[39]

The IRS uses the following criteria in determining whether a particular individual is an employee or self-employed:

> Anyone who performs services that can be controlled by an employer (what will be done and how it will be done) is an employee. This is so even when the employer gives the employee freedom of action, if the employer has the legal right to control the method and result of the services. Employers usually provide the tools and place to work and have the right to fire an employee.[40]

In summary, the application of well-established legal principles would dictate in most instances that ministers be treated as employees, at least to the extent that the churches for which they work have the ultimate right to supervise, control, and discharge them. It should be assumed that this is the conclusion that will be reached by most courts. As a result, churches will in most cases be legally responsible for the negligence committed by their pastors in the pursuit of church affairs.

## 5. MISCELLANEOUS FEDERAL AND STATE STATUTES

The applicability of numerous other federal and state statutes and regulations is dependent upon the existence of an employer-employee relationship. Some of the more important of these laws include the following: wage and hour legislation,[41] employment discrimination laws,[42] federal occupational safety and

---

[39]*See* note 35, *supra*, and accompanying text.

[40]IRS Publication 15.

[41]The Fair Labor Standards Act of 1938 exempts "professional employees" from the minimum wage and overtime pay provisions of the Act. Ministers are considered professional employees. *See* 29 U.S.C. §§ 206, 207, and 213; 29 C.F.R. § 541.301.

[42]*See, e.g.*, Title VII of the Civil Rights Act of 1964, 42 U.S.C. §§ 2000e *et seq.*, and the Age Discrimination in Employment Act, 29 U.S.C., §§ 621-34.

health legislation,[43] workmen's compensation,[44] and unemployment compensation.[45]

## §C. Status—Ordained, Commissioned, or Licensed

It is sometimes important to determine whether a minister is ordained, commissioned, or licensed. To illustrate, the Internal Revenue Code exempts wages paid for services by "a duly ordained, commissioned, or licensed minister of a church" from income tax withholding;[46] permits a "duly ordained, commissioned, or licensed minister of a church" to apply for exemption from social security coverage under certain circumstances;[47] and excludes the costs of renting or maintaining a home from the gross income of most ordained ministers (and some unordained ministers).[48] The Military Selective Service Act exempts "duly ordained ministers" from training and service.[49] And the Federal Unemployment Tax Act and many state unemployment laws exempt "service performed by a duly ordained, commissioned, or licensed minister" from unemployment compensation coverage.[50]

The classic legal definition of *ordination* was given by the Supreme Court of Connecticut in an early decision: "To ordain, according to the etymology and general use of the term, signifies to appoint, to institute, to clothe with authority. When the word is applied to a clergyman, it means that he has been invested with ministerial functions or sacerdotal power."[51]

Similarly, one court has observed:

A duly ordained minister, in general acceptation, is one who has followed a prescribed course of study of religious principles, has been consecrated to the service of living and teaching that religion through an ordination ceremony under the auspices of an established church, has been commissioned by that church as

---

[43]*See* the Federal Occupational Safety and Health Act, 29 U.S.C. §§ 651 *et seq.*

[44]*See, e.g.,* ILL. REV. STAT. ch. 48, §§ 138.1 *et seq.;* MO. REV. STAT. ch. 287; TEX. STAT. ANN. arts. 8306 *et seq.*

[45]*See, e.g.,* ILL. REV. STAT. ch. 48, §§ 300 *et seq;* MO. REV. STAT. ch. 288; TEX. STAT. ANN. arts. 5221b-1 *et seq.*

[46]I.R.C. § 3401(a)(9).

[47]I.R.C. § 1402(e).

[48]*See generally* I.R.C. § 107; Treas. Reg. § 1.107; and Rev. Rul. 78-301, 1978-2 C.B. 103. Housing allowances will be discussed in detail in chapter 6, *infra.*

[49]50 U.S.C. App. § 456(g).

[50]*See, e.g.,* I.R.C. § 3309(b); MO. REV. STAT. § 288.034(9).

[51]Kibbe v. Antram, 4 Conn. 134, 139 (1821).

its minister in the service of God, and generally is subject to control or discipline by a council of the church by which he was ordained.[52]

The Military Selective Service Act defines *duly ordained minister of religion* as

> any person who has been ordained, in accordance with the ceremony, ritual, or discipline of a church, religious sect, or organization established on the basis of a community of faith and belief, doctrines and practices of a religious character, to preach and to teach the doctrines of such church, sect, or organization and to administer the rites and ceremonies thereof in public worship, and who as his regular and customary vocation preaches and teaches the principles of religion and administers the ordinances of public worship as embodied in the creed or principles of such church, sect, or organization.[53]

Webster's *Third New International Dictionary* defines *ordination* as "[investing] with ministerial or sacerdotal functions; [introduction] into the office of the Christian ministry by the laying on of hands or by other forms."

The legal definitions of *ordination* closely parallel those adopted by religious bodies themselves. Illustratively, *The Encyclopedia of the Lutheran Church* provides that "ordination is the solemn act of the church designating as ministers of the Gospel, and committing to them the holy office of the Word and Sacraments, certain ones who have been regularly called by God through the church to serve in a specific field or sphere of duty."[54] *The Episcopalian's Dictionary* defines *ordination* as "the ceremony in which an individual is commissioned and empowered for the work of the ministry."[55] *The Mennonite Encyclopedia* defines *ordination of ministers* as "an act of the church in which the minister-elect receives confirmation to his office by a ceremony of laying on of hands of a bishop and the intercession of the congregation, which gives him the right to lead the congregation in worship and life as pastor, to perform the duties of his office, whatever they may be, to preach the Word of God, to

---

[52]Buttecali v. United States, 130 F.2d 172, 174 (5th Cir. 1942).

[53]50 U.S.C. App. § 466(g)(1). *But cf.* Yeoman v. United States, 400 F.2d 793 (10th Cir. 1968) (exemption from armed services for ministers available only to leaders of religious faiths, not to members in general); United States v. Dyer, 272 F. Supp. 965 (N.D. W. Va. 1967), *aff'd*, 390 F.2d 611 (4th Cir. 1968) (seminary education not a prerequisite to obtaining ministerial exemption); United States v. Hestad, 248 F. Supp. 650 (W.D. Wis. 1965) (Selective Service Act's definition of *ordained* takes precedence over definition adopted by particular cult).

[54]THE ENCYCLOPEDIA OF THE LUTHERAN CHURCH 1857 (1965).

[55]H. HARPER, THE EPISCOPALIAN'S DICTIONARY 116 (1974).

perform marriages, to ordain, to administer baptism and communion, to administer discipline, to administer the alms fund, etc."[56]

*The Encyclopedia of World Methodism* defines *ordination* as "the name for the solemn act whereby men are set apart for office in the Christian ministry."[57] The *Encyclopedia of Southern Baptists* defines *ordination* as "[t]he ceremony whereby those who have a vocation and have given some evidence of ability for the ministerial office are set apart for the work of their calling."[58]

Where a particular statute or regulation pertaining to ordained ministers does not specifically define the term *ordained,* it is likely that the courts would defer to the definitions adopted by religious bodies themselves, provided that such definitions are reasonable. Where, however, a statute or regulation does define the term *ordained,* the legal definition will control to the extent that it conflicts with the definition adopted by a religious body. Thus, in one case, a Jehovah's Witness was denied exemption from military service on the ground that he was not an "ordained minister," despite his claim that he was engaged "full time" in the ministry.[59]

The term *licensed minister* is often used by religious bodies to denote a status inferior to and usually preliminary to ordination. Commissioning is a procedure commonly followed by independent churches which do not recognize formal ordination. It is usually an investiture of authority to perform religious functions on behalf of a congregation, and thus is analogous to ordination. Some religious bodies commission missionaries, even though the prospective missionaries are already licensed or ordained. The IRS has held that for purposes of the Internal Revenue Code, commissioned or licensed ministers of religious bodies that provide for ordination will not be included within the term *ordained, commissioned,* or *licensed minister* unless they "perform substantially all the religious functions within the scope of the tenets and practices of their religious denominations" as an ordained minister.[60]

---

[56]THE MENNONITE ENCYCLOPEDIA 73 (1959).

[57]THE ENCYCLOPEDIA OF WORLD METHODISM 1817 (1974).

[58]ENCYCLOPEDIA OF SOUTHERN BAPTISTS 1056 (1958).

[59]United States v. Hestad, 248 F. Supp. 650 (W.D. Wis. 1965).

[60]Rev. Rul. 78-301, 1978-2 C.B. 103.

# 2

# THE PASTOR-CHURCH RELATIONSHIP

## §A. Initiating the Relationship

Churches may be classified in terms of polity or organization as either congregational or hierarchical. The United States Supreme Court has defined a *congregational* church as "a religious congregation which, by the nature of its organization, is strictly independent of other ecclesiastical associations, and so far as church government is concerned, owes no fealty or obligation to any higher authority."[1] The Court has defined a *hierarchical* church as "a subordinate member of some general church organization in which there are superior ecclesiastical tribunals with a general and ultimate power of control . . . over the whole membership of that general organization."[2] Some churches combine elements of both forms of polity.[3]

In congregational churches, the minister is selected by the congregation itself according to the procedures set forth in the church's bylaws. If the bylaws do not address the subject, then the established practice of the church controls. Congregational churches usually select their ministers either by majority vote of the church's membership or by the decision of the church's deacons or trustees.[4] Although either method is legally acceptable, most congregational

---

[1]Watson v. Jones, 80 U.S. 679, 722 (1871).

[2]*Id.* at 722-23.

[3]*See* Annot., 52 A.L.R.3d 324, 361 n.5 (1973).

[4]*See, e.g.,* Holiman v. Dovers, 366 S.W.2d 197 (Ark. 1963) (majority of members of Baptist church have right to select pastor); De Jean v. Board of Deacons, 139 A.2d 205 (Dela. 1958) (common practice in Baptist churches to select ministers by majority vote of congregation); Franklin v. Hahn, 275 S.W.2d 776 (Ky. 1955) (ministers in Christian Church selected by majority vote of congregation); Sherburne Village Baptist Society v. Ryder, 86 N.Y.S.2d 853 (1949) ("Under the usages and custom of the Baptist Church, the authority to employ or dismiss a minister lies not in the corporation, the trustees, or the deacons, but in the congregation itself."); Atkins v. Walker, 200 S.E.2d

or independent churches select their ministers by majority vote of the congregation's membership.

Hierarchical churches generally select their ministers according to the rules and regulations of the parent denomination. Some denominations give subordinate churches complete freedom in selecting ministers. Other denominations dictate who will be the minister of each affiliated church. Many denominations provide for the selection of ministers by the combined efforts of both the denomination and the subordinate church.

Where a hierarchical body or official, pursuant to authority contained in the denomination's rules and regulations, selects a minister for a local congregation, the local congregation is without authority to affect or overrule that decision. In a leading case,[5] a Methodist bishop acting pursuant to authority granted him by the *Doctrines and Disciplines of the Methodist Church* appointed a minister to serve a Methodist congregation in New Orleans, Louisiana. The congregation refused to recognize the bishop's appointment, and recognized instead a minister selected by congregational vote. In ruling in favor of the bishop, the court observed that the congregation was subject to the discipline of its denomination and accordingly had to recognize the appointment made by the bishop even though a majority of the congregation disapproved of it.

In those instances where a minister may be selected by vote of the congregation, it is important that the congregational vote be conducted pursuant to the church's constitution and bylaws. If an unincorporated church has no constitution or bylaws, or its constitution and bylaws do not deal with elections, then the established practice of the church should be observed. Incorporated churches having no constitutional or bylaw provision dealing specifically with elections may be subject to the requirements of state corporation law. As an example, if an incorporated church has no constitution or bylaws, and the applicable state corporation law specifies quorum, notice, and voting requirements, then these requirements must be followed. If they are not, a congregational election may be voidable.

Most states have religious or nonprofit corporation laws that specify to varying degrees how elections are to be conducted.[6] The procedures specified by state law are generally effective only where the corporation has not provided oth-

---

641, 650 (N.C. 1973) ("[T]he congregation . . . had the right, by a majority vote, in a duly called and conducted meeting of the congregation . . . to call to its pastorate the man of its choice."); McCarther v. Pleasant Bethany Baptist Church, 195 S.W.2d 819 (Tex. 1946) (minister retained by action of board of deacons).

[5]Brooks v. Chinn, 52 So.2d 583 (La. 1951).

[6]*See, e.g.,* Ill. Rev. Stat. ch. 32, §§ 163a *et seq.;* Mo. Rev. Stat. chs. 352 and 355; Tex. Stat. Ann. arts. 1396 *et seq.*

erwise in its own constitution or bylaws.[7] Should an incorporated church's procedures for electing a minister conflict with state laws dealing with corporate formalities, authority exists for the proposition that an election in accordance with the church's bylaws will not be voided.[8]

## §B. The Contract

The relationship between a minister and his church is often regarded as *contractual.* One court has stated that "one becomes pastor of a church pursuant to a contract, made with the person or body having the authority to employ."[9] Another court has noted that "just as a church can contract with persons outside the church membership, it can contract with its own pastor."[10]

Ascertaining precisely when the contract between a minister and a church is created is important, for once a contract exists, each party possesses rights which will be protected by law. If, for example, a church agrees to employ a particular minister, but reverses its decision before the minister begins his duties, has a contract been created? If so, the church may be liable for breach of contract. If not, the minister is without a legal remedy. Or, is a contract created where a church offers a position to a particular minister who verbally accepts the appointment, only to repudiate it later? Again, if a contract did exist, the church may have legal recourse against the minister.

Unfortunately, it is often difficult to ascertain whether or when a contract has been created, because a minister rarely signs a formal contract setting forth all of the terms of employment. In one case, a church entered into the following contract with a prospective minister:

> *Section 1. Agreement on Salary.* The First Party does hereby agree to pay the Second Party One Hundred Seventy-Five ($175) Dollars per week. All church engagements are counted as part of salary. This is a starting salary. *Section 2. Engagements.* The Second Party cannot accept any outside engagements without first getting the approval of the First Party, even if it is a charitable affair. *Section 3. Length of Contract.* This contract shall be a one (1) year contract with the option to terminate, if both parties mutually agree. This contract contains the entire agreement between the parties and supersedes any and all other agreements, verbal or written, and the first party shall not be bound by any agreement or representation other than those contained herein.

The church repudiated the agreement before the minister began his duties,

[7] *See generally* chapter 8, *infra.*
[8] *See* Rector, et al. v. Melish, 168 N.Y.S.2d 952 (1957).
[9] Walker v. Nicholson, 127 S.E.2d 564, 566 (N.C. 1962).
[10] Waters v. Hargest, 593 S.W.2d 364, 365 (Tex. 1979).

and the minister sued the church for breach of contract. The court concluded that "in a contract for the performance of services by one party in consideration of the payment of money by the other party, the nature and character of the services to be performed as well as the place of performance and the amount to be paid must be certain and definite. The contract here contains no description of the nature and character of the services to be performed by the minister or when or where the duties are to be performed. It is so indefinite and vague that it is unenforceable."[11]

On the other hand, if the church's offer is in writing, and sets forth (1) the nature of the services to be performed, (2) compensation to be paid, and (3) the term of employment, an enforceable contract will be created on the day the minister mails his acceptance to the church. This assumes, of course, that the church had authority to make the offer and acted in conformance with its constitution and bylaws.[12] On that date, all of the requirements for a valid and enforceable contract exist—an offer and an acceptance, an exchange of mutually beneficial promises, and a lawful purpose.[13] The church or prospective minister may sue to enforce such a contract if the other party defaults, even if the minister never actually began to perform services under the contract.

Often, the church's offer of employment is oral, or expressed in a contract omitting an essential term or containing a material ambiguity. If either the church or the minister repudiates such an agreement before the minister is to begin his duties, an enforceable contract probably does not exist. The agreement is simply too indefinite.[14] But once a minister begins to perform services on

---

[11]McTerry v. Free For All Missionary Baptist Church, 200 S.E.2d 915, 916 (Ga. 1973).

[12]Most courts hold that acceptances are valid when deposited in the mail, assuming that the mail is an authorized means of acceptance. A minority of courts insist that actual delivery of the acceptance is necessary before a contract can be created. *See generally* Morrison v. Thoelke, 155 So.2d 889 (Fla. 1963); Reserve Insurance Co. v. Duckett, 238 A.2d 536 (Md. 1968); 1 A. CORBIN, CONTRACTS § 78 (1950 & Supp. 1982).

[13]*See generally* A. CORBIN, CONTRACTS vols. 1, 1A, and 2 (1950 & Supp. 1982).

[14]*See, e.g.*, Kassab v. Ragnar Benson, Inc., 254 F. Supp. 830, 832 (W.D. Pa. 1966) ("One of the elements required to prove the existence of a binding contract is that the rate of compensation be clearly established."); McTerry v. Free For All Missionary Baptist Church, 200 S.E.2d 915 (Ga. 1973); Metro-Goldwyn-Mayer, Inc. v. Scheider, 347 N.Y.S.2d 755, 761 (1972) ("[T]here is no contract if material financial or time elements involving compensation or . . . duration are left undetermined. The court cannot write a contract which the parties have not made."); McMichael v. Borough Motors, Inc., 188 S.E.2d 721, 722 (N.C. 1972) ("A contract for service must be certain and definite as to the nature and extent of the service to be performed, the place where and the person to whom it is to be rendered, and the compensation to be paid, or it will not be enforced."). *But cf.* Hawkins v. Delta Spindle of Blytheville, Inc., 434 S.W.2d 825 (Ark. 1968); Maimon v. Telman, 240 N.E.2d 652 (Ill. 1968); Indiana Bell Telephone Co. v. Ice Service, Inc., 231 N.E.2d 820 (Ind. 1967); Bartlett v. Sterling

behalf of a church, he will be entitled to reasonable compensation for services rendered, even though no binding contract existed prior to the time he actually began his duties. Some courts base this rule on contractual grounds, but others rely on noncontractual grounds.[15]

If a contract between a church and its minister does not specify the duration of employment, or in cases where a minister works for a church without a written agreement, how long will the minister be entitled to work for the church? In those instances where a church congregation selects a minister by congregational vote, the congregation may specify the term of office. Even though no formal contract is signed, the congregation's specification of a term of employment will be construed as a condition of employment by most courts.[16] The bylaws of many churches prescribe a minister's term of office, and this will control where a contract is silent or ambiguous or does not exist. But where the congregation does not specify the duration of employment, and where the church has no bylaws or its bylaws do not provide guidance, then either the pastor or the church can terminate the relationship at any time, orally or in writing, without advance notice.[17]

Most courts consider an agreement to work for a certain salary per week, month, or year to be so indefinite as to be terminable at will by either party.[18] A minister who agrees to work for a church for a stated annual salary is therefore not on that basis alone entitled to work for a full year. To illustrate, one church had its pastor sign a contract containing the following provision: "We promise and oblige ourselves . . . while you are dispensing spiritual blessings to us to pay you the sum of $____ in ____ payments, yearly and every year so long as you continue the minister of the church . . . ." The minister claimed that this contract was a "contract for life." The court disagreed: "[A] hiring on the

---

Construction Co., 499 P.2d 425 (Okla. 1972); 1 S. WILLISTON, CONTRACTS § 36 (1957 & Supp. 1982).

[15]See generally 3 A. CORBIN, CONTRACTS § 566 (1950 & Supp. 1982); 1 S. WILLISTON, CONTRACTS § 36 (1957 & Supp. 1982).

[16]Most courts hold that once a party begins to perform personal services for another, a contract is created although none previously existed. See note 15, supra, and accompanying text. A congregational specification of the duration of employment will be considered a condition of the subsequent contract.

[17]See generally 1 S. WILLISTON, CONTRACTS § 39 (1957 & Supp. 1982). See also Taylor v. Greenway Restaurant, Inc., 173 A.2d 211 (D.C. 1961) ("Appellant's employment was for no definite period and was subject to termination at the will of either party. Except when specifically so provided by agreement or by statute, neither employer nor employee is entitled to notice of termination.").

[18]1 S. WILLISTON, CONTRACTS § 39 (1957 & Supp. 1982).

basis of a yearly salary, if no period of employment is otherwise stated, is terminable, without cause, at the election of either employer or employee."[19]

As has been noted, if a valid contract exists between a church and its minister, then either party will be liable for breaching the contract, including any of the terms of employment set forth in the agreement. Employment contracts are breached most frequently by repudiation of the employment relationship prior to the expiration of the term specified in the contract. Where one party breaches the employment contract, what legal remedies are available to the innocent party? Before answering this question, it must be recognized that civil courts will involve themselves in a contractual dispute between a church and its pastor only if "the determination of the parties' rights can be accomplished by the application of neutral principles of law without the necessity of adjudicating matters of church doctrine or determining matters of church government in a hierarchical church."[20]

One court has held that where a church breaches an employment contract by discharging a minister prior to the expiration of his term of office, but after he has begun performing duties, the minister has three remedies:

> (1) He may immediately bring an action for damages for any special injury which he may have sustained; (2) he may treat the contract as rescinded and sue immediately in quantum meruit for the work and labor he actually performed; or (3) he may wait until the termination of the period for which he was employed and then sue upon the contract and recover his whole wages.[21]

If a minister selects the third alternative, two additional factors must be borne in mind. First, the suit must be filed within the time period specified in the applicable statute of limitations, which begins to run upon the expiration of the contract term.[22] Second, the wages not paid under the terminated contract will not necessarily be the measure of damages. The minister has a legal duty to mitigate the church's damages by accepting available alternative employment of the same or similar character.[23] If the minister diligently seeks alternative employment of the same or similar character, but none is available, he is entitled to sue for the full salary corresponding to the terminated portion of the employment term. If he does not seek other employment, then the church's

[19]Bethany Reformed Church v. Hager, 406 N.E.2d 93, 95 (Ill. 1980).

[20]Waters v. Hargest, 593 S.W.2d 364, 365 (Tex. 1979) (rule was mandated by First Amendment).

[21]Rosenstock v. Congregation Agudath Achim., 164 S.E.2d 283, 284-85 (Ga. 1968) (citations omitted).

[22]Id. at 285.

[23]See Annot., 44 A.L.R.3d 629 (1972).

liability will be reduced by the amount which the minister, with reasonable diligence, might have earned from other employment during the remaining contract term. If the minister finds work of the same or similar character during the remaining term of employment, then the church's liability will be reduced by the value of the compensation received by the minister from his new employer.

To illustrate, in one case a church discharged a minister who had served only four years of a seven-year term of employment. The discharged minister sued for breach of contract. In attempting to assess the proper monetary damages for breach of contract, the court observed:

> There is evidence . . . to the effect that . . . appellant saw Mr. Bailey, the secretary of the Gulf Coast Christian churches, and applied for a regular pastorate in some church, and none was available. The evidence also shows that appellant was advised that Mr. Bailey had a number of calls for interim pastorates. The evidence is insufficient to show that appellant made any effort to obtain employment in any of such interim pastorates and it is difficult to ascertain from the record just what diligence appellant exercised to obtain employment. There is nothing in the record to the effect that appellant would not be able to obtain employment from the date the case went to trial to the time the contract would expire but for the wrongful termination thereof.[24]

The church, as an employer, has the right to dismiss a minister before the expiration of a specified term of office under either of two theories. First, the minister can be dismissed if his behavior corresponds to a specific ground for dismissal expressed in his contract. A church should never discharge a minister for a contractual violation unless it has credible and convincing evidence. Churches should also avoid the use of vague terminology in reciting the grounds for termination of employment. Terms such as *dishonesty, immorality, incompetence, inefficiency,* and *unbecoming conduct* should be avoided. The grounds should be stated with sufficient clarity that neither the minister nor the church will be in doubt about their meaning. Second, a church may dismiss a minister prior to the expiration of a specified term of employment where the minister violates an implied condition of employment. Implied conditions of employment are not stated in the contract, but are reasonable inferences of the parties' unexpressed intentions and assumptions. One court has observed:

> The law implies a stipulation or undertaking by an employee in entering into a contract of employment that he is competent to perform the work undertaken and is possessed of the requisite skill and knowledge to enable him to do so, and that he will do the work of the employer in a careful manner. If he is not qualified

[24]Mayhew v. Vanway, 371 S.W.2d 90, 94 (Tex. 1963).

to do the work which he undertakes, if he is incompetent, unskillful or inefficient, or if he executes his work in a negligent manner or is otherwise guilty of neglect of duty, he may be lawfully discharged before the expiration of his term of employment.[25]

The courts have also held that an incapacitating illness of long duration or an intervening mental incapacity will also be sufficient grounds for termination of an employment contract before its expiration.[26]

It has been held that a wrongfully discharged minister may not sue to restrain his church from "breaching and terminating the contract." His appropriate remedy is a suit for breach of contract.[27]

A minister may also breach the employment contract. Again, the most frequent example is repudiation of the employer-employee relationship without justification prior to the expiration of the employment term. In such a case, the church may bring a legal action against the minister. The measure of damages will be the cost to the church of obtaining the services of another minister, plus any other damages resulting directly from the minister's repudiation of the contract, provided that such damages were foreseeable at the time the contract was entered into.[28]

Finally, an employment contract, like any contract, may be rescinded where one party fraudulently induced the innocent party to enter into the contract. In one case, a synagogue sought to rescind a contract with a rabbi on the ground that it had been defrauded by the rabbi's failure to disclose a criminal record and disbarment as an attorney. The court, in holding in favor of the synagogue, observed:

> Arrangements between a pastor and his congregation are matters of contract subject to enforcement in the civil courts. Contracts in general are subject to rescission when they are obtained by fraud. . . . Legal fraud consists of a material misrepresentation of a presently existing or past fact made with knowledge of its falsity, with the intention that the other party rely thereon, and he does so rely to his damage.[29]

The court concluded that "a prior criminal record and disbarment from the

---

[25]Seco Chemicals, Inc. v. Stewart, 349 N.E.2d 733, 738-39 (Ind. 1976).

[26]Fisher v. Church of St. Mary, 497 P.2d 882 (Wyo. 1972).

[27]Bennett v. Belton, 436 S.W.2d 161 (Tex. 1968).

[28]*See* Annot., 61 A.L.R.2d 1008 (1958).

[29]Jewish Center v. Whale, 397 A.2d 712 (N.J. 1978), *aff'd,* 411 A.2d 475 (1980).

practice of law must be disclosed by one seeking a rabbinical post involving the spiritual, religious and educational leadership of a religious congregation."[30]

## §C. Compensation

As was noted in the preceding section, a minister who works for a church without a written contract or with a contract which does not specify the compensation to be paid him is entitled to receive reasonable compensation for services actually performed. Where a church and its minister enter into a contract which specifies the compensation to be paid, the minister is legally entitled to receive that compensation. One court has stated: "[T]he question of liability for the salary of a minister or pastor is governed by the principles which prevail in the law of contracts, and it is generally held that a valid contract for the payment of such a salary will be enforced."[31] Thus, if a church fails to pay a minister the full compensation specified in a written contract, either because the minister is discharged before his term of office expires or because the church reduces his salary, the minister may sue for breach of contract.

As was noted in the preceding section, a minister discharged prior to the end of his term of office must generally wait until the end of the contract term before bringing an action for payment of the full compensation specified in the contract. And, he must generally attempt to mitigate the church's damages by seeking available alternative employment of the same or similar character.

If the salary specified by contract is reduced by action of a church, however, the minister may immediately sue for breach of contract. A minister who consents to a reduction in compensation will not be allowed to recover his losses. Thus, where a church was unable to pay its minister the full salary specified by contract because of financial difficulties, and the church and its minister mutually agreed to reduce the stated salary by nearly fifty percent, the minister could not later sue for the difference.[32] And where a minister waived full payment of his compensation by acquiescing in church budgets that reduced his salary, by voting for resolutions reducing his salary, and by returning a check to his church, he could not later recover the difference.[33]

The civil courts will entertain a suit by a minister for unpaid compensation despite his church's claim that such a controversy is purely ecclesiastical. In one case, a Catholic priest sued his diocese for wrongfully withholding his salary. The diocese maintained that the civil courts could not entertain suits

---

[30]*Id.* at 714.

[31]Way v. Ramsey, 135 S.E. 454, 455 (N.C. 1926).

[32]Norton v. Normal Park Presbyterian Church, 47 N.E.2d 526 (Ill. 1943).

[33]James v. Christ Church Parish, 185 P.2d 984 (Wash. 1947) (but as to later years, court held minister had not waived payment of contractual salary).

involving the administration of church affairs and the relationship of a church to its minister, even with respect to salary, since these are matters of purely ecclesiastical concern. The court, in deciding that it did have jurisdiction to hear the case, observed:

> It was not the intent of [the First Amendment] and it has been so held in many cases, that civil and property rights should be unenforceable in the civil courts simply because the parties involved might be the church and members, officers, or the ministry of the church. It was not intended as a shield to payment of a just debt when the purpose of the First Amendment is not being violated. Ministers have been awarded their salary in suits against the church.[34]

Compensation paid to a minister must be in the amounts authorized by appropriate action. If a church authorizes a specified salary, and the church treasurer pays the minister an amount in excess of the authorized salary, the minister will have to account for the difference.[35]

Where a minister receives money directly from church members, it has been held that such monies are gifts and not compensation, and accordingly the church's obligation to pay a stated salary is not diminished by the amount of such gifts.[36] However, it is doubtful that a minister could exclude the value of such gifts from his gross income for income tax purposes, since the IRS generally considers direct payments by church members to their ministers to be compensation for services rendered and not bona fide gifts.[37] A church member could not deduct the value of such gifts from his gross income, since such gifts are made directly to an individual and not to a charitable organization as required by the Internal Revenue Code.[38]

It has been held that a minister's salary takes priority over unusual church expenses, but not necessarily over customary church expenses, such as maintenance, insurance, and repairs.[39] And where a minister sued the trustees of an unincorporated church to recover an unpaid salary, one court held that such a suit must be dismissed since the trustees could not be personally liable.[40]

Finally, it is important to note that one of the conditions a church must meet in order to obtain and retain its federal income tax exemption is that no part

---

[34]Bodewes v. Zuroweste, 303 N.E.2d 509, 511 (Ill. 1973).

[35]Harrison v. Floyd, 97 A.2d 761 (N.J. 1953).

[36]*Id.*

[37]*See* chapter 6, § C, *infra.*

[38]I.R.C. § 170.

[39]Board of Trustees v. Richards, 130 N.E.2d 736 (Ohio 1954).

[40]McCall v. Capers, 105 S.W.2d 323 (Tex. 1937).

of its net earnings "inures to the benefit of any private . . . individual."[41] The courts have uniformly held that although payment of "reasonable compensation" by a tax-exempt organization to its employees does not constitute the inurement of net earnings to the benefit of a private individual, the payment of unreasonably high salaries does.[42] In one case, a small church was denied tax-exempt status on the ground that an excessive and unreasonable amount of its net earnings was paid to its pastor.[43] The reasonableness of compensation is a matter which must be decided in each case on the basis of the facts.

## §D. Termination

Congregational, or independent, churches may terminate a minister's employment at any time with or without cause so long as applicable procedures are followed and the minister's term of office is not specified by contract, church bylaw, or congregational vote.[44] One court, in approving the action of an independent church in discharging its minister, held that "a pastor may be deposed by a majority of the members at a congregational meeting at any time, so far as the civil courts are concerned, subject only to inquiry by the courts as to whether the church, or its appointed tribunal has proceeded according to the law of the church."[45]

If a church discharges a minister without following the procedures set forth in its constitution and bylaws, the discharge will not be legally effective. It has been held that the attempted discharge of a minister by congregational vote was invalid where the vote was conducted at an improperly called church meeting;[46] where the meeting was "so beset with confusion that no business could have been legally transacted";[47] or where the congregation had not been duly notified that a vote would be taken on whether to retain a minister.[48]

In many cases, there is disagreement about the class of lawful church members entitled to vote. In one case, a pastor ignored a congregational decision to terminate his services on the ground that most of those participating in the

---

[41]I.R.C. § 501(c)(3).

[42]*See, e.g.,* Harding Hospital, Inc. v. United States, 505 F.2d 1068 (6th Cir. 1974); Mabee Petroleum Corp. v. United States, 203 F.2d 872 (5th Cir. 1953). *See generally* chapter 14, § B, *infra.*

[43]Unitary Mission Church v. Commissioner, 74 T.C. 36 (1980).

[44]Watts v. Greater Bethesda Missionary Baptist Church, 154 N.E.2d 875 (Ill. 1958).

[45]In re Galilee Baptist Church, 186 So.2d 102, 106 (Ala. 1966). *Accord* Blauert v. Schupmann, 63 N.W.2d 578 (Minn. 1954).

[46]In re Galilee Baptist Church, 186 So.2d 102 (Ala. 1966).

[47]*Id.*

[48]St. John's Greek Catholic Hungarian Russian Orthodox Church v. Fedak, 233 A.2d 663 (N.J. 1967); Hayes v. Board of Trustees, 225 N.Y.S.2d 316 (1962).

congregational vote were not lawful members. The pastor alleged that most of those voting against him had ceased to be members by their failure to abide by an unwritten church "rule" requiring that members attend church regularly and contribute to the church's support. Those who had been "disfellowshiped" claimed that they were aware of no such rule, and that they were never notified that their membership was in jeopardy. The court concluded that the expulsion of the church members was improper, since the alleged rule was of doubtful existence, and since the members were not given a hearing on their status.[49] Where a church's constitution or bylaws specify the manner by which a member may lose his membership, this will be controlling. Thus, where a church's constitution provided that membership status could be severed only by "excommunication," and where no member voting to dismiss a minister had been excommunicated, the minister could not challenge his dismissal on the ground that several of the members voting against him had forfeited their membership through irregular attendance and inadequate support.[50] This was so despite the fact that the church's constitution also provided that "no one can . . . remain a member of this congregation . . . but such as partake of the Lord's Supper with due frequency . . . and contribute according to his ability toward the maintenance of the church." The court reasoned that the members' infrequent attendance and minimal support was justified by their belief that the pastor had deviated from the church's doctrines.

In another case, a minister challenged a congregational vote to dismiss him on the ground that many of the members who voted against him had lost their membership by holding separate services in another church under another minister. The court disagreed: "The constitution and bylaws nowhere specifically provide a procedure for determining whether a member has lost his membership because of his conduct or beliefs. However, we think it must be implied . . . that it is for the congregation to make this determination."[51]

Where a church has no bylaw provisions dealing with dismissal of ministers, it has been held that a majority vote of the church's membership will warrant dismissal.[52] This is so even if no notice was given that the dismissal of a minister was to be considered at a scheduled meeting, at least in the case where all members knew that the minister's continued employment would be discussed, and where the dismissed minister and his supporters did not object to the lack of notice.[53]

The courts will determine, if necessary, whether applicable church proce-

---

[49]Longmeyer v. Payne, 205 S.W.2d 263 (Mo. 1947).

[50]Blauert v. Schupmann, 63 N.W.2d 578 (Minn. 1954).

[51]Schumacher v. Giedt, 112 N.W.2d 898 (S.D. 1962).

[52]See note 50, supra.

[53]Id.

dures were followed in the dismissal of a minister, at least if the decision to dismiss is properly vested in the congregation. Such a determination obviously is a neutral act, involving no interpretation of religious doctrine.[54] And the courts will enjoin a properly dismissed minister from holding services in the event that he ignores a church's vote of dismissal.[55]

If a church votes to discharge a minister before the expiration of a stated term of office, the minister generally may proceed against the church for breach of contract if the church lacked good cause for discharging him. A church obviously is not required to keep a minister for the duration of a stated term where good cause exists to discharge him, and thus when a church discharges a minister before the end of his employment term on the basis of good cause the minister has no legal recourse against the church. Significant doctrinal deviation, moral misconduct, and incompetence are the kinds of grounds that normally will justify the discharge of a minister before the end of his term, at least where these terms are defined with sufficient clarity. A church should be capable of demonstrating, by competent and convincing evidence, the existence of "good cause" if it chooses to discharge a minister before the end of his term.

In hierarchical churches, the authority to dismiss a minister is sometimes vested in an ecclesiastical tribunal or commission superior to the local congregation. Where an ecclesiastical tribunal is vested with such authority, the First Amendment prevents the civil courts from ascertaining whether such a tribunal acted in accordance with prescribed procedures in dismissing a minister, even if it is claimed that the tribunal acted arbitrarily.[56] The United States Supreme Court has held:

> [T]he First and Fourteenth Amendments permit hierarchical religious organizations to establish their own rules and regulations for internal discipline and government, and to create tribunals for adjudicating disputes over these matters. When this choice is exercised and ecclesiastical tribunals are created to decide disputes over the government and direction of subordinate bodies, the Constitution requires that civil courts accept their decisions as binding upon them.[57]

[54]Providence Baptist Church v. Superior Court, 251 P.2d 10 (Cal. 1952); Waters v. Hargest, 593 S.W.2d 364 (Tex. 1979). *Contra* Simpson v. Wells Lamont Corp., 494 F.2d 490 (5th Cir. 1974) (federal courts without jurisdiction to determine "who will preach from the pulpit").

[55]Rush v. Yancey, 349 S.W.2d 337, 338-39 (Ark. 1961) ("[W]here a minister of a congregational church is dismissed by action of the majority of the church, and thereafter usurps the pastoral duties, such majority are entitled to an injunction to restrain him, and to prevent him and his adherents from occupying and using the church without consent of the majority.").

[56]Serbian Eastern Orthodox Diocese v. Milivojevich, 426 U.S. 696 (1976).

[57]*Id.* at 724-25.

Where a hierarchical body or official dismisses the minister of a subordinate congregation, the congregation has no authority to retain the minister.[58] But if no hierarchical body or official has such authority, then the church congregation alone has the right to dismiss its minister.[59]

### §E. Nature of the Relationship

A minister who performs services on behalf of a church is treated as an employee of the church if he satisfies the common law definition of an employee discussed in chapter 1. This has important consequences. Perhaps most important, it means that a church may be legally responsible for most of the civil wrongs committed by its minister in the course of church business. It also means that many laws which pertain to the employer-employee relationship— such as employment discrimination, occupational safety and health legislation, workmen's compensation, and unemployment compensation—may apply, in whole or in part, to the pastor-church relationship. Finally, it means that the church may be responsible for the contractual obligations incurred by its minister in the pursuit of church business.

[58]Eastern Orthodox Catholic Church v. Adair, 141 N.Y.S.2d 772 (1955), aff'd, 161 N.Y.S.2d 826 (1957); Rector, et al. v. Melish, 88 N.Y.S.2d 764 (1949), aff'd, 96 N.Y.S.2d 496 (1950).

[59]St. John's Greek Catholic Hungarian Russian Orthodox Church v. Fedak, 233 A.2d 663 (N.J. 1967).

# 3

# AUTHORITY, RIGHTS, AND PRIVILEGES

## §A. In General

What authority does a minister possess by virtue of his office? In general, a minister will have the authority to do those things specifically authorized in his employment contract, in the church's constitution and bylaws, or by specific delegation of authority from the church board or trustees. Obviously, a minister has the right to enter the church building for the purpose of conducting worship services, at least until his services are terminated by appropriate action. One court has observed that "a minister has a right in the nature of an easement to enter the church . . . for divine services."[1] A minister is also entitled to reasonable compensation for services rendered, and generally may occupy the church's parsonage.[2]

## §B. Officer of the Church Corporation

A minister has no inherent right to be the president of his church corporation. The office of president is one that is filled according to the constitution and bylaws of the church. Although the minister is customarily named president of the corporation, this is not a legal requirement.

## §C. Property Matters

Where no authority over the business and property affairs of a church has been delegated to a minister, he may not lawfully act for the church in such matters. In one case, a minister declared himself to be the absolute religious

[1]Skinner v. Holmes, 33 A.2d 819, 820 (N.J. 1943).
[2]Fuchs v. Meisel, 60 N.W. 773 (Mich. 1894).

leader of a congregation and thereafter exercised complete control over all of the church's spiritual and business activities. The minister's conveyance of church properties was challenged by members of the congregation who questioned his authority in business matters. The court concluded that the minister's "proclaiming . . . of himself as the religious superior of the congregation may suffice to establish that fact in spiritual matters of his church, but it does not effect legal superiority in secular matters."[3] The court emphasized that there must be "clear and convincing" evidence of congregational acceptance of legal superiority by a minister over church business and property matters before such authority will be recognized by the courts. In a related case, a minister who was the sole trustee of a church was not permitted to convey church property for his own benefit.[4] And where a minister attempted to lease church properties without authorization from the church board, the lease was found to have no legal effect.[5]

A church may of course ratify the unauthorized actions of its pastor. Ratification may be by express action of the congregation or church board, or it may be implied if the church has knowledge of unauthorized action but does nothing to repeal it.[6] Thus, where a minister commits some unauthorized act and the church knows of the act but does not object within a reasonable time, the church may be left without legal recourse.

## §D. Performance of Marriage Ceremonies

A minister has the authority, in most states, to perform marriages. This authority is granted by state law. One typical statute provides that "[m]arriages may be celebrated . . . by a minister of the gospel in regular standing in the church or society to which he belongs."[7] Some states require that the minister be ordained;[8] others require that the minister be either licensed or ordained;[9] and others omit any specific reference to either licensure or ordination.[10]

In most states, it is a criminal offense for one to perform a marriage ceremony who is not authorized to do so by state law. Thus, if a state law authorizes only

[3]Gospel Tabernacle Body of Christ Church v. Peace Publishers & Co., 506 P.2d 1135, 1138 (Kan. 1973).

[4]Dawkins v. Dawkins, 328 P.2d 346 (Kan. 1958).

[5]American Legion v. Southwest Title Insurance Co., 207 So.2d 393 (La. 1968).

[6]Hill v. Hill, 241 S.W.2d 865 (Tenn. 1951).

[7]ILL. REV. STAT. ch. 89, § 4.

[8]See, e.g., KAN. STAT. § 23-104(a); OKLA. STAT. title 43, § 7.

[9]See, e.g., TEX. FAMILY CODE ANN. title 1, § 1.83.

[10]See, e.g., ILL. REV. STAT. ch. 89, § 4; KY. REV. STAT. § 402.050; MO. REV. STAT. § 451.100.

ordained ministers to perform marriage ceremonies, an unordained minister will be criminally liable for performing a marriage. Criminal penalties for the unauthorized performance of a marriage ceremony generally include a small fine or short prison sentence. [11]

Many states also impose criminal penalties upon ministers for the following acts:

1. failure to maintain a record of marriage ceremonies performed
2. failure to return promptly to the proper authorities a properly completed certificate of marriage and the license to marry
3. marrying persons without a marriage license
4. marrying persons not legally capable of marrying

Misspelling a name, inserting the wrong date, or having less than the required number of witness signatures on the marriage certificate will not affect the validity of the marriage. It is generally held that a marriage will be considered valid even though the minister fails to complete and return a marriage certificate. And, a marriage will be valid even though the minister performing the ceremony was not authorized to do so, at least if the parties did not know that he lacked authority. [12]

Many states permit members of religious sects to be married according to the rites and customs of their sect, even though such ceremonies may not be consistent with state marriage laws. [13] Such laws do not dispense with licensing and reporting requirements, however.

## §E. Exemption From Military Duty

The Military Selective Service Act exempts "regular or duly ordained ministers of religion" from military training and service. [14] Ministers are not exempted from the Act's registration requirements. The Act defines the term *duly ordained minister of religion* as

> a person who has been ordained, in accordance with the ceremonial [sic], ritual, or discipline of a church, religious sect, or organization established on the basis of a community of faith and belief, doctrines and practices of a religious character, to preach and to teach the doctrines of such church, sect, or organization and to administer the rites and ceremonies thereof in public worship, and who as his regular and customary vocation preaches and teaches the principles of religion

[11] *See, e.g.,* ILL. REV. STAT. ch. 38, § 32-6 (imprisonment of one to three years); MO. REV. STAT. § 451.120 (up to $500 fine); OKLA. STAT. title 43, § 15 (fine of $100 to $500, imprisonment of thirty days to one year).

[12] *See, e.g.,* UNIFORM MARRIAGE AND DIVORCE ACT § 206.

[13] *See, e.g.,* ILL. REV. STAT. ch. 89, § 5.

[14] 50 U.S.C. App. § 456(g).

and administers the ordinances of public worship as embodied in the creed or principles of such church, sect, or organization.[15]

The Act defines the term *regular minister of religion* as

one who as his customary vocation preaches and teaches the principles of religion of a church, a religious sect, or organization of which he is a member, without having been formally ordained as a minister of a religion, and who is recognized by such church, sect, or organization as a regular minister.[16]

It has been held that the definitions of *ordained* and *regular ministers* contained in the Act will take precedence over the definitions adopted by a church or religious organization.[17] It also has been held that a minister is entitled to the exemption if he meets the definition of either an ordained or regular minister, even if he has no college or seminary training.[18]

The most important element in the definition of both ordained and regular ministers is the requirement that the minister's "customary vocation" be preaching and teaching the principles of his church or sect. The United States Supreme Court has held that the Act's definitions do "not preclude all secular employment," since many ministers who are employed by small churches must seek part-time secular employment in order to adequately support themselves. The Court specifically held that a minister's vocation could be preaching and teaching the principles of his church although he supported himself by working five hours a week as a radio repairman.[19] Other cases make it plain that ministers may pursue minimal amounts of secular employment without jeopardizing their exemption from military service.

But where a minister spends substantial amounts of time in secular employment, he may not be entitled to the exemption. To illustrate, the following ministers were denied an exemption from military service on the ground that their customary vocation was not the ministry: a minister who worked twenty-eight hours a week as a busboy and thirty hours a month as a minister;[20] a minister who worked forty-five hours a week as a carpenter and fifteen hours a month as a minister;[21] a minister employed full-time in secular employment

[15]50 U.S.C. App. § 466(g)(1).

[16]50 U.S.C. App. § 466(g)(2).

[17]United States v. Novak, 475 F.2d 180 (7th Cir. 1973), *cert. denied,* 412 U.S. 930 (1973).

[18]United States v. Dyer, 272 F. Supp. 965 (N.D. W.Va. 1967).

[19]Dickinson v. United States, 346 U.S. 389 (1953).

[20]Fore v. United States, 395 F.2d 548 (10th Cir. 1968).

[21]Leitner v. United States, 222 F.2d 363 (4th Cir. 1955).

and fourteen hours a week in the ministry;[22] and a minister employed full-time in secular employment and ten hours a week in the ministry.[23]

It is clear that a minister need not be the sole or principal religious leader of his congregation to be entitled to the exemption. Assistant or associate ministers are also entitled to the exemption if they are either ordained or regular ministers.[24] The motivation of an individual in becoming a minister is irrelevant. Thus, a minister cannot be denied an exemption on the ground that his sole purpose in becoming a minister was to evade military service.[25]

The exemption of ministers from military training and service does not violate the First Amendment of the United States Constitution.[26] The purpose of the exemption is not to benefit ministers, but rather "to assure religious leadership to members of [their] faith."[27]

The Military Selective Service Act further provides that

[s]tudents preparing for the ministry under the direction of recognized churches or religious organizations, who are satisfactorily pursuing full-time courses of instruction in recognized theological or divinity schools, or who are satisfactorily pursuing full-time courses of instruction leading to their entrance into recognized theological or divinity schools in which they have been preenrolled, shall be deferred from training and service, but not from registration . . . .[28]

Note that students preparing for the ministry are not granted an exemption. Rather, their military training and service is merely "deferred." This deferral may of course mature into an exemption if the student completes his training and becomes an ordained or regular minister.

Part-time theology students are not entitled to deferral. Thus, one student who worked full-time in a secular job and who attended only two hours of classes a week was found to be subject to military training and service.[29]

The military services provide for chaplains, and this practice has been upheld

[22]United States v. Burgueno, 423 F.2d 599 (9th Cir. 1970), *cert. denied,* 398 U.S. 965 (1970).

[23]*See generally* Annot., 1 A.L.R. Fed. 607 (1969).

[24]Wiggins v. United States, 261 F.2d 113 (5th Cir. 1958); United States v. Hull, 391 F.2d 257 (4th Cir. 1968), *cert. denied,* 392 U.S. 914 (1968).

[25]Rowell v. United States, 223 F.2d 863 (5th Cir. 1955).

[26]United States v. Branigan, 299 F.Supp. 225 (S.D.N.Y. 1969).

[27]United States v. Bittinger, 422 F.2d 1032 (4th Cir. 1969).

[28]50 U.S.C. App. § 456(g)(2).

[29]United States v. Bartelt, 200 F.2d 385 (7th Cir. 1952).

despite claims that it constitutes a violation of the religious neutrality required by the First Amendment.[30]

Finally, the Military Selective Service Act provides that no person who "by reason of religious training and belief is conscientiously opposed to participation in war in any form" shall be subject to combatant training and service in the armed forces.[31] One need not be a minister to qualify for conscientious objector status, and a person is not automatically entitled to such status because he is a minister.[32] The courts have greatly liberalized the meaning of "religious training and belief." The United States Supreme Court has held that conscientious objector status is properly available to any individual who is conscientiously opposed to war on the basis of "moral, ethical, or religious beliefs about what is right and wrong and [which are] held with the strength of traditional religious convictions."[33] Conscientious objector status is thus available to agnostics and even atheists, since belief in God is not a prerequisite to conscientious objector status.[34] Avowed humanists have been granted conscientious objector status.[35]

Conscientious objector status is available to an individual on the basis of religious conviction even though he is not a member of a religious society or organization.[36] And it is available even though an individual's opposition to war is based only partly on "religious training and belief."

To receive conscientious objector status, one must be opposed to participation in war in any form. It is not enough that an individual is opposed merely to a particular war.[37] One may be entitled to conscientious objector status even though he is willing to use force in defense of self, home, or family.[38]

The Military Selective Service Act does provide that conscientious objectors may be compelled to perform noncombatant military service or civilian work contributing to the maintenance of the national health, safety, or interest.

Those sections of the Military Selective Service Act pertaining to conscientious objectors have been upheld against claims that they constitute a vio-

[30]Elliott v. White, 23 F.2d 997 (D.C. Cir. 1928). The constitutionality of the military chaplaincy program is presently being litigated in Katcoff v. Marsh, No. 79-2986 (E.D.N.Y. filed Nov. 23, 1979).

[31]50 U.S.C. App. § 456(j).

[32]United States v. Bryan, 263 F.Supp. 895 (N.D. Ga. 1967).

[33]Welsh v. United States, 398 U.S. 333, 340 (1970).

[34]United States v. Wainscott, 496 F.2d 356 (4th Cir. 1974).

[35]United States v. Vlasits, 422 F.2d 1267 (4th Cir. 1970).

[36]United States v. Stock, 460 F.2d 480 (9th Cir. 1972).

[37]Gillette v. United States, 401 U.S. 437 (1971).

[38]Rosenfeld v. Rumble, 515 F.2d 498 (1st Cir. 1975), cert. denied, 423 U.S. 911 (1975).

lation of the religious neutrality required by the First Amendment,[39] and that they condone "involuntary servitude."[40]

## §F. Exemption From Jury Duty

One has a right to have a jury decide questions of fact in most civil and criminal cases. This right is recognized in the United States Constitution and in most state constitutions as well as in many state and federal statutes. Associated with the right to trial by jury is the corresponding obligation of jury service. Every citizen has a duty to serve as a juror when called upon to do so, unless specifically exempted or excused.

In many states, ministers are exempted from the duty of jury service. The exemption may be automatic,[41] or it may be available only upon timely application.[42] In the latter case, it has been held that a court is under no duty to inform a prospective juror of entitlement to an exemption[43]—the burden is upon the prospective juror to affirmatively claim it.

The exemption of ministers and various other occupations from the duty of jury service has been explained on the ground that "it is for the good of the community that their regular work should not be interrupted."[44]

Of course, an exempted minister has the right to waive the exemption and have his name placed on the list of eligible jurors.

In those states where a minister is not exempted from jury service, a minister may be excused from service upon a showing that undue hardship or extreme inconvenience would result, or that the public good would be impaired. Such a decision is entirely within the discretion of the presiding judge. Obviously, a minister who is not exempted from jury service should be excused if he has a funeral to perform, where several parishioners are in the hospital and in need of visitation, where the church is engaged in the construction of a new facility, or where there are urgent counseling needs.

---

[39]*See* note 37, *supra.*

[40]United States v. Fallon, 407 F.2d 621 (7th Cir. 1969), *cert. denied,* 395 U.S. 908 (1969).

[41]*See, e.g.,* ILL. REV. STAT. ch. 78, § 4: "The following persons shall be exempt from serving as jurors, to wit: . . . officiating ministers of the gospel . . . ."

[42]*See, e.g.,* ARK. STAT. ANN. § 39-108: "The following persons will not be required to serve as grand or petit jurors if they object to serving and make their objections known to the court prior to being sworn: . . . (b) persons whose principal activity is that of a clergyman." Exemptions of ministers from jury duty have been upheld against the claim that such exemptions violate the First Amendment. United States v. Butler, 611 F.2d 1066 (11th Cir. 1980), *cert. denied,* 449 U.S. 830 (1980).

[43]State v. Rogers, 324 So.2d 403 (La. 1975).

[44]Rawlins v. Georgia, 201 U.S. 638 (1906)(Holmes, J.).

A minister not otherwise exempt from jury service may be excused if he is properly challenged. A prospective juror may be challenged on the grounds of prejudice, direct interest in the litigation, previous knowledge of the facts, acquaintance with a party to the lawsuit, prior jury service in the same or a related case, or preconceived opinions about the lawsuit.

It has been held that persons whose religious beliefs prohibit them from serving on juries must be excused from jury service, at least if this does not create a serious threat to the effective functioning of the jury system.[45]

## §G. Confidential Communications

The great majority[46] of states consider certain communications made to ministers to be privileged. This means that a minister cannot be forced to testify in a judicial proceeding about the content of the communication. Not every communication made to a minister is protected from disclosure. The typical statute applies only to (1) communications (2) confidentially made (3) to a minister (4) acting in his professional capacity as a spiritual adviser (5) "in the course of discipline." These elements will be considered in turn.

### 1. COMMUNICATIONS

The privilege against divulging confidential communications extends only to actual communications between an individual and a clergyman. Communications obviously include verbal statements, but they also have been held to include nonverbal forms of communication. One court has held that the act of a murder suspect in displaying a gun to a minister was a "communication." The court reasoned that the word *communication* is not limited to conversation but includes "any act by which ideas are transmitted from one person to another."[47]

But acts that are not intended to "transmit ideas" are not deemed communications. Thus, it has been held that a minister's personal impressions of a person's mental capacity were not privileged,[48] nor were a minister's personal observations of the demeanor or reactions of another.[49]

---

[45]In re Jenison, 125 N.W.2d 588 (Minn. 1963).

[46]In 1981, 43 states recognized the privilege in some form. *See* 8 J. WIGMORE, EVIDENCE § 2396 (McNaughton ed. 1961 & Supp. 1981).

[47]Commonwealth v. Zezima, 310 N.E.2d 590 (Mass. 1974).

[48]Buuck v. Kruckeberg, 95 N.E.2d 304 (Ind. 1951). *Contra* Boyles v. Cora, 6 N.W.2d 401 (Iowa 1942).

[49]State v. Kurtz, 564 S.W.2d 856 (Mo. 1978).

## 2. Confidentiality

To be entitled to the privilege against the disclosure of confidential communications made to a minister, a communication must be made in confidence. This is generally interpreted to mean that a communication must be made under circumstances which imply that it would forever remain a secret. Otherwise, the privilege does not apply. Thus, statements made to a minister in the presence of other persons generally will not be privileged.[50]

Where, however, the presence of a third person is legally required, (e.g., a prisoner who cannot communicate with a minister unless a guard is present), the privilege has been held to apply.[51] And there is authority that communications made to a minister in the presence of elders, deacons, or other church officers are privileged, at least where the communication involved a confession of sin made in the course of a disciplinary proceeding.[52] It has also been held that statements made to a minister by a spouse during marriage counseling are privileged despite the fact that the other spouse is present.

Ordinarily, however, statements made to a minister in the presence of deacons, elders, church members, or any other persons will not be privileged.[53] Statements made to a minister in the course of friendly, informal conversation ordinarily are not privileged, since the circumstances do not suggest that the conversation will be kept in confidence.[54] Communications made to a minister with the understanding that he will transmit them to a third party obviously lack confidentiality, and are not considered privileged.[55]

In summary, privileged communications to a minister must not only be made in private, but they must also be made subject to an express or implied understanding that they will never be disclosed. The substance of the communication, the place where it is made, and the relationship, if any, between the minister and the one making the communication are all factors to be considered.

## 3. Made to a Clergyman

The typical statute provides that only those confidential communications made to clergymen, priests, or ministers of the gospel are privileged. Communications made to nuns,[56] an elder and deacon in the Christian Church,[57]

---

[50]State v. Berry, 324 So.2d 822 (La. 1975).

[51]People v. Brown, 368 N.Y.S.2d 645 (1974).

[52]Reutkemeier v. Nolte, 161 N.W. 290 (Iowa 1917).

[53]Milburn v. Haworth, 108 P. 155 (Colo. 1910).

[54]Angleton v. Angleton, 370 P.2d 788 (Idaho 1962).

[55]United States v. Wells, 446 F.2d 2 (2nd Cir. 1971).

[56]In re Murtha, 279 A.2d 889 (N.J. 1971).

[57]Knight v. Lee, 80 Ind. 201 (1881).

and lay religious counselors whose services are not indispensable[58] have been held not to be privileged. But communications made to lay religious counselors whose services are necessary because of the number of people requiring counseling,[59] and to elders in the Presbyterian Church,[60] have been deemed privileged.

It has been held that the IRS could not be prevented from inspecting church records on the basis of the privilege against disclosure of confidential communications to clergymen, since the term *clergyman* applies only to natural persons and not to church corporations.[61]

Finally, it is interesting to observe that the Federal Rules of Evidence, which are applicable in all trials in federal court, provide that the privilege will extend to communications made to an individual reasonably believed to be a clergyman by the person making the communication.[62]

### 4. ACTING IN HIS PROFESSIONAL CAPACITY

Most state laws require that the communication be made to a clergyman acting in his professional capacity as a spiritual adviser. Certainly there can be no expectation of confidentiality—and therefore no privilege—unless a statement is made to a clergyman acting in his professional capacity.

If a statement is made to a clergyman as a mere friend, the privilege does not apply. To illustrate, a murder suspect's incriminating admissions made to a clergyman who was a friend and frequent companion were held not to be privileged. The court reasoned that the statements had been made to the clergyman as a friend and not as a professional spiritual adviser.[63]

In another case, statements made to a clergyman by an individual who was attempting to sell him a watch were held not to be privileged.[64]

Many, perhaps most, of the communications made to a minister are not made to him in his professional capacity as a spiritual adviser. They are made to him, by church members and nonmembers alike, at church functions, following church services, in committee rooms, in hospital rooms, at funeral homes, on street corners, and at social and recreational events. Such communications

---

[58]People v. Diercks, 411 N.E.2d 97 (Ill. 1980).

[59]In re Verplank, 329 F.Supp. 433 (C.D. Cal. 1971).

[60]Cimijotti v. Paulsen, 219 F.Supp. 621 (N.D. Iowa 1963), *appeal dismissed,* 323 F.2d 716 (8th Cir. 1963).

[61]United States v. Luther, 481 F.2d 429 (9th Cir. 1973) (the court so held because no evidence presented in favor of extending privilege to church corporations).

[62]FED. R. EVID. 506.

[63]Burger v. State, 231 S.E.2d 769 (Ga. 1977).

[64]State v. Berry, 324 So.2d 822 (La. 1975).

ordinarily are not privileged. Even strictly private conversations may be made for purposes other than spiritual advice, and thus are not privileged.

A minister must inquire into the purpose or objective of a conversation in determining whether a communication is privileged. Was the minister sought out primarily for spiritual advice? Were the statements of a type that could have been made to anyone? Where did the conversation take place? Was the conversation pursuant to a scheduled appointment? What was the relationship between the minister and the person making the communication? These are the kinds of questions which help to clarify the purpose of a particular conversation, thereby determining the availability of the privilege.

### 5. THE COMMUNICATION WAS MADE IN THE COURSE OF DISCIPLINE

Several state laws require that the communication be made to a clergyman "in the course of discipline enjoined by the rules or practice" of his church. Some courts have interpreted this language strictly. As a result they apply the privilege only to communications "made in the understood pursuance of that church discipline which gives rise to the confessional relation, and, therefore, in particular to confessions of sin only, not to communications of other tenor."[65]

Other states construe such language broadly, so as to extend the privilege to all confidential communications made to a clergyman acting in his professional capacity as a spiritual adviser. In a leading case, one court, in interpreting the phrase *in the course of discipline enjoined by the rules or practice of the religious body to which he belongs,* observed:

> The word "discipline" . . . has no technical legal meaning. . . . The "discipline enjoined" includes the "practice" of all clergymen to be trained so as to . . . concern themselves in the moral training of others, and to be as willing to give spiritual aid, advice, or comfort as others are to receive it . . . . So it is in the course of "discipline enjoined" by the "practice" of their respective churches that the clergyman is to show the transgressor the error of his way; to teach him the right way; to point the way to faith, hope, and consolation; perchance, to lead him to seek atonement.
> . . . .
> It is important that the communication be made in such spirit and within the course of "discipline," and it is sufficient whether such "discipline" enjoins the clergyman to receive the communication or whether it enjoins the other party . . . to deliver the communication. Such practice makes the communication privileged, when accompanied by the essential characteristics.
> . . . .
> The fundamental thought is that one may safely consult his spiritual adviser. . . .

[65]In re Estate of Soeder, 220 N.E.2d 547, 568-69 (Ohio 1966).

When any person enters that secret chamber, this statute closes the door upon him, and civil authority turns away its ear.[66]

At least one state has recognized that a narrow interpretation of the requirement that confidential communications be made "in the course of discipline enjoined by the rules or practice" of a church would largely restrict the privilege to the Roman Catholic Church, since most Protestant denominations have no formalized system of "discipline."[67] One court has labeled any such limitation of the privilege to the clergy of one denomination an "absurdity."[68] Such an interpretation, favoring the clergy of one sect, would present serious constitutional problems, since the First Amendment prevents states from passing laws which arbitrarily favor one sect to the disadvantage of others.[69]

Most states broadly interpret the requirement that the confidential communication be made in the course of discipline. It may be safely assumed in most states that the privilege will extend to any communication made in confidence to a clergyman acting in his professional capacity as a spiritual adviser. Such an interpretation is not only permissible in view of the lack of any technical legal definition of the term, but it is also a socially desirable interpretation, since it encourages spiritual counseling. Some of the more recent state laws recognizing the privilege have avoided any reference to the term *discipline*. Rule 505 of the Uniform Rules of Evidence, which has been adopted in several states, provides that the privilege extends to any confidential communication made "to a clergyman in his professional character as spiritual adviser." Rule 506 of the Federal Rules of Evidence, which applies in all cases in the federal courts, uses substantially this same language.

Finally, it should be noted that some states protect confessions from compulsory disclosure in court. This term generally has been broadly interpreted. One court has observed that "[t]he 'confession' contemplated by the statute has reference to a penitential acknowledgment to a clergyman of actual or supposed wrongdoing while seeking religious or spiritual advice, aid, or comfort, and . . . it applies to a voluntary 'confession' as well as to one made under a mandate of the church."[70]

[66]In re Swenson, 237 N.W. 589 (Minn. 1931).

[67]In re Estate of Soeder, 220 N.E.2d 547 (Ohio 1966).

[68]In re Swenson, 237 N.W. 589 (Minn. 1931).

[69]Everson v. Board of Education, 330 U.S. 1 (1947); *see generally* Stoyles, *The Dilemma of the Constitutionality of the Priest-Penitent Privilege—The Application of the Religion Clauses,* 29 U. PITT. L. REV. 27 (1967).

[70]In re Swenson, 237 N.W. 589 (Minn. 1931).

## 6. MISCELLANEOUS CONSIDERATIONS

### a. *Clergyman-Parishioner Relationship*

It is held by most courts that a clergyman-parishioner relationship is not necessary to invoke the privilege.[71] Thus, even though the person making the communications is not a member of the minister's church, his confidential communications to that minister generally will be privileged. This would appear to be the correct view, for the purpose underlying nondisclosure of confidential communications made to clergymen applies with equal force to all who seek out a minister in confidence for spiritual guidance and help.[72]

### b. *Marriage Counseling*

Many courts have had difficulty in deciding whether to apply the privilege to communications made to clergymen in the course of marriage counseling. The prevailing view is that such statements will be privileged so long as all of the various elements of the privilege are satisfied. Most courts have assumed that statements made to a minister in the course of marriage counseling are made to the minister in his professional capacity as a spiritual adviser, and in the course of discipline.[73] Some courts have reached the opposite conclusion.[74]

### c. *Who May Assert the Privilege*

In most states, only the person who made the communication and the minister to whom it was made may claim the privilege. Many states permit the person who made the communication to prevent the minister or any other person from disclosing the communication.[75]

---

[71]Kohloff v. Bronx Savings Bank, 233 N.Y.S.2d 849 (1962).

[72]Professor Wigmore has listed four preconditions to the existence of any privilege: (1) the parties assumed that the communication would forever be kept secret; (2) communications would often not be made if the privilege did not exist; (3) in the opinion of the community, the secrecy of a particular kind of communication (*e.g.*, confidential communications to clergymen) should be preserved; (4) the injury which would attend elimination of the privilege outweighs the benefits to justice. 8 J. WIGMORE, EVIDENCE § 2396 (McNaughton ed. 1961 & Supp. 1981). These conditions would apply equally to church members and nonmembers.

[73]People v. Pecora, 246 N.E.2d 865 (Ill. 1969), *cert. denied*, 397 U.S. 1028 (1970); Kruglikov v. Kruglikov, 217 N.Y.S.2d 845 (1961), *appeal dismissed*, 226 N.Y.S.2d 931 (1962).

[74]Simrin v. Simrin, 43 Cal. Rptr. 376 (Cal. 1965).

[75]*See, e.g.*, UNIFORM RULE OF EVIDENCE § 505.

### d. When to Assert the Privilege

The privilege does not excuse a minister or the person making the communication from appearing in court. It merely excuses him from disclosing the communication in court against his will. The proper time to assert the privilege is when the person who made the communication or the minister to whom it was made is asked about the communication in court. The question must be objected to prior to an answer on the ground that it seeks to elicit privileged information. If the privilege is not claimed, it is waived. Thus, if the person who made the communication answers questions about the communication on the witness stand, without objecting, the privilege will be deemed waived, even if the question is later challenged. If a timely objection is overruled, it will serve as a basis for appeal.

### §H. Visiting Privileges at Penal Institutions

Many states allow ministers to enter correctional institutions for purposes of religious counseling and instruction.[76] However, much discretion is vested in prison authorities to determine the conditions under which a particular visit will be allowed. It is customary to allow a prisoner to visit with a minister prior to the infliction of the death penalty, and some states provide for the presence of clergymen at executions.

It has been held that the First Amendment does not forbid outsiders from entering prisons in order to conduct religious services and to "witness" to prisoners, at least where prisoners are not forced to participate.[77]

The practice of many prisons in employing chaplains has also been upheld against the claim that it constitutes a violation of the First Amendment.[78]

### §I. Miscellaneous

Ministers are eligible for various benefits under federal tax laws. Most importantly, they are permitted to exclude from their gross income the cost of owning or maintaining a residence; they can elect to be exempt from social security; and they are not considered to be "employees" subject to federal unemployment taxes.[79] Most states similarly exempt ministers from unemployment taxes. Several states exempt parsonages from property taxes, although nearly all of such states require that a parsonage be owned by the church and not by the minister in order to be qualified for the exemption.

---

[76]See, e.g., ILL. REV. STAT. ch. 38, § 1003-7-2.

[77]Campbell v. Cauthron, 623 F.2d 503 (8th Cir. 1980).

[78]Theriault v. Silber, 547 F.2d 1279 (5th Cir. 1977), cert. denied, 434 U.S. 871 (1977).

[79]See chapters 5, 6, and 10, infra.

Several states exempt ministration to the sick by prayer from the prohibition against unauthorized practice of medicine and exempt ministers from the penalties imposed upon persons who practice psychology without a license.[80] As a result, a minister is not in violation of law when he prays for the sick. But if a minister persuades a sick person to forego medical treatment and rely completely upon prayer for recovery, the minister may be responsible for any adverse consequences which could have been prevented by conventional medical treatment.[81]

The Interstate Commerce Act permits common carriers to provide transportation without charge or at discounted rates to "a minister of religion."[82] Various states likewise permit common carriers to provide free or discounted transportation to ministers.[83]

[80]TEX. HEALTH CODE ANN. title 71, §§ 4504, 4512c.
[81]*See generally,* chapter 4, § E, and chapter 18, § F, *infra.*
[82]49 U.S.C. § 10723.
[83]*See, e.g.,* KAN. STAT. § 66-707.

# 4

# LIABILITIES, LIMITATIONS, AND RESTRICTIONS

Ministers increasingly are being sued in their professional capacities for a variety of reasons. Some of the bases of liability are new and in the process of formation. Others are well-established. In this chapter the more common bases of legal liability will be reviewed.

## §A. Negligence

Perhaps the most likely basis of legal liability for a minister acting in the course of his ministry is negligence. *Negligence* has been defined as "the failure to observe, for the protection of the interests of another person, that degree of care, precaution and vigilance which the circumstances justly demand, whereby such other person suffers injury."[1] Stated simply, negligence is conduct which creates an unreasonable risk of harm to another's person or property, and which does in fact result in injury or damage. Negligent conduct need not be and usually is not intentional. It may consist either of a specific act or failure to act.

Although negligence can arise in innumerable ways, it is most often associated with carelessness in the operation of an automobile. But a minister may create unreasonable risks of harm to another's person or property in countless other ways, such as entrusting a dangerous article to one who, because of inexperience or immaturity, cannot safely handle it; authorizing a children's activity or retreat without adequate adult supervision; knowing of a dangerous condition on the church property but failing to warn members and visitors; failing to take

---

[1]T. COOLEY, TORTS 1324-25 (3d ed. 1906). This definition has been quoted by several courts, and has been characterized as the "best definition." Keefe v. Strauss, 155 N.Y.S. 530 (1915).

reasonable action to have ice and snow removed from the church's sidewalks and parking lot; or failing to have an excessively slippery floor made safe.

Even if a minister's conduct or failure to act creates an unreasonable risk of harm to others, and harm does in fact result, the minister may assert various defenses which may insulate him from liability. Perhaps the most common defense is that of "contributory negligence." Contributory negligence is simply negligence on the part of the injured party that contributes to the injury. Obviously, if the victim is himself negligent, and except for his negligence the accident would not have occurred, the party whose negligence directly caused the accident cannot be fully accountable for the injury.

Traditionally, contributory negligence on the part of a victim was a complete defense to liability. Such a rule proved to be inequitable, however, for it entirely insulated from legal liability the party whose negligence directly caused the injury. To remedy this situation, several states have adopted "comparative negligence" laws. These laws seek to apportion damages and liability on the basis of the relative fault of the parties involved. Under the doctrine of comparative negligence, a negligence victim who himself was contributorily negligent will not necessarily be denied recovery. Instead, his recovery will be reduced in proportion to his fault. Comparative negligence laws vary widely. Some states have adopted "pure" comparative negligence. Such laws allow a proportionate recovery to all negligence victims, including those whose own contributory negligence was equal to or greater than the negligence of the person directly causing the injury. Other states have adopted a "fifty percent" rule, under which a victim may recover proportionate damages only if his contributory negligence was less than fifty percent of the combined negligence resulting in his injury.

Another defense to negligence is the doctrine of "assumption of risk." Under this doctrine, one who voluntarily exposes himself to a known and appreciated danger created by the negligence of another will not be allowed to recover damages for resulting injuries. Assumption of risk is distinct from contributory negligence and is not affected by comparative negligence laws.

Finally, a minister whose negligence results in injury to another's person or property may defend himself on the basis of "imputed negligence." Under certain circumstances the law permits the negligence of one party to be imputed to another, even though the other was not negligent. The most common example involves the negligence of employees committed in the course of employment. It is well-settled that the negligence of an employee acting in the course of employment is imputed to his employer. The reason for such a rule has been stated as follows:

> The losses caused by the negligence of employees, which as a practical matter are sure to occur in the conduct of the employer's enterprise, are placed upon

the enterprise itself, as a required cost of doing business. They are placed upon the employer because, having engaged in an enterprise which will, on the basis of past experience, involve harm to others through the [negligence] of employees, and sought to profit by it, it is just that he, rather than the injured plaintiff, should bear them; and because he is better able to absorb them and to distribute them, through prices, rates or liability insurance, to society, to the community at large.[2]

If a minister is an employee of the church for which he works, it follows that the minister's negligence will be imputed to the church. Unfortunately, very few courts have faced this issue. Of those courts that have, nearly all have concluded that a minister is an employee of his church, and that the minister's negligence committed in the course of employment is imputed to the church. In the leading case of *Malloy v. Fong*,[3] Justice Traynor, speaking for the California Supreme Court, observed that "no compelling reason" existed for not imputing the negligence of church employees to churches themselves. In resolving the issue of whether a minister of a Presbyterian missions church was an employee of his presbytery, the Court applied the same test applied in other contexts:

> Whether a person performing work for another is an [employee] . . . depends primarily upon whether the one for whom the work is done has the legal right to control the activities of the alleged [employee] . . . . It is not essential that the right of control be exercised or that there be actual supervision of the work . . . . The existence of the right of control and supervision establishes the existence of an employment relationship.[4]

The Court concluded that a Presbyterian minister working in a newly created church mission is an employee of his presbytery since the presbytery exercises control over him. The Court noted in particular that the presbytery had the right "to install and remove its ministers, to approve or disapprove their transfer to other jurisdictions, and to supervise and control the activities of local churches, particularly those in the missions stage . . . ."[5]

The *Malloy* case has been relied on by several courts in imputing the negligence of a minister to his church or to a parent ecclesiastical body or official. To illustrate, one court has held that the negligence of a minister committed while driving to a regional meeting of his denomination was attributable to his church.[6] Another court imputed the negligence of a minister to his denomina-

---

[2]W. PROSSER, TORTS § 69 (4th ed. 1971).

[3]Malloy v. Fong, 232 P.2d 241 (Cal. 1951).

[4]*Id.* at 249 (citations omitted).

[5]*Id.* at 249-50.

[6]Vind v. Asamblea Apostolica De La Feen Christo Jesus, 307 P.2d 85 (Cal. 1957).

tion since the denomination exercised general supervision and control over its ministers.[7] The negligence of a minister in permitting a religious service to continue despite disorder and physical danger was imputed to his church.[8] And it has been held that the negligence of a Roman Catholic priest can be imputed to his bishop.[9] In the only recent case reaching an opposite result, one court refused to hold a church liable for injuries suffered by a church member who tripped over a defective condition in the minister's parsonage.[10]

It would be wrong to conclude that such cases establish that a minister is an employee of his church and that his negligence will be imputed to his church. The Court in *Malloy*, and each court that has followed *Malloy*, reached that conclusion only after carefully applying well-established criteria for determining whether or not an individual is an employee. And although this may be the conclusion reached by most courts, it is only because the cases involved instances of direct church control over the activities of a minister.

The fact that the minister's negligence may be imputed to his church does not necessarily shield the minister from all liability. In some states, a church could require a minister to indemnify or reimburse it for damages paid as a result of imputed negligence. Further, most negligence victims sue the individual who directly caused the injury as well as his employer. Thus, it is common for the victim of a minister's negligence to sue both the minister individually and his employing church. If for any reason the suit against the church is dismissed, the minister may still be liable.

## §B. Defamation

*Defamation* may be defined simply as words that tend to injure the reputation of another. If the words are oral, the defamation generally is referred to as slander. If the words are written, the defamation generally is referred to as libel. Although this terminology is still frequently employed, there is a tendency to refer to slander and libel collectively as defamation. The words must also be communicated to another individual or group, and in fact diminish the esteem, respect, goodwill, or confidence in which the defamed person is held.

It is important to observe that defamation is injury to one's reputation, not to one's feelings. To illustrate, the courts have held that it is defamatory to say of another that he refuses to pay his just debts, that he is immoral, about to

[7]Miller v. International Church of the Foursquare Gospel, Inc., 37 Cal. Rptr. 309 (1964).

[8]Bass v. Aetna Insurance Co., 370 So.2d 511 (La. 1979).

[9]Stevens v. Roman Catholic Bishop, 123 Cal. Rptr. 171 (1975).

[10]Allen v. College Street Church of God, 217 S.E.2d 196 (Ga. 1975).

be divorced, a hypocrite, a liar, a scoundrel, a crook, or a swindler.[11] In each instance, a court concluded that the victim's esteem or reputation had in fact been adversely affected.

## 1. THE PASTOR AS DEFENDANT

It is clear from the preceding definition that a minister will be liable for defamation if, in the presence of one or more persons, he makes an unprivileged statement that adversely affects the reputation of another. In a famous case, a minister publicly charged a member of his congregation with a "vile spirit and utter disrespect for leadership," and declared that another member had associated himself with a pastor who "under the role of minister of Jesus, is one of Satan's choicest tools." The court found such remarks to be defamatory.[12] In another notable case, a Roman Catholic archbishop was found guilty of defaming a priest by publicly referring to him as an "irresponsible and insane" person who was "morally blind" and "disobedient to the laws of the church."[13]

One minister was found guilty of defaming a former member by publicly referring to him as a "lost sheep" who had attempted to put the minister "out of the church."[14] In another case, one minister wrote a letter to another minister, recommending that a particular foreign missionary's endorsement be withdrawn. In the letter, the minister stated that the missionary in question was a liar; that he failed to pay his debts; that he was engaged in a program of destruction, hatred, and "tyrancy"; that his nature was to rule as a dictator; that his aim was to divide and split the churches; and that he was carrying out Satan's plan of division and destruction. The court concluded that such allegations standing alone would be defamatory. The court held, however, that communications made by one minister to another minister involving matters of common concern enjoy a "qualified privilege." This means that they will not be considered defamatory unless they are made with legal malice. The court defined *legal malice* as either knowledge that a statement is false or reckless disregard concerning the truth or falsity of a statement. Since the court could not say that the statements concerning the missionary were known by the minister to be false or were made with a reckless disregard concerning their truth or falsity, it denied the missionary's motion for a verdict in his behalf.[15]

The above-cited cases suggest that ministers refrain from making public remarks that might diminish the reputation, respect, goodwill, or esteem of

[11]*See generally* Annot., 87 A.L.R.2d 453 (1963).
[12]Brewer v. Second Baptist Church, 197 P.2d 713 (Cal. 1948).
[13]Hellstern v. Katzer, 79 N.W. 429 (Wis. 1899).
[14]Servatius v. Pichel, 34 Wis. 292 (1876).
[15]Murphy v. Harty, 393 P.2d 206 (Ore. 1964).

other persons. However, if a minister does communicate a disparaging remark about another, he may be able to assert one or more defenses to a charge of defamation. These defenses are described later in this section.

## 2. THE PASTOR AS PLAINTIFF

In recent years, the law has made it increasingly difficult for public figures to successfully sue others for defamatory remarks. The courts reason that when a person voluntarily thrusts himself into the public eye, he must expect to be the target of some criticism. Although few reported cases have addressed the question, it is likely that the courts will consider ministers to be public figures. Accordingly, they will be required to show more than a mere impairment of reputation in order to win a defamation suit. They must also demonstrate that the allegedly defamatory remark was uttered with malice—malice in this context meaning either actual knowledge that the remark was false or a reckless disregard concerning its truth or falsity.

The courts have found that it is defamatory to publicly accuse a minister of willful deceit, a greatly confused mind, and the grossest type of moral misconduct;[16] heresy and disturbing the peace of the church;[17] low moral character and scandalous and evil conduct that was so bad that it could not be described publicly;[18] lying, hatred, "tyrancy," failure to pay debts, and satanic motives;[19] adultery or fornication;[20] improper handling of church finances;[21] and being unable to keep his word for twenty-four hours.[22] Similarly, the courts have held that it is defamatory to say of a minister that "there has not to our knowledge appeared in public within the memory of the present generation of North Carolinians a more ignorant man,"[23] or that " I would not have anything to do with him or touch him with a ten foot pole."[24] In most of such cases, the minister was able to demonstrate that the person who uttered the defamatory remarks did so either with the knowledge that they were false or with a reckless disregard concerning their truth or falsity. In the future, it should be assumed that ministers will be required to make such a showing as a precondition to defamation suits.

[16]Stewart v. Ging, 327 P.2d 333 (N.M. 1958).
[17]Creekmore v. Runnels, 224 S.W.2d 1007 (Mo. 1949).
[18]Loeb v. Geronemus, 66 So.2d 241 (Fla. 1953).
[19]Murphy v. Harty, 393 P.2d 206 (Ore. 1964).
[20]Haynes v. Robertson, 175 S.W. 290 (Mo. 1915).
[21]Curtis v. Argus Co., 156 N.Y.S. 813 (1916).
[22]Boling v. Clinton Cotton Mills, 161 S.E. 195 (S.C. 1931).
[23]Pentuff v. Park, 138 S.E. 616 (N.C. 1927).
[24]Cole v. Millspaugh, 126 N.W. 626 (Minn. 1910).

## 3. Defenses

A person charged with uttering a defamatory remark has an array of defenses available to him, the most common of which are the following:

### a. *Truth*

The maxim that "truth is an absolute defense" to defamation is correct in most states. If an allegedly defamatory remark is true, it is simply not regarded as defamation by most courts. This defense is most commonly justified on the ground that the dissemination of truth should not be impeded by the fear of damage suits. In recent years, courts have devised a new tort (invasion of the right of privacy) to punish statements which, though true, disclose private facts about another person under circumstances making such disclosure highly offensive to a reasonable person. Thus, while truth is a defense to defamation, it does not necessarily insulate one from all legal liability.

### b. *Judicial Proceedings*

Remarks uttered during the course of judicial proceedings generally will not constitute defamation.

### c. *Consent*

One who consents to a defamatory communication will not be permitted to assert later that it was defamatory. For example, one who asks an acquaintance to provide a prospective employer with a letter of recommendation cannot later complain if the letter is derogatory. The consent, to be effective, must of course be voluntary and knowing.

### d. *"Self-Defense"*

Many courts permit a person who was defamed to respond to the defamation in a manner which, if viewed independently, might constitute defamation. The person must be careful to confine his remarks to the charges made against him.

### e. *Statements Concerning Church Matters*

Ordinarily, charges directed against ministers, church officers, or church members, and uttered before a church tribunal or council in the course of church disciplinary proceedings, or entered into the minutes or records of such a proceeding, will not be deemed defamatory unless legal malice is proven. As has been noted before, malice in this context means that the person making a disparaging remark either knew the statement to be false or made it with a reckless disregard concerning its truth or falsity.

More generally, there is legal precedent for the proposition that communications uttered between church members and relating to a matter of mutual concern to members of the church will not be considered defamatory if legal malice is absent. To illustrate, statements made under the following circumstances have been held not to be defamatory: a communication made between officers of a church or denomination on any subject in which they both have an interest;[25] communications between members of a religious organization concerning the conduct of other members or officers;[26] charges made against a church member during a church investigation into his character;[27] reading a sentence of excommunication of a church member in the presence of a church congregation;[28] and charges made by an officer of a church against the church's minister.[29]

### f. *Mitigating Factors*

Although technically not defenses to a charge of defamation, public retraction of a defamatory statement or proof that the allegedly defamed individual provoked a defamatory statement will be admissible for the purpose of mitigating or minimizing damages.

### §C. Undue Influence

If the recipient of a gift unduly influenced the donor who made the gift, the donor or his representative may have the gift canceled. This rule applies both to direct gifts made during one's lifetime and to gifts contained in documents (such as wills) which take effect at the donor's death. Undue influence is more than persuasion or suggestion. It connotes total dominion and control over the mind of another. As one court has noted, "undue influence is that influence which, by force, coercion or overpersuasion destroys the free agency" of another.[30]

Undue influence generally must be inferred from the circumstances surrounding a gift, since it seldom can be proven directly. Circumstances commonly considered in determining whether a donor was unduly influenced in the making of a gift include (1) whether the gift was the product of hasty action; (2) whether the gift was concealed from others; (3) whether the person or

---

[25]Church of Scientology v. Green, 354 F.Supp. 800 (S.D.N.Y. 1973).

[26]Willenbucher v. McCormick, 229 F.Supp. 659 (D. Colo. 1964).

[27]Cimijotti v. Paulsen, 219 F.Supp. 621 (N.D. Iowa 1963), *appeal dismissed*, 323 F.2d 716 (8th Cir. 1963).

[28]*Id.*

[29]Browning v. Gomez, 332 S.W.2d 588 (Tex. 1960).

[30]In Matter of Soper's Estate, 598 S.W.2d 528, 538 (Mo. 1980).

organization benefited by the gift was active in securing it; (4) whether the gift was consistent or inconsistent with prior declarations and planning of the donor; (5) whether the gift was reasonable rather than unnatural in view of the donor's circumstances, attitudes, and family; (6) the donor's age, physical condition, and mental health; (7) whether a confidential relationship existed between the donor and the recipient of the gift; and (8) whether the donor had independent advice.[31]

It is generally held that the burden of proving undue influence is upon the one seeking to invalidate the gift and that undue influence must be proven by "clear and convincing" or "clear and satisfactory" evidence. Proof by a mere preponderance of the evidence will not suffice.[32] However, many courts hold that a "presumption" of undue influence arises whenever a gift is made by a church member directly to his minister. Even so, this presumption is rebuttable.

To illustrate, in one case a seventy-year-old invalid dying from cancer was visited several times a week by a pastor of her church. Three days before her death, the pastor persuaded her to execute a will leaving most of her property to him. The pastor's personal attorney was called upon to draft the instrument. Two days later, the pastor attempted to have the donor give him additional property by a deed of gift, but by this time the donor was in a stupor and was physically unable to sign her name. She died a day later. The gift to the pastor was challenged on the ground that it was the product of undue influence. The court concluded that undue influence was established by the age and feeble mental and physical condition of the donor, the involvement of the pastor in procuring the gift to himself, the confidential "clergyman-parishioner" relationship that existed between the pastor and the donor, and the lack of any independent advice.[33]

In another case, a gift by a seventy-nine-year-old spinster to her church was invalidated because the evidence demonstrated that the church's minister visited the donor daily and preyed upon her fear that other churches in the community might exceed her own in size and prosperity.[34]

But in the great majority of cases, gifts to churches have been upheld despite the claim that they were the product of undue influence. Thus, in one case, a court in upholding a gift to a church observed:

> If a determined old lady, who knows her own mind and without consulting her children, carries out her own wishes in that regard and buys an annuity contract, can have her wishes held for naught and the contract set aside . . . then no such

[31]In re Estate of McCauley, 415 P.2d 431 (Ariz. 1966).
[32]See generally 25 AM. JUR. 2d Duress and Undue Influence § 48 (1966).
[33]In re Miller's Estate, 60 P.2d 492 (Cal. 1936).
[34]Whitmire v. Kroelinger, 42 F.2d 699 (W.D.S.C. 1930).

annuity can stand in this state against such attack. The entire evidence discloses that the conduct of the officer of this church or organization was above reproach, for, even after she sought them out and asked for the investment, they did not press the matter, but gave her every opportunity to seek other advice and change her desires.[35]

Other courts have rejected a charge of undue influence where a donor, though ninety years of age, was well-educated and predisposed to making a gift to her church;[36] where an elderly donor had long considered making a gift to his church and was not close to his parish priest;[37] where an elderly donor was mentally competent and experienced in business affairs, and was the first to suggest making a gift to his church;[38] where a donor's lifetime gifts to her church and minister left her with ample assets for her own support, were not the result of active solicitation by her minister, and were acknowledged with satisfaction several times by the donor during her life;[39] and where a donor frequently gave to her church, was capable of making independent business decisions, and was not close to any of her relatives.[40]

If a gift to a church is not found to be the product of undue influence, it will not be invalidated on the ground that the donor disinherited his children.[41]

One who would challenge a gift made to a church on the basis of undue influence must not delay seeking redress for an unreasonable length of time, since unreasonable delay will bar any recovery.[42]

In summary, a minister should refrain from soliciting gifts to himself from aged or mentally infirm church members, and should be very cautious in soliciting gifts for his church. Gifts to a church will be valid if the minister merely suggests and does not actively solicit a gift, the donor is mentally competent, the donor was predisposed to conveying the gift, and the donor had independent advice and assistance in implementing the gift.

### §D. Invasion of Privacy

#### 1. DEFINITIONS

In the past few decades, the subject of invasion of privacy has achieved

---

[35]Wixson v. Nebraska Conference Association of Seventh-Day Adventists, 241 N.W. 532 (Neb. 1932).

[36]Klaber v. Unity School of Christianity, 51 S.W.2d 30 (Mo. 1932).

[37]Coughlin v. St. Patrick's Church, 209 N.W. 426 (Iowa 1926).

[38]Severson v. First Baptist Church, 208 P.2d 616 (Wash. 1949).

[39]Lindley v. Lindley, 356 P.2d 455 (N.M. 1960).

[40]Umbstead v. Preachers' Aid Society, 58 N.E.2d 441 (Ind. 1944).

[41]West v. Iowa Seventh-Day Adventist Association, 189 N.W. 765 (Iowa 1922).

[42]Nelson v. Dodge, 68 A.2d 51 (R.I. 1949).

considerable attention. Actually, the term *invasion of privacy* encompasses four separate kinds of conduct.

### a. *Public Disclosure of Private Facts*

One who gives publicity to the private life of another is subject to liability for invasion of his privacy if the matter publicized is of a kind that would be highly offensive to a reasonable person and is not of legitimate concern to the public.[43] The key elements of this form of invasion of privacy are (1) publicity (2) of a highly objectionable kind (3) given to private facts about another. *Publicity* is defined as a communication to the public at large, or to so many persons that the matter is substantially certain to become one of public knowledge. Thus, it is not an invasion of privacy to communicate a fact concerning another's private life to a single person or even to a small group of persons.[44] But a statement made to a large audience, such as a church congregation, does constitute "publicity."

The facts that are publicly disclosed must be private. There is no liability if one merely repeats something that is a matter of public record or has already been publicly disclosed. Thus, a minister who makes reference in a sermon to the prior marriage or prior criminal acts of a particular church member has not invaded the member's privacy; such facts are matters of public record. Many other facts—such as, dates of birth, military service, divorce, licenses of various kinds, pleadings in a lawsuit, ownership of property, and various debts—are matters of public record. References to such facts will not invade another's privacy.

Finally, the matter that is communicated must be such that a reasonable person would feel justified in feeling seriously aggrieved by its dissemination.

This type of invasion of privacy is perhaps the most significant for ministers, since ministers typically are apprised of many private facts about members of their congregations and they have innumerable opportunities to divulge such facts. Ministers must exercise caution in divulging private facts about members of their congregations, even when the communication is positive in nature. For example, a minister publicly comments on the sordid immorality of a recent convert to his church, intending his remarks to be complimentary. He nonetheless has publicized private facts about the member under circumstances that may be highly offensive. The minister under these circumstances may well have invaded the privacy of the church member.

[43]RESTATEMENT (SECOND) OF TORTS § 652D (1977).
[44]RESTATEMENT (SECOND) OF TORTS § 652D comment a (1977).

### b. *Use of Another's Name or Likeness*

Another type of *invasion of privacy* is defined as the unauthorized use of another's name or likeness for personal or commercial advantage. To illustrate, if a company uses a child's name or picture in its advertisements without consent of the child or his parents, the company has invaded the child's privacy. The person whose name or likeness is used need not be a public figure. Churches may commit this type of invasion of privacy by publishing a picture of a person without his consent.

### c. *False Light in the Public Eye*

One who gives publicity to a matter that places another before the public in a false light is subject to liability for invasion of that person's privacy. However, the false light in which the person was placed must be highly offensive to a reasonable person, and it must have been publicized either with a knowledge that it was false or with a reckless disregard concerning its truth or falsity.[45]

A minister who ascribes to another person beliefs or positions that he does not in fact hold may have invaded his privacy. In preparing sermons or articles, ministers must be careful not to attribute to other persons opinions, statements, or beliefs that are not in fact held.

### d. *Intruding Upon Another's Seclusion*

One who intentionally intrudes upon either the solitude or private affairs of another is subject to liability to the other for invasion of his privacy if the intrusion would be highly offensive to a reasonable person.[46] This is committed if one without consent enters another's home, inspects another's private records, eavesdrops upon another's private conversation, or makes persistent and unwanted telephone calls to another. In some cases, it can be committed by unauthorized entry into a hospital room. To illustrate, a minister who enters a hospital room without consent and peers behind a closed screen may have invaded the privacy of the patient.

### 2. DEFENSES

If the victim consents to the invasion of his own privacy, this is an absolute defense. Statements that are made in judicial proceedings, that are required by law, or that are exchanged between husband and wife or attorney and client ordinarily cannot constitute an invasion of privacy. Further, statements relating to a matter of common interest—such as statements between members of a

[45]RESTATEMENT (SECOND) OF TORTS § 652E (1977).
[46]RESTATEMENT (SECOND) OF TORTS § 652B (1977).

church relating to the qualifications of church officers and members—generally cannot serve as the basis for invasion of privacy.

### 3. THE PRIVACY ACT OF 1974

Considerable confusion surrounds the scope of the Privacy Act of 1974. The Privacy Act was enacted to permit persons (1) to know of any records about them the government is collecting, maintaining, and distributing; (2) to prevent government records about them from being used without consent and for purposes other than those for which the records were first acquired; and (3) to correct and amend such records if necessary. Significantly, the Privacy Act applies only to records maintained by the federal government and some federal contractors. It has no relevance to church records.

### 4. "SUNSHINE" LAWS

Related to the Privacy Act are the various public meeting or "sunshine" laws that have been enacted by the federal government[47] and several states.[48] Such laws typically provide that meetings of all governmental bodies will be open to the public unless specifically exempted. One court has held that a state public meeting law applied to a private, nonprofit corporation organized to perform a governmental function and supported almost exclusively by tax revenues.[49] It is unlikely that such laws will ever be amended or construed to apply to churches and religious organizations.

## §E. Clergyman Malpractice

May a pastor be sued for malpractice? Should a pastor obtain malpractice insurance? These are questions of increasing relevance to many ministers.

*Malpractice* is generally defined as a failure to exercise an accepted degree of skill in the performance of professional duties that results in injury to another. In the past, malpractice suits were restricted almost exclusively to doctors and lawyers—a doctor prescribed the wrong medication or made a faulty diagnosis; a lawyer missed a pleading deadline or made an error in a title search. But in recent years, a small number of malpractice suits have been brought against pastors.

In the most significant case to date, a California church and its pastoral staff were sued by the parents of a young suicide victim who allegedly had been dissuaded by his pastors from seeking professional psychiatric help. The parents

[47]5 U.S.C. § 552b.
[48]*See generally* Annot., 38 A.L.R.3d 1070 (1971).
[49]Seghers v. Community Advancement, Inc., 357 So.2d 626 (La. 1978).

alleged that their son's pastors had been remiss in (1) discouraging psychiatric help, (2) representing that psychiatric help was of little or no value, (3) failing to disclose to the parents certain statements made by the victim, and (4) failing to refer the victim to a professional psychiatrist or psychologist. The trial court dismissed the suit as frivolous.

Future clergyman malpractice cases will likely make similar charges—some dereliction in counseling that leads directly to someone's injury, a failure to disclose to relatives the substance of counseling interviews, or a failure by a pastor to refer an individual with serious psychiatric problems to a psychiatrist or psychologist. Three factors, however, suggest that such suits will not be successful.

First, and most important, the First Amendment would be a bar to such suits, for the courts ultimately would have to determine the legitimacy of the counseling advice given by a pastor. This is clearly a prohibited inquiry under the First Amendment. The United States Supreme Court has stated:

> Men may believe what they cannot prove. They may not be put to the proof of their religious doctrines or beliefs. Religious experiences which are as real as life to some may be incomprehensible to others. Yet the fact that they may be beyond the ken of mortals does not mean that they can be made suspect before the law. Many take their gospel from the New Testament. But it would hardly be supposed that they could be tried before a jury charged with the duty of determining whether those teachings contained false representations. The miracles of the New Testament, the Divinity of Christ, life after death, the power of prayer are deep in the religious convictions of many. If one could be sent to jail because a jury in a hostile environment found those teachings false, little indeed would be left of religious freedom.[50]

Second, clergyman malpractice would in many cases clash with the pastor's duty to maintain the secrecy of communications shared with him in the privacy of counseling sessions.

Third, clergyman malpractice would suggest that a pastor should recognize that psychiatrists and psychologists are more capable of helping individuals with severe psychiatric problems than pastors. This assumption is untenable for at least two reasons: (1) Statistics indicate that the clinical success rate of psychiatric treatment is extremely low. It is also revealing to note that the suicide rate among psychiatrists is among the highest of any profession. (2) Psychological disorders are not beyond the competence of spiritual counselors. Many psychiatrists have acknowledged the therapeutic value of religion. One psychiatrist has observed:

---

[50]United States v. Ballard, 322 U.S. 78, 86-87 (1944).

I regard prayer as a master mind cure and personal religious experience as *the highest and truest form of psychotherapy*. There can be no question that the religion of Jesus, when properly understood and truly experienced, possesses power both to prevent and cure numerous mental maladies, moral difficulties, and personality disorders. . . .

The sincere acceptance of the principles and teachings of Christ with respect to the life of mental peace and joy, the life of unselfish thought and clean living, would at once wipe out more than one half the difficulties, diseases, and sorrows of the human race.[51]

Finally, the following considerations should guide a pastor or his church in determining whether or not to obtain clergyman malpractice insurance: (1) the cost is minimal; (2) the common acceptance of such insurance will encourage clergyman malpractice lawsuits; (3) the general liability insurance policies of many churches may be broad enough to cover clergyman malpractice, particularly if an allegation of personal injury is involved; (4) no pastor has yet been successfully sued for clergyman malpractice; (5) malpractice insurance would pay for the cost of defending a malpractice case.

## §F. Contract Liability

Whether the minister of an incorporated church will be personally liable on a contract that he signs depends upon two factors: (1) whether the identity of the minister's church is disclosed in the contract, and (2) whether the minister signs in a representative capacity, such as "Rev. John Smith, President." If both elements are observed, generally a minister of an incorporated church will not be personally liable. The church's identity is usually disclosed by listing the church as one of the parties to the contract. There is legal precedent for the proposition that omission of a signer's title will not render him personally liable if his corporation is identified in the contract and where the circumstances clearly reveal that he signed in an official capacity.[52] This view, however, is

---

[51]W. SADLER, MODERN PSYCHIATRY 759-760 (1949) (emphasis added). Dr. Sadler also gives the following account:

"Several years ago I had as a patient a young man, twenty-two years of age, who was fighting what he thought was a great moral battle. He became very much discouraged; broke off his marriage engagement; severed his connection with the church; and at the time I met him, seriously contemplated suicide. Having unsuccessfully tried various methods of helping him, I finally advised him that he was in need of spiritual strength and suggested that he would find great help in systematic prayer." *Id.* at 762.

[52]Kenneally v. First National Bank of Anoka, 400 F.2d 838 (8th Cir. 1968), *cert. denied,* 393 U.S. 1063 (1969).

not universally accepted. A minister, therefore, should be careful to disclose his representative capacity when signing a contract on behalf of his church.

Occasionally, contracts refer only to "the undersigned parties," in which case the minister must be careful to link the church's name with his signature. This commonly is done by placing the church name directly above the signature line. The signature line either is preceded by the word *by* or specifically refers to the minister's representative capacity. Thus, if a church is not specifically mentioned in the body of a contract, the minister may avoid personal liability on the contract by signing in either of the following two ways:

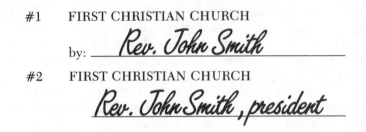

#1 FIRST CHRISTIAN CHURCH

by: _Rev. John Smith_

#2 FIRST CHRISTIAN CHURCH

_Rev. John Smith, president_

One authority has stated that "if there is no disclosure of the [corporation] in the body of the contract, the mere appending of words descriptive of the signer as, for example, the word 'president,' would not be sufficient of itself to relieve the signer of individual liability."[53]

The above discussion assumes that the contract was authorized by appropriate church action. If a minister signs a contract that has not been so authorized, the prevailing rule is that he will be personally liable on the contract. The church, of course, can "ratify" an unauthorized contract, in which case the church becomes liable on it.

In many cases it is unclear whether a minister in fact has been authorized to sign a contract on behalf of his church. This obviously is a very important question, for if the minister has not been authorized to sign the contract, he may be personally liable on it. The minister should be certain that the contract has been duly authorized by appropriate action and that he, as the church's minister, is authorized to sign. The church's charter and bylaws must be reviewed, as well as pertinent state laws. To illustrate, many churches have adopted bylaws requiring that disposition of church property be authorized only by congregational vote. Even if the board of deacons or trustees of such a church independently approves the disposition of church property, any subsequent contract of sale would be unauthorized. And even if the church congregation has approved the sale in a church business meeting, the minister

---

[53]W. FLETCHER, CYCLOPEDIA OF THE LAW OF PRIVATE CORPORATIONS § 3034 (1978).

should be satisfied that all of the procedural requirements for such a meeting—such as notice and quorum—have been met.

Unless a minister has satisfied himself that a particular contract has been properly authorized, and unless he is certain that he has been authorized to sign on behalf of the church, he should refrain from doing so.

In no event should a minister assume that he is authorized to enter into contracts on behalf of his church simply by virtue of his position. One court has held that:

> The mere proclaiming of [oneself] as the religious superior of the congregation may suffice to establish that fact in spiritual matters of his church, but it does not effect legal superiority in secular matters. There must be clear and convincing evidence of congregational acknowledgement of and acquiescence in the concept of legal superiority and authority over church business and property matters.[54]

Finally, a minister of an unincorporated church who signs a contract on behalf of the church may be personally liable on the contract even if the church is identified in the contract and the minister signs in a representative capacity. Several courts have concluded that ministers and trustees of unincorporated churches who sign contracts on behalf of their churches will be personally liable thereon.[55]

## §G.  Securities Law Violations

The subject of church securities is discussed in detail elsewhere.[56] In this chapter, only the potential legal liability of a minister under federal and state securities laws will be considered.

A minister exposes himself to legal liability under state or federal securities law in two principal ways: through the sale of church securities without first becoming registered as a salesman or agent, and through the use of any fraudulent or deceptive practice in the sale of church securities. These two grounds will be considered in turn.

---

[54]Gospel Tabernacle Body of Christ Church v. Peace Publishers & Co., 506 P.2d 1135, 1138 (Kan. 1973). *See also* American Legion v. Southwest Title and Insurance Co., 207 So.2d 393 (La. 1968), *reversed on other grounds,* 218 So.2d 612 (La. 1969) (lease entered into by minister without knowledge of church was held to be a "nullity"); Hill v. Hill, 241 S.W.2d 865 (Tenn. 1951).

[55]*See, e.g.,* I.W. Phillips & Co. v. Hall, 128 So. 635 (Fla. 1930); Abrams v. Brent, 362 S.W.2d 155 (Tex. 1962); Mitterhausen v. South Wisconsin Conference Assoc. of Seventh-Day Adventists, 14 N.W.2d 19 (Wis. 1944).

[56]*See* chapter 11, section C, *infra.*

### 1. SALESMAN REGISTRATION

The Uniform Securities Act, which has been adopted by a majority of the fifty states, provides that "it is unlawful for any person to transact business in this state as a broker-dealer or agent unless he is registered under this act."[57] Registration involves the filing of a detailed application with the state securities commission, payment of the prescribed fee, and, in many states, the successful completion of a securities law examination.

Some states exempt the sellers of church securities from the salesman registration requirements.[58] The majority, however, require registration—and only a few of these states waive the examination requirement.[59] A minister contemplating the offer or sale of securities to his church should assume that he must register as a salesman until he receives adequate assurance that he is exempt. And even if he does not expect to do any selling himself, virtually any promotion of church securities, no matter how indirect, may suffice to set in motion the salesman registration requirements for him.

Section 410 of the Uniform Securities Act provides that any person who offers or sells a security in violation of the salesman registration requirement

> is liable to the person buying the security from him, who may sue either at law or in equity to recover the consideration paid for the security, together with interest at the rate of six percent per year from the date of payment, costs, and reasonable attorneys' fees, less the amount of any income received on the security, upon the tender of the security, or for damages if he no longer owns the security.

Section 410 further provides that the employer of an unregistered salesman is also liable. Thus, both a minister and his church will be liable under this section if the minister sells church securities in violation of a salesman registration provision.

Section 409 imposes criminal penalties ranging up to a fine of $5,000 or imprisonment of three years upon any person who "willfully violates" the salesman registration requirement.

### 2. FRAUDULENT PRACTICES

Section 101 of the Uniform Securities Act and section 17 of the federal Securities Act of 1933 provide that it is unlawful for any person in connection with the offer, sale, or purchase of any security, directly or indirectly

---

[57]UNIFORM SECURITIES ACT § 201(a).

[58]See, e.g., ARIZ. REV. STAT. ANN. § 44-1843; ILL. REV. STAT. ch. 121½, § 137.8(A); KY. REV. STAT. § 292.310(2)(a); NEB. REV. STAT. § 8-1101(2).

[59]See, e.g., Delaware Securities Commission Rule 14B(d); Maryland Securities Commission Rule .02B(4).

a. to employ any device, scheme, or artifice to defraud,
b. to make any untrue statement of a material fact or to omit to state a material fact necessary in order to make the statements made, in the light of the circumstances under which they are made, not misleading, or
c. to engage in any act, practice, or course of business which operates or would operate as a fraud or deceit upon any person.

Neither the federal Securities Act of 1933 nor the Uniform Securities Act exempts ministers or religious organizations from this provision. Ministers may violate these antifraud provisions by making false or misleading statements about church securities; failing to disclose material risks associated with church securities; manipulating the church's financial records in order to facilitate the sale of church securities; failing to establish a debt service or sinking fund out of which church securities will be retired; making false predictions; recommending securities transactions to investors without regard to their financial situation; inducing transactions that are excessive in view of an investor's financial resources; borrowing money from an investor; commingling investors' funds with one's own personal funds; deliberately failing to follow an investor's instructions; making unfounded guarantees; misrepresenting to investors the true status of their funds; or stating that securities are insured or secured when they are not.

To illustrate, one minister was found guilty of engaging in fraudulent practices when it was established that he failed to disclose to investors of church securities that he had $116,000 in unsatisfied debts; he had incurred $700,000 in unsatisfied debts on behalf of a previous church through the sale of securities; and church financial statements were in error.[60]

Although a minister may not have intended to defraud investors, that is no defense. A defrauded investor need not prove intent to defraud in order to recover.

Section 410 of the Uniform Securities Act permits a defrauded investor to recover the purchase price of any security that he purchased plus interest, costs, and attorneys' fees, less the amount of income received on the security. If a defrauded investor no longer owns the security, he may sue for general damages.

Section 409 imposes criminal penalties ranging up to a $5,000 fine and three years imprisonment for willful violations of the antifraud provisions.

In addition, the federal Securities Act of 1933 provides civil remedies for defrauded investors and imposes criminal penalties ranging up to a $10,000 fine and five years imprisonment for willful violations.[61]

[60]Order of Florida Comptroller No. 78-1-DOS (February 17, 1978).
[61]15 U.S.C. § 77x.

## §H. Failure to Report Child Abuse

In an effort to reduce the incidence of child abuse, several states have enacted laws requiring the reporting of actual or suspected cases of child abuse. Most state reporting laws impose a duty to report only on certain designated professions. For example, most reporting laws impose a duty to report on physicians and related health care personnel, psychologists, social workers, teachers, and law enforcement officials. Some states specifically include ministers in the class of persons who are under a duty to report.

Other state reporting laws do not specifically include ministers in the class of persons under a duty to report, but define the class so broadly that it may be construed to include ministers. For example, one state imposes a duty to report on "any person having cause to believe that a child's physical or mental health or welfare has been or may be adversely affected by abuse or neglect . . . ."[62] Many state laws are similar to this in breadth.[63]

It is important to note that most reporting laws require reports of both actual and imminent cases of child abuse. A person under a duty to report must not wait until the actual abuse occurs to file his report if he is aware of information that gives him reasonable cause to believe that an act of abuse may occur in the near future. Also, it should be observed that *child abuse* is usually defined to include mental and emotional as well as physical abuse.

Nearly every state law requiring the reporting of child abuse gives the reporter immunity from any legal liability that might otherwise have resulted from his report. A typical state law provides that any person participating in good faith in the making of a report "shall have immunity from any liability, civil or criminal, that otherwise might result by reason of such actions."[64] Most reporting laws also state that no one shall be relieved of the duty to report because of the privileged or confidential nature of communications that he has received.[65] A minister, therefore, may not excuse his failure to report on the basis that the information he received was "confidential" or privileged.

Penalties for violation of the duty to report often involve fines or prison sentences.[66]

[62]TEX. FAMILY CODE ANN. title 2, § 34.01.

[63]*See, e.g.,* KAN. STAT. § 38-717; KY. REV. STAT. § 199.335(2); OKLA. STAT. title 21, § 846; TENN. CODE ANN. § 37-1203. *See generally* V. DE FRANCIS & C. LUCHT, CHILD ABUSE LEGISLATION IN THE 1970's (1974).

[64]MO. REV. STAT. § 210.135.

[65]*See, e.g.,* KY. REV. STAT. § 199.335(7); OKLA. STAT. title 21, § 848; TEX. FAMILY CODE ANN. title 2, § 34.04.

[66]*See, e.g.,* MO. REV. STAT. § 210.165 (up to $1,000 and one year imprisonment); TENN. CODE ANN. § 37-1212 ($50 and up to three months imprisonment).

# 5

# SOCIAL SECURITY FOR MINISTERS

## §A. Introduction

The Social Security Act currently provides an array of benefits designed to assist aged and disabled persons and their dependents. In addition, the Social Security Act and related laws provide unemployment benefits, black lung benefits, and various welfare services to the poor.[1]

Social security benefits are financed primarily through two separate tax systems. Under the Federal Insurance Contributions Act (FICA) a tax is levied against employers and employees. Under the Self-Employment Contributions Act, a tax is levied against the net earnings of self-employed persons.

## §B. Ministers Deemed Self-Employed

For social security purposes, a duly ordained, commissioned, or licensed minister of a church in the exercise of his ministry has always been treated as a self-employed person, not as an employee.[2] As a result, a church is not considered an employer and thus is not obligated to pay any social security taxes attributable to the minister's income. And, the minister pays the tax applicable to self-employed persons unless he is exempt from social security coverage.

## §C. Coverage Rules

Until 1968, service performed by a duly ordained, commissioned, or licensed minister of a church in the exercise of his ministry was considered exempt from social security tax.[3] A minister was permitted to file a certificate (Form 2031)

[1]1981 SOCIAL SECURITY HANDBOOK.

[2]I.R.C. §§ 3121(b)(8), 1402.

[3]I.R.C. § 1402(c)(4) prior to its amendment by P.L. 90-248, § 115, effective January 2, 1968.

with the IRS, electing to have social security coverage extended to such work, but filing was purely voluntary. Moreover, the certificate had to be filed by the due date of the minister's federal income tax return for the second tax year in which the minister had net earnings from self-employment of $400 or more, any part of which consisted of remuneration for service performed in the exercise of his ministry.[4] Finally, the certificate electing social security coverage was considered irrevocable.

In 1967, Congress amended the provisions of the social security law applicable to ministers. Under the new law, which took effect in 1968, social security coverage was extended to services performed by a duly ordained, commissioned, or licensed minister of a church in the exercise of his ministry. A minister who began his ministry before 1968 is automatically covered, unless he filed an application for exemption (Form 4361—see illustration at end of chapter) by the later of the following two dates: April 15, 1970, or the due date of the federal income tax return for the second tax year after 1953 in which the minister had net earnings from self-employment of $400 or more, any part of which was derived from the performance of service as a minister.[5] Ministers who filed a certificate before 1968 electing social security coverage may not file an exemption application.[6]

The exemption application permits a minister to withdraw from social security coverage if he meets all of the following conditions:

1. He is an ordained, commissioned, or licensed minister of a church. Licensed ministers of a church or denomination that both licenses and ordains ministers are eligible for the exemption only if they perform substantially all of the religious functions of an ordained minister under the tenets and practices of their religious denomination.[7]

2. The church or denomination that ordained, commissioned, or licensed the minister qualifies as a tax-exempt religious organization.[8]

3. The minister must affirm that because of religious principles he is conscientiously opposed to accepting (for services performed as a minister) any governmental insurance that makes payments in the event of death, disability, old age, or retirement, or makes payments toward the cost of, or provides services for, medical care, including the benefits of any insurance system established by the Social Security Act.[9] Ministers who object to social security coverage on the basis of economic considerations rather than religious principles

[4]Treas. Reg. § 1.1402(e)(2)-1.
[5]I.R.C. § 1402(e); *see also* Allison v. Commissioner, 39 T.C.M. 268 (1979).
[6]I.R.C. § 1402(e)(1).
[7]Rev. Rul. 78-301, 1978-2 C.B. 103.
[8]Rev. Rul. 80-59, 1980-1 C.B. 191.
[9]I.R.C. § 1402(e)(1). *See generally* IRS Publication 517.

are not eligible for an exemption. In one case, a minister who filed an exemption application solely on the basis of economic considerations was found to have made an invalid application, and he was found liable for social security taxes for every year beginning with 1968.[10]

4. As noted earlier in this chapter, an exemption application must be filed by the later of the following two dates: April 15, 1970, or the due date of the federal tax return for the second tax year after 1953 in which the minister has net earnings from self-employment of $400 or more, any part of which was derived from the performance of service as a minister.

An exemption is irrevocable.[11] A minister will not be allowed to change his mind at a later time and request that social security coverage be extended to his services as a minister. Congress did allow ministers who were exempt as of December 20, 1977, to revoke their exemptions by the due date of their federal income tax return for 1978 (generally April 15, 1979) by filing a Form 4361-A. But Congress has not otherwise given ministers the opportunity to revoke a duly filed exemption application.

Several constitutional challenges have been brought against the exemption of ministers from social security coverage. Thus far, none has been successful. The courts have consistently held that the exemption of those ministers who oppose social security on religious grounds is mandated by the constitutional guaranty of freedom of religion.[12]

These coverage rules may be illustrated by the following examples:

*Example 1. X,* a licensed minister, is engaged by *Y* Church as a minister of music. Assuming that he is otherwise qualified, *X* is eligible for exemption from social security coverage if he performs substantially all of the religious functions that an ordained minister in his church or church denomination may perform.[13]

*Example 2. X,* an ordained minister, is opposed to social security on the basis of economic considerations, not on the basis of religious principles. *X* is not entitled to an exemption from social security coverage.

*Example 3. X,* an ordained minister, is opposed to social security on the basis of nonreligious conscientious objection. *X* is not entitled to an exemption from social security coverage.[14]

*Example 4. X,* a duly ordained minister since 1957, earned more than $400 from services performed in the exercise of his ministry for each year from 1957 to the present. He never filed a Form 2031 electing social security coverage.

[10]Rev. Rul. 70-197, 1970-1 C.B. 181.

[11]I.R.C. § 1402(e)(3).

[12]*See, e.g.,* Linger v. Commissioner, 42 T.C.M. 1068 (1981).

[13]Rev. Rul. 78-301, 1978-2 C.B. 103.

[14]Rev. Rul. 75-189, 1975-1 C.B. 289.

X had until April 15, 1970, to file an exemption application (Form 4361). If he failed to do so by that date, his services in the exercise of his ministry automatically became subject to social security.[15]

*Example 5.* X, an unordained layman, conducts religious services. He is not eligible for the exemption, since he is not a duly ordained, commissioned, or licensed minister. If X subsequently becomes ordained, commissioned, or licensed, he has until the due date of his federal tax return for the second year in which his net earnings from self-employment (a portion of which constituted earnings from the exercise of his ministry) exceeded $400 to file an exemption application. His previous service as a layman does not affect this deadline.

*Example 6.* X, a duly ordained minister, pastored a church from 1955 to 1965. In 1965, X left the ministry to accept secular employment. He retained his status as an ordained minister. In 1971, X left secular employment to return full-time to the ministry. He filed an exemption application in 1971. His application was not timely filed.[16]

*Example 7.* X, who was ordained in 1980, had net earnings as a minister in excess of $400 in 1980 and 1981. He had until April 15, 1982, to file an exemption application. However, if X did not file an exemption application by April 15, 1981, his self-employment tax for 1980 was due by that date.[17]

*Example 8.* Same facts as Example 7, except that X was licensed and not ordained in 1980. The answer is the same provided that X performs substantially all of the religious functions of an ordained minister in his church or church denomination.

*Example 9.* X was ordained in 1975. He had net earnings as a minister in excess of $400 in 1975 and 1980. He had until the due date of his 1980 federal income tax return (April 15, 1981) to file an exemption application.

## §D. Services to Which Exemption Applies

A duly ordained, commissioned, or licensed minister of a church is permitted to exclude from social security coverage only services performed by him in the exercise of his ministry. The income tax regulations define *service by a minister in the exercise of his ministry* to include

> the ministration of sacerdotal functions and the conduct of religious worship, and the control, conduct, and maintenance of religious organizations (including the

---

[15]Kinney v. Commissioner, 40 T.C.M. 883 (1980); Williams v. United States, 79-1 U.S.T.C. 9279 (Ct. Cl. 1979).

[16]Strang v. United States, 591 F.2d 381 (6th Cir. 1979).

[17]IRS Publication 517.

religious boards, societies and other integral agencies of such organizations), under the authority of a religious body constituting a church or church denomination.[18]

The regulations defining *service by a minister in the exercise of his ministry* further stipulate:

1. Service performed by a minister constitutes "the ministration of sacerdotal functions and the conduct of religious worship" based upon the tenets and practices of the particular religious body constituting his church or church denomination.[19]

2. Service performed by a minister in "the control, conduct, and maintenance of religious organizations" relates to directing, managing, or promoting the activities of such organizations.[20]

3. Any religious organization is deemed to be "under the authority of a religious body constituting a church or church denomination" if it is organized for and dedicated to carrying out the tenets and principles of faith of a church or denomination.[21]

4. If a minister is performing service in "the conduct of religious worship" or "the ministration of sacerdotal functions," such service is in the exercise of his ministry whether or not it is performed for a religious organization.[22]

5. If a minister is performing service for an integral agency of a religious organization under the authority of a church or denomination, all service performed by him—in the conduct of religious worship, in the ministration of sacerdotal functions, or in the control, conduct, and maintenance of the agency— is in the exercise of his ministry.[23]

6. Even though a minister's service is performed for a secular institution and no religious activity is involved, if it is at the direction of his church or denomination, it is in the exercise of his ministry.[24]

The regulations further specify that if a minister is performing service for an organization that is neither a religious organization nor operated as an integral agency of a religious organization and his service is not performed at the direction of his denomination or church, then only his conduct of religious worship or ministration of sacerdotal functions is in the exercise of his ministry.[25]

The following examples will illustrate the rules just discussed:

[18]Treas. Reg. § 1.1402(c)-5(b)(2).
[19]Treas. Reg. § 1.1402(c)-5(b)(2)(i).
[20]Treas. Reg. § 1.1402(c)-5(b)(2)(ii).
[21]*Id.*
[22]Treas. Reg. § 1.1402(c)-5(b)(2)(iii).
[23]Treas. Reg. § 1.1402(c)-5(b)(2)(iv).
[24]Treas. Reg. § 1.1402(c)-5(b)(2)(v).
[25]Treas. Reg. § 1.1402(c)-5(c)(2).

*Example 10. X* pastors a small rural church. To help support himself, he also works part-time in secular employment. *X* files a timely exemption application. *X's* exemption application removes only his services performed in the exercise of his ministry from social security coverage. Therefore, he must still pay social security tax on earnings from his secular employment.[26]

*Example 11. X* is an ordained minister who is employed in an administrative capacity by his denomination. X's work for his denomination constitutes the exercise of his ministry.[27]

*Example 12. X,* an ordained minister, is a full-time professor at a seminary under the authority of a church denomination. *X* is performing service in the exercise of his ministry, even if the seminary is under the authority of a denomination other than his own.[28]

*Example 13. X,* an ordained minister, is employed as a campus chaplain at a secular university. *X* devotes his entire time to performing his duties as a chaplain, which include conducting religious worship, offering spiritual counsel to university students, and teaching a class in religion. *X* is performing service constituting the exercise of his ministry.[29]

*Example 14. X,* a duly ordained minister, is assigned by his church denomination to perform advisory service to *Y* Company in connection with the publication of a book dealing with the history of *X's* church denomination. *Y* Company is neither a religious corporation nor operated as an integral agency of a religious organization. *X* performs no other service for his denomination or *Y* Company. X's work is construed as performance of his ministry.[30]

*Example 15. X,* a duly ordained minister, is engaged by *Y* University to teach mathematics. He performs no other service for *Y,* although from time to time he performs marriages and conducts funerals for relatives and friends. *Y* University is neither a religious organization nor operated as an integral agency of a religious organization. *X* is not performing service for *Y* University at the direction of his denomination. The service performed by *X* for *Y* University cannot be construed as the exercise of his ministry. However, his performance of marriages and conducting of funerals can be construed as the exercise of his ministry.[31]

*Example 16. X,* an ordained minister, temporarily leaves the ministry in order to pursue secular employment. He occasionally performs marriages and funerals for relatives and friends. He also conducts a weekly Bible study in

[26]Ross v. Commissioner, 40 T.C.M. 815 (1980).
[27]Rev. Rul. 57-129, 1957-1 C.B. 313.
[28]Rev. Rul. 57-107, 1957-1 C.B. 277.
[29]Treas. Reg. § 1.1402(c)-5(b)(2)(iii).
[30]Treas. Reg. § 1.1402(c)-5(b)(2)(v).
[31]Treas. Reg. § 1.1402(c)-5(c)(2).

his home. The service performed by *X* in his secular employment is not in the exercise of his ministry. However, service performed by *X* in performing marriages and conducting funerals and Bible studies is in exercise of his ministry.

## §E. Computation of Tax

The social security tax for ministers who have not filed a timely exemption application is computed by multiplying the applicable rate of tax times the minister's "net earnings from self-employment."[32] *Net earnings from self-employment* is defined as gross income derived from self-employment less various deductions. The principal deductions for a minister include the following:

1. Unreimbursed business expenses allowed only as itemized deductions on Form 1040, Schedule A. These include all ordinary and necessary expenses incurred by the minister in carrying on his profession which are not reimbursed by his church. Examples are the purchase of books and magazines, membership dues to professional societies, ministry-related home telephone costs, and entertainment expenses. In each case, the expense is allowable only to the extent that it is an ordinary and necessary expense of the minister in carrying on his profession. Note that such expenses are deductible in computing net earnings from self-employment whether or not the minister actually deducts them as an itemized deduction on Form 1040, Schedule A. Thus, if the minister's total itemized deductions do not exceed his "zero bracket amount" (standard deduction), and therefore he does not itemize his deductions for income tax purposes, he may still deduct such expenses in computing net earnings from self-employment.

2. Employee business expenses reported on Form 1040. Employees can deduct certain business expenses even if they do not itemize their deductions on Form 1040, Schedule A. These include meal and lodging costs incurred while on overnight business trips away from home, and expenses associated with business use of a car. These expenses are computed on IRS Form 2106 and reported on Form 1040.

3. Ministry-related deductions reported on Schedule C. Although ministers who meet the common law definition of an employee no longer report their church salary on Schedule C, they still should use Schedule C to report income and related expenses from such self-employment activities as the performance of marriages, baptisms, and funerals.

The law expressly *includes* within the definition of net earnings from self-employment the fair rental value of a parsonage furnished to a minister or the housing allowance paid to a minister. Thus, while a housing allowance is excludable by a minister in computing income taxes, it is not excludable in

---

[32]I.R.C. §§ 1401-1403.

computing social security taxes.[33] Also included in the definition of net earnings from self-employment is the value of meals and lodging furnished to a minister by or on behalf of his employer for the convenience of his employer, even though such amounts may be excluded in computing income taxes.[34]

After computing net earnings from self-employment, a minister multiplies this figure times the applicable rate of tax to determine his social security taxes. Note, however, that the law prescribes a maximum amount of net earnings from self-employment that are subject to social security tax. Any net earnings above this maximum taxable amount are not taxable. The maximum taxable net earnings from self-employment for tax years beginning with 1982 is determined by an "escalator" announced each year by the Secretary of the U.S. Department of Health and Human Services.[35]

Proposed self-employment tax rates are set forth below.[36]

### Self-Employment Tax Rates

| | |
|---|---|
| 1983 | 9.35% |
| 1984 | 14.00% |
| 1985 | 14.10% |
| 1986 | 14.30% |
| 1987 | 14.30% |
| 1988 | 15.02% |
| 1989 | 15.02% |
| 1990 | 15.30% |

To illustrate, a minister who has not filed a timely exemption application and whose net earnings from self-employment for 1983 are $30,000 will pay $2,805 ($30,000 × 9.35%) in social security taxes for the year.

There is no tax on net earnings from self-employment of less than $400 in a given year. However, if a person has more than $400 of self-employment earnings in a given year, he pays tax on the entire amount. Thus, if an individual's net earnings from self-employment for a given year is $1,000, he pays tax on the full $1,000 and not on the $1,000 less the minimum taxable amount of $400.

If an individual receives both income from self-employment and wages as an employee in a given year, his taxable self-employment earnings are the maximum taxable self-employment earnings for that year minus his wages as

[33]I.R.C. § 1402(a)(8).

[34]Id.

[35]The escalator is tied to increases in wage indexes. For 1983, maximum net earnings subject to tax were $35,700.

[36]The self-employed are eligible for a tax credit of 2.7% of their earnings in 1984, 2.3% in 1985, and 2.0% in 1986 through 1989.

an employee, assuming that the wages are subject to social security tax. For example, if an individual had $40,000 of self-employment income in a tax year for which the maximum taxable self-employment income was $35,000, and $5,000 in employee wages unrelated to his ministry, his taxable self-employment income could not exceed $30,000 ($35,000 less $5,000).

## §F. Tax Returns

Every taxpayer is required to prepay his taxes each year either by making estimated tax payments or by having his employer withhold a portion of his income. Since a minister's income derived from the exercise of ministry is exempt from withholding, he is required to estimate and prepay his taxes. This is done on IRS Form 1040-ES.[37] Both federal income taxes and social security taxes must be estimated and prepaid since federal law requires that ministers include social security taxes in computing and paying estimated tax installments.[38] At the end of the current tax year, a minister computes his actual income and social security taxes on IRS Form 1040 and Schedule SE.

## §G. Postscript—Is Social Security a Good Investment?

Is social security a good investment? In a sense this question has no relevance since social security coverage is compulsory for all ministers of the gospel unless they object to participation on the basis of religious principles. Nevertheless, many ministers are interested in knowing what they are getting in return for their substantial tax payments.

As has been noted, Congress established the social security system to provide for the material needs of individuals and families, to protect aged and disabled persons against the expenses of illnesses that could otherwise exhaust their savings, to keep families together, and to give children the opportunity to grow up in health and security. These many benefits are provided through retirement insurance, survivors insurance, disability insurance, and hospital and medical insurance.

Although an individual conceivably could buy private insurance to cover most if not all of the benefits social security coverage provides, it is likely that the cost of such coverage would at best be comparable to the social security tax, and at the worst could cost considerably more. Furthermore, comparison of the value of alternative private insurance plans assumes that a person would have the discipline to purchase such insurance. This is a very dubious assumption. In fact, when Congress put social security coverage on a mandatory,

---

[37] See generally chapter 6, infra.
[38] I.R.C. § 6015(d).

involuntary basis, it rejected entirely the notion that Americans could be expected to discipline themselves into buying private insurance.

Many critics of social security compare the cost of social security with other retirement programs. They conclude that if a person invests his social security taxes in a private retirement program he can accumulate greater retirement benefits. This argument overlooks the fact that social security provides many more benefits than retirement benefits. Social security coverage also provides survivors benefits, disability insurance, and hospital and medical insurance. When these additional benefits are considered, the value of social security is considerably enhanced. Social security retirement benefits are also inflation-indexed, which virtually guarantees that a person who attains or exceeds his life expectancy will receive benefits far exceeding his contributions. Furthermore, it must be remembered that social security benefits ordinarily are not taxable, whereas benefits under most private retirement programs would be subject to tax.

To put social security retirement benefits into perspective, consider that a person who retired in 1981 at age sixty-five and who paid the maximum social security tax each year from 1937 through 1981 contributed a total of approximately $14,800.[39] His initial benefits of $735 a month will return every dollar of his contributions within twenty months. And if he lives until age seventy-nine—his life expectancy—he will collect $127,000, not counting cost-of-living increases. And this does not take into account survivors insurance, disability insurance, and hospital or medical insurance. Obviously, considerable evidence opposes those who maintain that social security is a bad investment.

It is true that in some cases a person will not receive back all of his contributions. The worker described in the preceding paragraph could have died in 1981, shortly after retiring at age sixty-five, not survived by a spouse or any dependents. Leaving no dependents, he would have received only the intangible benefit of having been insured throughout most of his working life under the survivors, disability, medical, and hospital insurance provisions. But such cases will be rare. The statistical probability is a normal life expectancy. And as noted earlier, a person who reaches or exceeds his life expectancy will receive benefits far exceeding his contributions.

---

[39]Compounding the value of this individual's contributions would not materially affect the example. The compounded value would be substantially less than his retirement benefits alone if he attains his life expectancy, even without compounding the value of such benefits to take into account cost-of-living increases.

| Form **4361** (Rev. September 1981) Department of the Treasury Internal Revenue Service | **Application for Exemption from Self-Employment Tax for Use by Ministers, Members of Religious Orders and Christian Science Practitioners** | OMB No. 1545-0168 Expires 8/31/84 |
|---|---|---|

Documentation required by Specific Instruction Item 4 MUST be attached to this form. Before filing this form see General Instructions.

**Please type or print**

| 1 Name | 2 Social security number |
|---|---|
| Address | |
| City or town, State and ZIP code | |

| 3 Check ONLY ONE box: ☐ Christian Science practitioner   ☐ Ordained minister, priest, rabbi ☐ Member of religious order not under a vow of poverty   ☐ Commissioned or licensed minister (see Item 7) | 4 Date ordained, licensed, etc. |
|---|---|

| 5 Legal name of ordaining, licensing, or commissioning body or religious order | Employer identification number |
|---|---|
| Address | |
| City or town, State and ZIP code | |

6 Enter the first two years after the date entered in Item 4, above, in which you had net earnings from self-employment of $400 or more, some part of which was from services as a minister, priest, rabbi, etc.; or as a member of a religious order; or as a Christian Science practitioner . . . . . . . . . . . . . . . . . . . ▶ | 19 ____ | 19 ____

**Caution:** *Form 4361 is not proof of any of the following: (a) the right to an exemption from Federal income tax withholding and social security tax; (b) the right to a parsonage allowance exclusion (section 107 of the Internal Revenue Code); or (c) assignment by your religious superiors to a particular job.*

7 If you are applying for the exemption as a licensed or commissioned minister, and your denomination provides for the ordination of ministers, please indicate to what extent your ecclesiastical powers differ from those of an ordained minister of your denomination and attach a copy of your denomination's by-laws relating to the powers of ordained, and commissioned or licensed ministers.

-------------------------------------------------------------------------------------------------------

8 I certify that, because of my religious principles, I am conscientiously opposed to the acceptance (with respect to services performed by me as a minister, member, or practitioner) of the benefits of any public insurance that makes payments in the event of death, disability, old-age, or retirement or makes payments toward the cost of, or provides services for, medical care (including the benefits of any insurance system established by the Social Security Act).

I certify that I did not file an effective waiver certificate (Form 2031) electing social security coverage on earnings as a minister, member, or practitioner.

I hereby request an exemption from payment of self-employment tax with respect to my earnings from services as a minister, member, or practitioner, pursuant to the provisions of section 1402(e) of the Internal Revenue Code. I understand that the exemption, if granted, will apply only to such earnings. Under penalties of perjury, I declare that this application has been examined by me and to the best of my knowledge and belief it is true and correct.

Signature ▶ _____   Date ▶ _____

**Note:** The exemption is granted only if the application is approved by Internal Revenue Service, and Copy C is returned to you marked "approved."

| **For Internal Revenue Service Use** | **COPY A** |
|---|---|
| ☐ Approved for exemption from self-employment tax (see Caution above) ☐ Disapproved for exemption from self-employment tax | **To be retained by Internal Revenue Service** |
| By ......................................................................................................  (Director's signature)                           (Date) | |

## General Instructions

This form *must be filed in triplicate with the Internal Revenue Service.*

**Paperwork Reduction Act Notice.**—The Paperwork Reduction Act of 1980 says we must tell you why we are collecting this information, how we will use it, and whether you have to give it to us. We ask for the information to carry out the Internal Revenue laws of the United States. We need it to ensure that you are complying with these laws and to allow us to figure and collect the right amount of tax. You are required to give us this information.

If you are a member of a religious order **who has taken a vow of poverty,** do not file this form because you are automatically exempt from the payment of self-employment tax for amounts earned for services performed for your church or an integral agency thereof. **However,** members of a religious order who are under a vow of poverty and are paid to perform services for an

organization other than the church or an integral agency of it are treated as regular employees of this organization for Federal employment tax purposes (Federal income tax withholding, social security and Federal unemployment tax). The automatic exemption from self-employment tax does not apply to amounts earned during such employment.

**A. Purpose of This Form.**—This form should be used to request exemption under the Self-Employment Contributions Act for services performed by a minister, member of a religious order, or Christian Science practitioner.

**B. Who May File for Exemption.**—Any duly ordained, commissioned, or licensed minister of a church, member of a religious order (who has not taken the vow of poverty), or Christian Science practitioner may file for exemption from self-employment tax. To be eligible for the exemption, the applicant must establish that the or-

daining, commissioning, or licensing body (or religious order) is a church that is exempt from Federal income tax under section 501(a) of the Internal Revenue Code as a religious organization described in section 501(c)(3), and must also establish that the church (or convention or association of churches) is one described in section 170(b)(1)(A)(i). The request must be based on a conscientious opposition, because of the applicant's religious principles, to accepting (for services performed as a minister, member, or practitioner) public insurance (including social security benefits) that makes payments in the event of death, disability, old-age, or retirement or provides services for, medical care. However, if the minister, member, or practitioner has previously filed an effective waiver certificate Form 2031, an application for exemption may **NOT** now be filed.

Commissioned or licensed ministers of a church or church denomination that pro-

*(Continued on back)*

vides for ordination of ministers may file an application for exemption if they are invested with the authority to perform substantially all of the religious duties of their church or church denomination.

For more information, see **Publication 517,** Social Security for Members of the Clergy and Religious Workers.

**C. Earnings to Which This Exemption Applies.**—An exemption that is effective for a duly ordained, commissioned, or licensed minister of a church applies only to service performed in the exercise of the ministry.

Service performed by a minister in the exercise of the ministry includes the ministration of sacerdotal functions, the conduct of religious worship, and the control, conduct, and maintenance of religious organizations (including the religious boards, societies, and other integral agencies of such organizations), under the authority of a religious body constituting a church or church denomination. The following rules apply in determining whether services performed by a minister are performed in the exercise of the ministry.

If a minister is performing service in the conduct of religious worship or the ministration of sacerdotal functions, this service is in the exercise of the ministry whether or not it is performed for a religious organization.

If a minister is performing service for an organization that operates as an integral agency of a religious organization under the authority of a religious body constituting a church or church denomination, all service performed by the minister in the conduct of religious worship, in the ministration of sacerdotal functions, or in the control, conduct, and maintenance of such organization is in the exercise of the ministry. The following example illustrates this rule:

**Example:** M, a duly ordained minister, is engaged by the N Religious Board to serve as director of one of its departments. M performs no other service. The N Religious Board is an integral agency of O, a religious organization operating under the authority of a religious body constituting a church denomination. M is performing service in the exercise of M's ministry.

If a minister, under an assignment or designation by a religious body constituting the minister's church, performs service for an organization that is neither a religious organization nor operated as an integral agency of a religious organization, all service performed by the minister, even though this service may not involve the conduct of religious worship or the ministration of sacerdotal functions, is in the exercise of the ministry. Ordinarily, the services of a minister are not assigned or designated services if any of the following circumstances are present: (1) the organization for which the minister performs the services did not arrange with the minister's church for the minister's services; (2) the minister is performing services for the organization that other employees of the organization who have not been so designated are performing; or (3) the minister performed the same services before and after the designation.

**D. Earnings to Which This Exemption Does Not Apply.**—An exemption that is effective for a duly ordained, commissioned, or licensed minister of a church does not apply to service performed that is not in the exercise of the ministry.

If a minister is performing service for an organization that is neither a religious organization nor operated as an integral agency of a religious organization and the service is not performed under an assignment or designation by the minister's ecclesiastical superiors, then only the service performed by the minister in the conduct of religious worship or the ministration of sacerdotal functions is in the exercise of the ministry. The following example illustrates this rule:

**Example:** M, a duly ordained minister, is engaged by N University to teach history and mathematics. M performs no other service for N although from time to time M performs marriages and conducts funerals for relatives and friends. N University is neither a religious organization nor operated as an integral agency of a religious organization. M is not performing the service for N under an assignment or designation by M's ecclesiastical superiors. The service performed by M for N University is not in the exercise of M's ministry. However, service performed by M in performing marriages and conducting funerals is in the exercise of M's ministry.

Service performed by a duly ordained, commissioned, or licensed minister of a church as an employee of the United States, or a State, territory, or possession of the United States, or the District of Columbia, or a foreign government, or a political subdivision of any of the foregoing, is not considered to be in the exercise of the ministry for purposes of the tax on self-employment income, even though this service may involve the ministration of sacerdotal functions or the conduct of religious worship. For example, service performed by a chaplain in the Armed Forces of the United States is considered to be performed by a commissioned officer in this capacity and not by a minister in the exercise of the ministry. Similarly, service performed by a chaplain in a State prison or State University is considered to be performed by a civil servant of the State and not by a minister in the exercise of the ministry.

**E. Time Limitation for Filing Application for Exemption.**—An application for exemption must be filed with the Internal Revenue Service by the later of the two following dates: (1) the due date of your tax return (including extensions) for the second tax year in which you have net earnings from self-employment of $400 or more, any part of which was derived from services as a minister, member of a religious order or Christian Science practitioner; or (2) the due date (including extensions) of your tax return for your second tax year ending after 1967.

**Example:** Reverend Aker, ordained in 1965, had net ministerial earnings of $400 or more in all years after 1965 and had not filed a waiver certificate electing social security coverage (Form 2031). He should have filed an application for exemption by April 15, 1970, or extended date.

Reverend Beeker, ordained in 1978, had ministerial income of $400 or more in 1978 and in 1979. He should have filed an application for exemption not later than April 15, 1980, or extended date.

**F. Effective Date of Exemption.**—An exemption from self-employment tax is effective for the first tax year ending after 1967, and all succeeding tax years in which you have net earnings from self-employment of $400 or more, any part of which is derived from services as a minister, member, or practitioner. Thus, if you had qualified net earnings of $400 or more in 1968 and not again until 1979, a valid application for exemption from self-employment tax filed by April 15, 1980, would be effective for 1968 and all years thereafter. However, contact an IRS office to see if you are entitled to file a claim for refund of self-employment taxes paid in prior tax years.

**G. Where to File.**—Mail your application to the **Internal Revenue Service Center** for the place where you live.

| | |
|---|---|
| New Jersey, New York City and counties of Nassau, Rockland, Suffolk, and Westchester | Holtsville, NY 00501 |
| New York (all other counties), Connecticut, Maine, Massachusetts, New Hampshire, Rhode Island, Vermont | Andover, MA 05501 |
| Alabama, Florida, Georgia, Mississippi, South Carolina | Atlanta, GA 31101 |
| Michigan, Ohio | Cincinnati, OH 45999 |
| Louisiana, New Mexico, Arkansas, Kansas, Oklahoma, Texas | Austin, TX 73301 |
| Alaska, Arizona, Colorado, Idaho, Minnesota, Montana, Nebraska, Nevada, North Dakota, Oregon, South Dakota, Utah, Washington, Wyoming | Ogden, UT 84201 |
| Illinois, Iowa, Missouri, Wisconsin | Kansas City, MO 64999 |
| California, Hawaii | Fresno, CA 93888 |
| Indiana, Kentucky, North Carolina, Tennessee, Virginia, West Virginia | Memphis, TN 37501 |
| Delaware, District of Columbia, Maryland, Pennsylvania | Philadelphia, PA 19255 |

If you have no legal residence in the United States then mail this form to the Internal Revenue Service Center, Philadelphia, PA 19255.

**H. Extensions of Time for Filing and Noncalendar Year Taxpayers.**—In general, the filing dates stated do not apply if you file your tax return for other than a calendar year or you are granted an extension of time to file your return. Contact the nearest Internal Revenue Service office for applicable dates.

**I. How to Indicate Exemption on Form 1040.**—If your only income subject to self-employment tax is from ministerial services, and **Copy C has been returned to you approved by the Internal Revenue Service,** write "Exempt-Form 4361" on the self-employment line in Other Taxes section of Form 1040. However, if you have other income subject to self-employment tax, see Schedule SE (Form 1040).

**J. Revocation of Exemption.**—You **may** not revoke the exemption once it is received.

## Specific Instructions

**Item 2.**—Enter your social security number as it appears on your social security card. If you have no number, file application Form SS–5 with the local office of the Social Security Administration. If you do not receive your card in time, file Form 4361 and enter "Applied for" in the space provided for the number.

**Item 4.**—Enter the date you were duly ordained, commissioned, or licensed as a minister of a church, or date you became a member of a religious order, or date you commenced practice as a Christian Science practitioner. No application for exemption should be filed prior to this date. *A copy of the certificate (or a letter from the governing body of your church if you did not receive a certificate) establishing your status as a duly ordained, commissioned, or a licensed minister, or a member of a religious order, or Christian Science practitioner, must be attached to the form.*

**Item 5.**—If you are a minister or a member of a religious order, enter the legal name, address, and employer identification number of the church denomination that ordained, commissioned, or licensed you or the order of which you are now a member. The employer identification number should be obtained from the ordaining, licensing, or commissioning body or religious order.

# 6

# INCOME TAXES AND THE MINISTER

Since several excellent resources dealing with federal income taxes are available to ministers,[1] a comprehensive treatment of the subject in this text is not necessary. This chapter accordingly will be restricted to those matters of special relevance to ministers.

## §A. Preliminary Considerations

### 1. EMPLOYEE OR SELF-EMPLOYED

The status of a minister for income tax purposes is a question that has caused considerable confusion. As was noted in chapter 1, if a minister is considered to be self-employed he may deduct his business expenses on Schedule C and reduce his adjusted gross income by reporting his net business income on Form 1040. Thus, a self-employed minister will be able to deduct his business expenses even if he does not itemize his deductions. If a minister is considered an employee, he must report his church salary on Form 1040, and he may deduct only travel and transportation expenses in computing adjusted gross income. A minister who is deemed to be an employee, therefore, must itemize his deductions on Schedule A in order to claim many business-related expenses. Furthermore, his employing church must issue him a W-2 form each year.

The IRS has stated:

Under the common law rules, whether you perform services as an employee or as a self-employed person depends on all the facts and circumstances. Generally,

[1] Two excellent summaries dealing specifically with ministers' income taxes are C. TEITELL, MINISTER'S GUIDE FOR INCOME TAX (printed yearly) and ABINGDON CLERGY INCOME TAX GUIDE (printed yearly). In addition, the IRS will provide upon request Publication 17 (a comprehensive guide to completing the federal income tax return) and Publication 517 (a guide to income tax and social security for ministers).

if you perform services subject to the will and control of an employer, both as to what will be done and how it will be done, you are an employee. It does not matter if the employer allows you considerable discretion and freedom of action, as long as the employer has the legal right to control both the method and the result of the services.

. . . .

For example, if you are hired and paid by a church to perform ministerial services for it, subject to its right of control, under the common law rules you are an employee of the church in the performance of those services and your wages are reported on Form W-2.[2]

The IRS traditionally has regarded ministers as self-employed. However, in Revenue Ruling 80-110 and in Publication 517, the IRS specifically held that it is possible for a minister to be an employee under the common law test (quoted above). These holdings have caused considerable confusion about the status of ministers since some commentators have interpreted the holdings to mean that the IRS now views all ministers as employees. This, however, does not appear to be the case. Revenue Ruling 80-110 held that a minister who is an employee of a church may not deduct unreimbursed business expenses on Schedule C, but rather must use Schedule A. In Publication 517, the IRS lists a comprehensive example of how a minister who is an employee of a church should report his income and business deductions. In neither case did the IRS hold that all ministers are employees. It merely stated various income tax consequences if employee status was assumed. Perhaps the greatest significance of Revenue Ruling 80-110 and Publication 517 is that the IRS recognized that ministers working for local church congregations may under some circumstances be considered employees. Previously, the IRS had regarded ministers as self-employed for income tax purposes.

Some ministers would not satisfy the common law definition of *employee* developed by the IRS. Full-time evangelists obviously would not. Conceivably neither would some ministers serving in local churches, particularly if these churches lack the legal authority to control the method, means, and results of the ministers' services and lack the authority to terminate those services.

The IRS has recognized that a minister can be an employee for some purposes and self-employed for others. Publication 517 notes that ministers who are common law employees of their churches may be self-employed in the performance of services outside their activities as employees. For example, a minister may receive fees for performing marriages, baptisms, or other personal

---

[2]IRS Publication 517. The IRS also states in Publication 517 that "[i]f you have a question as to whether you are an employee or a self-employed person, you may get a ruling from the Internal Revenue Service by filing Form SS-8 . . . ." *See also* chapter 1, § B.2, *supra*, for the IRS test for employment status contained in regulation 31.3401(c)-1(b).

services directly from church members. These fees are considered earnings from self-employment for all tax purposes.

In summary, if a minister does not meet the common law test for an employee developed by the IRS, he logically should continue to be treated as self-employed for income tax purposes. Revenue Ruling 80-110 and Publication 517 would not appear to affect this result since in both cases the IRS simply made an assumption that a particular minister was an employee rather than self-employed. In neither case did the IRS make a substantive determination that all ministers are to be treated as employees. If the existence of an employer-employee relationship is in doubt, the IRS has stated that the particular facts of each case will be determinative.[3]

## 2. Who Must File

The Internal Revenue Code stipulates that individuals earning less than a prescribed amount do not have to file a federal income tax return. The amount of income necessitating a return varies, depending on whether an individual is married, and whether he (or his spouse) is sixty-five years of age or older.[4] The law also stipulates that persons earning self-employment income in excess of the designated minimum must file a federal income tax return even if they otherwise would not be required to do so.[5] Some of these amounts are frequently adjusted, so they should be checked at least yearly.

## 3. Which Form Should Be Filed

A minister must use Form 1040, since neither Form 1040A (the short form) nor Form 1040EZ is available to persons, such as ministers, who pay estimated tax.

## 4. W-2 Forms

Section 6051 of the Internal Revenue Code lists three categories of employers who must issue W-2 forms to their employees: (1) employers who are required to deduct and withhold federal income or social security taxes from employees' wages, (2) employers who would have been required to deduct and withhold federal income taxes if an employee had claimed no more than one withholding exemption, and (3) employers engaged in a trade or business who pay wages for services performed by employees.

If a minister does not satisfy the common law definition of an employee

[3]Treas. Reg. § 31.3401(c)-1(d).
[4]I.R.C. § 6012.
[5]*Id.*

discussed earlier in this chapter, then his church cannot be characterized as his employer and no W-2 form is necessary. A church can report a self-employed minister's compensation on Form 1099-NEC (Nonemployee Compensation).

If a minister does satisfy the common law definition of an employee, then the IRS maintains that his employing church or other religious organization must issue him a W-2 form.[6] The validity of this position is not clearly established. Since churches are not required to deduct and withhold federal income or social security taxes from a minister's wages even if he reported only one withholding exemption,[7] they do not fit within either of the first two categories of employers required to issue W-2 forms to employees. The third category of employer includes all those employers engaged in a "trade or business" who pay wages to employees for services rendered. Although the term *trade or business* is not defined in the Internal Revenue Code, the IRS has defined the term as

(1) A pursuit carried on for livelihood or profit.
(2) A pursuit in which a profit motive is present and where there is some type of economic activity involved. As to the profit motive, an activity will be considered a business if it is entered into and carried on in good faith for the purpose of making a profit, as opposed to an activity engaged in purely for self-satisfaction.
(3) An enterprise that is characterized by regularity of activities and transactions and the production of income. The absence of income, in itself, will not prevent an enterprise from being classified as a trade or business.[8]

Although a church would not fit within the first two of these definitions, it may be argued that it fits within the third. This is apparently the reasoning of the IRS, for it has held that "form W-2 is the correct form to use to report the wages paid by the church to its employee, the minister."[9] This position is merely an opinion, however. The view that churches are not engaged in a trade or business and therefore are exempt from the requirement of issuing W-2 forms to employee-ministers would appear to be just as valid an interpretation of the Internal Revenue Code, especially since many courts would reject the third definition of a trade or business suggested by the IRS.[10]

Nevertheless, issuance of W-2 forms would be more consistent with the requirement that minister-employees report their church salaries on Form

[6]IRS Publication 517.
[7]I.R.C. § 3401(a)(9).
[8]IRS Publication 334.
[9]IRS Publication 517.
[10]*See generally* MERTENS, LAW OF FEDERAL INCOME TAXATION § 25.08 (1972 & Supp. 1982).

1040. A minister-employee who reports his church salary as wages on Form 1040 without attaching a Form W-2 to his return may have his Form 1040 returned to him. In addition, the IRS may attempt to impose a penalty upon a church-employer for failing to furnish W-2 forms to employees. For willfully failing to do so, section 6674 of the Internal Revenue Code imposes a $50 fine and section 7204 imposes a criminal penalty of $1,000 or imprisonment for not more than one year.

## 5. WITHHOLDING

Beginning in 1943, Congress required most employers to withhold federal income taxes from employees' wages. However, Congress specifically exempted "services performed by a duly ordained, commissioned, or licensed minister of a church in the exercise of his ministry."[11] As a result, churches are not required to withhold income taxes from wages paid to their ministers. But churches must withhold federal income taxes and social security taxes from the wages paid to other employees, such as organists, janitors, and secretaries.[12]

The income tax regulations[13] define *services performed by a duly ordained, commissioned, or licensed minister of a church in the exercise of his ministry* to include (1) the ministration of sacerdotal functions and the conduct of religious worship, and (2) the control, conduct, and maintenance of religious organizations, including the religious boards, societies, and other integral agencies of such organizations, under the authority of a religious body constituting a church or church denomination. The regulations specify that a minister is performing service in the exercise of his ministry if he performs religious worship or the ministration of sacerdotal functions, whether or not such services are performed for a religious organization. But if a minister works for a secular institution, and his service is not at the direction of ecclesiastical superiors, then only the service performed by him in the conduct of religious worship or the ministration of sacerdotal functions is construed as the exercise of his ministry.

## 6. ESTIMATED TAX

Beginning in 1943, Congress attempted to place the federal income tax system on a pay-as-you-go basis. It did this by requiring most employers to withhold income tax on their employees' wages and by requiring most individuals whose wages are not subject to income tax withholding to periodically estimate and

---

[11]I.R.C. § 3401(a)(9).

[12]Eighth Street Baptist Church, Inc. v. United States, 295 F. Supp. 1400 (D. Kan. 1969). The social security amendments of 1983, effective as of January 1, 1984, automatically extended social security coverage to all nonministerial church employees.

[13]Treas. Reg. § 31.3401(a)(9)-1(b).

prepay their taxes. Since compensation paid to ministers for services performed in the exercise of their ministry ordinarily is not subject to withholding, ministers must estimate and prepay their taxes.[14] Their reporting is done on IRS Form 1040-ES.

Before 1983, Form 1040-ES consisted of detailed instructions, a worksheet, and four *declaration-vouchers.* Ministers used the worksheet to calculate their income tax and any social security tax for the current year. By April 15 of each year, a minister had to submit to the IRS a declaration-voucher listing his estimated tax for the year, accompanied by a check for either the entire amount or one-fourth of the total. Ministers who elected to pay only one-fourth of their estimated taxes by the April 15 deadline were required to pay the remaining three-fourths in equal installments on the following June 15, September 15, and January 15. Each installment had to be accompanied by one of the four vouchers contained in the Form 1040-ES package.

On July 23, 1982, the IRS proposed a new regulation that would have required estimated tax payments to be made directly to authorized commercial banking institutions rather than to IRS service centers. This regulation was withdrawn on November 24, 1982, due to widespread criticism from banking institutions.

For tax years beginning in 1983, the IRS modified the procedure for reporting and paying estimated taxes. Declaration-vouchers listing estimated taxes for the year are no longer used. Under the revised system, a minister still computes his estimated federal income taxes and any social security taxes on a worksheet included with Form 1040-ES. In general, this is done by estimating adjusted gross income and then subtracting estimated credits, deductions, and exemptions. Using one's prior year income and deductions as a starting point is often helpful. To determine estimated taxes for the year, estimated taxable income is multiplied by the applicable tax rate contained in the Tax Rate Schedule of Form 1040-ES. If estimated taxes are equal to or greater than $300 in 1983, $400 in 1984, or $500 in 1985 and later years, the minister completes a *payment-voucher* contained in Form 1040-ES and remits it along with payment following the previously described procedure. If a filing date falls on a Saturday, Sunday, or legal holiday, the next regular workday is considered to be the deadline.

A minister who pays one-fourth of his estimated taxes on April 15 automatically will be sent a package by the IRS containing preprinted payment-vouchers listing his name, address, and social security number. The four blank payment-vouchers included with the Form 1040-ES are used only for the initial April 15 payment and thereafter only if a minister does not receive a package of preprinted vouchers.

A minister may become liable for estimated tax payments midway through

[14]*See generally* IRS Publication 505.

a year, for example, if he accepts his first pastorate during the summer. In such a case, the minister should submit a payment-voucher by the next filing deadline accompanied by a check for the entire estimated tax liability or for a prorated portion. To illustrate, a minister who does not become subject to the estimated tax procedures until July 1 would use the blank September 15 payment-voucher and pay at least one-half of the estimated tax liability for the year.

At the end of the tax year, a minister computes his actual tax liability on Form 1040. Neither Form 1040A nor Form 1040EZ may be used. If a minister overpaid his taxes for the year, he can elect to have the overpayment credited against his estimated tax for the next tax year. It can be credited against his first installment or spread evenly over each of the four quarterly installments.

If a minister's estimated tax payments prove to be less than his actual income tax and any social security tax, he may be charged a penalty on the amount of underpayment. Ministers should use Form 2210 to figure any underpayment and penalty. The penalty will not apply to ministers who fit within certain exceptions. For example, no penalty is imposed on taxpayers whose withheld taxes and estimated tax payments for the current year equal or exceed the prior year's tax.

If a minister files a Form 1040 before February 1, and he pays the balance of any tax due for the preceding year, he is not required to pay the last quarterly installment of his estimated tax on the preceding January 15.

Finally, ministers may request a reasonable extension of time to file a payment-voucher. However, an extension will not relieve a minister from liability for underpayment penalties. It merely extends the dates for filing payment-vouchers and paying the estimated tax.

## §B. Housing Allowances

### 1. Introduction

Section 107 of the Internal Revenue Code currently states:

> In the case of a minister of the gospel, gross income does not include—(1) the rental value of a home furnished to him as part of his compensation; or (2) the rental allowance paid to him as part of his compensation, to the extent used by him to rent or provide a home.

Before 1954, a minister of the gospel could exclude from his gross income only the rental value of a parsonage and its appurtenances which were actually furnished to him as part of his compensation. He could not exclude a rental allowance paid in cash in lieu of the use of a dwelling. Thus, a minister who did not live in a church-owned parsonage was not eligible for the exclusion even though he received a cash housing allowance from his church which he used to rent or purchase a home.

The exclusion of the rental value of a parsonage "in the case of a minister of the gospel" goes back to section 213(b)(11) of the Revenue Act of 1921. It subsequently became section 22(b)(6) of the Internal Revenue Code of 1939 and was incorporated into section 107(1) of the Internal Revenue Code of 1954 (quoted above).[15]

Section 107(2) of the 1954 Code for the first time permitted a minister to exclude from his gross income a "rental allowance paid to him as part of his compensation, to the extent used by him to rent or provide a home." With respect to the housing allowance exclusion, a minister who purchases or rents his own home is now treated the same as a minister living in a church-owned parsonage.[16]

Congress has never explained its rationale in enacting the housing allowance exclusion, other than to note that it enacted the 1954 amendment to section 107 to abolish the discrimination that existed against churches that could not furnish a parsonage but did pay a housing allowance.

## 2. ELIGIBILITY

The income tax regulations specify that "to qualify for the exclusion, the home or rental allowance must be provided as remuneration for services which are ordinarily the duties of a minister of the gospel."[17] The regulations further state:

> Examples of specific services the performance of which will be considered duties of a minister for purposes of section 107 include the performance of sacerdotal functions, the conduct of religious worship, the administration and maintenance of religious organizations and their integral agencies, and the performance of teaching and administrative duties at theological seminaries. Also, the service performed by a qualified minister as an employee of the United States (other than as a chaplain in the Armed Forces . . .), or a State, Territory, or possession of the United States . . . is in the exercise of his ministry provided the service performed includes such services as are ordinarily the duties of a minister.[18]

---

[15]*See* Rev. Rul. 59-270, 1959-2 C.B. 44.

[16]Before 1954, the allowance was referred to as the "parsonage allowance" since it applied only to parsonages. Since 1954, the allowance has gone by several names, including *parsonage allowance, rental allowance,* and *housing allowance.* In this chapter, only the term *housing allowance* will be used. This term is broad enough to apply to most situations, and the use of a single term will reduce confusion.

[17]Treas. Reg. § 1.107-1(a).

[18]*Id.*

The IRS has held that the regulations defining *service performed by a minister in the exercise of his ministry* for purposes of the self-employment or social security tax will be applicable in defining those services that are "ordinarily the duties of a minister of the gospel."[19] Thus, the materials presented in chapter 5 will be relevant in determining a minister's eligibility for the housing allowance.

It has been held that a full-time, commissioned Jewish cantor employed by a congregation to perform religious teaching and worship in accordance with the tenets of the Jewish faith is a "minister of the gospel" within the meaning of section 107.[20] One court has noted that "the statutory term 'minister of the gospel,' which generally refers to one proclaiming the teachings of Christ in the New Testament, is applied with difficulty to a faith, such as Judaism, rooted exclusively in the Old Testament."[21] Nevertheless, the court concluded that the term must apply to "persons holding an equivalent status in other religions."

It has also been held that a minister of music and a minister of education were not entitled to a housing allowance since neither was an ordained, commissioned, or licensed minister of the gospel, despite their performance of various ministerial duties.[22] And, it has been held that a minister who is licensed by a church or denomination that ordains some of its ministers is eligible for the housing allowance only if he performs "substantially all of the religious functions" of an ordained minister.[23]

The IRS has determined that ministers who work for a seminary that is not under the authority of a religious body constituting a church or church denomination are ineligible for the housing allowance exclusion.[24] However, ministers who are employed by seminaries that are under such authority are eligible.[25] In the latter case, the IRS noted that the college was controlled by a board of directors under the authority of the elders of the denomination; all faculty members were members of the same denomination; and the college trained ministers primarily for the denomination. The element of church or denominational control is not specifically mentioned in section 107 or the associated regulations. However, as mentioned earlier, the regulations do specify that the self-employment tax regulations will be applicable in deciding what ministerial

---

[19]*Id.*

[20]Rev. Rul. 78-301, 1978-2 C.B. 103.

[21]Silverman v. Commissioner, 57 T.C. 727 (1972).

[22]Rev. Rul. 59-270, 1959-2 C.B. 44. *See also* Kirk v. Commissioner, 425 F.2d 492 (D.C. Cir. 1970).

[23]Rev. Rul. 78-301, 1978-2 C.B. 103.

[24]Rev. Rul. 63-90, 1963-1 C.B. 27.

[25]Rev. Rul. 70-549, 1970-2 C.B. 16.

services will be eligible for the housing allowance exclusion. One such regulation states:

> [S]ervice performed by a minister in the exercise of his ministry includes the ministration of sacerdotal functions and the conduct of religious worship, and the control, conduct, and maintenance of religious organizations (including the religious boards, societies and other integral agencies of such organizations), under the authority of a religious body constituting a church or church denomination.[26]

The IRS has ruled that ministers of the gospel who teach or hold administrative positions at parochial schools that are under the authority of a church or church denomination are eligible for the housing allowance exclusion.[27] But, it has been held that a minister who taught data processing courses at a secular university was not eligible for the allowance.[28] Similarly, an ordained minister who served as the administrator of a nursing home was held to be ineligible since the nursing home was not under the authority of a church or church denomination.[29] And, an ordained minister who worked for a charitable corporation that had no affiliation with a church or church denomination was held to be ineligible for the allowance, even though the corporation had been created to furnish advice to churches.[30]

Widows and widowers of deceased ministers are not eligible for the allowance.[31] Retired ministers are eligible for a housing allowance only if they meet all of the following conditions:

1. They are members of a retirement plan operated by a church, a national church organization, or an organization acting on behalf of a church or national church organization.

2. The housing allowance is designated in advance of payment by the church or religious organization which operates the retirement plan, and applies only to retirement income paid under such plan.

3. Retirement income must compensate retired ministers for past services to local churches or religious denominations.[32]

[26]Treas. Reg. § 1.1402(c)-5(b)(2).
[27]Rev. Rul. 62-171, 1962-2 C.B. 39.
[28]Boyer v. Commissioner, 69 T.C. 521 (1978).
[29]Toavs v. Commissioner, 67 T.C. 897 (1977).
[30]Rev. Rul. 78-172, 1978-1 C.B. 35.
[31]Rev. Rul. 72-249, 1972-1 C.B. 36.
[32]Rev. Rul. 75-22, 1975-1 C.B. 49.

### 3. CONDITIONS

A minister who is eligible for a housing allowance must still satisfy the following conditions before he is entitled to exclude the allowance from his gross income.

#### a. *Home*

The allowance is available only with respect to a home. The term *home* is defined by the regulations as "a dwelling place (including furnishings) and the appurtenances thereto, such as a garage."[33] The regulations further stipulate that if "a minister rents, purchases, or owns a farm or other business property in addition to a home, the portion of the rental allowance expended in connection with the farm or business property shall not be excluded from his gross income."[34]

#### b. *Advance Designation*

With respect to ministers who receive a cash allowance instead of a parsonage, the housing allowance must be designated *in advance* of payment by official action of the employing church or religious organization.[35] It is important to observe that the law requires designation in advance of payment, not in advance of the tax or calendar year. Therefore, a church that neglects to designate a housing allowance by the first day of a new year is not prevented from doing so later. But, its designation will be effective only for the remainder of the year. Similarly, when a minister joins a church midway through a year, and the church designates an allowance in advance of his first wage payment, he will be entitled to a housing allowance for the remainder of the year.

The housing allowance designation must be in writing, and may be contained in an employment contract, minutes, a resolution, or in any other appropriate document. The regulations state that a designation is sufficient if it "permits a payment or a part thereof to be identified as a payment of rental allowance as distinguished from salary or other remuneration."[36] Adequate designation would include a percentage of gross income, or a specific dollar amount. In either case, the housing allowance could be distinguished from salary. Paying a minister's housing allowance and salary in two separate checks is not necessary for an employing church that has made an adequate designation; the advance designation itself serves to distinguish salary from the housing allowance. The

[33]Treas. Reg. § 1.107-1(b).
[34]Treas. Reg. § 1.107-1(c).
[35]Treas. Reg. § 1.107-1(b).
[36]*Id.*

employing church does *not* report the designated housing allowance on the minister's W-2 form.

It has been held that a minister is not entitled to exclude a housing allowance from his gross income if his church simply paid him a salary without designating a housing allowance.[37] In a related case, a church's retroactive designation of a housing allowance was held to be ineffective.[38]

The designation must be made by the minister's immediate employer, assuming of course that it is either a church or religious organization. Thus, a designation by the national headquarters of a religious denomination is an ineffective designation for ministers employed by local congregations affiliated with the denomination.[39] The national headquarters of a denomination may of course designate housing allowances for its qualifying minister-employees. And, it has been held that a denominational headquarters that maintains a retirement program may designate as a housing allowance a portion of the retirement income paid to retired ministers.[40]

Ministers living in church-owned parsonages are permitted to exclude the rental value of the parsonage from their gross income without any church designation.[41] However, a minister living in a parsonage may not exclude the cost of utilities or furnishings unless the church has specifically designated a housing allowance for such items.[42]

### c. *Maximum Exclusion*

A minister may not necessarily exclude the full amount of the housing allowance designated by his employing church. The regulations require that a housing allowance "must be included in the minister's gross income in the taxable year in which it is received, to the extent that such allowance is not used by him during such taxable year to rent or otherwise provide a home."[43] The excludable housing allowance for a given year is thereby limited to the *actual expenses* a minister incurs in that year to rent or provide a home. The regulations define *expenses incurred to rent or provide a home* to include all amounts expended for the rent of a home, for the purchase of a home, and for costs directly relating to providing a home. The last category is very broad, and has been held to include furnishings, appurtenances, utilities, property

---

[37]Eden v. Commissioner, 41 T.C. 605 (1964).

[38]Ling v. United States, 200 F. Supp. 282 (D. Minn. 1961).

[39]Rev. Rul. 62-117, 1962-2 C.B. 38.

[40]Rev. Rul. 75-22, 1975-1 C.B. 49.

[41]Rev. Rul. 59-350, 1959-2 C.B. 45.

[42]*Id.*

[43]Treas. Reg. § 1.107-1(c).

taxes, home insurance, and repairs. It does not, however, include the cost of food, maid service, or automobiles. In 1962 the IRS ruled that a minister who itemized his federal income tax deductions could deduct interest and taxes incurred in purchasing and maintaining a home even though these same items were excluded from gross income by means of the housing allowance exclusion.[44] In effect, home-owning ministers could receive a "double deduction."

In 1983 the IRS reversed itself and eliminated the double deduction for tax years beginning in 1983 by ruling that mortgage interest and property taxes cannot be deducted as itemized expenses on Schedule A of Form 1040 to the extent that they are excluded from gross income as a housing allowance.[45] The IRS based its ruling on section 265 of the Internal Revenue Code, which specifies that expenses allocable to income that is exempt or excluded from federal income taxes must be allocated to such income and may not be deducted from adjusted gross income as itemized expenses on Schedule A. This principle, ignored by the IRS in its 1962 ruling, dictates that expenses fully allocable to the housing allowance exclusion, such as mortgage interest and property taxes, may not be deducted from taxable income as itemized expenses. In support of its position, the IRS cited a decision of the Supreme Court which held that the Internal Revenue Code should not be interpreted to allow the practical equivalence of double deductions without a clear declaration of intent by Congress.[46]

The practical effect of the 1983 ruling is to deny any itemized deduction for mortgage interest and property taxes to a home-owning minister who excludes all of his actual expenses in owning and maintaining a home. A minister who is not able to exclude all of the expenses incurred in owning and maintaining his home—because his actual expenses exceed either his church-designated allowance or the fair rental value of his home plus the cost of utilities—is able to deduct a portion of his mortgage interest and property taxes as itemized deductions on Schedule A. The amounts of the deductions are determined by decreasing actual expenses to the extent that they are allocable to the housing allowance. The IRS gives the following illustration on how to make this computation:

> During the taxable year, a minister of a [sic] gospel who is employed as a pastor of a church received $19,000 as compensation from the church and a combined

---

[44]Rev. Rul. 62-212, 1962-2 C.B. 41.

[45]Rev. Rul. 83-3, 1983-1 I.R.B. 10. Implementation of the new ruling, which was to take effect in 1983, was postponed recently by the IRS in Announcement 83-100 until January 1, 1985, for ministers who owned and occupied their present home prior to January 3, 1983, and who continue to occupy their present home until January 1, 1985.

rental and utility allowance of $6,300. . . . During the year, the minister used the rental and utility allowance, together with other funds, to make monthly payments for the residence in which the minister lived. Those payments totaled $8,400 and consisted of principal ($500), insurance ($400), real estate taxes ($1,400), interest ($4,000), and utility costs ($2,100), . . . the amount of the itemized deductions otherwise allowable for the interest and real estate taxes must be decreased to the extent the expenses are allocable to the rental allowance received from the church. . . . [T]he $4,000 of interest otherwise deductible [as an itemized expense] is decreased by $3,000, computed by multiplying $4,000 (the amount of the interest otherwise deductible) by a fraction, the numerator of which is $6,300 (the combined rental and utility allowance) and the denominator of which is $8,400 (the total of all expenditures to which the rental and utility allowance is applicable), or $4,000 × $6,300/$8,400 = $3,000. Therefore, the deduction for interest allowable . . . is $1,000 ($4,000-$3,000). . . . [T]he $1,400 of real estate taxes otherwise deductible [as an itemized expense] is decreased by $1,050 computed by multiplying $1,400 (the amount of the real estate taxes otherwise deductible) by a fraction, the numerator of which is $6,300 and the denominator of which is $8,400 . . . or $1,400 × $6,300/$8,400 = $1,050. Therefore, the itemized deduction for real estate taxes . . . is $350 ($1,400-$1,050).

There are two other limitations on how much of the church-designated housing allowance a minister may exclude from his gross income. First, the IRS maintains that a minister who owns his home may never exclude more than the fair rental value of his home (including furnishings) plus the actual cost of utilities.[47] To hold otherwise, the IRS claims, would discriminate against ministers who rent their homes. The fair rental value of a minister's home is a question of fact to be determined on a case-by-case basis. Second, the IRS has ruled that a housing allowance may not exceed the reasonable value of a minister's services to a church or religious organization.[48]

The rules previously discussed may be summarized as follows:

### Maximum Housing Allowance

| | |
|---|---|
| Minister owns home | Actual expenses incurred in providing and maintaining home, including down payment, mortgage principal and interest payments, real estate taxes, repairs, improvements, furnishings, utilities, and homeowners insurance, but not to exceed either (1) church-designated allowance, or (2) fair rental value of home (including furnishings) plus cost of utilities |

[47]Rev. Rul. 71-280, 1971-2 C.B. 92.
[48]Rev. Rul. 78-448, 1978-2 C.B. 105.

| | |
|---|---|
| Minister rents home | Actual expenses incurred by minister in providing and maintaining home, including rental payments, utilities, and furnishings, but in no event more than church-designated allowance |
| Minister lives in church-owed parsonage | Fair rental value of parsonage is excludable without necessity of church designation; actual expenses incurred by minister in maintaining parsonage, including utilities and furnishings, are excludable, but only if church designates housing allowance with respect to such items |

The following problems will further clarify the rules discussed above.

*Example 1. X,* an ordained minister, purchased a home in 1982 for $50,000. During 1982, he paid $15,000 down on the home, and in addition paid $500 in principal and $4,500 in interest on the mortgage loan. X also paid $2,000 for utilities, $1,000 for home furnishings, $750 for repairs, $500 for property taxes, and $200 for homeowners insurance. His church board designated 40 percent of his salary of $20,000 as a housing allowance. The annual fair rental value of the home is $6,500. How much can X exclude as a housing allowance?

As a homeowner, X is entitled to exclude only his actual expenses to the extent that they do not exceed the lower of the church-designated allowance or the fair rental value of his home plus the cost of utilities. *X's* actual expenses in providing and maintaining a home in 1982 were $24,450. The church-designated allowance was $8,000 (40 percent of $20,000) and the fair rental value of his home plus the cost of utilities was $8,500 ($6,500 plus $2,000). X may exclude only $8,000.

*Example 2. X,* an ordained minister, bought a home several years ago. His actual expenses in maintaining and providing the home for the current year were mortgage payments (principal and interest) of $6,000, property taxes of $500, utilities of $1,500, furnishings of $750, insurance of $300, and repairs of $500. *X's* salary for the year was $20,000, and his church-designated housing allowance was $100 per week. The annual fair rental value of the house was $5,000. How much can X exclude as a housing allowance?

As a homeowner, X is entitled to exclude only his actual expenses to the extent that they do not exceed the lower of the church-designated allowance or the fair rental value of the home plus the cost of utilities. *X's* actual expenses in providing and maintaining a home for the year were $9,550. The church designated allowance was $5,200 ($100 x 52 weeks) and the fair rental value of the home plus the cost of utilities was $6,500 ($5,000 plus $1,500). X may exclude only $5,200.

*Example 3.* Same facts as in Example 2, except that the church-designated allowance was $200 per week. X may exclude $6,500 of his actual expenses.

*Example 4.* X, an ordained minister, rented a home for $400 per month. He also incurred $1,500 in utilities and spent $1,000 on furnishings. His church designated 50 percent of his annual salary of $20,000 as a housing allowance. How much can X exclude?

Ministers who rent a home are entitled to exclude their actual expenses in providing and maintaining their home, including rental payments, utilities, and furnishings, as long as the excluded allowance does not exceed the church-designated allowance. X's actual expenses in providing and maintaining his home were $7,300 for the year. X may exclude this entire amount since it does not exceed his church-designated allowance of $10,000 (50 percent of $20,000).

*Example 5.* X, an ordained minister, lives in a parsonage owned by his church. He pays the church no rent for the home. X is required to pay for his own furnishings and utilities. During the current year, X spent $1,000 on furnishings and $2,000 on utilities. How much can X exclude as a housing allowance?

Ministers who live in church-owned parsonages may exclude the fair rental value of the parsonage as a housing allowance. This is true whether or not the church specifically designates an allowance. However, ministers living in parsonages may exclude the cost of furnishings and utilities only to the extent that such cost does not exceed a church-designated allowance. If X's church did not specify a housing allowance by appropriate action, X would not be entitled to exclude any of the cost of his furnishings or utilities.

4. REPORTING

As noted previously, a minister excludes his housing allowance by not reporting it on his federal income tax return. Of course, he must report his housing allowance as income to the extent that it is not excludable under the rules discussed in this chapter. If a minister's employing church issues the minister a W-2 form, the W-2 form should not list any portion of the church-designated housing allowance. Thus, if a minister's annual salary is $15,000, and the church designates 40 percent of the salary as a housing allowance, the minister's W-2 form should list only $9,000 ($15,000 less the housing allowance of $6,000) as income. But if the minister is not entitled to exclude the entire church-designated allowance, the difference between the church-designated allowance and his actual housing exclusion must be reported as income.

If a minister is considered to be self-employed, then his church should reduce the compensation reported on his Form 1099 by the amount of the church-designated allowance. Again, if the minister is not able to exclude the entire church-designated allowance, then the difference must be reported as income.

It is also important to note that the church-designated housing allowance is *not* excludable in computing self-employment earnings.

## §C. Special Occasion Gifts to Ministers

Churches occasionally collect special offerings to honor a minister on a birthday, an anniversary, a holiday, or retirement. Should a minister treat such offerings as taxable income and include them in his gross income? Or, is he entitled to exclude them?

The answers to these questions depend upon whether the special occasion offering is characterized as a gift or as compensation for services rendered. If the offering is regarded as compensation, then it must be reported as income on the minister's federal income tax return. If the offering is regarded as a bona fide gift, then it may be excluded inasmuch as section 102 of the Internal Revenue Code excludes the value of gifts from gross income.

Characterizing a particular offering as a gift or as compensation for services rendered is often difficult. The United States Supreme Court has provided some clarification by noting the following characteristics of a gift under the Internal Revenue Code: "A gift in the statutory sense . . . proceeds from a 'detached and disinterested generosity' . . . 'out of affection, respect, admiration, charity or like impulses . . . .' The most critical consideration . . . is the transferor's intention."[49]

Under the Supreme Court's test, if intentions are to compensate the minister for services rendered, then the offering must be treated as taxable compensation.

It is well-settled that payments made to a retired minister will constitute a gift and not taxable compensation if all of the following conditions are satisfied: (1) the payments are made by a local church congregation with which the minister was associated; (2) the payments are not made in accordance with any enforceable agreement or established plan; (3) the payments are authorized at or about the time of the minister's retirement; (4) the minister does not perform any further services for the church and is not expected to do so; and (5) the minister was adequately compensated during his previous working relationship with the church.[50] Under these circumstances it is clear that the intention or motivation prompting the payment is "affection, respect, admiration, charity or like impulses," not a desire to compensate the recipient for services rendered.

However, it has been held that payments received by a retired minister

[49]Commissioner v. Duberstein, 363 U.S. 278, 285 (1960) (citations omitted).

[50]*See, e.g.,* Hershman v. Kavanagh, 120 F. Supp. 956 (E.D. Mich. 1953), *aff'd,* 210 F.2d 654 (6th Cir. 1954); Mutch v. Commissioner, 209 F.2d 390 (3rd Cir. 1954); Rev. Rul. 55-422, 1955-1 C.B. 14.

under an established pension plan of his denomination are to be treated as taxable compensation.[51]

A Christmas offering on behalf of a minister is a more difficult question. It is fairly clear that Christmas distributions based mechanically upon service, salary, and length of employment and made directly by an employing church are to be treated as taxable compensation.[52] An even more difficult question is presented when a congregation voluntarily gives a special offering to provide a Christmas distribution to its minister. If the primary intention was to compensate the minister for services rendered to the congregation, then the offering must be treated as taxable income. If, however, the intention to give was based upon "affection, respect, admiration, charity or like impulses," then a gift may be implied. Although a determination of a congregation's intention presents unique problems, the following factors would likely be relevant: the length of the minister's tenure; whether his annual salary was clearly prescribed, and, if so, the extent to which it had been paid; and the characterization of the offering by the congregation.

The discussion pertaining to Christmas offerings would also be applicable in characterizing other special occasion offerings.

### §D. Travel Expenses

A minister may deduct ordinary and reasonable expenses incurred while traveling away from home in the pursuit of ministerial duties. If the expenses are incurred in connection with self-employment activities such as the performance of weddings, funerals, and baptisms, or if a minister is not deemed to satisfy the common law definition of an employee, the travel expenses are reported on Schedule C of Form 1040. If a minister is deemed to be an employee and the expenses are incurred while traveling on behalf of his employing church, then the expenses are computed on Form 2106 and reported directly on Form 1040 as a deduction from gross income. Overnight trips away from home for business purposes obviously qualify. But a trip need not be overnight so long as at some point the minister needs to be and is released from his duties long enough to obtain sleep or rest. Resting in one's car, however, does not suffice.

Deductible travel expenses include the following:

1. air, rail, and bus fares

2. operating and maintaining a car

3. taxi fares or other costs of transportation between an airport or station and one's hotel

4. transportation from the place where one eats or sleeps to a temporary work assignment

[51]Perkins v. Commissioner, 34 T.C. 117 (1960).
[52]Painter v. Campbell, 110 F. Supp. 503 (N.D. Tex. 1953).

5. baggage charges and transportation costs for sample and display material
6. meals and lodging when one is away from home on business
7. cleaning and laundry expenses
8. telephone and telegraph expenses
9. public stenographers' fees
10. operating and maintaining house trailers
11. tips that are incidental to any of these expenses
12. other similar expenses related to qualifying travel[53]

If a particular trip within the United States is entirely for business, the minister may deduct all ordinary and necessary travel expenses. However, if a trip is primarily personal, the minister may not deduct travel expenses to and from the destination even if he had some business activity at the destination. If a trip is primarily for business and, while at the business destination, a minister extends his stay for a vacation, makes a nonbusiness side trip, or has other nonbusiness activities, he may deduct his travel expenses to and from the destination. Whether the primary purpose of a trip is business or pleasure, a minister may deduct the business expenses incurred at his destination.

Note that travel expenses incurred by a minister acting as an employee of his church are deducted from gross income when computing adjusted gross income on Form 1040. Therefore, they are deductible whether or not a minister itemizes deductions. As has been indicated, travel expenses attributable to self-employment activities of a minister, such as performing weddings, funerals, and baptisms, are reported on Schedule C. And, the travel expenses of a minister who does not satisfy the common law definition of an employee are also reported on Schedule C.

Travel expenses incurred by a minister in attending a convention are deductible if the minister can demonstrate that attending the convention benefits his own work or business.[54] However, expenses incurred by a minister's spouse are deductible only if a real business purpose was served in bringing the spouse along. Incidental services, such as typing notes or assisting in entertainment, are insufficient grounds to warrant a deduction.

It is important to ascertain the extent to which a minister's employing church reimburses him for travel expenses incurred while traveling away from home on behalf of the church. Ministers who are considered to be employees and who receive no reimbursement from their churches for travel expenses may deduct the full value of their reasonable and necessary travel expenses on Form 1040. Form 2106 is used to compute the exact amount of the deduction. If a

---

[53]IRS Publication 463.
[54]Shutter v. Commissioner, 2 B.T.A. 23 (1925).

minister receives reimbursement from his employing church for travel expenses, then he reports the amount of the reimbursement along with his travel expenses on Form 2106. Then, to the extent that his expenses exceed the reimbursement received from his employing church, he deducts his travel expenses on Form 1040 as an employee business expense. Ministers whose reimbursements exceed their expenses report the surplus as income on Form 1040. If a minister reports reimbursements on Form 2106, his employing church need not include the value of such reimbursements on his W-2 form. Ministers who are deemed to be self-employed report allowable travel expenses on Schedule C.

A minister is not required to report travel expenses or reimbursements if he is required to and does account to his church for travel expenses, if he does not deduct travel expenses on his return, or if his travel expenses equal or exceed the value of church reimbursements. It should also be noted that a minister who does not claim a reimbursement to which he is entitled may not claim a deduction for the expenses to which the reimbursement applies, and that all reimbursements for personal expenses must be reported as income on Form 1040.

All travel expenses must be properly substantiated or the deduction will not be allowed. Proof of travel expenses should be kept in an account book, diary, statement of expense, or similar record, supported by adequate documentary evidence, which together will support each element of an expense. For example, unsupported entries on a desk calendar are not proper proof. A minister does not need to record information in an account book that duplicates information shown on a receipt. Records must be dated. Record entries made after the fact ordinarily are not acceptable. Deductions are not allowed for approximations or estimates, or for expenses that are lavish, extravagant, or otherwise unreasonable. In summary, travel expense records must establish these things:

1. Each separate amount that was spent for travel away from home, such as the cost of transportation or lodging. It is acceptable to total the daily cost of breakfast, lunch, dinner, and other incidental expenses of such travel if listed in reasonable categories such as meals, gas and oil, and taxi fares.

2. The dates one departed from and returned home, and the number of days spent on business away from home.

3. The destination or locality of the travel away from home, described by name of city or similar designation.

4. The business reason for one's travel or the business benefit derived or expected to be gained from the travel.[55]

---

[55]I.R.C. § 274.

In denying a minister's travel expenses in attending out-of-state conferences, the United States Tax Court recently observed:

> With regard to the taxpayers' automobile and travelling expenses, the court found that they failed to substantiate their expenses for travel away from home to the conferences and for their meals and lodging while on those trips. The sparse information recorded on their kitchen calendar was insufficient to satisfy the substantiation requirements.[56]

### §E. Transportation Expenses

Transportation expenses include the cost of travel by air, rail, bus, taxi, and the cost of driving and maintaining a car, but not the costs of meals and lodging. Transportation expenses are deductible whether or not the minister was "away from home." However, transportation expenses may be deductible only to the extent that they are (1) ordinary and necessary, and (2) incurred in the performance of professional duties. If the expenses are incurred in connection with self-employment activities such as the performance of weddings, funerals, and baptisms, they are reported on Schedule C of Form 1040. The business-related transportation expenses of a minister who does not satisfy the common law definition of an employee are also reported on Schedule C. Transportation expenses incurred by a minister who is deemed to be an employee of a church are computed on Form 2106 and reported directly on Form 1040 as a deduction from gross income. Since transportation expenses incurred by a minister while acting as an employee are deductible directly from gross income in computing adjusted gross income, they are deductible whether or not a minister itemizes his deductions.

In no event may commuting expenses be deducted as a transportation expense. Thus, a minister may not deduct the cost of taking a bus, subway, taxi, train, or car between his home and church. Such expenses are nondeductible personal expenses. They may not be deducted no matter how far a minister must commute.

Since automobile expenses constitute the most common kind of transportation expense, they alone will be considered in this section. To determine deductible automobile expenses, a minister must first determine the percentage of total miles driven for business purposes during the tax year in question. After determining the percentage of business use, the minister must decide between two methods of computing the automobile expense deduction. The first method generally is referred to as the actual expenses method. Under this approach, a minister deducts the actual expenses incurred in connection with

---

[56]Onstott v. Commissioner, 41 T.C.M. 827 (1981).

the business use of his car. Deductible items include the cost of gas, oil, repairs, supplies, cleaning, depreciation, interest on a car loan, taxes, licenses, garage rent, parking fees, and tolls. The cost of major capital items, such as a new engine, an air conditioner, a car stereo system, or the cost of the car itself, are not deductible as operating expenses. Such items must be capitalized and deducted as depreciation or cost recovery allowances.

After determining the total automobile expenses for a particular year, a minister simply multiplies the total actual expenses times the percentage of business use to determine his automobile expense deduction. Of course, if a minister is reimbursed by his employing church for some or all of his automobile expenses, or if he receives an automobile allowance from his church, the reimbursement rules discussed in the preceding section in connection with travel expenses would be applicable. The substantiation and recordkeeping requirements discussed in connection with travel expenses also apply to automobile expenses.

The second method of computing the automobile expense deduction is referred to as the optional, or standard mileage rate, method. Under this method, a minister computes his automobile expense deduction by multiplying his total business miles for a particular tax year by the standard mileage rates. The rates as of the publication date of this book are 20¢ per mile for the first 15,000 business miles and 11¢ per mile for any additional business miles. These rates are subject to change.

The following rules apply to the optional, or standard mileage rate, method:

1. It is available only for passenger cars, vans, pickup trucks, and panel trucks.

2. The minister must own the car, not use the car for hire, and use only the straight-line method when claiming its depreciation.

3. As of the publication date of this book, a minister can deduct only 11¢ per mile for all business mileage if his car is fully depreciated.

4. The standard mileage rate is used instead of actual operating and fixed expenses and depreciation. However, the business portion of parking fees, tolls, taxes, and interest on car loans may still be deducted.

5. The standard mileage rate method may be used even if a minister's reimbursement for expenses is less than the amount figured using the standard mileage rate. However, if a minister is reimbursed by his church for automobile expenses or receives an automobile allowance he may deduct only the expense that exceeds the reimbursement or allowance. The reimbursement rules discussed in the preceding section should be consulted.

6. The substantiation rules discussed in the preceding section are applicable.

## §F. Educational Expenses

Under certain circumstances a minister may deduct his educational expenses. To be deductible, educational expenses must be ordinary and necessary and the educational instruction must satisfy one or both of the following tests:

1. It meets the express requirements of one's employer, or the requirements of law or regulations, for keeping one's salary, status, or job, if the requirements imposed serve a business purpose.

2. It maintains or improves skills required in doing one's present work.

Even if one or both of the preceding requirements is met, a minister may *not* deduct educational expenses if the education (1) is required in order to meet the minimum educational requirements for qualification in one's work or business, or (2) is part of a program of study that will lead to qualifying one in a new trade or business—regardless of whether the minister intends to enter that trade or business.

Educational expenses include amounts spent for tuition, books, supplies, laboratory fees and similar items, and certain travel and transportation costs. If a minister's educational expenses qualify for deduction, he may deduct transportation expenses incurred in going between (1) the general area where he works and a school located beyond that general area, or (2) the place of work and a school within the same general area. However, if a minister goes home before going to school, he may deduct the expense of going from home to school only to the extent that it is not more than the transportation expense that he would have had if he had gone from work to school. The cost of local transportation between home and school on a nonworking day may never be deducted.

If a minister travels "away from home" to obtain education, he may deduct his expenses for travel, meals, and lodging while away from home.[57] If a trip is mainly for personal reasons, travel expenses are not deductible.

Most educational expenses are deducted as miscellaneous deductions on Schedule A of Form 1040. This means that they are deductible only by ministers who itemize their deductions. A minister may not deduct amounts for which he has been reimbursed. Whether or not a minister itemizes deductions, he may deduct unreimbursed travel and transportation expenses incurred in attending qualifying educational instruction.

## §G. Professional Expenses

Ministers who are treated as employees for income tax purposes no longer report unreimbursed professional expenses such as entertainment, subscrip-

---

[57]The term *away from home* is explained in the previous section dealing with travel expenses.

tions to professional journals, religious books, conference registrations, business telephone use, and professional dues on Schedule C. All of such expenses are listed on Schedule A of Form 1040 to the extent that they have a legitimate business purpose. Such expenses are not reported as employee business expenses on Form 2106, and therefore they may be deducted only if a minister's aggregate itemized deductions exceeds the available "zero bracket amount" (standard deduction). Any reimbursement a minister receives from his employing church for professional expenses must be reported as income on Form 1040 and on the minister's W-2 form.

Ministers who do not satisfy the definition of a common law employee (discussed earlier in this chapter) report professional expenses on Schedule C.

In 1964 the Tax Court ruled that because a minister's housing allowance is excluded from gross income, that portion of his unreimbursed professional expenses attributable to earning his tax-exempt housing allowance is not deductible as an itemized expense on Schedule A of Form 1040.[58] This ruling was based on section 265 of the Internal Revenue Code, which specifies that expenses allocable to income that is excluded from federal income taxes must be allocated to such income and may not be deducted from adjusted gross income as itemized expenses on Schedule A. The IRS has not enforced this allocation rule, but there is no assurance that it will not do so in the future. Enforcement would be consistent with Revenue Ruling 83-3, discussed earlier in the present chapter, in which the IRS ruled that mortgage interest and property taxes that are fully allocable to a minister's housing allowance exclusion cannot be deducted as itemized expenses.

[58]Deason v. Commissioner, 41 T.C. 465 (1964).

# Part Two

---

# Law and the Church

# 7

# DEFINITIONS

Since many state and federal laws use the term *church,* it is important to define the term with precision. To illustrate, the Internal Revenue Code uses the term *church* in many contexts, including the following:

1. charitable giving limitations[1]
2. church pension plans under the Employee Retirement Income Security Act of 1974 (ERISA)[2]
3. exemption from the necessity of applying for recognition of tax-exempt status[3]
4. unemployment tax exemptions[4]
5. exemption from filing annual information returns[5]
6. exemption from filing returns regarding liquidation, dissolution, or termination[6]
7. restrictions on the examination of financial records[7]

The Internal Revenue Code occasionally uses the term *church* in connection with the term *minister.* For example, service performed by a duly ordained, commissioned, or licensed minister of a church is expressly exempted from federal employment taxes,[8] unemployment taxes,[9] income tax withholding re-

[1]I.R.C. § 170(b)(1)(A)(i).
[2]I.R.C. §§ 410(d), 414(e).
[3]I.R.C. § 508(c)(1).
[4]I.R.C. § 3309(b)(1).
[5]I.R.C. § 6033(a)(2)(A).
[6]I.R.C. § 6043(b)(1).
[7]I.R.C. § 7605(c).
[8]I.R.C. § 3121(b)(8)(A).
[9]I.R.C. § 3309(b)(2).

quirements,[10] and self-employment taxes (if a valid waiver has been timely filed).[11] Despite these many references to the term *church,* the Internal Revenue Code contains no definition of the term.[12]

In addition, federal law prescribes the position and manner of display of the United States flag in church buildings;[13] imposes penalties upon persons who cross state lines to avoid prosecution for damaging or destroying church buildings, or who refuse to testify in any criminal proceeding relating to such an offense;[14] and describes the benefits available to churches under the National Flood Insurance Act.[15]

Many state and local laws contain specific references to the term *church.* These laws govern such matters as zoning, nonprofit corporations, state and local revenue, the use of church buses, the desecration of church buildings, the sale of intoxicating liquors within a specified distance from a church, building codes, property ownership, and interference with church services.

Every law that uses the term *church* raises definitional problems. To illustrate, one city enacted a zoning ordinance permitting only single-family dwellings, churches, schools, libraries, and farms in areas classified as "residential." A church purchased seven acres of undeveloped land in a residential zone, and constructed a church building, parking lot, and recreational complex consisting of two softball diamonds. The softball diamonds were surrounded by banks of high-intensity electric lights, which made nighttime games possible. Soon after the softball diamonds were completed, the church conducted a softball tournament over a two-week period. Games lasted until 11:30 p.m. Several neighbors complained of the bright lights, noise, dust, traffic, and stray softballs. The city discontinued electrical service to the softball fields, defending its action on the ground that the lighted softball fields were not a permissible activity in a residential zone.

The church sued the city, arguing that the softball fields were a legitimate extension of the church itself, and therefore were permissible. The court agreed with the church: "The activities conducted on this field are an integral part of the church program and are sufficiently connected with the church itself that the use of this property for recreational purposes is permissible."[16] The court emphasized that "the term 'church' is broader than the church building itself"

[10]I.R.C. § 3401(a)(9).

[11]I.R.C. § 1402(e).

[12]*See generally* Whelan, *"Church" in the Internal Revenue Code,* 45 FORDHAM L. REV. 885 (1977).

[13]36 U.S.C. § 175(k).

[14]18 U.S.C. § 1074.

[15]42 U.S.C. § 4013(b)(1)(C).

[16]Corporation of the Presiding Bishop v. Ashton, 448 P.2d 185, 189 (Idaho 1968).

and must be interpreted to include "uses customarily incidental or accessory to church uses . . . if reasonably closely related, both in substance and in space, to the main church purpose."[17]

Many other courts have been asked to decide whether a particular use or activity comes within the definition of *church* in the context of municipal zoning laws. The following activities and uses have been held to come within that definition: use of a home across the street from a church for women's fellowship meetings and religious education classes;[18] a single-family residence used by the United Presbyterian Church as a religious coffeehouse for university students;[19] a priest's home, convent, and parochial school;[20] a twenty-four-acre tract of land containing a large mansion that was used as a synagogue and a meeting place for the congregation's social groups and youth activities;[21] a kindergarten, play area, and parochial school;[22] a thirty-seven-acre estate used by an Episcopal church as a religious retreat and center for religious instruction;[23] and a private school operated by a Baptist church.[24]

Other courts have concluded that certain activities do not constitute a church in the context of zoning laws. To illustrate, one court has held that an area restricted to residential and church uses could not accommodate temporary, open-air camp meetings.[25] The court observed that not every place in which religious services are conducted is a church. It inferred that a church at the least must consist of "a building set apart for public worship," and thus could not include camp meetings. Another court held that a dwelling of sixteen bedrooms and twelve bathrooms occupied by twenty-five people comprising four different families, all members of the American Orthodox Catholic Church, was not a church or parish house even though religious instruction was given daily for one hour to the children and three times a week to the adults.[26] The court reasoned that "the principal use of the building . . . is that of a dwelling

---

[17]*Id.* at 188.

[18]Twin-City Bible Church v. Zoning Board of Appeals, 365 N.E.2d 1381 (Ill. 1977).

[19]Synod of Chesapeake, Inc. v. Newark, 254 A.2d 611 (Del. 1969).

[20]Board of Zoning Appeals v. Wheaton, 76 N.E.2d 597 (Ind. 1948).

[21]Community Synagogue v. Bates, 154 N.Y.S.2d 15 (1956).

[22]Diocese of Rochester v. Planning Board, 154 N.Y.S.2d 849 (1956).

[23]Diocese of Central New York v. Schwarzer, 199 N.Y.S.2d 939 (1960), *aff'd,* 217 N.Y.S.2d 567 (1961).

[24]City of Concord v. New Testament Baptist Church, 382 A.2d 377 (N.H. 1978).

[25]Portage Township v. Full Salvation Union, 29 N.W.2d 297 (Mich. 1947).

[26]People v. Kalayjian, 352 N.Y.S.2d 115 (1973). *See also* Heard v. Dallas, 456 S.W.2d 440 (Tex. 1970) (child care center operated in minister's residence held not to be a "church").

for residential purposes" and that "the incidental religious instruction provided to the families does not change this fact."[27]

Similarly, when a farmers' organization purchased a church building for meetings promoting agriculture and "higher ideals of manhood, womanhood, and citizenship," a court concluded that the building no longer could be considered a church.[28] A "church," observed the court, is "a place or edifice consecrated to religious worship, where people join together in some form of public worship."[29]

Finally, one court has held that the use of a twenty-eight-acre tract by a Jewish foundation for a conference center, leadership training center, and children's retreat did not constitute a church despite the claim that some religious instruction would be conducted on the property.[30]

The term *church* has also been construed frequently in the context of tax exemptions. In one case, a religious radio station argued that it was exempt from state sales and use taxes since it was a church.[31] The radio station's corporate purpose was to "exalt the Lord Jesus Christ and to maintain facilities for the worship of God and for the teaching and preaching of the Gospel." The station actively engaged in religious activities, including broadcasting of predominantly religious programming, missions promotion, child evangelism, establishment of Bible study groups, and personal counseling. In addition, the station owned an auditorium that was used frequently for interdenominational worship services and related programs. The state tax commissioner challenged the station's exemption on the ground that it was not a church. In particular, the commissioner argued that the radio station could not be a church since it did not have "a body of communicants gathered together in an order, or united under one form of government."[32] The court, acknowledging that the term *church* is "not susceptible to a precise definition," summarily concluded that the radio station was entitled to the exemption since it "exhibited the essential qualities of a church," despite the fact that it did not have a definite congregation.[33]

In another case,[34] a county tax assessor determined that a private residence was not a church, despite the homeowners' contention that monthly meetings

---

[27]*Id.* at 118.

[28]In re Upper St. Clair Township Grange No. 2032, 152 A.2d 768 (Pa. 1959).

[29]*Id.* at 771.

[30]State ex rel. B'nai B'rith Foundation v. Walworth County, 208 N.W.2d 113 (Wis. 1973).

[31]Maumee Valley Broadcasting Assoc. v. Porterfield, 279 N.E.2d 863 (Ohio 1972).

[32]*Id.* at 865.

[33]*Id.*

[34]Ideal Life Church v. County of Washington, 304 N.W.2d 308 (Minn. 1981).

of the eleven-member Ideal Life Church were held in the home and the church had received a charter from the mail-order Universal Life Church. The tax assessor's determination was upheld by the state supreme court, which quoted with approval the reasoning of a lower court in the same case:

> [T]he proper test for determination of a "church" depends upon an analysis of all the facts and circumstances of each particular case. In the present action the following factors . . . lead to the clear conclusion that Petitioner is not a "church" . . .
>
> 1. In substance, the preconceived and primary, if not the sole motive behind Petitioner's organization and operation was tax avoidance in favor of the private individuals who control the corporation . . . .
> 2. Petitioner's doctrine and beliefs, such as they are, are intentionally vague and non-binding upon its members.
> 3. Petitioner's members freely continue to practice other religions.
> 4. Petitioner has no formally trained or ordained ministry.
> 5. Petitioner has no sacraments, rituals, education courses or literature of its own.
> 6. Petitioner has no liturgy, other than simple meetings which resemble mere social gatherings or discussion groups rather than religious worship.
> 7. Petitioner is not an institution which advances religion (as that term is commonly understood) as a way of life for all men.
> 8. Petitioner does not require a belief in any Supreme Being or beings.[35]

Another court upheld the property tax exemption of a sixty-five-acre tract of land containing a religious hermitage and retreat center. While noting that the property was "not a church in the narrow sense," the court concluded that "a church is more than merely an edifice affording people the opportunity to worship God . . . . To limit a church to being merely a house of prayer and sacrifice would, in a large degree, be depriving the church of the opportunity of enlarging, perpetuating and strengthening itself and the congregation."[36]

One court has held that an evangelistic association is not a church and thus is not exempt from unemployment insurance payroll taxes.[37] The court noted that the evangelistic association was exempt from federal income tax, was established for avowedly religious purposes, conducted worship services in cities throughout the country, had a mailing list in excess of 25,000 persons, and relied upon contributions for its support. However, concluded the court, the association could not be deemed a church since "there was no group of believers who had voluntarily bound themselves together in an organized association for

---

[35]*Id.* at 315.
[36]Order Minor Conventuals v. Lee, 409 N.Y.S.2d 667, 669 (1978).
[37]Vic Coburn Evangelistic Assoc. v. Employment Division, 582 P.2d 51 (Ore. 1978).

the purpose of shared and regular worship."[38] Another court ruled that an interdenominational Christian youth organization that conducted religious services and administered sacraments was a church and thus was exempt from payment of unemployment taxes.[39] The court concluded that a comprehensive definition of the term *church* was not possible. Instead, the court opted for a functional approach: If an organization performs church functions, such as the conduct of worship and the promulgation of a creed, it will be deemed a church.

The IRS often must decide whether a particular individual, group, or organization is a bona fide church. For example, in one case the IRS maintained that a husband and wife and their minor child were not a church despite the family's insistence to the contrary. The family alleged that it was a church since the father often preached and disseminated religious instruction to his son; the family conducted "religious services" in their home; and the family often prayed together at home. A federal court agreed with the IRS that the family was not a church. The court quoted the fourteen criteria utilized by the IRS in determining whether a particular group or organization is in fact a church:

1. a distinct legal existence
2. a recognized creed and form of worship
3. a definite and distinct ecclesiastical government
4. a formal code of doctrine and discipline
5. a distinct religious history
6. a membership not associated with any other church or denomination
7. an organization of ordained ministers
8. ordained ministers selected after completing prescribed studies
9. a literature of its own
10. established places of worship
11. regular congregations
12. regular worship services
13. Sunday schools for religious instruction of the young
14. schools for the preparation of ministers

No single factor is controlling, although all fourteen may not be relevant to a given determination.[40]

In concluding that the family was not a church, the court observed: "At a minimum, a church includes a body of believers or communicants that assem-

[38] *Id.* at 52.

[39] Young Life Campaign v. Patino, 176 Cal. Rptr. 23 (1981).

[40] American Guidance Foundation v. United States, 490 F. Supp. 304 (D.D.C. 1980). These fourteen criteria were contained in an earlier edition of IRS Publication 557. They currently are set forth in Internal Revenue Manual 7(10)69, §§ 321.3:(3) and 321.3:(4).

bles regularly in order to worship. Unless the organization is reasonably available to the public in its conduct of worship, its educational instruction, and its promulgation of doctrine, it cannot fulfill this associational role."[41]

The IRS has successfully challenged a variety of tax-evasion schemes that have operated under the guise of a church. These schemes usually involve some or all of the following characteristics: An individual forms his own church, assigns all or a substantial part of his income to the church, takes a vow of poverty, declares himself to be the minister, retains control over all church funds and property, designates a substantial housing allowance for himself, and reports the income that he has assigned to his church as a charitable contribution deduction on his federal tax return. In most cases the church has no building other than the personal residence of the minister, and it conducts few if any religious activities. Since the minister often purchases his credentials and church charter by mail, such schemes commonly are referred to as mail-order churches. The IRS consistently has refused to recognize such entities as entitled to exemption from federal income taxation. This determination, however, usually is made on the basis that the net earnings of the alleged church inure to the benefit of private individuals, not because the organization does not constitute a church. The IRS treatment of mail-order churches is considered in detail in a later chapter.

In construing the phrase *church or convention or association of churches,* which appears several times in the Internal Revenue Code,[42] the courts have concluded that the word *church* may include a private elementary and secondary school maintained and operated by a church,[43] a seminary,[44] and conventions and associations of churches.[45] The term *convention or association of churches* has not been construed with precision. The income tax regulations define *a convention or association of churches* to mean "a convention or association of churches."[46]

In summary, although no comprehensive definition of the term *church* has been devised that will apply in every context, it is clear that the term includes the following: (1) a building and property used primarily for worship or religious activities, (2) a society of persons who regularly congregate in a church building

[41]*Id.* at 306.

[42]I.R.C. §§ 170(b)(1)(A)(i), 410(d), 414(e)(1)(A), 414(e)(3)(A), 508(c)(1)(A), 512(b)(14), 514(b)(3)(E), 3309(b)(1), 6033(a)(2)(A)(i), 6043(b)(1), and 7605(c).

[43]St. Martin Evangelical Lutheran Church v. South Dakota, 451 U.S. 772 (1981).

[44]EEOC v. Southwestern Baptist Theological Seminary, 651 F.2d 277 (5th Cir. 1981).

[45]De La Salle Institute v. United States, 195 F. Supp. 891 (N.D. Cal. 1961); Senate Report 2375, 81st Congress, 2d Session, p. 27.

[46]Treas. Reg. § 1.170A-9(a).

for worship and religious activities, or (3) a religious denomination, or a convention or association of churches.

The term *integrated auxiliary* occasionally occurs in the Internal Revenue Code and income tax regulations in connection with the term *church*. Integrated auxiliaries of churches are exempted from the requirements of applying for tax-exempt status,[47] filing annual information returns,[48] and filing returns regarding dissolution.[49] An integrated auxiliary of a church is defined by the income tax regulations as an organization that is exempt from taxation under section 501(c)(3); that is affiliated with a church; and whose principal activity is exclusively religious.[50] The regulations further state that an organization's principal activity will not be considered to be exclusively religious if that activity is educational, literary, charitable, or of a nature other than religious that would serve as a basis for exemption under section 501(c)(3) of the Internal Revenue Code, and that an integrated auxiliary is "affiliated" with a church if it is either controlled by or associated with a church or with a convention or association of churches.[51]

The regulations cite men's and women's organizations, seminaries, missions societies, and youth groups as examples of integrated auxiliaries. The regulations cite the following examples of organizations that are not integrated auxiliaries: hospitals, separately incorporated elementary schools, orphanages, old age homes, and liberal arts colleges that are affiliated with churches. In each case the activity performed by the affiliated organization is educational, literary, charitable, or of a nature other than "exclusively religious" that would serve as a basis for exemption under section 501(c)(3) of the Code.[52]

---

[47]I.R.C. § 508(c)(1)(A).
[48]I.R.C. § 6033(a)(2)(A)(i).
[49]I.R.C. § 6043(b)(1).
[50]Treas. Reg. § 1.6033-2(g)(5)(i).
[51]Treas. Reg. § 1.6033-2(g)(5)(iv).
[52]*Id.*

# 8

# ORGANIZATION AND ADMINISTRATION

A church can exist as either a corporation or an unincorporated association. This chapter will explore the essential features of both forms of organization, discuss the advantages and disadvantages of each, and summarize the incorporation process.

## §A. Unincorporated Associations

### 1. IN GENERAL

In general, any church that is not a corporation is an unincorporated association. The term *unincorporated association* is defined as any group "whose members share a common purpose, and . . . who function under a common name under circumstances where fairness requires the group be recognized as a legal entity."[1]

One court has observed:

> A church or religious society may exist for all the purposes for which it was organized independently of any incorporation of the body . . . and, it is a matter of common knowledge that many do exist and are never incorporated. For the promotion of religion and charity, they may subserve all the purposes of their organization, and, generally, need no incorporation except incidentally to further these objects.[2]

Traditionally, unincorporated associations had no legal existence. This fact had many important consequences. First, an association could not own or transfer property in its own name; second, an association could not enter into

---

[1]Barr v. United Methodist Church, 153 Cal. Rptr. 322, 328 (1979), *cert. denied,* 444 U.S. 973 (1980).

[2]Murphy v. Traylor, 289 So.2d 584, 586 (Ala. 1974).

contracts or other legal obligations; and third, an association could not sue or be sued.

The inability to sue or be sued had many important ramifications. It meant, for example, that a church association could not sue its members. Thus, if a church member's negligence caused fire damage to a church building, neither the church nor the church's insurance company, as a subrogee of the insured church, could sue the member.[3] It also meant that a church association could not be sued by its members. In one case, a church member who was injured because of the negligence of her church was denied recovery against the church on the ground that a member of an unincorporated church is engaged in a joint enterprise and may not recover from the church any damages sustained through the wrongful conduct of another member.[4] Finally, since an association could not sue or be sued, it generally was held that an association's members were personally responsible for the acts of other members or agents of the association committed in the course of the association's business.[5] One court stated the general rule as follows:

> The members of an unincorporated association are engaged in a joint enterprise, and the negligence of each member in the prosecution of that enterprise is imputable to each and every other member, so that the member who has suffered damages to his person, property, or reputation through the tortious conduct of another member of the association may not recover from the association for such damage although he may recover individually from the member actually guilty of the tort.[6]

These legal disabilities, particularly the personal liability of every member for the acts of other members, rendered the unincorporated association form of organization highly undesirable for churches and most other nonprofit organizations. Many states have enacted laws that remove some or all of these traditional disabilities.[7] Thus, while most states still prohibit an association from owning or transferring title to property in its own name, many states do permit an association to hold or transfer title to property in the name of "trustees"

---

[3]Employers Mutual Casualty Co. v. Griffin, 266 S.E.2d 18 (N.C. 1980).

[4]Goard v. Branscom, 189 S.E.2d 667 (N.C. 1972), cert. denied, 191 S.E.2d 354 (1972).

[5]See generally H. OLECK, NONPROFIT CORPORATIONS, ORGANIZATIONS, AND ASSOCIATIONS 95-132 (4th ed. 1980); P. Kauper & Ellis, Religious Corporations and the Law, 71 MICH. LAW REV. 1500 (1973).

[6]Williamson v. Wallace, 224 S.E.2d 253 (N.C. 1976).

[7]See generally OLECK, supra note 5, at 95-132; P. Kauper & S. Ellis, supra note 5, at 1541-43; Barr v. United Methodist Church, 153 Cal. Rptr. 322 (1979), cert. denied, 444 U.S. 973 (1980).

acting on behalf of the association.[8] Some states permit unincorporated associations to sue and be sued in the association name.[9] Other states permit some members of an association to bring suit as representatives of the entire membership.[10] Some courts, under limited circumstances, permit an association to bring suit in its own name as representative of its members. One court has held that a church association may bring suit on behalf of its members when "(a) its members would otherwise have standing to sue in their own right; (b) the interests it seeks to protect are germane to the organization's purpose; and (c) neither the claim asserted nor the relief requested requires the participation of individual members in the lawsuit."[11] Finally, a number of states permit associations to enter into contracts.

Even so, unless state law provides otherwise, unincorporated associations remain incapable of suing or being sued, holding or transferring title to property, and entering into contracts and other legal obligations. In those states where some or all of the traditional legal disabilities persist, an association generally may act only through its membership.

It is also important to observe that most if not all states still hold that members of an unincorporated association are personally responsible for the acts of other members or agents of the corporation, at least if the acts occur in the course of association activities or if the members knew or should have known of the acts and thus by implication approved them. This potential legal liability of each member is doubtless the principal disadvantage of the association form of organization.

Finally, it is interesting to observe that although the Internal Revenue Code restricts tax-exempt status to corporations, community chests, funds, and foundations organized and operated exclusively for religious and other charitable purposes,[12] the IRS construes the term *corporations* to include unincorporated associations.[13]

---

[8]P. Kauper & S. Ellis, *supra* note 5 at 1542; Adams v. Bethany Church, 361 So.2d 510 (Ala. 1978); Ervin v. Davis, 199 S.W.2d 366 (Mo. 1947); African Methodist Episcopal Church v. Independent African Methodist Episcopal Church, 281 S.W.2d 758 (Tex. 1955).

[9]Enterprise Lodge v. First Baptist Church, 264 So.2d 153 (Ala. 1972); Adams v. Bethany Church, 361 So.2d 510 (Ala. 1978).

[10]Rock Zion Baptist Church v. Johnson, 47 So.2d 397 (La. 1950).

[11]Church of Scientology v. Cazares, 638 F.2d 1272, 1279 (5th Cir. 1981).

[12]I.R.C. § 501(c)(3).

[13]Treas. Reg. § 1.501(c)(3)-1(b)(2); IRS Publication 557.

## 2. CREATION AND ADMINISTRATION

In general, an unincorporated association is created by the voluntary association of two or more individuals under a common name for a particular purpose. The creation of an unincorporated association ordinarily does not require compliance with state laws, although several states have enacted laws allowing associations to organize in a more formal way.[14] Such laws typically confer many of the rights and privileges enjoyed by corporations upon associations that choose to formally organize.

It is customary and desirable for the members of an unincorporated association to adopt rules for the internal management of the affairs of the association. Although these rules usually are called bylaws, they occasionally are called articles of association, constitution, or charter. Such terminology is not important.[15] In this chapter, the rules and regulations of an unincorporated association will be referred to as bylaws. The bylaws of an unincorporated association typically contain provisions dealing with meetings; election, qualification, and tenure of officers and trustees; qualification and acceptance of members; the acquisition and transfer of property; the status of property upon the dissolution of the association; and the rights and duties of members between themselves and with the association.

It is well-settled that the bylaws of an unincorporated association constitute a contract between the association and its members, and that the rights and duties of members, as between themselves and in their relation to the association in all matters affecting its internal government and the management of its affairs, are measured by the terms of such bylaws.[16] By becoming a member an individual agrees to be bound by the association's bylaws, and to have his rights and duties determined by them.[17]

It is also clearly established that if a dispute occurs an association's bylaws are to be construed by the association itself, not by the courts.[18] The courts may interfere with the enforcement of an association's bylaws only when a particular provision is contrary to established public policy or is so patently arbitrary and unreasonable as to be beyond the protection of the law.[19] If an

[14]P. Kauper & S. Ellis, *supra* note 5, at 1541 n.213.

[15]Cunningham v. Independent Soap & Chemical Workers, 486 P.2d 1316 (Kan. 1971).

[16]Savoca Masonry Co., Inc. v. Homes & Son Construction Co., Inc., 542 P.2d 817, 820 (Ariz. 1975).

[17]Libby v. Perry, 311 A.2d 527 (Me. 1973).

[18]Kentucky High School Athletic Association v. Hopkins County Board of Education, 552 S.W.2d 685 (Ky. 1977).

[19]Pinsker v. Pacific Coast Society of Orthodontists, 526 P.2d 253 (Cal. 1974).

association's bylaws do not deal specifically with a particular issue, the issue is determined by a majority vote of the association's members.

## §B. Corporations

### 1. IN GENERAL

The legal disabilities connected with the unincorporated association form of organization cause many churches to incorporate. Unlike many unincorporated churches, church corporations are capable of suing and being sued, entering into contracts and other legal obligations, and holding title to property. Perhaps most important, the members of a church corporation ordinarily are shielded from personal liability for the debts and misconduct of other members or agents of the church.

Two forms of church corporation are in widespread use in the United States. By far the more common form is the membership corporation, which is composed of and controlled by church members. Several states also recognize trustee corporations. The trustees of a trustee corporation constitute and control the corporation. A few states also permit certain officers of hierarchical churches to form corporations sole,[20] a *corporation sole* being defined as a corporation consisting of a single individual.

### 2. THE INCORPORATION PROCESS

Although procedures for the incorporation of churches vary from state to state, most states have adopted one or more of the following procedures:

#### a. *Model Nonprofit Corporation Act*

The Model Nonprofit Corporation Act, adopted in whole or in part by several states,[21] provides a uniform method of incorporation for several kinds of nonprofit organizations, including religious, scientific, educational, charitable, cultural, and benevolent organizations. The procedure consists of the following steps: (1) preparation of duplicate articles of incorporation setting forth the corporation's name, period of duration, address of registered office within the state, name and address of a registered agent, purposes, and names and addresses of the initial board of directors and incorporators; (2) notarized signature of the duplicate articles of incorporation by the incorporators; and (3) submission of the prescribed filing fee and duplicate articles of incorporation to the secretary

---

[20]*See generally* P. Kauper & S. Ellis, *supra* note 5, at 1538-41.

[21]1W. FLETCHER, CYCLOPEDIA OF THE LAW OF PRIVATE CORPORATIONS §§ 2.4, 68, 80 (1974 & Suppl. 1982). Many other states have adopted the Nonprofit Corporation Act. Since this Act is based on and closely parallels the Model Nonprofit Corporation Act, only the latter Act is considered in this chapter.

of state. The secretary of state reviews the articles of incorporation to ensure compliance with the Act. If the articles of incorporation are satisfactory, the secretary of state endorses both duplicate copies, files one in his office, and returns the other along with a certificate of incorporation to the church.[22] The church's corporate existence begins at the moment the certificate of incorporation is issued.[23] After the certificate of incorporation has been issued, the Act specifies that an organizational meeting of the board of directors shall be held at the call of a majority of the incorporators for the purpose of adopting the initial bylaws of the corporation and for such other purposes as may come before the meeting.[24]

The incorporators and directors can be the same persons in most states. Many states require at least three directors. Incorporators and directors must have attained a prescribed age and be citizens of the United States. They ordinarily do not have to be citizens of the state in which the church is incorporated.

The Model Nonprofit Corporation Act governs many aspects of a nonprofit corporation's existence, including meetings of members, notice of meetings, voting, quorum, number and election of directors, vacancies, officers, removal of officers, books and records, merger or consolidation with other organizations, and dissolution. In most of these matters, a corporation is bound by the Act's provisions only if it has not provided otherwise in its articles of incorporation or bylaws. For example, a corporation may stipulate in its bylaws the percentage of members constituting a quorum, but if it fails to do so the Act provides that a quorum consists of ten percent of the voting membership.[25] Similarly, the Act provides that directors shall serve for one-year terms unless a corporation's articles of incorporation or bylaws provide otherwise.[26]

Certain provisions in the Act may not be altered by a corporation. For example, the Act mandates that corporations have a minimum of three directors.[27] Although a corporation may require more than three directors, it may not require less. The Act also prohibits corporations from making loans to officers or directors.[28]

The Act requires all nonprofit corporations to file an annual report with the secretary of state's office. The report is filed on a form provided by the secretary of state, and ordinarily sets forth the name of the corporation, the address of

[22]MODEL NONPROFIT CORPORATION ACT § 30.

[23]*Id.* at § 31.

[24]*Id.* at § 32.

[25]*Id.* at § 16.

[26]*Id.* at § 18.

[27]*Id.*

[28]*Id.* at § 27.

the corporation's registered office in the state of incorporation, the name of the registered agent at such address, the names and addresses of the directors and officers, and a brief statement of the nature of the affairs the corporation is actually conducting. A nominal fee must accompany the report.

States that have adopted the Act differ with regard to the penalties imposed upon corporations that fail to file the annual report by the date prescribed. Some states impose only a nominal fine.[29] Others call for the cancellation of a corporation's certificate of incorporation.[30] Cancellation of a certificate of incorporation has the effect of terminating the existence of a corporation. This is an extraordinary penalty, generally available only after the secretary of state's office has sent the corporation a written notice of the impending cancellation. If a corporation fails to respond to the written notice, the secretary of state issues a certificate of cancellation, which is the legal document terminating both the certificate of incorporation and the corporation's legal existence. Many states permit reinstatement of terminated corporations. Reinstatement generally is available upon the filing of a formal application within a prescribed time.

It is important to distinguish between the terms *nonprofit* and *tax-exempt*. Nonprofit corporations generally are defined to include any corporation whose income is not distributable to its members, directors, or officers.[31] The fact that an organization incorporates under a state's nonprofit corporation law does not in itself render the corporation exempt from federal, state, or local taxes. Exemption from tax generally is available only to those organizations that have applied for and received recognition of tax-exempt status. In some cases the law recognizes the tax-exempt status of certain nonprofit organizations and waives the necessity of making formal application for recognition of exempt status. For example, "churches, their integrated auxiliaries, and conventions or associations of churches" are exempted from federal income tax without the need of making formal application.[32] Thus, unless a nonprofit corporation applies for and receives recognition of tax-exempt status or is expressly recognized by law to be exempt from tax without the necessity of making formal application, it will not be considered tax-exempt.

Many churches prefer not to incorporate under the Model Nonprofit Corporation Act. This decision ordinarily is based upon two considerations. First, churches do not want to be bothered with the annual reporting requirements. Although these requirements normally are not burdensome, they must be

[29]VT. NONPROFIT CORPORATION ACT § 85.

[30]IOWA CODE § 504A.87.

[31]ARIZ. REV. STAT. ANN. § 10-1002(21); COLO. REV. STAT. § 7-20-102(10); GA. CODE § 22-2102(c).

[32]I.R.C. § 508(c).

rigidly followed if a church is to avoid loss of its corporate status. Many church corporations have been terminated through disregard of the reporting requirements. Second, many churches regard the Model Nonprofit Corporation Act to be too restrictive since it regulates virtually every aspect of corporate organization and administration. The Act does specify that most of its provisions are applicable only if a corporation has not provided otherwise in its charter or bylaws. However, churches often are unwittingly controlled by the Act through their failure to adopt bylaws dealing with particular aspects of organization and administration that are addressed in the Act. Some churches of course consider this to be an advantage, for it means that there will be authoritative direction on most questions of church administration.

Some states permit churches incorporated under the Model Nonprofit Corporation Act to convert to another form of corporation available under state law.

### b. Special Statutes

Several states have adopted statutes that pertain exclusively to the incorporation and administration of specific religious denominations. Such statutes typically apply only to the Roman Catholic Church, the Eastern Orthodox Church, Methodist churches, and the Protestant Episcopal Church. New York, however, has statutes covering over thirty-five religions and denominations, and Michigan and New Jersey each provides for over twelve.[33] Most of the states providing for the incorporation of churches of specified denominations also have enacted general nonprofit corporation laws. Churches generally can elect to incorporate under either the general nonprofit or the special religious corporation law.

### c. Court-Approved Corporations

Some states allow churches to incorporate by submitting articles of incorporation or articles of agreement to a local state court for approval. If the court determines that the church is organized for religious purposes and its objectives are consistent with the laws of the state, a certificate of incorporation is issued, which ordinarily is filed with the local recorder's office and with the secretary of state. This form of incorporation provides a minimum of state control over the operation of church corporations, since ordinarily no annual reporting is required and the corporation law regulates only a few areas of corporate organization and administration.

[33]P. Kauper & S. Ellis, *supra* note 5, at 1534.

### d. *Religious Corporation Laws*

Many states have adopted general laws pertaining to the incorporation and administration of religious corporations without any specific reference to particular denominations. Incorporation under such statutes ordinarily is simpler than incorporating under the general nonprofit corporation law. Typically, a church may incorporate under a general religious corporation statute by adopting articles setting forth the church's name, address, purposes, and the names and addresses of church officers and directors, and filing the articles with either the county recorder or the secretary of state. A church's corporate existence ordinarily begins upon the filing of the articles with the appropriate government agency.

Churches are free to incorporate under either the Model Nonprofit Corporation Act or a general religious corporation law in those states where both forms of incorporation are available. One court rejected the claim that churches must incorporate under a state's general religious corporation law.[34] Obviously, a church that incorporates under the Model Nonprofit Corporation Act rather than under a general religious corporation law will be governed exclusively by the model Act.

### e. *"De Facto" Corporations*

Even if a church fails to comply with one or more technical requirements of incorporation, it will be considered a de facto corporation if the following three requirements are satisfied:

> (1) a special act or general law under which a corporation may lawfully exist, (2) a bona fide attempt to organize under the law and colorable compliance with the statutory requirements, and (3) actual use or exercise of corporate powers in pursuance of such law or attempted organization.[35]

Thus, when church trustees failed to sign a certificate of incorporation as required by state law, and the certificate was duly filed with the proper state authorities and remained on file without challenge for over thirty years, a court rejected the contention that the church was not a corporation.[36] Once the de facto status of a corporation is established, it may be attacked only by the state in a *quo warranto* proceeding.

[34]Bible Presbyterian Church v. Harvey Cedars Bible Conference, Inc., 202 A.2d 455 (N.J. 1964).

[35]Trustees of Peninsular Annual Conference of the Methodist Church, Inc. v. Spencer, 183 A.2d 588, 592 (Del. 1962).

[36]*Id.*

### 3. CHARTER, CONSTITUTION, BYLAWS, AND RESOLUTIONS

The application for incorporation generally is called the articles of incorporation or articles of agreement. This document, when approved and certified by the appropriate government official, is commonly referred to as the corporate charter.[37] It is often said that the corporate charter includes by implication every pertinent provision of state law.[38]

Although church charters typically set forth the name, address, period of duration, and purposes of the corporation; the doctrinal tenets of the church; and the names and addresses of incorporators and directors; they rarely contain rules for the internal government of the corporation. For this reason, it is desirable and customary for churches to adopt rules for their internal operation. One court has observed that "it has been uniformly held that religious organizations have the right to prescribe such rules and regulations as to the conduct of their own affairs as they may think proper, so long as the same are not inconsistent with . . . the law of the land."[39] Such rules ordinarily are called bylaws, although occasionally they are referred to as a constitution or a constitution and bylaws. The terms *bylaws* and *constitution* often are used synonymously. Technically, however, the terms are distinguishable—*bylaws* referring generally to the rules of internal government adopted by a corporation, and *constitution* referring to the supreme law of a corporation.[40] Correctly used, the term *constitution* refers to a body of rules that is paramount to the bylaws. It may refer to the charter or to a document separate and distinct from both the charter and bylaws. Church corporations that differentiate between constitution and bylaws ordinarily do so on the basis of amendment procedures, with the amendment of the church constitution requiring a larger majority vote than an amendment of the bylaws.

It makes no sense for a church corporation to have a constitution and a separate body of bylaws unless the constitution is made superior to the bylaws either by express provision or by a more restrictive amendment procedure. Identifying a single body of rules as the constitution and bylaws without any attempt to distinguish between the two is a common but inappropriate practice. Obviously, the best practice would be to set forth the corporation's purposes and beliefs in the corporate charter, and to have a single body of rules for internal government identified as bylaws. At a minimum, church bylaws should cover the following matters: selection of members; time and place of annual

---

[37]W. FLETCHER, *supra* note 21, at § 164.

[38]*Id.*

[39]Ohio Southeast Conference of Evangelical United Brethren Church v. Kruger, 243 N.E.2d 781, 787 (Ohio 1968).

[40]W. FLETCHER, *supra* note 21, at § 4167.

business meetings; calling of special business meetings; notice for annual and special meetings; quorums; voting rights; selection, tenure, and removal of officers and directors; filling of vacancies; responsibilities of directors and officers; method of amending bylaws; and purchase and conveyance of property.[41] It is also helpful to adopt by reference a specific body of parliamentary procedure for use in all church meetings.

Income tax regulations require the assets of a church, upon its dissolution or termination, to pass to another tax-exempt organization.[42] The IRS has stated that the following paragraph will satisfy this requirement if contained in a church corporation's articles of incorporation or bylaws:

> Upon the dissolution of the corporation, the Board of Trustees shall, after paying or making provision for the payment of all of the liabilities of the corporation, dispose of all of the assets of the corporation exclusively for the purposes of the corporation in such manner, or to such organization or organizations organized and operated exclusively for charitable, educational, religious, or scientific purposes as shall at the time qualify as an exempt organization or organizations under section 501(c)(3) of the Internal Revenue Code of 1954 (or the corresponding provision of any future United States Internal Revenue Law), as the Board of Trustees shall determine. Any such assets not so disposed of shall be disposed of by the Court of Common Pleas of the county in which the principal office of the corporation is then located, exclusively for such purposes or to such organization or organizations, as said Court shall determine, which are organized and operated exclusively for such purposes.[43]

The IRS also suggests that the following two paragraphs be placed in a church corporation's articles of incorporation:

> Said corporation is organized exclusively for charitable, religious, and educational purposes, including, for such purposes, the making of distributions to organizations that qualify as exempt organizations under section 501(c)(3) of the Internal Revenue Code of 1954 (or the corresponding provision of any future United States Internal Revenue Law).

> No part of the net earnings of the corporation shall inure to the benefit of, or be distributable to its members, trustees, officers, or other private persons, except that the corporation shall be authorized and empowered to pay reasonable compensation for services rendered and to make payments and distributions in furtherance of the purposes set forth in [these articles]. No substantial part of the activities of the corporation shall be the carrying on of propaganda, or otherwise

---

[41]*See generally* the MODEL NONPROFIT CORPORATION ACT BYLAWS.
[42]Treas. Reg. § 1.501(c)(3)-1(b)(4).
[43]IRS Publication 557.

attempting to influence legislation, and the corporation shall not participate in, or intervene in (including the publishing or distribution of statements) any political campaign on behalf of any candidate for public office. Notwithstanding any other provision of these articles, the corporation shall not carry on any other activities not permitted to be carried on (a) by a corporation exempt from Federal income tax under section 501(c))(3) of the Internal Revenue Code of 1954 (or the corresponding provision of any future United States Internal Revenue Law) or (b) by a corporation contributions to which are deductible under section 170(c)(2) of the Internal Revenue Code of 1954 (or the corresponding provision of any future United States Internal Revenue Law).[44]

The preceding paragraphs ensure the continued recognition of a church's tax-exempt status. They will be considered in detail in another chapter.[45] It is advisable for a church to state its purposes in terms of "charitable, religious, and educational" activities, since this will allow the greatest flexibility and will minimize problems. For example, if a church wishes to establish an elementary school its authority to do so will be indisputable if its purposes are "charitable, religious, and educational." Similarly, a church clearly has the authority to build a nursing home if its purposes are "charitable, religious, and educational," since care for the aged is without question a charitable function. A church may believe that education and nursing care are religious functions too, but the IRS does not agree with this conclusion.

Corporate resolutions are not bylaws. A resolution is an informal and temporary enactment for disposing of a particular item of business, whereas bylaws are rules of general applicability.

Occasionally, conflicts develop among provisions in a corporation's charter, constitution, bylaws, and resolutions. It is well-settled that provisions in a corporate charter take precedence over conflicting provisions in a corporation's constitution, bylaws, or resolutions. Thus, when a church charter provided for seven trustees and the church's bylaws called for nine, the charter provision was held to control.[46] Another court has held that "religious and quasi-religious societies may adopt a constitution and bylaws for the regulation of their affairs, if conformable and subordinate to the charter and not repugnant to the law of the land . . . ."[47] If the constitution is separate and distinct from the bylaws and is of superior force and effect either by expressly so providing or by reason of a more difficult amendment procedure, then provisions in a corporation's

---

[44]*Id.*

[45]*See* chapter 14, *infra.*

[46]Morris v. Richard Clark Missionary Baptist Church, 177 P.2d 811 (Cal. 1947).

[47]Leeds v. Harrison, 87 A.2d 713, 720 (N.J. 1952).

constitution take precedence over conflicting provisions in the bylaws.[48] Thus, where a church constitution specified that a pastor was to be elected by a majority vote of the church membership and the bylaws called for a two-thirds vote, the constitution was held to control.[49]

Resolutions are of course inferior to, and thus may not contradict, provisions in a corporation's charter, constitution, and bylaws.

The power to enact and amend bylaws is vested in the members, unless the charter or bylaws grants this authority to some other body. Occasionally, trustees or directors are given the authority to enact and amend bylaws. Procedures to be followed in amending the bylaws should be and usually are set forth in the bylaws. Such procedures must be followed.

The state law under which a church is incorporated will specify the procedure to be followed in amending the corporate charter. Generally, a charter amendment must be filed with and approved by the state official who approved the charter.

## §C. Records and Reporting

### 1. IN GENERAL

Each church should maintain (1) correct and complete books and records of account, (2) minutes of the proceedings of its members, (3) minutes of the proceedings of its board of directors, (4) resolutions of its board of directors, (5) minutes of the proceedings of committees, and (6) a current list of voting members. These documents, in addition to the corporate charter, constitution, bylaws, certificate of incorporation, and business correspondence, constitute the records of a church corporation. The Model Nonprofit Corporation Act, under which many churches are incorporated, states:

> Each corporation shall keep correct and complete books and records of account and shall keep minutes of the proceedings of its members, board of directors and committees having any of the authority of the board of directors; and shall keep at its registered office or principal office in this State a record giving the names and addresses of its members entitled to vote. All books and records of a corporation may be inspected by any member, or his agent or attorney, for any proper purpose at any reasonable time.[50]

Churches incorporated under statutes other than the Model Nonprofit Corporation Act, and unincorporated churches, generally are under no legal obligation to maintain records.

[48]W. FLETCHER, supra note 21, at § 4195.
[49]Pelzer v. Lewis, 269 A.2d 902 (Pa. 1970).
[50]MODEL NONPROFIT CORPORATION ACT § 25.

All records should be as complete as possible, which means that each record should be dated and indicate the action taken, the persons present, and the voting results if any. It is often helpful to include a brief statement of the purpose for each action if it would not otherwise be clear. The secretary of the board of directors usually is the custodian of the corporate records; records of account customarily are maintained by the treasurer.

Finally, the income tax regulations state that "any person subject to tax . . . shall keep such permanent books of account or records, including inventories, as are sufficient to establish the amount of gross income, deductions, credits, or other matters required to be shown by such person in any return of such tax. . . ."[51]

## 2. INSPECTION

Section 25 of the Model Nonprofit Corporation Act, previously quoted, gives members of an incorporated church the right to inspect corporate records for any proper purpose at any reasonable time. Members of churches not incorporated under the Model Nonprofit Corporation Act rarely have a statutory right to inspect church records. Such a right may be given by the bylaws or charter of a church corporation or association. Some courts have held that members inherently possess a limited right of inspection even if the right is not expressly granted by statute, bylaw, or charter.

A right of inspection, however, generally applies only to members. Persons who are not members of a church have no right to demand inspection of church records. As has been mentioned elsewhere, the Privacy Act and Freedom of Information Act have no application to religious organizations.[52]

Churches, however, that raise funds by issuing securities, such as bonds or promissory notes, may be required by state securities laws to allow investors—whether members or not—to inspect the financial statements of the church.

Members and nonmembers alike may compel the production (i.e., disclosure) or inspection of church records as part of a lawsuit against a church if the materials to be produced or inspected are relevant and not privileged. For example, Rule 34 of the Federal Rules of Civil Procedure, adopted by several states and used in all federal courts, specifies that any party to a lawsuit

> may serve on any other party a request (1) to produce and permit the party making the request, or someone acting on his behalf, to inspect and copy, any designated documents . . . which are in the possession, custody or control of the party upon whom the request is served; or (2) to permit entry upon designated land or other

[51]Treas. Reg. § 1.6001-1(a).
[52]See chapter 4, § D, supra.

property in the possession or control of the party upon whom the request is served for the purpose of inspection . . . .

Similarly, Rule 45(b) states that a subpoena may command the person to whom it is directed "to produce the books, papers, documents, or tangible things designated therein . . . ." Rule 45 also stipulates that a subpoena may be quashed or modified if it is "unreasonable and oppressive." Federal, state, and local government agencies are also invested with extensive investigative powers, including the right to subpoena and inspect documents. However, this authority generally may not extend to privileged or irrelevant matters.

Since church records are not inherently privileged, they are not immune from production or inspection. Although most states consider confidential communications to be privileged when they are made to a clergyman acting in his professional capacity as a spiritual adviser, several courts have held that the privilege does not apply to church records. For example, in upholding an IRS subpoena of the records of a religious corporation over its objection that its records were privileged, one federal court observed that the "contention of violation of a penitent-clergyman privilege is without merit. A clergyman must be a natural person."[53] Another court, in upholding the admissibility of a church membership registration card over an objection that it was privileged, noted that "this information by any flight of the judicial imagination cannot conceivably be considered as a confession made to [a clergyman] in his professional character in the course of discipline . . . and, of course, is not privileged."[54]

Other courts have rejected the claim that the First Amendment to the United States Constitution insulates church records from inspection. To illustrate, members of one church sought a court order authorizing them to examine the church's financial records. The church was incorporated under the state's general nonprofit corporation law, which gave members the right to inspect corporate records at any reasonable time. The church and its pastor objected to the inspection on the ground that the First Amendment prohibits the courts from involving themselves in church affairs. The court disagreed with this contention, concluding that "First Amendment values are plainly not jeopardized by a civil court's enforcement of a voting member's right to examine these records."[55]

There have been several cases involving the power of the IRS to inspect church records. Section 7602 of the Internal Revenue Code gives the IRS the

[53]United States v. Luther, 481 F.2d 429, 432 (9th Cir. 1973) (the court did state that its holding would not prevent "a later determination at a time when the issue is properly raised and supported by a proper showing").

[54]In re Estate of Soeder, 220 N.E.2d 547, 572 (Ohio 1966).

[55]Burgeois v. Landrum, 396 So.2d 1275, 1277-78 (La. 1981).

authority to examine or subpoena the books and records of any person or organization for the purposes of (1) ascertaining the correctness of any federal tax return, (2) making a return where none has been filed, (3) determining the liability of any person or organization for any federal tax, or (4) collecting any federal tax. This authority has been held to apply to churches.[56]

As part of the Tax Reform Act of 1969, Congress amended section 511 of the Internal Revenue Code to extend the federal tax on the unrelated business income of tax-exempt organizations to churches and religious denominations. In general, unrelated business income constitutes income from a regularly carried on trade or business not substantially related to the exempt purposes of a tax-exempt organization. The amendment of section 511 represented a major change in the treatment of churches and denominations, previously exempt from most federal taxes, including unrelated business income taxes. The Tax Reform Act also added section 7605(c) to the Internal Revenue Code:

> No examination of the *books of account* of a church or convention or association of churches shall be made to determine whether such organization may be engaged in the carrying on of an unrelated trade or business or may be otherwise engaged in activities which may be subject to [the tax on unrelated business income] unless the Secretary (such officer being no lower than a principal internal revenue officer for an internal revenue region) [1] believes that such organization may be so engaged and [2] so notifies the organization in advance of the examination. No examination of the *religious activities* of such an organization shall be made except to the extent necessary to determine whether such organization is a church or a convention or association of churches, and no examination of the *books of account* of such an organization shall be made other than to the extent necessary to determine the amount of tax imposed by this title.[57]

Because amended section 511 created new tax liability for churches and denominations, the addition of section 7605(c) was considered necessary to protect such organizations from excessive tax audits by IRS agents investigating unrelated business activities. Accordingly, the first sentence of section 7605(c) shields the *books of account* of churches and denominations from any IRS examination for the purpose of determining any unrelated business income tax liability unless the IRS (1) has some basis for believing that such an organization is engaged in an unrelated trade or business, and (2) notifies the organization in advance of the examination.

Some churches have argued that unless an examination is undertaken to

---

[56] *See, e.g.,* United States v. Coates, 692 F.2d 629 (9th Cir. 1982); United States v. Dykema, 666 F.2d 1096 (7th Cir. 1981); United States v. Freedom Church, 613 F.2d 316 (1st Cir. 1979).

[57] I.R.C. § 7605(c) (emphasis added).

determine whether a church is engaged in an unrelated trade or business, section 7605(c) prohibits IRS examinations of any church records.[58] Such a contention has been rejected by the courts. It is true that the protection of churches afforded by the first sentence of section 7605(c) extends to any IRS examination of the *books of account* of a church or denomination conducted to enforce section 511, but section 7605(c) was not intended to restrict IRS investigations for other purposes. In connection with section 7605(c), the House Report on the Tax Reform bill stated: "New subsection (c) does not preclude an agent, for example, from examining an organization to determine if it is, in fact, a church."[59]

The last sentence of section 7605(c) states that the IRS can examine the *religious activities* of a church or religious denomination to the extent necessary to determine if it is in fact a bona fide church or denomination. This sentence also gives the IRS authority to examine the *books of account* of such organizations to the extent necessary to determine the amount of tax imposed under any internal revenue law (including income taxes, estate and gift taxes, employment taxes, and excise taxes). Income tax regulation 301.7605-1(c)(2) parallels section 7605:

No examination of the *books of account* of an organization which claims to be a church or a convention or association of churches shall be made except after the giving of notice as provided in this subparagraph and except to the extent necessary (i) to determine the initial or continuing qualification of the organization under section 501(c)(3); (ii) to determine whether the organization qualifies as one, contributions to which are deductible . . . ; (iii) to obtain information for the purpose of ascertaining or verifying payments made by the organization to another person in determining the tax liability of the recipient, such as payments of salaries, wages, or other forms of compensation; or (iv) to determine the amount of tax, if any, imposed by the Code upon such organization. No examination of the *books of account* of a church or convention or association of churches shall be made unless the Regional Commissioner believes that such examination is necessary and so notifies the organization in writing at least 30 days in advance of examination. The Regional Commissioner will conclude that such examination is necessary only after reasonable attempts have been made to obtain the information from the *books of account* by written request and the Regional Commissioner has determined that the information cannot be fully or satisfactorily obtained in that matter. In any examination of a church or convention or association of churches for the purpose of determining unrelated business income tax liability

---

[58]*See, e.g.,* United States v. Coates, 526 F. Supp. 248 (E.D. Cal. 1982), *aff'd in part and rev'd in part,* United States v. Coates, 692 F.2d 629 (9th Cir. 1982).

[59]H.R. REP. No. 413, 91st Cong., 1st Sess. (1969).

pursuant to such notice, no examination of the *books of account* of the organization shall be made except to the extent necessary to determine such liability.[60]

This regulation clearly permits the examination of a church's *books of account* for purposes other than the determination of unrelated business income tax liability.

Similarly, regulation 301.7605-1(c)(3) permits IRS examination of a church's *religious activities* for purposes other than the determination of unrelated business income tax liability:

No examination of the *religious activities* of an organization which claims to be a church or convention or association of churches shall be made except (i) to the extent necessary to determine the initial or continuing qualification of the organization under section 501(c)(3); (ii) to determine whether the organization qualifies as one, contributions to which are deductible . . . ; or (iii) to determine whether the organization is a church or convention or association of churches subject to the [tax on unrelated business income]. The requirements . . . that the Regional Commissioner give notice prior to examination of the *books of account* of an organization do not apply to an examination of the *religious activities* of the organization for any purpose described in this subparagraph. Once it has been determined that the organization is a church or convention or association of churches, no further examination of its *religious activities* may be made in connection with determining its liability, if any, for unrelated business income tax.[61]

This regulation confirms the IRS view that the limitations imposed by the first sentence of section 7605(c) on IRS examinations of churches' *books of account* for purposes of determining unrelated business income tax liability do not apply to examinations of churches' *religious activities*. Thus, the IRS need not give advance notice of its intention to examine the *religious activities* of a church or religious denomination.

The courts have repeatedly affirmed the authority of the IRS to examine the *books of account* and *religious activities* of churches and denominations for any of the purposes cited in previously quoted regulation 301.7605-1(c).[62] To illustrate, the courts have upheld IRS examinations of the books, records, and

---

[60]Treas. Reg. § 301.7605-1(c)(2) (emphasis added).

[61]Treas. Reg. § 301.7605-1(c)(3) (emphasis added).

[62]*See, e.g.,* United States v. Coates, 692 F.2d 629 (9th Cir. 1982); United States v. Dykema, 666 F.2d 1096 (7th Cir. 1981); United States v. Freedom Church, 613 F.2d 316 (1st Cir. 1979); United States v. Life Science Church of America, 636 F.2d 221 (8th Cir. 1980); United States v. Holmes, 614 F.2d 985 (5th Cir. 1980).

papers of churches, including *books of account,* in connection with investigations of a church's qualification for tax-exempt status.[63]

The fact that the IRS has the authority to examine the *books of account* and *religious activities* of a church or religious denomination does not necessarily establish its right to do so. The courts have held that an IRS summons or subpoena directed at church records must satisfy the following conditions to be enforceable:

1. It is issued in good faith. *Good faith* in this context means that (1) the investigation will be conducted pursuant to a legitimate purpose, (2) the inquiry is necessary to that purpose, (3) the information sought is not already within the IRS' possession, and (4) the proper administrative steps have been followed.[64] The IRS need only make a minimal showing of the relevancy of the information sought, and then the burden shifts to the church to establish that the subpoena is invalid.

2. It does not violate the church's First Amendment right to freely exercise its religion. An IRS subpoena will not violate a church's First Amendment rights if it only incidentally burdens the free exercise of religion and is supported by some overriding governmental interest, such as maintenance of the integrity of the government's fiscal policies.[65]

---

[63]United States v. Freedom Church, 613 F.2d 316 (1st Cir. 1979). *See also* United States v. Coates, 692 F.2d 629 (9th Cir. 1982); United States v. Dykema, 666 F.2d 1096 (7th Cir. 1981).

[64]In United States v. Powell, 379 U.S. 48 (1964), the United States Supreme Court held that the IRS must make the following showing in order to obtain judicial enforcement of a summons or subpoena: "[T]hat the investigation will be conducted pursuant to a legitimate purpose, that the inquiry may be relevant to the purpose, that the information sought is not already in the Commissioner's possession, and that the administrative steps required by the Code have been followed . . . ." *Powell* did not involve an IRS examination of church records. In United States v. Holmes, 614 F.2d 985 (5th Cir. 1980), a federal appeals court held that section 7605(c) narrowed the scope of the second part of the *Powell* test from mere relevancy to necessity in the context of church records since it required that an examination of church records be limited "to the extent necessary."

[65]*See, e.g.,* United States v. Coates, 692 F.2d 629 (9th Cir. 1982); United States v. Life Science Church of America, 636 F.2d 221 (8th Cir. 1980); United States v. Holmes, 614 F.2d 985 (5th Cir. 1980); United States v. Freedom Church, 613 F.2d 316 (1st Cir. 1979).

3. It does not create an impermissible entanglement of church and state.[66]

Even under these limitations the IRS has extensive authority. In one case, it was allowed to demand production of the following church records:

All books, records, and papers . . . including but not limited to organizational documents and bylaws; *books of accounts,* bank records, bank statements, including cancelled checks, and records of receipts and disbursements with information indicating the source and nature of such receipts and purposes for the disbursements. All correspondence to the church and records relating to any and all assets owned or used by the [church] and the manner in which such assets were acquired. Records regarding the nature and specific extent of all *religious activities* conducted by the church to include but not limited to a list of all members of the congregation and members of the Sacerdotal Order of the church and the manner by which such members are selected. Records to indicate which members if any have taken a vow of poverty, with records of all, if any, of the assets or income turned over or to be turned over to the church. All records and information on the specific activities conducted by such members to the extent that such activities are attributed to the religious purpose or creed of the church. . . . All records and information concerning any contracts and agreements entered into by the church with its pastor. Documents and records related to the background of your ministers and trustees to include a precis of curriculum completed by the ordained ministers who are members of the church and the circumstances pertaining to their ordination.[67]

Although IRS authority to examine and subpoena church records is very broad, it has limits. To illustrate, one subpoena was issued against all documents relating to the organizational structure of a church since its inception; all correspondence files for a three-year period; the minutes of the officers, directors, trustees, and ministers for the same three-year period; and a sample of every piece of literature pertaining to the church.[68] A court concluded that this sub-

[66]*See generally* United States v. Coates, 692 F.2d 629 (9th Cir. 1982); United States v. Grayson County State Bank, 656 F.2d 1071 (5th Cir. 1981); United States v. Freedom Church, 613 F.2d 316 (1st Cir. 1979); *cf.* Surinach v. Pesquera de Busquets, 604 F.2d 73 (1st Cir. 1979) (subpoena issued against Catholic schools in Puerto Rico held violative of First Amendment, for no compelling governmental interest justified the investigation); EEOC v. Southwestern Baptist Theological Seminary, 651 F.2d 277 (5th Cir. 1981) (application of 1964 Civil Rights Act's reporting requirements to seminary did not violate First Amendment).

[67]United States v. Freedom Church, 613 F.2d 316, 318 (1st Cir. 1979).

[68]United States v. Holmes, 614 F.2d 985 (5th Cir. 1980). *See also* United States v. Trader's State Bank, No. 81-3275 (9th Cir. 1983) (IRS summons seeking production of all of a church's bank statements, correspondence, and records relating to bank accounts, safe deposit boxes, and loans held to be overly broad).

poena was "too far reaching" and declared it invalid. It noted, however, that a "properly narrowed" subpoena would not violate the First Amendment.

Whether the government has the right to compel religious organizations to release the names of members and contributors is a hotly contested issue. In 1958, the United States Supreme Court held that the freedom to associate with others for the advancement of beliefs and ideas is a right protected by the First Amendment against governmental infringement, whether the beliefs sought to be advanced are political, economic, religious, or cultural.[69] The Court acknowledged that the right of association is nowhere mentioned in the First Amendment, but it reasoned that such a right must be inferred in order to make the express First Amendment rights of speech and assembly more secure. The Court concluded that an order by the State of Alabama seeking to compel disclosure of the name of every member of the National Association for the Advancement of Colored People in Alabama constituted an impermissible restraint upon members' freedom of association, since

> on past occasions revelation of the identity of its rank-and-file members has exposed these members to economic reprisal, loss of employment, threat of physical coercion, and other manifestations of public hostility. Under these circumstances, we think it apparent that compelled disclosure of [the NAACP's] Alabama membership is likely to affect adversely the ability of [the NAACP] and its members to pursue their collective effort to foster beliefs which they admittedly have the right to advocate, in that it may induce members to withdraw from the Association and dissuade others from joining it . . . .[70]

It is clear that governmental actions that may have the effect of curtailing the freedom of association are subject to the closest scrutiny.[71] Yet case law makes it clear that the right to associate is not absolute; a "significant interference" with the right may be tolerated if the government (1) avoids unnecessary interference, (2) demonstrates a sufficiently important interest, and (3) employs the least intrusive means of achieving its interests.[72]

The Supreme Court has observed that "[d]ecisions . . . must finally turn, therefore, on whether [the government] has demonstrated so cogent an interest in obtaining and making public the membership lists . . . as to justify the substantial abridgement of associational freedom which such disclosures will effect. Where there is a significant encroachment upon personal liberty, the

---

[69]National Association for the Advancement of Colored People v. Alabama, 357 U.S. 449 (1958).

[70]*Id.* at 462-63.

[71]*Id.* at 460-61.

[72]Cousins v. Wigoda, 419 U.S. 477, 488 (1975).

State may prevail only upon showing a subordinating interest which is compelling."[73]

Government demands for the production and inspection of membership and contributor lists frequently are approved on the ground that a compelling governmental interest exists. For example, in one case, a federal appeals court upheld the enforcement of an IRS summons seeking the name of every individual who had contributed property other than securities to Brigham Young University (BYU) for the tax years 1976, 1977, and 1978.[74] Before issuing the summons, the IRS had audited the returns of 162 taxpayers who had contributed property to the university during the years in question. In each instance the amount of the contribution claimed by the taxpayer was overvalued, in many cases grossly overvalued. As a result, the IRS surmised that many of the remaining contributors had overvalued their contributions.

The university challenged the summons on the ground that the IRS was without a reasonable basis for believing that the remaining contributors had overvalued their contributions. The university further asserted that the information sought was readily available to the IRS through its own files, and that enforcement of the summons would infringe upon the contributors' freedom of association under the First Amendment.

The court, in upholding the summons, observed that "having previously examined the returns of some 162 donors of gifts in kind to BYU and having found that all were overvalued, the IRS has established a reasonable basis for believing that *some* of the remaining donors of in kind gifts *may* have also overvalued their gifts."[75]

In another case, the Federal Communications Commission (FCC) received complaints that a religious broadcaster was not expending contributed funds as indicated in over-the-air solicitations. As part of its investigation, the FCC ordered the broadcaster to divulge the names of all contributors and the amount of each contribution. The broadcaster refused to comply on the ground that such information was protected by the First Amendment freedoms of religion and association. An FCC administrative tribunal ruled that under the circumstances the agency had a compelling interest in obtaining disclosure of the names of contributors and the amounts of contributions, and that this interest outweighed the freedoms of religion and association.[76]

It is clear, however, that when the identities of all members or contributors

---

[73]Bates v. Little Rock, 361 U.S. 516, 524 (1960).

[74]United States v. Brigham Young University, 679 F.2d 1345 (10th Cir. 1982).

[75]*Id.* at 1349.

[76]In re Application of Faith Center, Inc., 82 F.C.C.2d 1 (1980), *aff'd*, Faith City, Inc. v. F.C.C., Nos. 81-1648, 81-1649 (D.C. Cir. April 7, 1982), *cert. denied*, 51 U.S.L.W. 3611 (U.S. Feb. 22, 1983).

are not reasonably relevant to a particular governmental investigation, then the government's interest in disclosure will not be sufficiently compelling to outweigh the constitutionally protected interests of members and contributors.[77]

## 3. REPORTING REQUIREMENTS

### a. *State Law*

As was noted in the preceding section, many state nonprofit corporation laws require the filing of an annual report with the secretary of state's office. Generally, this report calls for the name of the corporation, the address of its registered office in the state of incorporation and the name of its registered agent at such address, a brief statement of the nature of the affairs that the corporation is actually conducting, and the names and addresses of directors and officers. A nominal fee usually must accompany the report. Annual reports are prepared on forms provided by the secretary of state's office.

In addition, many states have attempted to regulate charitable solicitations by requiring charitable organizations to register with a state agency prior to soliciting donations. Many states require, in addition to the initial registration, the filing of annual reports. Churches and other religious organizations are exempted from the registration and reporting requirements of most charitable solicitation laws.[78] An exemption under such laws is apparently required by the First Amendment. To illustrate, a Minnesota charitable solicitation law exempted religious organizations that received more than half of their contributions from members. The law was challenged by the Unification Church as an unconstitutional infringement upon the First Amendment rights of religious organizations not receiving more than half of their contributions from members. A federal appeals court agreed with the church and ordered the exemption expanded to cover all religious organizations "in light of the traditional governmental reluctance to intrude unnecessarily in the affairs of religious organizations."[79] On appeal, the United States Supreme Court agreed that the church was exempt. It reached its decision, however, not by expanding the exemption but by invalidating the entire law. The Court concluded that in discriminating against certain religious organizations the law ran afoul of the First Amendment.[80]

---

[77]*See, e.g.,* Savola v. Webster, 644 F.2d 743 (8th Cir. 1981); Familias Unidas v. Briscoe, 619 F.2d 391 (5th Cir. 1980).

[78]*See, e.g.,* MASS. ANN. LAWS ch. 68, § 20; N.J. REV. STAT. § 45:17A-5(a); VA. CODE § 57-48(2).

[79]Valente v. Larson, 637 F.2d 562 (8th Cir. 1981).

[80]Valente v. Larson, 102 S. Ct. 1673 (1982).

In a related case, a North Carolina charitable solicitation law that exempted only those religious organizations that received most of their financial support from members was challenged by two religious organizations that received most of their support from nonmembers.[81] The North Carolina Supreme Court concluded that the solicitation of funds by religious organizations is an activity protected by the First Amendment, that the preferred treatment of religious organizations receiving most of their support from members unconstitutionally discriminated against religious organizations receiving substantial support from nonmembers, and that the charitable solicitation law as a whole violated the First Amendment because of the "excessive entanglement" that it created between church and state.

Many cities have enacted ordinances regulating the public solicitation of funds. The United States Supreme Court has held repeatedly that any limitations on local solicitation by religious organizations, whether through a licensing or reporting scheme, will be carefully scrutinized.[82]

### b. *Federal Law*

Federal law imposes several reporting requirements on charitable organizations. Among them are the following:

### (1) *Application for Recognition of Tax-Exempt Status*

Most organizations seeking recognition of exemption from federal income tax must file an application with the IRS. This is done on IRS Form 1023 or 1024, depending on the nature of the applicant. Churches, their "integrated auxiliaries," and conventions or associations of churches are exempted by law from payment of federal income tax and therefore they are not required to file an application with the IRS.[83] Such organizations nevertheless may find it advantageous to obtain IRS recognition of exempt status since this would avoid the need of substantiating the deductibility of contributions. A church may obtain recognition of exemption in either of two ways: (1) by filing a Form 1023 with the IRS, or (2) by being a member of a convention or association of churches that has obtained a "group-exemption ruling" from the IRS.

If a church independently applies for and receives IRS recognition of exemption, it must notify the IRS of any material changes in its sources of support, purposes, character, or methods of operation. Churches that are included in the group exemption ruling of a convention or association of churches must

---

[81]Heritage Village Church & Missionary Fellowship v. State, 263 S.E.2d 726 (N.C. 1980).

[82]*See* chapter 18, *infra.*

[83]I.R.C. § 508(c)(1)(A).

annually notify their convention or association of any changes in their purposes, character, or methods of operation. The procedures for obtaining an exemption from federal income taxes are discussed in detail in another chapter.[84]

### (2) Annual Information Returns

Section 6033 of the Internal Revenue Code imposes upon most tax-exempt organizations the obligation of filing an annual information return with the IRS. The annual information return is prepared on IRS Form 990 and sets forth gross income; expenses; disbursements for exempt purposes; assets and liabilities; net worth; contributions received, including the names and addresses of substantial contributors; and compensation paid to certain employees. Section 6033 exempts "churches, their integrated auxiliaries, and conventions and associations of churches" from the annual information return requirements.

### (3) Tax on Unrelated Business Income

Even though a church is recognized as tax-exempt, it still may be liable for tax on its unrelated business income, that is, income from a regularly carried on trade or business that is not substantially related to the purposes constituting the basis for the church's exemption. A church that has $1,000 or more in gross income from an unrelated trade or business must file an IRS Form 990-T. In computing unrelated business taxable income, churches are entitled to deduct all reasonable and necessary expenses directly associated with the unrelated business. The tax on unrelated business income is considered in detail in another chapter.[85]

### (4) Employment Taxes

### (a) Pre-1984 Rules

Every employer, including organizations exempt from federal income tax, that pays taxable wages to employees is responsible for withholding, depositing, paying, and reporting federal income tax, social security tax, and federal unemployment tax from such wage payments unless specifically exempted by law. Churches are exempted from paying federal unemployment taxes on their employees.[86] As has been noted elsewhere,[87] the law exempts churches from the requirement of withholding income taxes from the wages of "a duly ordained, commissioned, or licensed minister of a church in the exercise of his

[84] See chapter 14, § B, infra.
[85] See chapter 14, § B, infra.
[86] I.R.C. § 3306(c)(6).
[87] See chapter 6, § A, supra.

ministry."[88] However, churches must withhold taxes from the wages of non-minister employees. Withholding of taxes from the wages of nonminister employees is discussed in detail elsewhere.[89] It will suffice for purposes of the present chapter to say that a church must (1) obtain an employer identification number, (2) have each employee complete a Form W-4 listing withholding allowances, (3) compute each employee's taxable wages, and (4) compute the amount of tax to be withheld by utilizing IRS tables. A church must also file a quarterly return with the IRS on Form 941E for the first quarter in which it is required to withhold income taxes and for every quarter thereafter. Form 941E reports wages and withheld taxes.

Smaller employers with accumulated withheld taxes of less than $500 at the end of any calendar quarter pay the withheld taxes by the end of the following month. The payment ordinarily accompanies the employer's quarterly Form 941E. Employers with accumulated withheld taxes of more than $500 but less than $3,000 at the end of any month must deposit the taxes with an authorized financial institution by the fifteenth day of the following month. Employers with accumulated withheld taxes of more than $3,000 at the end of any "eighth-monthly" period (eighth-monthly periods end on the 3rd, 7th, 11th, 15th, 19th, 22nd, 25th, and the last day of each month) must deposit the taxes with an authorized financial institution within three banking days after the close of that eighth-monthly period. Deposits must be accompanied by a federal tax deposit form. The bank forwards deposits directly to the Department of the Treasury, which in turn credits the employer's account. Employers subject to the tax deposit requirements must still file a Form 941E each quarter.

Only federal income taxes withheld from the wages of nonminister employees are reported on Form 941E. Until January 1, 1984, services performed in the employ of a church or other religious organization are excepted from liability for social security taxes. However, a church or other religious organization can elect to extend social security coverage to services performed by its employees. This may be done either by filing a Form SS-15 and a Form SS-15a with the IRS or by paying, either inadvertently or intentionally, social security taxes for at least three consecutive calendar quarters for any nonminister employee. The latter method is termed *constructive filing.* A church that has so waived its exemption from social security taxes must use Form 941 rather than Form 941E to report withheld federal income and social security taxes. In general, the amount of social security taxes to be withheld for any payroll period is determined by multiplying the current FICA-Medicare combined tax rate times the employee's taxable wage base. A maximum annual taxable wage base is deter-

---

[88]I.R.C. § 3401(a)(9).

[89]*See* chapter 6, § A, *supra,* and chapter 10, § A, *infra.*

mined each year by the Secretary of the Department of Health and Human Services.

A church or other religious organization that has waived its exemption from social security is permitted to revoke its waiver at the end of a specified quarter by giving two years' advance notice in writing to the IRS office with which it is required to file its returns. This provision is applicable, however, only if the certificate of waiver has been in effect for a period of at least eight years.

An ordained, commissioned, or licensed minister of a church is considered to be self-employed for purposes of social security taxes. Unless he personally files a timely exemption application with the IRS on Form 4361, he remains subject to social security taxes even if his church does not elect to extend social security coverage to its employees.[90]

The IRS maintains that churches must prepare a Form W-2 for every employee. As has been noted elsewhere, ministers may be considered employees for purposes of federal income taxes.[91] A Form W-2 reports an employee's annual wages and all withheld federal income and social security taxes. Churches should delete the minister's housing allowance in reporting his wages whether or not he is deemed to be an employee. Churches should also delete from Form W-2 any reimbursements that are reported by an employee on Form 2106. A church should provide triplicate copies of Form W-2 directly to employees before February 1 of the following year, and submit an additional copy to the Social Security Administration before March 1 of the following year for every employee who is covered by social security. The Social Security Administration's copy is transmitted with a Form W-3.

Although a church that has not waived its exemption from social security taxes and that has no nonminister employees is not required to withhold taxes or file a Form 941E, if its minister is treated as an employee it may wish to file a Form 941E each quarter in order to reconcile the church's W-2 forms.

Finally, under the Federal-State Tax Collection Act of 1972, states can elect to have the federal government collect state income taxes through wage withholding.

### (b) Post-1983 Rules

The pre-1984 rules discussed above generally apply after December 31, 1983—with one major exception. In 1983, Congress amended the Social Security Act by deleting the exemption of "service performed in the employ of a religious . . . organization described in section 501(c)(3) which is exempt from income tax under section 501(a) . . . ." This amendment, which takes effect on

[90]*See* chapter 5, § C, *supra.*
[91]*See* chapter 1, § B, and chapter 6, § A, *supra.*

January 1, 1984, automatically extends social security coverage to all nonminister employees of every religious organization, including churches, church schools, and denominations. It allows no exceptions or exemptions. The constitutionality of this amendment, which imposes a direct, involuntary tax on churches and religious organizations, is questionable.

As a result, churches and religious organizations must withhold both federal income and social security taxes from the wages of nonminister employees, and file a quarterly Form 941 with the IRS. Form 941E is no longer used since the exemption from social security coverage has been repealed. Churches remain exempt from paying federal unemployment taxes on their employees, and they are still exempted from withholding taxes from the wages of "a duly ordained, commissioned, or licensed minister of a church in the exercise of his ministry."

The pre-1984 tax deposit rules generally apply, with the exception that Congress may amend the amount of withheld taxes that initiates the monthly or eighth-monthly deposit requirements.

### (5) Information Returns

The IRS maintains that churches are required to prepare and submit information returns on the appropriate series of Form 1099 in order to report payments of $600 or more in the form of compensation to persons who are not employees of the church or payments of $10 or more in interest income to any individual.[92] For example, if a church pays $1,000 to an evangelist or guest speaker, this amount should be reported to the IRS by the church on Form 1099-NEC (Nonemployee Compensation) before March 1 of the following tax year. Similarly, if a church issues bonds or notes to finance construction it must report on Form 1099-INT (Interest Income) interest payments exceeding $10 that it makes to any investor. Form 1096 is used to summarize and transmit Forms 1099. Obviously, the purpose of Form 1099 is to ensure that the IRS is notified of all distributions of taxable income.

If a minister does not satisfy the common law definition of an employee discussed in chapter 1, then the appropriate way for his church to report his income would be by use of Form 1099-NEC rather than Form W-2.

### (6) Returns Regarding Dissolution or Termination

Section 6043 of the Internal Revenue Code requires a corporation to file a return (Form 966) within thirty days after the adoption of any resolution or plan concerning the dissolution of the corporation. Churches, their integrated auxiliaries, and conventions and associations of churches, however, are exempted by section 6043 from this reporting requirement.

[92]I.R.C. §§ 6041 and 6049.

## (7) EEOC Reports

Title VII of the Civil Rights Act of 1964 prohibits employers from discriminating in any employment decision—including hiring, discharge, compensation, and the terms, conditions, or privileges of employment—on the basis of race, color, religion, sex, or national origin.[93] Title VII applies to every employer, including churches, having fifteen or more employees for at least twenty weeks in a year. Part-time employees are to be included in making the calculation. The Act does exempt religious organizations, including churches, from the prohibition against discrimination based on religion, although the constitutionality of this provision has been challenged at least with respect to positions not involving religious duties.[94]

The Equal Employment Opportunity Commission (EEOC), an agency created by Congress to enforce Title VII of the Civil Rights Act of 1964, requires all employers, including religious organizations, having 100 or more employees to submit annually an Employer Information Report. This report is prepared on Standard Form 100, which is also known as Employer Information Report EEO-1. Among other things, this report provides the EEOC with the racial composition of the employer's work force.

## §D. Church Names

Occasionally, a new church will acquire a name that is so similar to the name of another church in the same locality that public confusion is likely to result. For example, a new congregation calling itself Calvary Presbyterian Church establishes a church in a community already having a Presbyterian church called Calvary Church. A confusion of names may occur in other ways, such as a new sect or religious organization acquiring a name similar to that of an existing one, or a local church withdrawing from a parent religious body but continuing to employ a name associating itself with the parent body. In any of these situations, does the preexisting church body have any legal basis for halting further use of the similar name by the other church or religious organization?

The courts have long protected the names of existing commercial enterprises against unauthorized use of confusingly similar names by other commercial organizations.[95] In many instances, the courts are simply enforcing state corporation laws that, in most states, prohibit new corporations from using names

[93]42 U.S.C. § 2000e-2(a). *See generally* chapter 10, § E, *infra.*

[94]*See* chapter 11, § I, *infra.*

[95]Couhigs' Pestaway Co., Inc. v. Pestaway, Inc., 278 So.2d 519 (La. 1973); Virginia Manor Land Co. v. Virginia Manor Apartments, Inc., 282 A.2d 684 (Pa. 1971); Annot., 115 A.L.R. 1241 (1938).

that are identical or confusingly similar to those of existing organizations.[96] Other courts have emphasized that such name protection statutes are merely embodiments of the underlying common law of unfair competition, which protects existing corporate names independently of any provisions in state corporate laws.[97] The courts have consistently protected the names of nonprofit corporations as well on the basis of one or more of the following theories: (1) the applicable nonprofit corporation statute contains a provision protecting the preexisting names of nonprofit corporations in much the same way as business corporation statutes protect the names of business corporations;[98] (2) extension of the name protection provided by business corporation statutes to nonprofit corporations when the state nonprofit law does not specifically provide such protection;[99] (3) the common law of unfair competition;[100] and (4) trademark protection.

In states having a name protection statute protecting the names of religious corporations, a church's name generally will be protected against later use of the same or a confusingly similar name in either of two ways: (1) the state official charged with the duty of reviewing applications for incorporation can reject the application of an organization whose name is either identical or

---

[96]See, e.g., ILL. REV. STAT. ch. 32, § 157.9 ("The corporate name . . . [s]hall not be the same as, or deceptively similar to, the corporate name or assumed name of any domestic corporation existing under any Act of this State or of any foreign corporation authorized to transact business in this State . . . ."); KAN. STAT. ANN. § 17-6002 ("The articles of incorporation shall set forth . . . [t]he name of the corporation which . . . shall be such as to distinguish it upon the records in the office of the secretary of state from the names of other corporations and partnerships organized, reserved or registered under the laws of this state . . . ."); KY. REV. STAT. § 271A.040 ("The corporate name . . . [s]hall not be the same as, or deceptively similar to, the name of any domestic corporation existing under the laws of this state or any foreign corporation authorized to transact business in this state . . . ."); MO. REV. STAT. § 351.110 ("The corporate name . . . [s]hall not be the same as, or deceptively similar to, the name of any domestic corporation existing under any law of this state or any foreign corporation authorized to transact business in this state . . . .").

[97]Massachusetts Mutual Life Ins. Co. v. Massachusetts Life Ins. Co., 218 N.E.2d 564, 570 (Mass. 1966) ("It is our view, however, that the corporate name protection statute is a statutory declaration and clarification of a portion of the extant common law of unfair competition . . . ."); Virginia Manor Land Co. v. Virginia Manor Apartments, Inc., 282 A.2d 684, 687 (Pa. 1971) ("The right of the corporation to the exclusive use of its own name exists at common law, and includes the right to prohibit another from using a name so similar to the corporate name as to be calculated to deceive the public.").

[98]ILL. REV. STAT. ch. 32, § 163a(6); MODEL NONPROFIT CORPORATION ACT § 7(b).

[99]First Congressional District Democratic Party Organization v. First Congressional District Democratic Organization, Inc., 177 N.W.2d 224 (Mich. 1970).

[100]Oklahoma District Council of the Assemblies of God v. New Hope Assembly of God, 597 P.2d 1211 (Okla. 1979).

deceptively similar to the name of an existing corporation; or (2) if the state official chooses to recognize the corporate status of an organization whose name is either identical or deceptively similar to that of an existing corporation, the offended corporation may sue to stop further use of the name.

As noted above, a church may also seek legal protection of its name through the law of unfair competition. Unfair competition is civil wrong created to protect existing organizations from the deceptive or unfair practices of competitors. It is entirely separate and distinct from trademark law. Among other things, unfair competition means the use of a name that is either identical with or confusingly similar to that of a preexisting organization. As one court has observed:

> In the law of unfair competition, a corporate or trade name used in connection with the business to which it relates may become an asset of great value. When it does, it partakes of the nature of a property right, and equity will enjoin the appropriation and use of such name if confusion of identity is likely to result.[101]

Courts have consistently protected charitable as well as business organizations from unfair competition. In a leading case one court observed:

> We hold that the common law principles of unfair competition protecting business corporations against another's use of the same or similar name are applicable to charitable or religious associations and corporations. . . . The right to this protection rests generally upon the fact that the use of identical or similar terms or names is likely to result in confusion or deception.[102]

To successfully establish that the name chosen by another organization constitutes unfair competition, a church must demonstrate

1. Prior use of the name.

2. Subsequent use of the same or a confusingly similar name by another religious organization.

3. The church with prior use of the name will be injuriously affected by continued use of the same or a confusingly similar name by the other religious organization. It has been held that anything that diverts members or donations from one church to another causes injury. Thus, injury generally will be established by the unauthorized use of a name identical or confusingly similar to that of a preexisting corporation.

4. The church with prior use of the name did not delay for an unreasonable

[101] *Id.* at 1214.

[102] *Id.* at 1215. *See also* National Board of YWCA v. YWCA of Charleston, 335 F. Supp. 615 (D.S.C. 1971).

time in seeking to enjoin further use of the same or a confusingly similar name by the other religious organization.[103]

Generic or highly generalized names are not protected from misappropriation under the doctrine of unfair competition unless a secondary meaning has been established. A generic name acquires a secondary meaning through such continued use that it is commonly associated with a particular church or religious organization in the public mind. Proof of a secondary meaning is a question of fact to be established on a case-by-case basis.

Finally, in some cases the name of a church or religious organization can be protected under federal trademark law. *Trademark* is defined by the Trademark Act of 1946 as "any word, symbol, or device, or any combination thereof adopted and used by a manufacturer or merchant to identify his goods and distinguish them from those manufactured and sold by others."[104] Trademark protection is thus available to any church or religious organization that uses a particular name to identify goods or services it offers to the public. For example, if a religious denomination publishes religious literature for its churches, and affixes its name to such literature, the name identifies the goods and therefore is eligible for trademark registration. Similarly, if a church establishes a counseling center, correspondence school, private elementary or secondary school, nursing home, radio or television station, or magazine that is identified by the church's name, the name may be entitled to trademark protection.

Of course, trademark protection is not available for a name or mark that so resembles a mark already registered with the Patent and Trademark Office, or previously used in the United States by another and not abandoned, as to be likely to cause confusion or to deceive. There are two ways of determining whether a proposed name conflicts with a preexisting name that is entitled to protection. First, a commercial search service can be retained which, for a fee, will render an opinion on the availability of a specified name. Second, an application for registration can be filed with the Patent and Trademark Office in Washington, D.C. Although the Patent and Trademark Office takes several months to evaluate an application, it eventually will notify the applicant whether its proposed name or mark conflicts with a preexisting mark.

Generic or highly generalized names and marks are not eligible for registration unless a secondary meaning can be established. A secondary meaning is established by proof of public association of a generic name or mark with a particular church or religious organization.

An application for trademark registration is a relatively simple procedure consisting of the following elements:

[103]*See generally* Annot., 37 A.L.R.3d 277 (1971).
[104]15 U.S.C. § 1127.

1. Preparation of a written application stating the applicant's name, address, state of incorporation or organization; the goods or services in connection with which the name or mark is used; the class of goods or services according to the official international classification system; the date of the first use of the name or mark on or in connection with the goods or services; the date of the first use of the name or mark as a trademark "in commerce"; the mode or manner in which the mark is used on or in connection with the goods.

2. A drawing of the mark, unless the mark consists solely of a name—in which case the name may be typed in capital letters on a piece of paper.

3. Five specimens of the goods bearing the name or mark. No specimens are required for names or marks associated with services.

4. The required filing fee.[105]

If a church name is not used in connection with any specific goods or services, trademark protection is unavailable.

## §E. Officers, Directors, and Trustees

### 1. IN GENERAL

Churches and religious organizations can conduct their temporal and spiritual affairs only through individuals. Unincorporated churches generally elect or appoint trustees to hold title to church property and to transact the business affairs of the church. The term *trustees* itself indicates that title to church property is held "in trust" for the members of the church and not for the private benefit of the trustees. It is customary for unincorporated churches to elect officers, consisting of a president, secretary, and treasurer.

State laws generally require that church corporations appoint an initial board of directors which in turn elects the corporation's first president, secretary, and treasurer. The initial board of directors typically adopts a set of bylaws that specifies the term of office of both officers and directors and sets forth the procedure for electing successors. Directors of church corporations occasionally are called "trustees," although such terminology technically is not appropriate for church corporations which are capable of holding title to their own property. Directors of church corporations occasionally are called deacons, although it is common for churches to have both directors and deacons—directors having oversight of the temporal affairs of the church and deacons having oversight of the spiritual.[106]

The Model Nonprofit Corporation Act specifies that a corporation shall have a president, one or more vice-presidents, a secretary, a treasurer, and such

---

[105]The filing fee, as of the date of publication of this book, is $175.

[106]Hayes v. Board of Trustees, 225 N.Y.S.2d 316 (1962).

other officers or assistant officers as the corporation deems necessary. The Act permits the same person to hold two or more offices except the offices of president and secretary.

The term *officer* is often interpreted broadly to include directors. Thus, for example, it has been held that a director may sign some corporate documents that by law must be signed by an officer of the corporation.[107] Normally, however, a church president, secretary, treasurer, and vice-president (if any) are the only officers having any authority to perform specific acts on behalf of the church.

There are no legal requirements regarding the number of trustees an unincorporated association must appoint or elect. Some states require that church corporations have a minimum number of directors.[108]

## 2. ELECTION OR APPOINTMENT

It is customary for directors and trustees to be elected by the church membership and for officers to be elected by the board of directors or trustees. There is of course considerable deviation from this rule. It is, for example, common for directors to nominate officers who are then elected by the voting membership.

Incorporated and unincorporated churches must follow the procedures in their charter or bylaws and in applicable state laws regarding the election or appointment of church officers, directors, and trustees. It is well-settled that a church member who claims that directors or officers were not elected according to such procedures has a right to have his claim heard in the courts, and that judicial resolution of such a claim does not violate the First Amendment. To illustrate, members of a church were allowed to challenge in court the legality of a congregational election of directors that allegedly did not conform to the procedural requirements in the church bylaws.[109] And, when a board of directors sought to perpetuate itself in office by refusing to call an election, church members were allowed to obtain legal redress because the state law under which the church was incorporated required annual elections of directors.[110]

Unless stated otherwise in either the bylaws or state law, officers, directors, and trustees are elected by a majority vote of the congregation's membership. Thus, it has been held that where a church had no constitution or bylaws

[107]W. FLETCHER, *supra* note 21, at § 271.
[108]MODEL NONPROFIT CORPORATION ACT § 18.
[109]Wilkerson v. Battiste, 393 So.2d 195 (La. 1980).
[110]Burnett v. Banks, 279 P.2d 579 (Cal. 1955).

granting authority to the board of deacons to elect a church treasurer, the congregation, not the board of deacons, had such authority.[111]

Many churches have adopted a "staggered system" of electing directors whereby a minority (often a third) of the directors are elected at each annual meeting. This normally is accomplished by classifying directors in the bylaws according to tenure: the first class holding office for one year, the second class for two years, and the third class for three years. Thereafter successors for each class of directors are elected for three-year terms. This system helps to ensure that a majority of the board at all times will be experienced. Unless forbidden by charter, bylaw, or statute, a director or officer may succeed himself in office.

Vacancies occurring in any office or on the board of directors or board of trustees are filled according to applicable provisions in state law or in the church's charter or bylaws. Church bylaws often permit vacancies in the board of directors to be filled by the board itself except for vacancies created by an increase in the number of directors. Vacancies typically are filled only for the unexpired term of the predecessor in office.

If the filling of vacancies is not provided for by state law or a church's charter or bylaws, there is no alternative but to await the next annual meeting of the congregation or to call a special meeting of the congregation expressly for the purpose of filling the vacancy for the unexpired term.

A minister is not entitled to serve as president of a church or even as a director or trustee unless specifically authorized in the church's charter or bylaws.[112]

### 3. AUTHORITY

#### a. *Officers*

It is often said that church officers may perform only those acts for which they have authority, and that the authority of church officers is analogous to that exercised by officers of private corporations.[113] It is a well-settled rule of law that the authority of a corporate officer may derive from four sources: express, implied, inherent, and apparent authority. The most basic kind of authority possessed by a church officer consists of *express authority* deriving from those powers and prerogatives conferred by statute, charter, bylaw, or resolution. Statutes occasionally confer certain powers upon the officers of church corporations, but by far the greatest sources of express authority are a

[111]Gervin v. Reddick, 268 S.E.2d 657 (Ga. 1980).

[112]Allen v. North Des Moines Methodist Episcopal Church, 102 N.W. 808 (Iowa 1905).

[113]Lewis v. Wolfe, 413 S.W.2d 314 (Mo. 1967).

church's charter, bylaws, and resolutions. Article V of the Model Nonprofit Corporation Bylaws lists the powers of corporate officers as follows:

*President.* The President shall be the principal executive officer of the corporation and shall in general supervise and control all of the business affairs of the corporation. He shall preside at all meetings of the Board of Directors. He may sign, with the Secretary or any other proper officer of the corporation authorized by the Board of Directors, any deeds, mortgages, bonds, contracts, or other instruments which the Board has authorized to be executed, except in cases where the signing and execution thereof shall be expressly delegated by the Board of Directors or by these bylaws or by statute to some other officer or agent of the corporation; and in general shall perform all duties incident to the office of President and such other duties as may be prescribed by the Board of Directors from time to time.

*Vice President.* In the absence of the President or in the event of his inability or refusal to act, the Vice President (or, in the event that there be more than one Vice President, the Vice Presidents in the order of their election) shall perform the duties of the President, and when so acting, shall have all powers of and be subject to all the restrictions upon the President. Any Vice President shall perform such other duties as from time to time may be assigned to him by the President or by the Board of Directors.

*Treasurer.* If required by the Board of Directors, the Treasurer shall give a bond for the faithful discharge of his duties in such sum and with such surety or sureties as the Board of Directors shall determine. He shall have charge and custody of and be responsible for all funds and securities of the corporation; receive and give receipts for moneys due and payable to the corporation from any source whatsoever, and deposit all such moneys in the name of the corporation in such banks, trust companies or other depositories as shall be selected in accordance with the provisions of . . . these bylaws; and in general perform all the duties incident to the office of Treasurer and such other duties as from time to time may be assigned to him by the President or by the Board of Directors.

*Secretary.* The Secretary shall keep the minutes of the meetings of the Board of Directors in one or more books provided for that purpose; see that all notices are duly given in accordance with the provisions of these bylaws or as required by law; be custodian of the corporate records and of the seal of the corporation and see that the seal of the corporation is affixed to all documents, the execution of which on behalf of the corporation under its seal is duly authorized in accordance with the provisions of these bylaws . . . and in general perform all duties incident to the office of Secretary and such other duties as from time to time may be assigned to him by the President or by the Board of Directors.

Officers also possess *implied authority* to perform all those acts that are necessary in performing an express power. The law essentially implies the existence of such authority, without which the express powers would be frustrated. To illustrate, the courts have held that express authority to manage a business includes the power to enter into contracts and to make purchases on behalf of the company. Authority to sell property has been held to include the power to execute a mortgage necessary for the sale of the property. And, authority to borrow money has been held to include the power to execute a guaranty.

Certain powers often are said to be *inherent* in a particular office, whether or not expressly granted in an organization's charter, bylaws, or resolutions. For example, it commonly is said that the president has inherent authority to preside at meetings of the corporation, that the vice-president has inherent authority to act as president if the president is absent or incapacitated, that the secretary has inherent authority to maintain the corporate seal and records and to serve as secretary in all corporate meetings, and that the treasurer has inherent authority to receive money for the corporation.[114] Some courts are beginning to recognize a broader inherent power in the office of corporate president, including the authority to enter into contracts on behalf of the corporation.[115] This is not universally accepted, however.

Finally, officers occasionally possess *apparent authority:* authority that has not actually been granted by the corporation but which the corporation through its actions and representations leads others to believe has been granted.[116] The doctrine of apparent authority rests on the principle of estoppel, which forbids one by his acts to give an officer or agent an appearance of authority that he does not have and to benefit from such misleading conduct to the detriment of one who has relied thereon.

If an officer performs an act for which he had no authority, the directors of the corporation can ratify the unauthorized act by consenting to it. Ratification generally is held to consist of three elements: acceptance by the corporation of the benefits of the officer's action, with full knowledge of the facts, and circumstances or affirmative conduct indicating an intention to adopt and approve the unauthorized action. Ratification may not occur before an unauthorized action, and must take place within a reasonable time after such action. Ratifications generally are considered to be irrevocable, unless one of the preceding three elements is absent, in which case the ratification never legally occurred.

Only that body possessing the power to perform or authorize an officer's

---

[114]W. FLETCHER, *supra* note 21, at § 441; Note, *Inherent Powers of Corporate Officers: Need for a Statutory Definition,* 61 HARV. L. REV. 867 (1948).

[115]W. FLETCHER, *supra* note 21, at § 559.

[116]Continental-Wirt Electronics Corp. v. Sprague Electric Co., 329 F. Supp. 959 (E.D. Pa. 1971).

unauthorized action has the power to ratify it. This generally is the board of directors. Ratification can be express, such as by formal, recorded action of the board of directors, or it can be implied from the acts and representations of the board. Implied ratification often occurs when a corporation knows or should have known of an unauthorized act and does nothing to repudiate it. Thus, when a church's parish committee should have known of various mortgages executed by the church's minister on behalf of the church but did nothing to disavow them, it was held to have ratified them by implication.[117]

### b. *Directors and Trustees*

Since directors and trustees generally are considered to be officers, all of the preceding discussion concerning the authority of officers applies to them. Thus, the authority of directors and trustees is to be found primarily in the express provisions of state law or in a church's charter or bylaws. In addition, directors and trustees will be deemed to have implied authority to do those things that are necessary to fulfill their express powers, and they will be clothed with apparent authority when a church through its actions or representations leads others to believe that authority to perform a particular act has been granted. To illustrate, five persons designated by a pastor as trustees of a church were held to have apparent authority to obligate the church even though they had not been properly elected.[118] Directors and trustees possess no inherent power.

The United States Supreme Court has stated that "the first place one must look to determine the powers of corporate directors is in the relevant State's corporation law. Corporations are creatures of state law . . . and it is state law which is the font of corporate directors' powers."[119] The Model Nonprofit Corporation Act states that "the affairs of a corporation shall be managed by a board of directors."[120] Many states that have not adopted the Act have similar provisions in their religious or nonprofit corporation laws. Most state laws thus confer general managerial authority upon the directors or trustees of incorporated churches. This authority often is very broad, even to the point of empowering the board to act on behalf of the church in the ordinary business of the corporation without the necessity of obtaining the consent or approval of the membership. Thus, the board of a church corporation ordinarily has the authority to enter into contracts; elect officers; hire employees; authorize notes,

---

[117]Perkins v. Rich, 429 N.E.2d 1135 (Mass. 1982).

[118]Straughter v. Holy Temple of Church of God and Christ, 150 So.2d 124 (La. 1963), *cert. denied,* 151 So.2d 693 (La. 1963).

[119]Burks v. Lasker, 441 U.S. 471, 478 (1979).

[120]MODEL NONPROFIT CORPORATION ACT § 16.

deeds, and mortgages; and institute and settle lawsuits. The powers of the board, however, may be limited by church charter, bylaw, or resolution.

The boards of unincorporated churches generally derive little or no authority from state law.

The courts have often held that a church board occupies a position analogous to the managing directors of a business corporation, at least with respect to the temporal affairs of a church, and that the board has authority to act only at regularly assembled meetings.[121] Thus, it has been held that where four out of seven directors met informally and agreed to change the location of an annual church meeting, the election of directors at such meeting was invalid.[122] Similarly, it has been held that "only when acting as a board may trustees of a religious corporation perform or authorize acts binding on the corporation," and therefore the attempt by an individual trustee of a church to employ an attorney on behalf of the church was invalidated.[123]

Directors and trustees may not perform acts not authorized either by state law or the church's charter or bylaws. Thus, when a church charter gave the board of trustees authority to institute lawsuits in the corporation's name only after being directed to do so by a majority vote of the church membership, a lawsuit instituted by the board itself without congregational approval was held to be unauthorized.[124] It has also been held that the trustees of a church corporation do not possess the authority to adopt bylaws for the church unless the charter or constitution of the church specifically gives them such authority.[125]

4. MEETINGS OF DIRECTORS AND TRUSTEES

It is a well-settled rule of law that the power to do particular acts and the general authority to manage the corporate affairs is vested in the directors or trustees, and that their acts are binding on the corporation only when done as a board at a legal meeting. Thus, neither a minority nor a majority of the board has the authority to meet privately and take action binding upon the corporation.[126] The reason for this rule has been stated as follows: "The law believes that the greatest wisdom results from conference and exchange of individual views, and it is for this reason that the law requires the united wisdom of a

---

[121]Coates v. Parchman, 334 S.W.2d 417 (Mo. 1960).

[122]*Id.*

[123]Krehel v. Eastern Orthodox Catholic Church, 195 N.Y.S.2d 334, 336 (1959), *aff'd*, 221 N.Y.S.2d 724 (1961).

[124]Honey Creek Regular Baptist Church v. Wilson, 92 N.E.2d 419 (Ohio 1950).

[125]Lewis v. Wolfe, 413 S.W.2d 314 (Mo. 1967).

[126]In re McCanna's Estate, 284 N.W. 502 (Wis. 1939).

majority of the several members of the board in determining the business of the corporation."[127]

This rule of course has exceptions. For example, if he has authority to act as an agent of the corporation, a single director may obligate the corporation. Further, it has been held in some jurisdictions that if all the directors convene and take action by majority vote, such action is binding upon the corporation even if the directors were not assembled in a legal meeting. In such a case, the directors typically waive any notice requirements and declare the meeting to be a special meeting of the board.

Corporate bylaws often contain provisions authorizing the board to meet informally and take action, provided that certain conditions are met. Such conditions generally deal with the number of directors that must be present in order for the board to act informally. Some state nonprofit corporation laws permit directors to take action without a meeting if they all submit written consents to a proposed action.[128] And some states permit directors to conduct meetings by conference telephone call.[129] The entire board of directors can of course take action at a duly convened meeting to ratify an action taken by a minority or majority of the board acting separately and not in a legal meeting.

The corporate bylaws ordinarily specify that regular meetings of the directors or trustees shall occur at specified times and at a specified location. The designation in the bylaws of the time and place for regular meetings of the board generally will be considered sufficient notice of such meetings. In addition, special meetings may be convened by those officers or directors who are authorized by the bylaws to do so. The bylaws ordinarily require that notice of a special meeting be communicated to all directors at a prescribed interval before the meeting. The notice also must be in the form prescribed by the bylaws.

A meeting of the directors or trustees will not be legal unless a quorum is present. A quorum refers to that number or percentage of the total authorized number of directors that must be present in order for the board to transact business. The bylaws typically state the quorum requirements. In the absence of a bylaw provision, the number of directors constituting a quorum may be prescribed either by the state statute under which the church is incorporated[130] or by the rule prevailing in a particular jurisdiction. In many states, a majority of the board will constitute a quorum in the absence of a bylaw or statutory

---

[127]Trethewey v. Green River Gorge, 136 P.2d 999, 1012 (Wash. 1943).

[128]WASH. REV. STAT. § 24.03.465.

[129]MO. REV. STAT. § 355.145.

[130]For example, § 163a19 of the Illinois General Nonprofit Corporation Act specifies that absent a provision to the contrary in the corporate charter or bylaws a majority of the directors constitutes a quorum.

provision to the contrary.[131] Some nonprofit incorporation laws specify that a quorum may not consist of less than a certain number. To illustrate, the non-profit corporation law of one state stipulates that in no event shall a quorum of directors consist of less than one-third of the whole board of directors.[132] If vacancies in the board reduce the number of directors to less than a quorum, some statutes permit the board to meet for the purpose of filling vacancies.[133]

Board meetings are often informal. The president of the corporation generally presides at such meetings, and the secretary keeps minutes. Actions of the board may be in the form of a resolution, although this is not necessary since it has been held that actions taken by the board and recorded in the minutes constitute corporate actions as effectively as a formal resolution.[134]

If a board meeting does not comply with the requirements in the corporation's bylaws or in state law, it will be invalid and its actions will have no legal effect. Thus, meetings will be invalid and ineffective if notice requirements are not satisfied, unless all of the directors waive the defect in notice either verbally or implicitly by their attendance without objection at the meeting. Meetings will also be invalid if quorum requirements are not satisfied, and an action taken by the board even at a duly called meeting will be invalid if it was adopted by less than the required number of votes.

## 5. REMOVAL OF OFFICERS, DIRECTORS, AND TRUSTEES

A corporation possesses the inherent power to remove an officer, director, or trustee for cause.[135] Thus, the courts have held that a church congregation has the inherent authority to remove a director for cause even though the church bylaws lacked provision for removal of directors.[136] In the context of church corporations, good cause will consist of material doctrinal deviation, immoral conduct, incompetency, and incapacity. The church membership itself and not the board generally has the authority to remove directors or trustees for cause. Officers elected by the board may be removed by the board. Officers or directors removed for cause generally have no right to compensation for the unexpired term of office.

A church has no authority to remove an officer or director without cause prior to the expiration of his term unless a bylaw or statute specifically grants

---

[131]W. FLETCHER, *supra* note 21, at § 419.

[132]ILL. REV. STAT. ch. 32, § 163a19.

[133]MODEL NONPROFIT CORPORATION ACT § 19.

[134]W. FLETCHER, *supra* note 21, at § 418.

[135]Rodyk v. Ukrainian Autocephalic Orthodox Church, 296 N.Y.S.2d 496 (1968), *aff'd*, 328 N.Y.S.2d 685 (1972).

[136]Mangum v. Swearingen, 565 S.W.2d 957 (Tex. 1978).

such authority. But if an officer or director is elected for an unspecified term, he may be removed at any time with or without cause by the body that elected him. And, when an officer's or director's term of office expires, a church congregation can fill the vacancy without demonstrating that good cause existed for not reelecting the former officer or director.[137]

State laws under which incorporated churches are organized often provide for removal of officers and directors. For example, the Model Nonprofit Corporation Act states that a director may be removed by any procedure set forth in the corporation's articles of incorporation,[138] and that an officer may be removed by the persons authorized to elect or appoint such officer whenever in their judgment it serves the best interests of the corporation.[139]

Provisions in state law or a church's bylaws for removal of officers and directors must be followed. Thus, if a statute specifies that any ten members of a church can call for a congregational meeting for the purpose of removing directors from office, any action taken at a meeting called by only eight members will be ineffective.[140] And, if a church votes to remove certain officers at a meeting conducted in violation of church bylaws, the removal of the officers will be without effect.[141]

Finally, it is the general rule that provisions in statutes, charters, or bylaws calling for an officer or director to serve for a prescribed term and until his successor is chosen do not prevent an officer or director from resigning; a resignation is complete upon its receipt by the corporation even though the corporate charter states that the office is to be held until a successor is elected and qualified.[142] Furthermore, the resignation of an officer or director will be effective even if not accepted at a formal meeting of the board of directors, at least if the board knew of the resignation and acquiesced in it.[143]

### 6. Personal Liability of Officers, Directors, and Trustees

It is a fundamental principle of corporate law that officers and directors lawfully acting on behalf of their corporation should do so at no risk of personal expense or liability. Nevertheless, a corporate officer is individually liable for the wrongs he personally commits and cannot shield himself behind a corpo-

---

[137]Morris v. Richard Clark Missionary Baptist Church, 177 P.2d 811 (Cal. 1947).

[138]MODEL NONPROFIT CORPORATION ACT § 18.

[139]*Id.* at § 24.

[140]Miles v. Wilson, 181 N.Y.S.2d 585 (1958).

[141]Tybor v. Ukrainian Autocephalic Orthodox Church, 151 N.Y.S.2d 711 (1956).

[142]Koven v. Saberdyne Systems, Inc., 625 P.2d 907 (Ariz. 1980).

[143]Anderson v. K.G. Moore, Inc., 376 N.E.2d 1238 (Mass. 1978), *cert. denied,* 439 U.S. 1116 (1979).

ration when he is the perpetrator.[144] The fact that an officer or director is acting for a corporation may also make the corporation secondarily liable,[145] but this does not relieve the individual of his personal responsibility.

However, an officer or director may not be found liable for the company's wrongs unless he culpably participated in the unlawful activities or somehow authorized or approved them. An officer or director may not claim total ignorance of corporate affairs, particularly those matters disclosed at directors meetings and those corporate records accessible to officers and directors. Thus, an officer or director may be found responsible for the unlawful act of a corporate agent if the act was discussed at a directors meeting and no formal action was taken to prevent it.

## §F. Members

### 1. IN GENERAL

It is often important to determine which persons comprise the membership of a church since the church's charter and bylaws, and in some cases state nonprofit corporation law, ordinarily vest considerable authority in the members. In congregational churches, the members typically elect and depose directors and ministers, authorize the purchase and sale of property, adopt and amend the charter or bylaws, and approve budgets. Church members in hierarchical churches typically possess some or all of these powers.

### 2. SELECTION AND QUALIFICATIONS

The essence of the relation between members and a church consists of an agreement between the parties, a profession of faith, adherence to the doctrines of the church, and submission to its government.[146] The membership of a church is typically determined by reference to the church charter and bylaws and to any applicable state corporation law. It is well-settled that (1) the right to determine the qualifications for membership belongs to the church, (2) a determination as to who are members "in good standing" is an ecclesiastical question relating to the government and discipline of a church, and (3) a church's

---

[144]Donsco, Inc. v. Casper Corp., 587 F.2d 602 (3rd Cir. 1978); W. FLETCHER, *supra* note 21, at § 1158.

[145]Employers are generally responsible for the wrongs committed by employees in the course of business.

[146]Freshour v. King, 345 P.2d 689 (Kan. 1959); Henson v. Payne, 302 S.W.2d 44 (Mo. 1956); Second Baptist Church v. Mount Zion Baptist Church, 466 P.2d 212 (Nev. 1970); Western Conference of Original Free Will Baptists v. Creech, 123 S.E.2d 619 (N.C. 1962).

decision about either matter is binding on the courts.[147] Thus, when two purported members of a church sought an accounting of church funds and the
church defended its noncompliance on the ground that the plaintiffs were not
members in good standing, a court deferred to the church's determination that
the plaintiffs were not members and dismissed the case.[148] The court observed
that membership in a religious society is an ecclesiastical matter to be determined by the church, not the courts. The United States Supreme Court has
stated the general rule of judicial nonintervention in the ecclesiastical affairs
of churches, including membership determinations, as follows:

> But it is a very different thing where a subject matter of dispute, strictly and purely
> ecclesiastical in its character—a matter over which the civil courts exercise no
> jurisdiction—a matter which concerns theological controversy, church discipline,
> ecclesiastical government, or the conformity of the members of the church to the
> standard of morals required of them—becomes the subject of its action. It may be
> said here, also, that no jurisdiction has been conferred on the tribunal to try the
> particular case before it, or that, in its judgment, it exceeds the powers conferred
> upon it, or that the laws of the church do not authorize the particular form of
> proceeding adopted; and, in a sense often used in the courts, all of those may be
> said to be questions of jurisdiction. But it is easy to see that if the civil courts are
> to inquire into all these matters, the whole subject of the doctrinal theology, the
> usages and customs, the written laws, and fundamental organization of every re-
> ligious denomination may, and must, be examined into with minuteness and care,
> for they would become, in almost every case, the criteria by which the validity of
> the ecclesiastical decree would be determined in the civil court.[149]

The Supreme Court has also held that religious freedom encompasses the
"power of [religious bodies] to decide for themselves, free from state interference, matters of church government as well as those of faith and doctrine."[150]
And, the Court has stated that "religious controversies are not the proper
subject of civil court inquiry."[151] This rule is often followed even when it is

[147]Rodyk v. Ukrainian Autocephalic Orthodox Church, 296 N.Y.S.2d 496 (1968), aff'd,
328 N.Y.S.2d 685 (1972). See also Stewart v. Jarriel, 59 S.E.2d 368 (Ga. 1950); Fast v.
Smyth, 527 S.W.2d 673, 676 (Mo. 1975) ("the determination of who are qualified
members of a church is an ecclesiastical matter"); Eisenberg v. Fauer, 200 N.Y.S.2d
749 (1960).

[148]Taylor v. New York Annual Conference of the African Methodist Episcopal Church,
115 N.Y.S.2d 62 (1952).

[149]Watson v. Jones, 80 U.S. 679, 733-34 (1871).

[150]Kedroff v. St. Nicholas Cathedral, 344 U.S. 94, 116 (1952).

[151]Serbian Eastern Orthodox Diocese v. Milivojevich, 426 U.S. 696, 713 (1976).

alleged that a church deviated from its own charter or bylaws in making a membership determination.[152]

Some courts have acknowledged room for "marginal civil court review" of the ecclesiastical determinations of churches, including determinations regarding membership, in the following situations: (1) if the church determination was the product of fraud or collusion;[153] (2) if civil, contract, or property rights of members are affected;[154] or (3) if a legitimate dispute occurs over the meaning of the criteria for membership.[155]

### 3. AUTHORITY

In churches with a congregational form of government, the general rule is that a majority of the members represent the church and have the right to manage its affairs and to control its property for the use and benefit of the church, and that the law will protect such authority at least as it relates to civil,

---

[152]Evans v. Shiloh Baptist Church, 77 A.2d 160 (Md. 1950); Jenkins v. New Shiloh Baptist Church, 56 A.2d 788 (Md. 1948).

[153]Gonzalez v. Roman Catholic Archbishop, 280 U.S. 1 (1929). The United States Supreme Court has stated that "arbitrariness" is no longer a basis for civil court review of the ecclesiastical determinations of churches. Serbian Eastern Orthodox Diocese v. Milivojevich, 426 U.S. 696 (1976).

[154]Carden v. La Grone, 169 S.E.2d 168, 172 (Ga. 1969) ("a court of equity will not interfere with the internal management of a religious society where property rights are not involved"); Third Missionary Baptist Church v. Garrett, 158 N.W.2d 771, 776 (Iowa 1968) ("It is a general rule recognized here and in foreign jurisdictions that ordinarily the courts have no jurisdiction over, and no concern with, purely ecclesiastical questions and controversies, including membership in a church organization, but they do have jurisdiction as to civil, contract, and property rights which are involved in or arise from a church controversy."); Mitchell v. Albanian Orthodox Diocese, 244 N.E.2d 276, 278-79 (Mass. 1969) ("[C]ourts do not interfere in a controversy that is exclusively or primarily of an ecclesiastical nature. Where civil or property rights or the construction of legal instruments are involved, however, the courts have been less reluctant to interfere."); Fast v. Smyth, 527 S.W.2d 673, 676 (Mo. 1975) ("[T]he determination of who are qualified members of a church is an ecclesiastical matter. There is, however, a well recognized exception to this general rule in this state. Civil courts will review ecclesiastical matters where necessary to protect the property, contracts, or civil rights of members.").

[155]Second Baptist Church v. Mount Zion Baptist Church, 466 P.2d 212 (Nev. 1970) (where church bylaws stipulated that failure to attend church or make financial contributions "without a reasonable excuse" resulted in termination of membership, court resolved church dispute concerning the meaning of "without a reasonable excuse"); Honey Creek Regular Baptist Church v. Wilson, 92 N.E.2d 419 (Ohio 1950) (court agreed to hear church dispute concerning the issue of whether "extending the right hand of fellowship" was a requirement of church membership).

contract, or property rights.[156] One court has stated the rule as follows: "[T]he courts will give effect to the action of the majority of members of a congregational or independent religious organization . . . insofar as regards civil or property rights when they have acted in harmony with church rules, customs and practices at a meeting properly called."[157] Thus it has been held that a majority of a church's membership has the authority to sell a parsonage and acquire a new one;[158] to oust a minority group that had wrongfully and violently seized possession of the church building;[159] to call a meeting of the church;[160] to expel members;[161] to disaffiliate from one denomination and associate with another;[162] and to adopt bylaws.[163] The general authority possessed by the members of a congregational church exists whether the church is incorporated or unincorporated. However, state corporate law may grant the members of an incorporated church additional specific powers. For example, some nonprofit corporation laws under which churches may incorporate specifically grant to members the authority to inspect the books and records of a corporation.[164]

The authority of a majority of members in a church with a congregational form of government is limited. It is often stated that church members have only such authority as is vested in them by the church's charter or bylaws or by state corporation law. In a leading case, a court rejected a demand by several church members that their church conduct a meeting at which the pastor and trustees would give a complete accounting of the affairs of the church, since neither the church's charter nor bylaws conferred such authority upon the membership. The court concluded that the members "have only such powers, if any, in the management of the affairs of the corporation as may be conferred upon them by the charter and bylaws."[165]

The charter and bylaws of many congregational churches limit the authority of a simple majority of members. For example, some require that sales or purchases of property, elections of ministers, and amendments to the charter or bylaws be by a two-thirds or three-fourths vote of the church membership.

---

[156]Mitchell v. Dickey, 173 S.E.2d 695 (Ga. 1970); Wright v. Smith, 124 N.E.2d 363 (Ill. 1955); McHargue v. Feltner, 325 S.W.2d 349 (Ky. 1959).

[157]Willis v. Davis, 323 S.W.2d 847, 849 (Ky. 1959).

[158]McHargue v. Feltner, 325 S.W.2d 349 (Ky. 1959).

[159]Mitchell v. Dickey, 173 S.E.2d 695 (Ga. 1970).

[160]Willis v. Davis, 323 S.W.2d 847 (Ky. 1959).

[161]Moorman v. Goodman, 157 A.2d 519 (N.J. 1960).

[162]Douglass v. First Baptist Church, 287 P.2d 965 (Colo. 1955).

[163]Lewis v. Wolfe, 413 S.W.2d 314 (Mo. 1967).

[164]MODEL NONPROFIT CORPORATION ACT § 25.

[165]Evans v. Shiloh Baptist Church, 77 A.2d 160, 163 (Md. 1950). See also Katz v. Singerman, 127 So.2d 515 (La. 1961).

Clearly the courts will disregard the authority of a church's members when property rights or civil liberties protected under state or federal law are violated. The rights that exist by virtue of state or federal law "cannot be overridden by a majority rule of any organization—church or otherwise."[166]

Members are under no compulsion to adhere to the tenets of their church, but they cannot impose their beliefs upon a majority that rejects them.[167] Members of course have the right to withdraw from one church and join another.[168] But members who withdraw or whose membership is terminated by action of the church no longer possess any authority. They have no interest in church property, and they cannot represent members in any legal action against the church.[169]

It is often stated that when a person becomes a member of a church, he does so upon the condition of submission to its ecclesiastical jurisdiction, and however much he may be dissatisfied with the exercise of that jurisdiction, he has no right to invoke the supervisory power of a civil court so long as none of his property, contract, or civil rights is affected.[170] Nor may a member deny the existence of a church's bylaws.[171]

Church members generally have no personal interest in church property since title ordinarily is vested in the trustees of unincorporated churches and in the church itself if the church is incorporated. Thus, if a church acquires property by a deed naming the church as grantee, the conveyance is to the church and constitutes no benefit or interest to any individual member.[172] Prior to 1969 the courts commonly decided that church property was held in trust for the use and benefit of those members adhering to the original tenets of the church, and thus a majority of the members could not abandon the tenets of the church and retain the right to use the church's property so long as a single

---

[166]Stansberry v. McCarty, 149 N.E.2d 683, 686 (Ind. 1958). *See also* Serbian Eastern Orthodox Diocese v. Ocokoljich, 219 N.E.2d 343 (Ill. 1966).

[167]Katz v. Singerman, 127 So.2d 515 (La. 1961).

[168]Trett v. Lambeth, 195 S.W.2d 524 (Mo. 1946); Brady v. Reiner, 198 S.E.2d 812 (W. Va. 1973).

[169]Stewart v. Jarriel, 59 S.E.2d 368 (Ga. 1950); Brady v. Reiner, 198 S.E.2d 812 (W. Va. 1973).

[170]Stewart V. Jarriel, 59 S.E.2d 368 (Ga. 1950).

[171]State ex rel. Morrow v. Hill, 364 N.E.2d 1156 (Ohio 1977).

[172]Presbytery of Cimarron v. Westminster Presbyterian Church, 515 P.2d 211 (Okla. 1973).

member adhered to the original doctrines of the church.[173] This rule was abolished by the United States Supreme Court in 1969.[174]

Members of churches affiliated with an ecclesiastical hierarchy generally are subject to the same limitations on their authority discussed above in connection with members of congregational churches, but in addition they are limited by the bylaws and tribunals of the parent denomination.[175]

### 4. REMOVAL

#### a. *In General*

As noted in the preceding section, the United States Supreme Court has held that all who unite themselves with a religious organization do so with implied consent to its bylaws and procedures.[176] Another court has stated the prevailing rule as follows: "A party having voluntarily assented to becoming a member of the local church thereby subjects himself to the existing rules and procedures of said church and cannot deny their existence."[177] It is therefore held that a church may promulgate rules governing the expulsion or excommunication of its members, and such rules bind the church's members.[178]

Some states adhere to the principle that the removal of church members is exclusively a matter of ecclesiastical concern and thus the courts are without authority to review such determinations.[179] This position generally is based upon the First Amendment principle of separation of church and state, or upon the fact that by joining the church a member expressly or implicitly consents to the authority of the church to expel members.[180]

---

[173]Wright v. Smith, 124 N.E.2d 363, 365 (Ill. 1955) ("[c]ourts will raise and enforce an implied trust so that the majority faction cannot effect a fundamental change of doctrine").

[174]In Presbyterian Church in the United States v. Mary Elizabeth Blue Hull Memorial Presbyterian Church, 393 U.S. 440 (1969), the Court held that civil courts could no longer construe or apply religious doctrine in resolving church property disputes. *See generally* chapter 9, *infra.*

[175]Presbytery of Cimarron v. Westminster Presbyterian Church, 515 P.2d 211 (Okla. 1973).

[176]Watson v. Jones, 80 U.S. 679, 729 (1871).

[177]State ex rel. Morrow v. Hill, 364 N.E.2d 1156, 1159 (Ohio 1977).

[178]Bagley v. Carter, 220 S.E.2d 919 (Ga. 1975).

[179]St. John's Greek Catholic Hungarian Russian Orthodox Church v. Fedak, 213 A.2d 651 (N.J. 1965), *rev'd on other grounds,* 233 A.2d 663 (N.J. 1966).

[180]Nunn v. Black, 506 F. Supp. 444 (W.D. Va. 1981), *aff'd,* 661 F.2d 925 (4th Cir. 1981), *cert. denied,* 102 S. Ct. 1008 (1982); Simpson v. Wells Lamont Corp., 494 F.2d 490 (5th Cir. 1974); Konkel v. Metropolitan Baptist Church, Inc., 572 P.2d 99 (Ariz. 1977); Macedonia Baptist Foundation v. Singleton, 379 So.2d 269 (La. 1979).

b. *Grounds for Civil Court Review*

In a majority of states limited judicial review of the expulsion of church members is permitted in one or more of the following contexts:

(1) *Interference With Civil, Contract, or Property Rights*

Although nearly all courts recognize that they have no authority to review purely ecclesiastical matters, most courts are willing to review the expulsion of a church member if the expulsion affects "civil, contract, or property rights."[181] The precise meaning of the term *civil, contract, or property rights* is unclear. Many courts interpret the exception broadly. To illustrate, it has been held that church membership in itself constitutes a "property right" since church members comprise the body of persons entitled to the use and enjoyment of church properties, and therefore the courts have authority to review all expulsions of church members.[182] It also has been argued that civil rights are involved in the expulsion of church members because of "the humiliation and hurt to personality, the injury to character, reputation, feelings and personal rights and human dignity."[183] Similarly, it has been held that (1) the expulsion of a member from a church can constitute a serious emotional deprivation which, when compared to some losses of property or contract rights, can be far more damaging to an individual; (2) the loss of the opportunity to worship in familiar surroundings is a valuable right that deserves the protection of the law; and (3) except in cases involving religious doctrine, there is no reason for treating religious organizations differently from other nonprofit organizations, whose membership expulsions are routinely reviewed by the courts.[184]

A few courts take a far narrower view. Thus, it has been held that church membership in itself does not constitute a property right,[185] a contract right,[186] or a civil right.[187] The more common tendency, however, is for courts to construe broadly the concept of civil, contract, or property rights, and thus agree to review membership expulsions, at least where the expulsions were not based upon doctrinal considerations.

---

[181]*See generally* Annot., 20 A.L.R.2d 421 (1951).
[182]Randolph v. First Baptist Church, 120 N.E.2d 485 (Ohio 1954).
[183]*Id.* at 489.
[184]Baugh v. Thomas, 265 A.2d 675 (N.J. 1970).
[185]Sapp v. Callaway, 69 S.E.2d 734 (Ga. 1952).
[186]Cooper v. Bell, 106 S.W.2d 124 (Ky. 1937).
[187]Stewart v. Jarriel, 59 S.E.2d 368 (Ga. 1950).

### (2) Authority of Expelling Body

It is also well-established that courts may review membership expulsions for the purpose of determining whether members were expelled by the body authorized to do so by the church charter or bylaws. Thus, when certain members of a church were expelled and sought judicial review of their expulsion, a court ruled, over the protests of the church, that it did have jurisdiction to determine whether the expulsions were the act of an authorized and duly constituted body.[188] Another court, in agreeing to review a church's expulsion of certain members, commented:

> [I]f a decision is reached by some body not having ecclesiastical jurisdiction over the matter, then the civil court would not be bound by that decision. . . . Once [a] determination is made that the proper ecclesiastical authority has acted in its duly constituted manner, no civil review of the substantive ecclesiastical matter may take place as this would be prohibited by Amendments I and XIV of the Federal Constitution . . . .[189]

### (3) Compliance With Church Charter and Bylaws

Most courts show little reluctance to review church membership expulsions to determine whether a church acted in accordance with its own charter or bylaws. Thus, where former church members complained that they had been removed improperly from the membership roll at a church meeting convened off of church premises without notice to them of either the location of the meeting or the fact that their dismissal would be discussed, a court concluded that it did have jurisdiction to determine whether the members were expelled in accordance with the charter and bylaws of the church.[190] The court cautioned, however, that if the church had complied with its charter and bylaws, the court would have no jurisdiction to proceed in its review.

Expelled church members' allegations that their expulsions deviated from established church procedures have also been reviewed by the courts in the following contexts: (1) members who allegedly were ineligible to vote according to church bylaws were permitted to vote for the expulsion of certain members;[191] (2) a pastor conducted a church meeting without prior notice, and, without a hearing of any kind, members present voted to expel an opposing faction from

---

[188]Brown v. Mt. Olive Baptist Church, 124 N.W.2d 445 (Iowa 1963).
[189]Bowen v. Green, 272 S.E.2d 433, 435 (S.C. 1980).
[190]Konkel v. Metropolitan Baptist Church, Inc., 572 P.2d 99 (Ariz. 1977).
[191]Anderson v. Sills, 265 A.2d 678 (N.J. 1970).

membership;[192] and (3) members present at a special meeting for which no prior notice had been given voted to summarily expel all members of the church who identified themselves, through attendance or support, with any other church.[193]

### (4) Expulsion Based on Fraud or Collusion

The United States Supreme Court has held that "[i]n the absence of fraud, collusion, or arbitrariness, the decisions of the proper church tribunals on matters purely ecclesiastical . . . are accepted in litigation before secular courts as conclusive . . . ."[194] The Court later held that ecclesiastical determinations could not be reviewed for "arbitrariness."[195] Such decisions suggest room for marginal civil court review of church membership expulsions if the expulsions are allegedly the product of fraud or collusion.[196] It has been held that if malice can be shown, members whose expulsions are based on fraudulent charges can sue for defamation those persons who bring the charges.[197]

### (5) Interpretation of Contested Terminology

Occasionally a court will agree to review an expulsion based on some vague condition of membership. For example, when a church's bylaws stipulated that failure to attend church or make financial contributions "without a reasonable excuse" would result in termination of membership, a court agreed to resolve the disputed phrase "without a reasonable excuse."[198] Another court agreed to determine whether a church's charter or bylaws made "extending the right hand of fellowship" a condition of membership where this was a disputed question.[199]

In summary, the emerging rule appears to be that courts may review church membership expulsions just as they review membership expulsions from any

---

[192]Abyssinia Missionary Baptist Church v. Nixon, 340 So.2d 746 (Ala. 1976); Longmeyer v. Payne, 205 S.W.2d 263 (Mo. 1947); Randolph v. First Baptist Church, 120 N.E.2d 485 (Ohio 1954); First Baptist Church v. Giles, 219 S.W.2d 498 (Tex. 1949).

[193]David v. Carter, 222 S.W.2d 900 (Tex. 1949).

[194]Gonzalez v. Roman Catholic Archbishop, 280 U.S. 1, 16 (1929).

[195]Serbian Eastern Orthodox Diocese v. Milivojevich, 426 U.S. 696 (1976). The Court did not pass upon the constitutionality of marginal civil court review of ecclesiastical determinations in cases of fraud or collusion.

[196]Presbytery of the Covenant v. First Presbyterian Church, 552 S.W.2d 865 (Tex. 1977).

[197]Loeb v. Geronemus, 66 So.2d 241 (Fla. 1953).

[198]Second Baptist Church v. Mount Zion Baptist Church, 466 P.2d 212 (Nev. 1970).

[199]Honey Creek Regular Baptist Church v. Wilson, 92 N.E.2d 419 (Ohio 1950).

other nonprofit, voluntary organization, provided only that no interpretation of religious doctrine is required.[200] It is clear that the First Amendment forbids courts in any context, including church membership expulsions, from involving themselves in the resolution of controversies requiring the interpretation of religious doctrine.[201] Many church membership expulsions do not involve questions of religious doctrine, however, and as to these there is no compelling reason, constitutional or otherwise, why courts should not be permitted to review the expulsions upon the request of expelled members in the same manner that they review membership expulsions in the context of other nonprofit organizations. It has been aptly stated that "[i]f the civil courts are to be bound by any sheet of parchment bearing the ecclesiastical seal and purporting to be a decree of a church court, they can easily be converted into handmaidens of arbitrary lawlessness."[202] It has also been noted that "[w]hen a faction of the church arrogates authority to itself, disrupts the organization and sets at naught well-defined rules of church order, there is no recourse left for those who desire their rights settled through orderly processes but resort to the courts."[203]

### c. *Preconditions to Civil Court Review*

It is well-settled that the courts will not review church membership expulsions unless the expelled members have exhausted all available procedures within their church for obtaining review of their expulsion. Thus, if an expelled member of a local church has not pursued all remedies provided by his local

---

[200]Baugh v. Thomas, 265 A.2d 675 (N.J. 1970); Waters v. Hargest, 593 S.W.2d 364 (Tex. 1979).

[201]Presbyterian Church in the United States v. Mary Elizabeth Blue Hull Memorial Presbyterian Church, 393 U.S. 440 (1969).

[202]Serbian Eastern Orthodox Diocese v. Milivojevich, 426 U.S. 696, 727 (1976) (Justice Rehnquist, dissenting). Justice Rehnquist also observed, in the same opinion, that "[t]o make available the coercive powers of civil courts to rubber-stamp ecclesiastical decisions of hierarchical religious associations, when such deference is not accorded similar acts of secular voluntary associations, would . . . itself create far more serious problems under the Establishment Clause." *Id.* at 734.

[203]Epperson v. Myers, 58 So.2d 150, 152 (Fla. 1952). *See also* Jones v. Wolf, 443 U.S. 595 (1979) (United States Supreme Court suggests that judicial review is permissible if restricted to an analysis based exclusively on "neutral principles" of law devoid of any interpretation of religious doctrine); I. Ellman, *Driven From the Tribunal: Judicial Resolution of Internal Church Disputes*, 69 CAL. L. REV. 1380 (1981) (arguing that judicial review of internal church disputes should be permitted as long as doctrinal interpretation not required).

church and a parent denomination for the review of his expulsion, the courts will not intervene.[204]

The United States Supreme Court has held that membership determinations made by ecclesiastical tribunals in hierarchical churches may not be reviewed by the courts, presumably under any circumstances, including review to ensure compliance with a church's charter and bylaws. The Court held:

> In short, the First and Fourteenth Amendments permit hierarchical religious organizations to establish their own rules and regulations for internal discipline and government, and to create tribunals for adjudicating disputes over these matters. When this choice is exercised and ecclesiastical tribunals are created to decide disputes over the government and direction of subordinate bodies, the Constitution requires that civil courts accept their decisions as binding upon them.[205]

The prevailing view is that judicial review of the membership determinations of congregational churches and of local hierarchical churches having complete autonomy in membership determinations is not in violation of the First Amendment, at least if the courts do not engage in any interpretation of religious doctrine.[206]

### d. Remedies for Improper Expulsion

A person who believes that he has been improperly expelled from membership in his church has a number of potential remedies available to him. First, he may be able to obtain judicial review of the expulsion if he resides in a jurisdiction that permits marginal civil court review of church membership determinations. If a court agrees to review the expulsion and finds that it was deficient on the basis of one of the grounds discussed in this section, it may declare the expulsion void and reinstate the expelled member.[207] Second, a wrongfully expelled member may be able to recover monetary damages.[208] Third, he may petition a court for an injunction prohibiting a church from interfering with his rights or privileges as a member.[209] Fourth, he may seek

---

[204]State ex rel. Nelson v. Ellis, 140 So.2d 194 (La. 1962), aff'd, 151 So.2d 544 (La. 1963); Rodyk v. Ukrainian Autocephalic Orthodox Church, 296 N.Y.S.2d 496 (1968), aff'd, 328 N.Y.S.2d 685 (1972).

[205]Serbian Eastern Orthodox Diocese v. Milivojevich, 426 U.S. 696, 724-25 (1976).

[206]Randolph v. First Baptist Church, 120 N.E.2d 485 (Ohio 1954).

[207]Ragsdall v. Church of Christ, 55 N.W.2d 539 (Iowa 1952).

[208]Louison v. Fischman, 168 N.E.2d 340 (Mass. 1960).

[209]David v. Carter, 222 S.W.2d 900 (Tex. 1949).

a declaratory judgment setting forth his rights.[210] Fifth, in some cases he may sue his church or certain of its members for defamation whether or not his expulsion is upheld.

*Defamation* generally is defined to include the following elements: (1) a public statement, whether oral or in writing; (2) reference to another; (3) that is false; and (4) which injures the reputation of the other. Truth is generally held to be an absolute defense to a defamation action. Thus if the allegedly defamatory statements were true, an expelled member will not be able to sue for defamation even if his reputation has been injured.

Defamation actions are limited in another important way. Most jurisdictions recognize that statements made by a person in a reasonable manner and for a proper purpose to others having a common interest with him in the communication are "qualifiedly privileged" and immune from attack unless they are made with malice. Malice in this context refers to either a knowledge that the communication was false or a reckless disregard concerning its truth or falsity.

The common interest among church members about church matters is likely sufficient to create a qualified privilege for communications between members on subjects relating to the church's interests. To illustrate, where expelled church members had been publicly referred to by other members as "totally unworthy of the continued confidence, respect and fellowship of a great church"; as willing to lie in order to harm their church; and as possessed of a vile spirit; a court concluded that the remarks were entitled to a qualified privilege. The court nevertheless considered the remarks defamatory because they had been made either recklessly or with a knowledge of their falsity.[211] In another case, an expelled member alleged that at various times in meetings of his religious group other members had stated that he was a disgrace to his religion, that his conduct was scandalous, that he was guilty of evil conduct and was a man of low character, and that his conduct was so bad that it could not be described publicly. A court, in finding such statements malicious, stated the general rule as follows:

> [M]embers of such bodies may report on the qualifications of applicants, prefer charges against fellow members, offer testimony in support of the charges, and make proper publications of any disciplinary action that may be taken, without liability for any resultant defamation, *so long as they act without malice.* The rule relative to qualified privilege is always subject to the limitation, as stated, that in connection with such activities the parties must act without malice. When a matter which otherwise would be a qualifiedly privileged communication is published falsely, fraudulently, and with express malice and intent to injure the persons

---

[210]Epperson v. Myers, 58 So.2d 150 (Fla. 1952).
[211]Brewer v. Second Baptist Church, 197 P.2d 713 (Cal. 1948).

against whom it is directed, the communication loses its qualifiedly privileged character and the parties lay themselves liable to a suit for damages in an action for libel or slander.[212]

## 5. PERSONAL LIABILITY OF MEMBERS

It is a fundamental characteristic of corporations that individual members will not be personally responsible for the misconduct of other members, so long as they do not participate personally in the misconduct or meaningfully ratify or affirm it. Each member of course is personally responsible for his own misconduct, and the corporation itself may be derivatively responsible for a member's misconduct. But other members of the corporation who were not involved in and did not affirm the wrongful act of another member ordinarily will not be personally responsible for it.

## §G. Meetings

### 1. IN GENERAL

Church charters and bylaws typically bestow substantial powers upon a church's membership. Under the prevailing view church members may exercise the authority conferred upon them only when acting at a meeting convened according to procedural requirements in the church's charter and bylaws or in applicable state law. Actions taken at irregularly called meetings generally are considered invalid unless subsequently ratified or affirmed at a duly convened meeting.

Church bylaws commonly call for annual general meetings of the church membership, and for such special meetings as the congregation or board of directors considers appropriate.

The pastor of the church, or the senior pastor of a church having more than one pastor on its staff, is legally authorized to preside at membership meetings if authorized by (1) church charter or bylaws, (2) established church custom, (3) applicable state nonprofit corporation law, or (4) the doctrine of inherent authority.

Although a church is free to determine the order of business to be followed at general or special meetings, the following order is commonly followed:

1. reading and approval of minutes
2. reports of officers, boards, and standing (that is, permanently established) committees

---

[212]Loeb v. Geronemus, 66 So.2d 241, 244 (Fla. 1953) (citations omitted). *See also* Joiner v. Weeks, 383 So.2d 101 (La. 1980), *cert. denied,* 385 So.2d 257 (La. 1980); Moyle v. Franz, 46 N.Y.S.2d 667 (1944), *aff'd,* 47 N.Y.S.2d 484 (1944).

3. reports of special committees (that is, committees appointed to exist only until they have completed a specific task)
4. special orders (that is, matters which have previously been assigned a type of special priority)
5. unfinished business and general orders (that is, matters previously introduced which have come over from the preceding meeting)
6. new business (that is, matters initiated in the present meeting)[213]

It is generally held that members have a right to express their views at church meetings since the very purpose of such meetings is to arrive at decisions through a free and open exchange of ideas. Thus, it has been held that the leaders of two opposing factions within a church had no authority to agree that a church membership meeting would be conducted without discussion.[214]

## 2. Procedural Requirements

A church's charter or bylaws typically specifies procedures for the convening and administration of church membership meetings. State nonprofit corporation law may impose additional procedural requirements on incorporated churches, although in most cases state corporation law will apply only if the church's charter or bylaws are silent. Where there is no specific charter, bylaw, or statutory provision governing church meetings, the established custom of the church generally will control.[215] For example, where it was the established custom of a church to give notice of the annual church membership meeting by public announcement during Sunday morning services on the two Sundays before the date set for the proposed meeting, a court ruled that the election of officers at a purported annual meeting was invalid when the custom was not followed.[216]

The procedural requirements causing the greatest amount of controversy are notice, quorum, and voting requirements. These subjects will be considered in turn.

### a. Notice

Church bylaws generally require that notice of the time and place of church membership meetings be given to the church membership. Bylaws occasionally require notice of the purposes of a meeting as well, particularly if some extraordinary matter is to be discussed. If a church is incorporated and its bylaws do not require notice requirements, the state nonprofit corporation law ordi-

---

[213]See, e.g., H. Robert, Robert's Rules of Order 21 (newly revised ed. 1981).
[214]Randolph v. Mount Zion Baptist Church, 53 A.2d 206 (N.J. 1947).
[215]McDaniel v. Quakenbush, 105 S.E.2d 94 (N.C. 1958).
[216]Coates v. Parchman, 334 S.W.2d 417 (Mo. 1960).

narily will contain the applicable requirements. Unincorporated churches that have no bylaws or written regulations are bound by their established customs regarding notice of church membership meetings. However, some courts have held that notice requirements established by custom can be disregarded if the notice actually given is more likely to provide notice to all church members than the form of notice prescribed by custom.[217]

A church must comply with the manner and method of giving notice prescribed in its charter or bylaws, in applicable state nonprofit corporation law, or by established church custom. Failure to follow applicable notice requirements will render a meeting and any action taken therein invalid. To illustrate, church membership meetings and all actions taken therein have been declared void in the following contexts: (1) notice of a special meeting was read publicly by a church secretary instead of by a church trustee as required by the applicable state nonprofit corporation law;[218] (2) a pastor publicly notified his congregation during a worship service that a special meeting would be convened immediately following the service; however, church bylaws stipulated that notice of special meetings had to be mailed to members at a prescribed time in advance of a meeting;[219] (3) a pastor convened a special meeting following a Sunday morning service without any notice other than an oral announcement during the service, despite an applicable provision in state nonprofit corporation law requiring written notice to be posted in a conspicuous place near the main entrance of the church for at least seven days before the meeting;[220] and (4) a small number of members present at a Wednesday evening church service publicly called a special meeting of the church membership for the following Saturday, in violation of an established church custom requiring notice to be read publicly during at least two Sunday morning services prior to such a meeting.[221]

The courts have held that action taken at an improperly called meeting will be invalid no matter how many members are present, and that even a majority of church members present at an improperly called meeting cannot "validate" the meeting by waiving the notice requirements.[222] However, action taken at an improperly called meeting can be ratified or affirmed by the church membership at a properly called meeting.[223]

It has also been held that the notice of a meeting should specify any business

---

[217]State Bank v. Wilbur Mission Church, 265 P.2d 821 (Wash. 1954).

[218]Hayes v. Brantley, 280 N.Y.S.2d 291 (1967).

[219]Mount Zion Baptist Church v. Second Baptist Church, 432 P.2d 328 (Nev. 1967).

[220]Bangor Spiritualist Church, Inc. v. Littlefield, 330 A.2d 793 (Me. 1975).

[221]In re Galilee Baptist Church, 186 So.2d 102 (Ala. 1966).

[222]Hollins v. Edwards, 616 S.W.2d 801 (Ky. 1981); Bangor Spiritualist Church, Inc. v. Littlefield, 330 A.2d 793 (Me. 1975).

[223]Hill v. Sargent, 615 S.W.2d 300 (Tex. 1981).

of an extraordinary nature or of great importance to be transacted.[224] The reasons for this requirement are to bring members interested in the proposed action to the meeting, and to allow preparation for the meeting. The purpose of a meeting need not otherwise be stated unless the church's charter or bylaws, applicable state nonprofit corporation law, or established custom so requires.

If notice has been given according to a church's bylaws, a meeting may not be challenged by a disgruntled minority. Thus, when oral notice of a special church membership meeting was announced from the church pulpit in accordance with the church's bylaws, a minority of members who had ceased attending the church and therefore did not receive actual notice of the meeting were not permitted to overturn the actions taken at the meeting on the basis of inadequate notice.[225]

### b. Quorum

Churches should and often do prescribe in their charter or bylaws the number of members that must be present at general or special membership meetings in order for business to be transacted. This minimum number is generally referred to as a quorum. State nonprofit corporation law ordinarily specifies a quorum for incorporated churches that have not otherwise so provided. Established church custom will control in the case of unincorporated churches having no bylaws or written regulations.

It is a fundamental principle of law that a majority of a quorum has the authority to act on behalf of the entire membership provided the meeting was properly called and a greater number or percentage of votes is not mandated by church charter or bylaws. This of course means that in some cases a minority of members can bind a church.[226]

If a church has no bylaw provision or established custom concerning quorums, it is unnecessary to demonstrate that a majority or any other percentage of the total membership attended a particular meeting in order to validate the action taken at the meeting.[227]

### c. Voting

Unless otherwise restricted by charter, bylaw, statute, or custom, every member of a church congregation is entitled to vote at a membership meeting. As noted in the preceding section, courts generally do not interfere with the membership determinations of local churches unless one of the narrow grounds

[224]Randolph v. First Baptist Church, 120 N.E.2d 485 (Ohio 1954).
[225]Gelder v. Loomis, 605 P.2d 1330 (Okla. 1980).
[226]Padgett v. Verner, 366 S.W.2d 545 (Tenn. 1963).
[227]State Bank v. Wilbur Mission Church, 265 P.2d 821 (Wash. 1954).

for marginal civil court review is present. Thus, a church will be permitted to determine its own membership unless a particular determination (1) is challenged on the basis of fraud or collusion; (2) affects a property, contract, or civil right; (3) involves the interpretation of an ambiguous condition of membership; or (4) in the case of membership expulsions, was not made by the appropriate body or was not made in accordance with the church's bylaws. Membership determinations of hierarchical churches probably are more insulated from civil court review than the determinations of congregational churches.

Church charters, bylaws, and customs, and applicable state nonprofit corporation laws occasionally do impose limitations on the right to vote. To illustrate, some nonprofit corporation laws restrict the right to vote in church membership meetings to members who have contributed financially to the support of the church.[228] Churches themselves sometimes enact similar resolutions or bylaws. For example, a church can adopt a resolution restricting the right to vote to members who are "paid up" and who do not neglect their offerings for three consecutive months. Such a resolution will prohibit from voting any member who has neglected to pay offerings for three consecutive months even if the failure to pay was a matter of conscience.[229]

If the right to vote is not restricted by charter, bylaw, custom, or statute, there is authority that all members of a church may vote in a church membership meeting regardless of age.[230] And, where the signing of a church's bylaws was a condition of church membership, a person who joined the church but failed to sign the bylaws was ineligible to vote.[231] Churches occasionally restrict the right to vote to members who have attended the church for a prescribed period, and of course such limitations must be satisfied in order for a member to be eligible to vote.

A member's right to vote may be lost by voluntary withdrawal from a church. Certainly, a member who quits attending a church and publicly states that he

---

[228]First Slovak Church of Christ v. Kacsur, 65 A.2d 93 (N.J. 1949) (members held not qualified to vote because they did not satisfy the statutory requirement that they "contribute regularly" to the support of their church); Anthony v. Cardin, 398 N.Y.S.2d 215 (1977) (holding that contributions of 10 cents per week were inadequate to satisfy the statutory requirement that voting members contribute to the support of the church).

[229]Sixth Baptist Church v. Cincore, 91 So.2d 922 (La. 1957).

[230]Hopewell Baptist Church v. Gary, 266 A.2d 593, 597 (N.J. 1970) (rejected contention that only members who had attained the age of 21 years be permitted to vote despite fact that almost two-thirds of a church's 900 members were under 21, since "[s]ound policy dictates that this court refrain from establishing such a limitation by judicial fiat"). See also In re Galilee Baptist Church, 186 So.2d 102 (Ala. 1966); Randolph v. Mount Zion Baptist Church, 53 A.2d 206 (N.J. 1947).

[231]Kubilius v. Hawes Unitarian Congregational Church, 79 N.E.2d 5 (Mass. 1948).

has quit the church and will never be back has abandoned his membership and no longer is eligible to vote in membership meetings.[232] But in many cases determining with certainty whether a member has voluntarily withdrawn from a church is difficult, since withdrawal is often a process that sometimes is temporarily or permanently reversed. Churches can reduce confusion in this area by defining voting membership in terms of attendance or financial support.

After determining the qualified voting members of a church who are present at a church membership meeting, a church must ensure that all other voting requirements imposed by charter, bylaw, custom, or statute are satisfied. Persistent trouble comes from the number of votes required to adopt a particular action. For example, if the church bylaws require a particular vote to be by a "majority of members," does this mean a majority of the total church membership or a majority of those members present at a duly convened membership meeting? If only a majority of those present at a membership meeting is required, then it is possible for an action to be adopted by a minority of the total church membership. To illustrate, if 60% of the total church membership attend a duly convened meeting, and 55% of those present vote to take a particular action, then the church has taken an official action even though only 33% (i.e., 55% of 60%) of the total church membership assented to it. Can this be said to constitute a vote by a majority of members?

Of course, a church can and should define the term *majority of members* to avoid this confusion. For example, a provision in a church's bylaws requiring that a particular kind of vote be by majority vote of the church's total membership would preclude action by a majority of members present at a duly called meeting unless they comprised a majority of the church's entire membership. But if a church nowhere defines *majority of members,* or any other term relating to the required number of votes needed to adopt an action, the fraction or percentage of votes needed to adopt an action generally has reference to the members present at a duly called meeting and not to the entire church membership.[233]

Occasionally, a church's charter, bylaws, and, in some cases, its constitution contain conflicting provisions regarding the required number of votes necessary for adoption of a particular action. As has been noted elsewhere, provisions in the charter control over provisions in the constitution, bylaws, or resolutions; provisions in the constitution control over provisions in the bylaws or resolutions; and provisions in the bylaws control over provisions in resolutions.[234] In most cases, an incorporated church is bound by the provisions of state nonprofit

---

[232]Lewis v. Wolfe, 413 S.W.2d 314 (Mo. 1967).

[233]Mack v. Huston, 256 N.E.2d 271 (Ohio 1970). *See generally* W. FLETCHER, *supra* note 21, at § 2020; MODEL NONPROFIT CORPORATION ACT § 16.

[234]*See* chapter 8, § B, *supra.*

corporation law only where it has not expressly provided otherwise in its own charter, constitution, or bylaws.

Votes can be cast orally, by show of hands, or by secret ballot. The method used is governed by the church's charter or bylaws. If the charter and bylaws are silent, established church custom will control. The members present at a meeting can also approve of a particular manner of voting if the church charter or bylaws do not speak to the subject. It has been held that a vote will be upheld even if it was not conducted by secret ballot as required by the corporate bylaws if no one objected to the vote during the meeting.[235] Absentee voting is not ordinarily permitted unless expressly sanctioned by charter, bylaw, custom, or statute.

Finally, it should be noted that members wishing to contest some irregularity in a particular election or vote must object to the irregularity at the meeting. One court has held that objections to voting procedures must start when a vote is being taken, not months later when the events have passed from peoples' minds and the matters that were voted on have been executed.[236]

### 3. MINUTES

The church secretary should prepare written minutes of every church membership meeting, being careful to note (1) the date of the meeting, (2) the number of members present, (3) the progression of every action from motion to final action, (4) some statement that each adopted action was approved by the necessary number of votes (a tally of the votes for and against a particular action should be inserted in the minutes if the vote is close or the action is of an extraordinary nature), and (5) a verbatim transcript of each approved action. Minutes should be signed by the church secretary, but this is not a legal requirement.[237]

The purpose of the minutes is to memorialize in a permanent and official form the actions taken by a church's membership. It has been said that the minutes are the "voice" of the corporation, and that a corporation will be bound by representations contained in its minutes that are relied upon by outsiders, even if the minutes were irregular.[238]

### 4. PARLIAMENTARY PROCEDURE

An organization may adopt any procedure that it desires for the conduct of membership meetings. *Robert's Rules of Order* or any other body of parlia-

[235]W. FLETCHER, *supra* note 21, at § 2017.
[236]Cosfol v. Varvoutis, 213 A.2d 331 (Pa. 1965).
[237]*Id.*
[238]W. FLETCHER, *supra* note 21, at § 2190.

mentary procedure is not necessarily binding unless specifically adopted.[239] Churches can adopt a specific body of parliamentary procedure by express choice contained in the church charter, bylaws, or resolutions, or by custom. If no body of parliamentary procedure has been adopted, either expressly or by custom, it has been held that the ordinary rules of parliamentary law should be observed in the conduct of a meeting.[240] It has also been held that the courts may review an action taken at a church membership meeting to ensure compliance with applicable parliamentary procedure.[241]

5. EFFECT OF PROCEDURAL IRREGULARITIES

It is the prevailing view that material procedural irregularities—such as disregard of notice, quorum, or voting requirements in a church's charter or bylaws—will invalidate a membership meeting and any actions taken therein, and that the civil courts will uphold the rights of those challenging the validity of such a meeting provided that no interpretation of religious doctrine is necessary.[242] A small minority of courts refuse to permit any judicial interference with the internal affairs of churches, and accordingly hold that civil courts cannot review the determinations of churches even where a lawsuit is brought alleging that the church disregarded its own procedures in the conduct of a meeting.[243] This view generally is based on the assumption that the First Amendment prohibits courts from interfering with the purely internal affairs of churches. Such a rendering of the First Amendment would appear to be too broad under the prevailing interpretation of that Amendment by the United States Supreme Court. It is true that there is no room for civil court review of any internal church decision based on the interpretation of religious doctrine. On this point all courts would agree. But, many internal church disputes involve the interpretation of purely secular language in church charters, bylaws, deeds, and trusts. The Supreme Court has suggested that there is room for marginal civil court review of the internal decisions of churches and church tribunals where the reviewing court can resolve the dispute solely on the basis of "neutral

[239]Abbey Properties Co. v. Presidential Insurance Co., 119 So.2d 74 (Fla. 1960).

[240]Randolph v. Mount Zion Baptist Church, 53 A.2d 206 (N.J. 1947).

[241]Umberger v. Johns, 363 So.2d 63 (Fla. 1978).

[242]Third Missionary Baptist Church v. Garrett, 158 N.W.2d 771 (Iowa 1968); Hollins v. Edmonds, 616 S.W.2d 801 (Ky. 1981); Bangor Spiritualist Church, Inc. v. Littlefield, 330 A.2d 793 (Me. 1975); Fast v. Smyth, 527 S.W.2d 673 (Mo. 1975); Atkins v. Walker, 200 S.E.2d 641 (N.C. 1973).

[243]Rodyk v. Ukrainian Autocephalic Orthodox Church, 296 N.Y.S.2d 496 (1968), aff'd, 328 N.Y.S.2d 685 (1972); Hill v. Sargent, 615 S.W.2d 300 (Tex. 1981).

principles" of law.[244] The Court specifically held that "neutral principles" of law include nondoctrinal language in charters, deeds, and bylaws.[245] One court in upholding the majority view observed that "we have no hesitancy in holding that this controversy is properly before us, our decisions being controlled entirely by neutral principles of law."[246]

Procedural requirements pertaining to notice, quorums, and voting generally involve no references to religious doctrine and thus actions adopted at a church membership meeting convened or conducted in violation of a church's procedural requirements ordinarily may be invalidated by a court of law.[247] In the case of incorporated churches, this rule has been justified on the ground that a religious corporation is an artificial entity created by law and capable of acting only in the manner prescribed by state law or its own internal regulations, and therefore compliance with such procedural requirements is a prerequisite to a valid meeting.[248]

### 6. JUDICIAL SUPERVISION OF CHURCH ELECTIONS

A court generally has the authority to supervise a church election to ensure compliance with applicable procedural requirements if the church requests such supervision or if certain members allege that the church has disregarded procedural requirements in the past.[249] And, it is clear that a court has the authority to order an election when a church board refuses to call one.[250]

### §H. Powers

It is often necessary to determine the nature and extent of a church's powers, for a church's actions may be subject to challenge if they exceed the church's authority. As has been noted elsewhere,[251] unincorporated churches possess only such authority as is granted to them by state law. Many states have enacted

---

[244]Jones v. Wolf, 443 U.S. 595 (1979). The Court in *Jones* expressly repudiated the apparent holding in Serbian Eastern Orthodox Diocese v. Milivojevich, 426 U.S. 696 (1976), that the courts *must* defer to the determinations of religious tribunals within hierarchical churches, by noting that the First Amendment did not require such a rule where no issue of religious doctrine is involved.

[245]*Id.*

[246]Bangor Spiritualist Church, Inc. v. Littlefield, 330 A.2d 793 (Me. 1975).

[247]*Id.*

[248]*Id.*

[249]Fast v. Smyth, 527 S.W.2d 673 (Mo. 1975); Second Baptist Church v. Mount Zion Baptist Church, 466 P.2d 212 (Nev. 1970).

[250]Willis v. Davis, 323 S.W.2d 847 (Ky. 1959).

[251]*See* chapter 8, § A, *supra.*

legislation enabling unincorporated churches to sue and be sued and to hold property in the name of trustees. But without any specific delegation of authority from the state, an unincorporated church has no legal powers and must act in the name of its members.

Most states have enacted some form of corporation law under which churches may incorporate. Often, a church may incorporate under either a general non-profit corporation law or a religious corporations law. State corporation law ordinarily bestows several specific powers upon organizations that incorporate, including the power to exist perpetually, to sue and be sued, to receive gifts, to acquire and own real or personal property, to sell or mortgage any of its property, to enter into contracts and incur liabilities, to invest its funds, to make donations, to elect officers and directors, and to make bylaws.[252] It has been held that statutes governing religious corporations reflect the public policy of granting religious organizations wide latitude in the conduct of their affairs, both spiritual and temporal.[253]

It is important to recognize that corporations derive their existence and powers from the state. It follows that corporations are without authority to do any act not expressly authorized by statute or implied from a power specifically granted.[254]

Some states place restrictions on the power of religious corporations to own property. These restrictions include limitations on the number of acres a religious corporation may own, limitations on the total dollar value of the property a religious corporation may own, limiting the property a religious corporation may own to only such property as is reasonably necessary for the corporation's purposes, and limiting the kinds of property that a religious corporation may own.[255]

Some states limit the power of religious corporations to sell or encumber property. For example, some states limit the power of churches to sell property without court approval[256] or without a specified percentage of voter approval.[257] A number of states limit the power of religious corporations to receive testamentary gifts. These restrictions generally fall into two categories: statutes limiting the amount of property that a religious organization may receive under

[252]MODEL NONPROFIT CORPORATION ACT § 5.

[253]Hopewell Baptist Church v. Gary, 266 A.2d 593 (N.J. 1970), aff'd, 270 A.2d 409 (N.J. 1970).

[254]Succession of Fisher, 103 So.2d 276 (La. 1958).

[255]See generally P. Kauper & S. Ellis, supra note 5, at 1545-46.

[256]Application of Church of St. Francis De Sales, 442 N.Y.S.2d 741 (1981) (applying section 12 of the New York Religious Corporations Law).

[257]MODEL NONPROFIT CORPORATION ACT § 44 (requiring approval of a two-thirds majority for a sale of all or substantially all of the property of a corporation).

a will, and statutes invalidating any testamentary gift to a religious organization if the will was executed within a prescribed time before the grantor's death. For example, some states prohibit certain testamentary gifts to a church if the will was executed within ninety days before the grantor's death.[258] Many states invalidate certain testamentary gifts that exceed one-third of the total value of the grantor's estate.[259] The subject of state limitations on testamentary gifts to charity is discussed in detail elsewhere.[260]

The powers of churches affiliated with religious hierarchies often are restricted or regulated by the parent ecclesiastical body. For example, the local churches of some denominations possess either limited authority or no authority to purchase or sell property, incur obligations, elect officers, or adopt bylaws.[261]

In addition to conferring specific, express powers upon charitable corporations, state nonprofit corporation laws typically contain a provision granting to incorporated charities the power to have and exercise all powers necessary or convenient to effect any or all of the purposes for which the organization is organized. Such a provision enables a church corporation to list in its charter various powers not specifically delegated by state corporation law. Therefore, in determining whether a church is empowered to take a particular action, the church charter must be reviewed in addition to the statute under which the church was incorporated. It is important to note, however, that a church may not include a power in its charter that would contravene law or public policy.[262] It is a well-settled rule of law that religious corporations, like business corporations, also possess implied authority to take all actions that are reasonably necessary in order to accomplish those powers expressly granted by charter or statute.[263]

---

[258]GA. CODE § 113-107; MISS. CODE ANN. § 671.

[259]CAL. PROBATE CODE § 41; IDAHO CODE § 14-326.

[260]See chapter 11, § B, infra.

[261]See, e.g., The Constitution of the United Presbyterian Church in the United States of America, Part II, Chapter XLII, which provides: "A particular church shall not sell, mortgage, or otherwise encumber any of its real property and it shall not acquire real property subject to an encumbrance or condition without the written permission of the presbytery . . . ."

[262]See generally W. FLETCHER, supra note 21, at § 2477; Molasky Enterprises, Inc. v. Carps, Inc., 615 S.W.2d 83, 86-87 (Mo. 1981) ("[T]he powers and existence of a corporation are derived from the state creating it. It functions under its charter which is a contract between it and the state in which it is organized. The statutory laws of the state applicable to it enter into and become a part of its articles of incorporation.").

[263]Synod of Chesapeake, Inc. v. City of Newark, 254 A.2d 611, 613-14 (Del. 1969). ("[A]ny contemporary church group, to be worth its salt, must necessarily perform non-religious functions . . . . Accordingly, such activities may not be banned as unrelated to church ritual."); Sales v. Southern Trust Co., 185 S.W.2d 623 (Tenn. 1945).

In summary, in determining whether a church corporation possesses the authority to take a particular action, the following analysis should be employed:

1. Review the statute under which the church was incorporated to determine if the power was expressly granted.
2. Review the church's charter to see if the power was expressly granted.
3. If the proposed church action is not expressly authorized by either statute or the church's charter, determine whether the church possesses implied authority to perform the act.
4. A corporation is never authorized to perform an act that is prohibited by law or public policy.

The courts generally have held that a corporation's bylaws cannot confer powers upon the corporation that are not granted by statute or charter, although the bylaws may regulate the manner in which a corporation's powers are exercised.[264]

It is often said that corporations lack the authority to perform any act that is illegal, contrary to public policy, or that would constitute a public nuisance.[265] Thus, it has been held that a church has no authority to exercise powers, even those expressly granted, in such a way as to cause a disturbance of the peace.[266]

Since most church corporations are incorporated under statutes expressly limiting them to nonprofit or religious purposes, churches generally have no authority to engage in substantial commercial enterprises for profit.

An act performed by a church corporation in excess of its express and implied powers is referred to as ultra vires. Considerable confusion surrounds the legal status of ultra vires actions. A majority of states permit ultra vires acts of a corporation to be challenged in only the following three situations:

1. a proceeding by a member or director against the corporation seeking an injunction prohibiting the corporation from doing an unauthorized act
2. a proceeding by the corporation against the officers or directors of the corporation for exceeding their authority
3. a proceeding by the state to dissolve the corporation or to enjoin the corporation from performing unauthorized acts

If the ultra vires act was a contract that has already been executed, it is generally held that the parties to the contract are entitled to compensation for the loss

[264]W. FLETCHER, *supra* note 21, at § 2494.
[265]*Id.* at § 2491.
[266]*See* chapter 11, § G, *infra.*

or damages sustained by them as a result of a judicial determination setting aside or prohibiting the performance of the contract.[267]

## §I. Merger and Consolidation

Although the terms *merger* and *consolidation* frequently are used interchangeably, they have separate legal meanings. In a merger, one corporation absorbs the other and remains in existence while the other is dissolved, whereas in a consolidation a new corporation is created and the consolidating corporations are extinguished.

It has been held that the decision whether to merge or consolidate is a religious question that should be of concern to no one other than the congregations involved, that the choice is one to be made by the respective members in the exercise of their religious beliefs, and that their freedom to make this choice is guaranteed by the First Amendment against federal or state interference.[268] Although the state may not interfere with a church's decision to merge or consolidate, a church must nevertheless follow those procedures in its own internal regulations or in applicable state corporation law for a valid merger or consolidation to occur. It must be stressed that state corporation laws governing mergers and consolidations may be separate and distinct. Thus, a church seeking to merge with another church may not employ a state law governing consolidations, and two churches desiring to consolidate may not use a state law governing mergers. State corporation laws often do contain a single procedure governing both mergers and consolidations, but this must not be assumed.

Unincorporated congregational churches generally are not restricted by state corporation law, and thus they may merge or consolidate whenever the respective congregations of the merging or consolidating churches so desire, provided that applicable provisions in each church's bylaws are followed.

It is well-settled that incorporated churches, like any other form of corporation, derive their legal existence and powers from the state. It follows that an incorporated church has the power to merge or consolidate only if such power is expressly delegated by state corporation law. Most religious and nonprofit corporation laws do grant churches the power to merge or consolidate. Such laws typically prescribe the following procedure:

1. The board of directors of each church desiring to merge or consolidate

---

[267] *See generally* W. FLETCHER, *supra* note 21, at chapter 40; Free For All Missionary Baptist Church, Inc. v. Southeastern Beverage & Ice Equipment Co., Inc., 218 S.E.2d 169 (Ga. 1975).

[268] Mount Zion Baptist Church v. Second Baptist Church, 432 P.2d 328 (Nev. 1967).

adopts a resolution approving of the proposed plan and submits it to a vote of members having voting rights at a general or special meeting.

2. Written notice of the proposed plan is given to each member eligible to vote.

3. The proposed plan is adopted if at least two-thirds of the votes cast approve of the plan.

4. Upon approval of the plan by the voting members, each corporation executes either articles of merger or articles of consolidation on a form prescribed by the secretary of state. This document sets forth the plan of merger or consolidation, the date of the meeting at which the plan was approved, a statement that a quorum was present and that the plan received at least two-thirds voter approval. The articles of merger or articles of consolidation are filed with the secretary of state.[269]

Church charters or bylaws may impose further requirements that must be followed.[270] And, if a proposed merger or consolidation would alter the doctrines of a church, it is essential to the validity of such a merger or consolidation that the church congregation possess the authority to change its doctrine and that the required number of members assent to the change.[271]

Church corporations affiliated with religious hierarchies must of course comply with applicable procedures in the constitution or bylaws of the parent ecclesiastical body.

The legal effect of a merger or consolidation generally is determined by state corporation law and the terms of the merger or consolidation agreement. State corporation law typically stipulates that all the properties of a church corporation that merges with another congregation belong to the surviving corporation. Similarly, the properties of two consolidating churches belong to the new corporation resulting from the consolidation. The surviving corporation in the case of a merger or the new corporation in the case of a consolidation is responsible for all the liabilities and obligations of each of the corporations so merged or consolidated. Thus, neither the rights of creditors nor any liens upon the property of such corporations is affected by a merger or consolidation.

## §J. Dissolution

Unincorporated churches having no affiliation with a religious hierarchy are mere voluntary associations of persons and may dissolve on their own initiative by a vote of the membership, by abandonment of the church, or by withdrawal

---

[269]MODEL NONPROFIT CORPORATION ACT §§ 42 et seq.

[270]In re Estate of Trimmer, 330 N.E.2d 241 (Ill. 1975); In re First Methodist Church, 306 N.Y.S.2d 969 (1970).

[271]See generally W. FLETCHER, supra note 21, at chapter 61.

of all members from the church, assuming that all applicable provisions in the church's bylaws or other internal rules are followed. The property of unincorporated churches generally is in the name of trustees. The IRS maintains that an unincorporated church is not eligible for exemption from federal income taxes unless its organizational document stipulates that all assets held in trust for the use and benefit of the church will pass to another charitable, tax-exempt organization upon dissolution of the church. Obviously, neither the trustees nor former members have any personal claim to trust assets following the dissolution of a church. This requirement is based on the fact that the Internal Revenue Code prohibits tax-exempt status to any organization whose net earnings or assets are payable to or for the benefit of any private individual.[272] If an unincorporated church has failed to include a provision in its organizational document providing for disposition of trust assets following dissolution of the church, a court may nonetheless direct that all trust assets pass to another charitable organization having similar purposes to those of the dissolved church. This power of the courts to determine the status of the trust assets of a dissolved church is known as the cy pres doctrine.

The dissolution of incorporated churches generally is regulated by state corporation law inasmuch as the state alone has the authority to dissolve those organizations it has created.[273] Corporate dissolutions may be either voluntary or involuntary. A voluntary corporate dissolution is accomplished by the corporation itself. Most state religious and nonprofit corporation laws contain a specific procedure for voluntary dissolution, which generally consists of the following elements:

1. The board of directors adopts a resolution recommending that the corporation be dissolved and directing that the question of dissolution be submitted to the church membership.

2. All voting members are notified in writing that the question of dissolution will be discussed at a special or general meeting of the members.

3. A resolution to dissolve the corporation is adopted if it receives at least two-thirds voter approval.

4. Notice of the dissolution is mailed to all creditors of the former corporation.

5. All corporate liabilities are paid. Any assets remaining after payment of liabilities are transferred to the organization or organizations, if any, prescribed in the dissolved corporation's charter or in the controlling rules of a church hierarchy, if any, with which the church is affiliated. If neither the charter nor controlling rules of a religious hierarchy specifies how corporate assets are to

[272]I.R.C. § 501(c)(3).
[273]W. FLETCHER, supra note 21, at § 7971.

be distributed following dissolution, the assets are conveyed to one or more organizations engaged in activities substantially similar to those of the dissolving corporation.

6. The articles of dissolution are executed. The articles set forth the name of the corporation, the date of the meeting of members at which the resolution to dissolve was adopted, and an acknowledgment that a quorum was present, that the resolution was adopted by at least two-thirds of the members present at such meeting, that all debts of the corporation have been paid, and that all remaining assets of the corporation have been transferred to the organization specified in the corporation's charter, or, if no organization is specified, to an organization engaged in activities substantially similar to those of the dissolving corporation.

7. The articles of dissolution are filed with the secretary of state. If the articles of dissolution conform to all legal requirements, the secretary of state issues to a representative of the dissolved corporation a certificate of dissolution, which is recorded with the office of the recorder of deeds of the county in which the church had been located.[274]

It is important to recognize that the IRS maintains that every incorporated church must contain a provision in its charter ensuring that in the event of a dissolution the assets of the church will pass to a tax-exempt organization. The IRS has stated that the following provision will suffice:

> Upon the dissolution of the corporation, the Board of Trustees shall, after paying or making provision for the payment of all of the liabilities of the corporation, dispose of all of the assets of the corporation exclusively for the purposes of the corporation in such manner, or to such organization or organizations organized and operated exclusively for charitable, educational, religious, or scientific purposes as shall at the time qualify as an exempt organization or organizations under section 501(c)(3) of the Internal Revenue Code of 1954 (or the corresponding provision of any future United States Internal Revenue Law), as the Board of Trustees shall determine. Any such assets not so disposed of shall be disposed of by the Court of Common Pleas of the county in which the principal office of the corporation is then located, exclusively for such purposes or to such organization or organizations, as said Court shall determine, which are organized and operated exclusively for such purposes.[275]

A church may of course specify in its charter the tax-exempt organization to which its assets will pass upon dissolution. These dissolution clauses are necessary in order to ensure the tax-exempt status of churches, since a church will not be considered entitled to tax-exempt status if any part of its net earnings

[274]MODEL NONPROFIT CORPORATION ACT §§ 45 *et seq.*
[275]IRS Publication 557.

or assets is payable to or for the benefit of any private individual.[276] It is important to emphasize that the property of a dissolved church will be conveyed to a charitable organization having purposes and activities substantially similar to those of the dissolved church if neither the church charter nor controlling rules of an ecclesiastical hierarchy provide otherwise. Thus, the courts have held that the members of a dissolving church had no authority to distribute church assets to a theological seminary or a servicemen's center, since neither organization was substantially related in purpose or activity to the dissolving church.[277] And, if a dissolving church is affiliated with a religious hierarchy whose internal rules require that the assets of a dissolving local church revert to the parent organization, the members of a dissolving church have no authority to distribute the church's assets to another organization.[278]

In addition to the procedures specified by state corporation law, church corporations are also bound by the procedural requirements of their own char- ters and bylaws, or the controlling rules of a parent ecclesiastical body, in a dissolution proceeding.

The corporation law of many states provides that church corporations may be dissolved involuntarily by the attorney general upon the occurrence of one or more of several grounds, including failure to pay fees prescribed by law, failure to file an annual report, fraudulent solicitation of funds, and exceeding the authority conferred by state corporation law.[279] Such laws typically permit church corporations to be dissolved involuntarily by a director or member if the directors are so deadlocked in the management of the corporation that irreparable injury to the corporation is being suffered; the acts of the directors are illegal, oppressive, or fraudulent; the corporation's assets are being wasted; or the corporation is unable to carry out its purposes.[280] To illustrate, one court found that an involuntary dissolution of a church was warranted where dissension over the dismissal of one minister and the hiring of another was so bitter that the church could no longer conduct its operations.[281]

---

[276]I.R.C. § 501(c)(3). The income tax regulations also specify that an organization is not organized exclusively for exempt purposes if its assets are payable to individuals or nonexempt organizations upon dissolution.

[277]Metropolitan Baptist Church v. Younger, 121 Cal. Rptr. 899 (1975).

[278]Polen v. Cox, 267 A.2d 201 (Md. 1970); German Evangelical Lutheran St. Johannes Church v. Metropolitan New York Synod of the Lutheran Church in America, 366 N.Y.S.2d 214 (1975), *appeal denied,* 378 N.Y.S.2d 1025 (1975).

[279]MODEL NONPROFIT CORPORATION ACT § 51.

[280]*Id.* at § 54(a).

[281]Fuimaono v. Samoan Congregational Christian Church, 135 Cal. Rptr. 799 (1977).

Finally, if a church in the regular course of its affairs is unable to pay its debts and obligations as they come due, the nonprofit corporation laws of many states permit an incorporated church to be involuntarily dissolved by a creditor whose claims are unsatisfied.[282]

[282]MODEL NONPROFIT CORPORATION ACT § 54(b).

# 9

# CHURCH PROPERTY DISPUTES

A study of the law of church property disputes must begin with the United States Supreme Court's decision in *Watson v. Jones*,[1] for the methodology outlined in *Watson* served as the principal means of resolving such disputes for nearly a century and continues to exert considerable influence. In *Watson*, the Court was faced with the problem of determining which of two factions in the Third or Walnut Street Presbyterian Church of Louisville, Kentucky, which had split in 1863 over the slavery controversy, was entitled to ownership of the church property. The Court began its analysis by observing: "The questions which have come before the civil courts concerning the rights of property held by ecclesiastical bodies, may, so far as we have been able to examine them, be profitably classified under three general heads . . . ."[2]

1. The first of these is when the property which is the subject of controversy has been, by the deed or will of the donor, or other instrument by which the property is held, by the express terms of the instrument devoted to the teaching, support, or spread of some specific form of religious doctrine or belief.

2. The second is when the property is held by a religious congregation which, by the nature of its organization, is strictly independent of other ecclesiastical associations, and so far as church government is concerned, owes no fealty or obligation to any higher authority.

3. The third is where the religious congregation or ecclesiastical body holding the property is but a subordinate member of some general church organization in which there are superior ecclesiastical tribunals with a general and ultimate

---

[1] 80 U.S. 679 (1871) [hereinafter cited as *Watson*].
[2] *Id.* at 722.

power of control more or less complete, in some supreme judicatory over the whole membership of that general organization.[3]

As to the first type of case, the Court concluded that "it would seem . . . to be the obvious duty of the Court . . . to see that the property so dedicated is not diverted from the trust which is thus attached to its use,"[4] and

[t]hough the task may be a delicate one and a difficult one, it will be the duty of the court in such cases, when the doctrine to be taught or the form of worship to be used is definitely and clearly laid down, to inquire whether the party accused of violating the trust is holding or teaching a different doctrine, or using a form of worship which is so far variant as to defeat the declared objects of the trust.[5]

As to the second type of case, the Court concluded:

In such cases where there is a schism which leads to a separation into distinct and conflicting bodies, the rights of such bodies to the use of the property must be determined by the ordinary principles which govern voluntary associations. If the principle of government in such cases is that the majority rules, then the numerical majority of members must control the right to the use of the property.[6]

The Court went on to observe:

This ruling admits of no inquiry into the existing religious opinions of those who comprise the legal or regular organization; for, if such were permitted, a very small minority, without any officers of the church among them, might be found to be the only faithful supporters of the religious dogmas of the founders of the church. There being no such trust imposed upon the property when purchased or given, the Court will not imply one for the purpose of expelling from its use those who by regular succession and order constitute the church, because they may have changed in some respect their views of religious truth.[7]

In summary, *Watson* held that property disputes in a purely congregational church are to be decided by majority rule, and that this rule would apply even if the majority had defected from the faith of the church's founders.

As to the third type of case, the Court concluded:

---

[3]*Id.* at 722-23.
[4]*Id.* at 723.
[5]*Id.* at 724.
[6]*Id.* at 725.
[7]*Id.*

In this class of cases we think the rule of action which should govern civil courts
. . . is, that, whenever the questions of discipline, or of faith, or ecclesiastical
rule, custom, or law have been decided by the highest of these church judicatories
to which the matter has been carried, the legal tribunals must accept such decisions as final, and as binding on them, in their application to the case before
them.
. . . .

All who unite themselves to such a body do so with an implied consent to this
government, and are bound to submit to it. But it would be a vain consent and
would lead to the total subversion of such religious bodies, if anyone aggrieved
by one of their decisions could appeal to the secular courts and have them reversed. It is of the essence of these religious unions, and of their right to establish
tribunals for the decision of questions arising among themselves, that those decisions should be binding in all cases of ecclesiastical cognizance, subject only to
such appeals as the organism itself provides for.[8]

This third holding of *Watson* became known as the compulsory deference rule—
courts must defer to the determinations of church tribunals with respect to
"questions of discipline or of faith, or ecclesiastical rule, custom, or law," and,
by implication, to *any* decision of a church tribunal.

In the years following *Watson,* nearly every court that decided a church
property dispute cited *Watson* and claimed to be following its methodology.
In cases involving express trusts and hierarchical churches (the first and third
"general heads"), the professed adherence to *Watson* was largely real.

But soon after *Watson* was decided, cases involving the ownership of property
in divided congregational churches (the second "general head") began to deviate
from the rule enunciated in *Watson*—that the majority in such congregations
should dictate the ownership of church property whether or not that majority
remained faithful to the doctrine of the church's founders. The seeming inequity
of this rule prompted many courts to disregard *Watson.* Thus, many courts
adopted the implied trust doctrine, under which church properties were deemed
to be held in trust for the benefit of those members adhering to the original
doctrines of the church.[9] The property of congregational churches following a

---

[8]*Id.* at 727, 729.

[9]*See, e.g.,* Davis v. Ross, 53 So.2d 544 (Ala. 1951); Holiman v. Dovers, 366 S.W.2d
197 (Ark. 1963); Chatfield v. Dennington, 58 S.E.2d 842 (Ga. 1950); Sorrenson v. Logan,
177 N.E.2d 713 (Ill. 1961); Pentecostal Tabernacle of Muncie v. Pentecostal Tabernacle
of Muncie, 146 N.E.2d 573 (Ind. 1957); Ragsdall v. Church of Christ, 55 N.W.2d 539
(Iowa 1952); Huber v. Thorn, 371 P.2d 143 (Kan. 1962); Philpot v. Minton, 370 S.W.2d
402 (Ky. 1963); Davis v. Scher, 97 N.W.2d 137 (Mich. 1959); Protestant Reformed
Church v. Tempelman, 81 N.W.2d 839 (Minn. 1957); Mills v. Yount, 393 S.W.2d 96
(Mo. 1965); Reid v. Johnston, 85 S.E.2d 114 (N.C. 1954); Beard v. Francis, 309 S.W.2d
788 (Tenn. 1957); Baber v. Caldwell, 152 S.E.2d 23 (Va. 1967); Anderson v. Byers, 69
N.W.2d 227 (Wis. 1955).

church split thus went to the faction adhering to the original doctrines of the church, whether that faction represented a majority or a minority of the church membership. This obviously was contrary to the spirit if not the letter of *Watson,* wherein the Court had observed: "There being no such trust imposed upon the property when purchased or given, the Court will not imply one for the purpose of expelling from its use those who by regular succession and order constitute the church, because they may have changed in some respect their views of religious truth."[10]

Several other courts held that if a majority of the members of a congregational church voted to change the denominational ties of the congregation, church property would be vested in the minority desiring to remain faithful to the original denomination.[11] Some courts applied the law of corporations to vest ownership of property in a minority faction of a congregational church where the majority had voted to deviate from the original doctrines. To illustrate, one court observed:

> It is the law of all corporations that a mere majority of its members cannot divert the corporate property to uses foreign to the purposes for which the corporation was formed. There is no difference between church and other corporations in this regard. Where a church corporation is formed for the purpose of promoting certain defined doctrines of religious faith, which are set forth in its articles of incorporation, any church property which it acquires is impressed with a trust to carry out such purpose, and a majority of the congregation cannot divert the property to other inconsistent religious uses against the protest of a minority, however small. The matter of use of the property of the church corporation, within the range of its corporate powers, may be determined by the majority of the congregation, but no majority, even though it embrace all members but one, can use the corporate property for the advancement of a faith antagonistic to that for which the church was established and the corporation formed.[12]

A few courts remained true to the ruling in *Watson* and awarded title to congregational church property to the majority faction without any consideration of church doctrine.[13]

---

[10] 80 U.S. 679 at 725.

[11] *See, e.g.,* Holt v. Scott, 42 So.2d 258 (Ala. 1949); Ables v. Garner, 246 S.W.2d 732 (Ark. 1952); Wright v. Smith, 124 N.E.2d 363 (Ill. 1955); Hughes v. Grossman, 201 P.2d 670 (Kan. 1949); Scott v. Turner, 275 S.W.2d 421 (Ky. 1954); Blauert v. Schupmann, 63 N.W.2d 578 (Minn. 1954); Montgomery v. Snyder, 320 S.W.2d 283 (Mo. 1958); Reid v. Johnston, 85 S.E.2d 114 (N.C. 1954); Beard v. Francis, 309 S.W.2d 788 (Tenn. 1957).

[12] Lindstrom v. Tell, 154 N.W. 969 (Minn. 1915).

[13] *See, e.g.,* Booker v. Smith, 214 S.W.2d 513 (Ark. 1948); Ennix v. Owens, 271 S.W. 1091 (Ky. 1925); Holt v. Trone, 67 N.W.2d 125 (Mich. 1954).

The wholesale disregard of *Watson's* holding with respect to congregational churches was reformed by the United States Supreme Court nearly a century after *Watson* in the landmark decision of *Presbyterian Church in the United States v. Mary Elizabeth Blue Hull Memorial Presbyterian Church.*[14] The question presented in *Hull* was whether a local Presbyterian church could retain title to its property after disassociating itself from the Presbyterian Church in the United States. In 1966, the membership of the Hull Memorial Presbyterian Church of Savannah, Georgia, voted to withdraw from the parent body on the grounds that it had so departed from the original tenets of the Presbyterian faith that it could no longer be considered the Presbyterian Church. Specifically, the Hull church majority contended that the parent body had departed from Presbyterianism in "making pronouncements and recommendations concerning civil, economic, social and political matters, giving support to the removal of Bible reading and prayer by children in the public schools, . . . causing all members to remain in the National Council of Churches of Christ and willingly accepting its leadership which advocated . . . the subverting of all parental authority, civil disobedience and intermeddling in civil affairs," and also in "disseminating publications denying the Holy Trinity and violating the moral and ethical standards of faith." Accordingly, the local church argued that it had not disaffiliated itself from Presbyterianism, but rather that the Presbyterian Church in the United States had disassociated itself from Presbyterianism, and hence the parent denomination had no right to claim an interest in the property of the local church.

A state trial court ruled that the parent body had indeed abandoned Presbyterianism, and thus the Hull church was entitled to retain title to its property. The Supreme Court of Georgia affirmed. However, the United States Supreme Court reversed both rulings, concluding that

> the First Amendment severely circumscribes the role that civil courts may play in resolving church property disputes. It is obvious, however, that not every civil court decision as to property claimed by a religious organization jeopardizes values protected by the First Amendment. Civil courts do not inhibit free exercise of religion merely by opening their doors to disputes involving church property. And there are neutral principles of law, developed for use in all property disputes, which can be applied without "establishing" churches to which property is awarded. But First Amendment values are plainly jeopardized when church property litigation is made to turn on the resolution by civil courts of controversies over religious doctrine and practice. If civil courts undertake to resolve such controversies in order to adjudicate the property dispute, the hazards are ever present of inhibiting the free development of religious doctrine and of implicating secular interests in matters of purely ecclesiastical concern. Because of these hazards,

[14]393 U.S. 440 (1969) [hereinafter cited as *Hull*].

the First Amendment enjoins the employment of organs of government for essentially religious purposes . . . ; the Amendment therefore commands civil courts to decide church property disputes without resolving underlying controversies over religious doctrine. Hence, States, religious organizations, and individuals must structure relationships involving church property so as not to require the civil courts to resolve ecclesiastical questions.[15]

*Hull* may thus be reduced to the following two principles:

1. Civil courts *are forbidden* by the First Amendment to decide church property disputes if the resolution of such disputes is dependent upon the interpretation of religious doctrine.
2. Civil courts *can* decide church property disputes consistently with the First Amendment if they do so on the basis of principles involving no analysis of religious doctrine. Illustratively, the Court observed that there are "neutral principles of law developed for use in all property disputes, which can be applied without 'establishing' churches to which property is awarded." (Even so, the Court neither described what it meant by "neutral principles of law," nor mentioned other doctrinally neutral and hence acceptable grounds for resolving church property disputes.)

In effect, *Hull* wiped away much of the gloss that had been judicially applied to circumvent the second holding of *Watson:* that the majority faction in a congregational church has the right to all church property whether or not it supports or deviates from the original doctrines of the church. No longer could civil courts award congregational church property to a minority faction as a result of a judicial interpretation of religious doctrine. The first ruling in *Watson*— that property received by a church in an instrument expressly limiting the use of such property to the adherents of a particular religious doctrine or belief— was invalidated by *Hull* to the extent that civil courts are called upon to interpret religious doctrine. In many cases of course, the civil courts could determine the ownership of property conveyed to a church subject to an express trust, for no interpretation of religious doctrine would be involved. Thus, Justice Harlan, concurring in *Hull,* noted:

> I do not . . . read the Court's opinion to . . . hold that the Fourteenth Amendment forbids civilian courts from enforcing a deed or will which expressly and clearly lays down conditions limiting a religious organization's use of the property which is granted. If, for example, the donor expressly gives his church some money on the condition that the church never ordain a woman as a minister or elder . . . or never amend certain specified articles of the Confession of Faith, he is entitled

---

[15]*Id.* at 449.

to his money back if the condition is not fulfilled. In such a case, the church should not be permitted to keep the property simply because church authorities have determined that the doctrinal innovation is justified by the faith's basic principles.[16]

Finally, the Supreme Court failed to discuss the effect of its decision on the third ruling of *Watson*—that the decision of an ecclesiastical judicatory is binding upon a local church in a hierarchical denomination. This omission was unfortunate and gave rise to much confusion.

In summary, the Supreme Court's decision in *Hull* was deficient in three respects: (1) it sanctioned a "neutral principles of law" approach to resolving church property disputes, but failed to describe what it meant by the phrase; (2) it implied that the neutral principles of law approach was one of many acceptable methods of resolving church property disputes, but it failed to describe any other methods; and (3) it failed to explain the relationship between a neutral principles of law approach and the compulsory deference approach (*i.e.*, civil courts are compelled to defer to the rulings of church tribunals) of *Watson*.

Subsequent cases have provided further clarification. In *Maryland and Virginia Eldership of the Churches of God v. Church of God*,[17] the United States Supreme Court was asked to review the constitutionality of the methodology employed by the courts of Maryland in resolving church property disputes. The Maryland approach involved the inspection by the courts of nondoctrinal provisions in (1) state statutes governing the holding of property by religious corporations; (2) language in the deeds conveying the properties in question to the local church corporations; (3) the terms of the charters of the corporations; and (4) provisions in the constitution of a parent denomination relating to the ownership and control of church property. Maryland courts awarded title to disputed church property according to the wording and effect of such documents, provided that this could be done without any inquiries into religious doctrine. The Supreme Court, in a *per curiam* opinion, summarily approved of the Maryland approach to the resolution of church property disputes.

In a concurring opinion, Justice Brennan, who had written the Court's opinion in *Hull*, attempted to resolve some of the questions raised by the *Hull* decision. First, Justice Brennan attempted to define the term *neutral principles of law*:

[C]ivil courts can determine ownership by studying deeds, reverter clauses and general state corporation laws. Again, however, general principles of property law

---

[16]*Id.* at 452.
[17]396 U.S. 367 (1970) [hereinafter cited as *Maryland & Virginia Eldership*].

may not be relied upon if their application requires civil courts to resolve doctrinal issues. For example, provisions in deeds or in a denomination's constitution for the reversion of local church property to the general church, if conditioned upon a finding of departure from doctrine, could not be civilly enforced.[18]

Next, Justice Brennan suggested two other acceptable means of resolving church property disputes:

> [T]he States may adopt the approach of *Watson v. Jones* and enforce the property decisions made within a church of congregational polity "by a majority of its members or by such other local organism as it may have instituted for the purpose of ecclesiastical government," and within a church of hierarchical polity by the highest authority that has ruled on the dispute at issue, unless "express terms" in the "instrument by which the property is held" condition the property's use or control in a specified manner.[19]
> . . . .
> [Another] approach is the passage of special statutes governing church property arrangements in a manner that precludes state interference in doctrine. Such statutes must be carefully drawn to leave control of ecclesiastical polity, as well as doctrine, to church governing bodies.[20]

Finally, Justice Brennan emphasized that "a State may adopt *any* one of various approaches for settling church property disputes so long as it involves no consideration of doctrinal matters, whether the ritual and liturgy of worship or the tenets of faith."[21]

Thus, a court can properly resolve a church property dispute if it can do so solely on the basis of nondoctrinal language in deeds, state corporation laws, constitutions and bylaws of local churches or of parent ecclesiastical bodies, or state statutes pertaining to church property arrangements. Accordingly, a court could not intervene in a church property dispute involving a deed containing a reverter clause specifying that title to church property reverts to the parent ecclesiastical body if the local church deviates from the doctrine of the parent body, since the court would necessarily become involved in an interpretation

[18]*Id.* at 370.

[19]*Id.* at 369. Note that the concurring opinion emphasized that the civil courts "do not inquire whether the relevant church governing body has power under religious law to control the property in question. Such a determination, unlike the identification of the governing body, frequently necessitates the interpretation of ambiguous law and usage." *Id.* at 369. The concurring opinion concluded that "the use of the *Watson* approach is consonant with the prohibitions of the First Amendment only if the appropriate church governing body can be determined without the resolution of doctrinal questions and without extensive inquiry into religious polity." *Id.* at 370.

[20]*Id.* at 370.

[21]*Id.* at 368.

of religious doctrine. But a reverter clause conditioned on a disaffiliation of a local church could be enforced by the courts, since enforcement would involve the nondoctrinal determination of whether or not a disaffiliation had occurred.

Further, a minority faction in a congregational church remaining faithful to the original doctrines of the church can no longer contend that the state law of corporations is violated when a majority votes to divert corporate property to uses foreign to the purposes for which the corporation was formed, since this obviously will necessitate interpretation of religious doctrine. If the constitution and bylaws of a parent ecclesiastical body provide for the reversion of local church property to the parent body itself in the event of a disaffiliation by a local church, the civil courts will intervene and enforce such a provision since it would not involve a question of religious doctrine. However, if the reverter clause conditioned reversion upon a departure or deviation from the doctrines of the parent body, an interpretation of religious doctrine would become necessary and accordingly such a clause would not be judicially enforceable.

Finally, it should be noted that the Court in *Maryland & Virginia Eldership* commented that civil courts can examine the ecclesiastical rulings of church judicatories in church property disputes to ensure that such rulings are not the product of "fraud, collusion, or arbitrariness."

In *Adickes v. Adkins,*[22] the Supreme Court of South Carolina suggested that when a majority of the membership in a local church votes to disaffiliate the church from a parent denomination, a minority desiring to remain faithful to the parent church will receive title to church property. The court observed:

> Counsel . . . argues the lower court should be reversed because "neutral principles of law" require that the property in question should be in the possession and control of the appellants as representing the majority of the members of the First Presbyterian Church of Rock Hill . . . . For this proposition appellants rely largely on the case of *Presbyterian Church in the United States v. Mary Elizabeth Blue Hull Memorial Presbyterian Church* . . . . A review of that case convinces us that it is of no comfort to the appellants here . . . . By a determination of this case, this Court exercises no role in determining ecclesiastical questions. We merely settle a dispute on the question of identity, which in turn necessarily settles a dispute involving the control of property. . . .

> The appellants voluntarily associated themselves with the First Presbyterian Church of Rock Hill and became subject to the discipline and government of the Presbyterian Church in the United States. They voluntarily severed their connection, and when they did they forfeited any right to the use and possession of the property of that church under the long established law of the church and of South Caro-

22215 S.E.2d 442 (S.C. 1975), *cert. denied,* 423 U.S. 913 (1975).

lina. . . . By joining the First Presbyterian Church of Rock Hill the members did not acquire such an interest in the property that they are entitled to take with them upon seceding. The property belonged to the First Presbyterian Church of Rock Hill before the members joined the church, and it belongs to the same after they have withdrawn. They simply are not now a part of that church. There is nothing in the ruling of the lower court, nor in our ruling today, which establishes, sponsors, advances, or supports either the religious belief of the majority or the minority in this case. This Court has traditionally avoided any intrusion upon religious matters and has confined its rulings in such cases to identifying the faction which represents the church after the schism occurred. . . . In so doing, we applied neutral principles of law referred to in *Hull*.[23]

Identifying the church, when a majority faction votes to disaffiliate, involves no interpretation of religious doctrine. It is a doctrinally neutral act, and hence is consistent with *Hull*.

In *Serbian Eastern Orthodox Diocese v. Milivojevich*,[24] the Supreme Court strongly affirmed *Watson's* compulsory deference approach to resolving church property disputes:

In short, the First and Fourteenth Amendments permit hierarchical religious organizations to establish their own rules and regulations for internal discipline and government, and to create tribunals for adjudicating disputes over these matters. When this choice is exercised and ecclesiastical tribunals are created to decide disputes over the government and direction of subordinate bodies, the Constitution requires that civil courts accept their decisions as binding upon them.[25]

The Court also held that civil courts could not review the rulings of church tribunals for arbitrariness, although it did imply that courts could review such rulings for fraud or collusion.

The Court's emphatic endorsement of the compulsory deference rule in *Serbian* caused considerable confusion about the continuing validity of the

---

[23]*Id.* at 444-45. *Accord* Mills v. Baldwin, 362 So.2d 2 (Fla. 1978), *vacated,* 443 U.S. 914 (1979), *on remand,* 377 So.2d 971 (Fla. 1979), *cert. denied,* 446 U.S. 983 (1980); Church of God in Christ, Inc. v. Stone, 452 F. Supp. 612 (D. Kan. 1976); Colin v. Iancu, 267 N.W.2d 438 (Mich. 1978); Diocese of Newark v. Burns, 417 A.2d 31 (N.J. 1980), *cert. denied,* 449 U.S. 1131 (1981); Protestant Episcopal Church v. Graves, 391 A.2d 563 (N.J. 1978), *aff'd,* 401 A.2d 548 (N.J. 1979), *aff'd,* 417 A.2d 19 (N.J. 1980), *cert. denied,* 449 U.S. 1131 (1981); Presbytery of the Covenant v. First Presbyterian Church of Paris, Inc., 552 S.W.2d 865 (Tex. 1977). *But see* Protestant Episcopal Church v. Barker, 171 Cal. Rptr. 541 (1981), *cert. denied,* 454 U.S. 864 (1982).

[24]426 U.S. 696 (1976) [hereinafter cited as *Serbian*].

[25]*Id.* at 724-25.

neutral principles of law approach. What, for example, would be the effect of a church tribunal's ruling in a church property dispute in a jurisdiction that followed the neutral principles of law approach? Would neutral principles supersede the church tribunal's ruling? Once again, the need for clarification was evident.

In *Jones v. Wolf*,[26] which was decided in 1979, the Supreme Court again turned its attention to church property disputes. Before analyzing *Jones*, it would be helpful to summarize the law of church property disputes as it existed prior to that decision:

1. Where property is conveyed to a local church by an instrument that contains an express provision restricting the use of such property, such a restriction will be recognized by the civil courts if this can be done without any consideration of religious doctrine. If a consideration of religious doctrine would be necessary, then the courts will not be able to resolve the question of ownership on the basis of the restrictive provision.[27]

2. When a split occurs in a local congregational church, and a dispute arises as to the ownership of such property, courts may resolve the dispute in any of the following four ways:

*Method 1.* Civil courts may resolve the dispute on the basis of neutral principles of law, provided that this can be done without inquiries into religious doctrine. Neutral principles of law include nondoctrinal language in the following types of documents:

    a. deeds[28]
    b. local church charters[29]
    c. constitution and bylaws of local church, and of parent ecclesiastical body[30]

*Method 2.* Civil courts may resolve the dispute on the basis of the *Watson* rule of deference to the will of a majority of the members of a congregational church.[31]

*Method 3.* Civil courts may resolve the dispute on the basis of state statutes governing the holding of property by religious corporations, provided that application of such statutes involves no inquiries into religious doctrine.[32]

*Method 4.* Civil courts may resolve the dispute on the basis of any other

[26]443 U.S. 595 (1979) [hereinafter cited as *Jones*].

[27]*Maryland & Virginia Eldership*, 396 U.S. 367, 369 (1970) (Brennan, J., concurring).

[28]*Maryland & Virginia Eldership*, 396 U.S. 367, 370 (1970) (Brennan, J., concurring).

[29]*Id.*

[30]*Id.*

[31]*See* note 6, *supra*, and accompanying text.

[32]*See* note 20, *supra*, and accompanying text.

methodology that they may devise "so long as it involves no consideration of doctrinal matters, whether the ritual and liturgy of worship or the tenets of faith."[33]

When a split occurs in a local hierarchical church, and a dispute arises as to the ownership of church property, courts may resolve the dispute in any of the following three ways:

*Method 1.* Civil courts may resolve the dispute on the basis of neutral principles of law, provided that this can be done without inquiries into religious doctrine. Neutral principles of law include nondoctrinal language in the following types of documents:

    a. deeds[34]

    b. local church charter[35]

    c. constitution and bylaws of local church, and of parent ecclesiastical body[36]

*Method 2.* Civil courts may resolve the dispute on the basis of the *Watson* compulsory deference rule, under which courts defer to the rulings of church tribunals in matters involving religious doctrine and polity, as well as in church property controversies.[37]

*Method 3.* Civil courts may resolve the dispute on the basis of state statutes governing the holding of property by religious corporations, provided that application of such statutes involves no inquiries into religious doctrine.

In *Jones,*[38] the United State Supreme Court was confronted with a dispute over the ownership of property following a schism in a local church affiliated with the Presbyterian Church in the United States (PCUS). The church had been organized in 1904, and had always been affiliated with the PCUS (a hierarchical denomination). In 1973, the church membership voted (164 to 94) to separate from the PCUS. The majority informed the PCUS of its decision, and then united with another denomination, the Presbyterian Church in America. The PCUS appointed a commission to investigate the dispute. The commission ultimately issued a ruling declaring the minority faction to be "the true congregation" and withdrawing from the majority faction "all authority" to continue to hold services at the church. The majority took no part in the commission's inquiry, and did not appeal the ruling to a higher PCUS tribunal.

---

[33]*Maryland & Virginia Eldership,* 396 U.S. 367, 368 (1970) (Brennan, J., concurring).

[34]*See* note 28, *supra,* and accompanying text.

[35]*See* note 29, *supra,* and accompanying text.

[36]*See* note 30, *supra,* and accompanying text.

[37]*See* note 8, *supra,* and accompanying text.

[38]443 U.S. 595 (1979).

The minority faction brought suit against the majority, after it became obvious that the majority was not going to honor the commission's ruling. The Georgia courts held that there was no neutral principle of law vesting any interest in the church property in the PCUS, and that as a result the local congregation itself had to determine the disposition of the property. On the ground that religious associations are generally governed by majority rule, the Georgia Supreme Court ultimately awarded the property to the majority faction that wanted to disaffiliate. The minority appealed the matter directly to the United States Supreme Court. The Court accordingly was confronted with a situation in which a church tribunal's decision in a property dispute conflicted with the decision reached by the courts. The Court characterized the issue as "whether civil courts . . . may resolve the dispute on the basis of 'neutral principles of law,' or whether they must defer to the resolution of an authoritative tribunal of the hierarchical church."

The Supreme Court began its opinion by reiterating the principles enunciated in *Hull* and *Watson* that "the First Amendment prohibits civil courts from resolving church property disputes on the basis of religious doctrine and practice,"[39] and that civil courts must "defer to the resolution of issues of *religious doctrine or polity* by the highest court of a hierarchical church organization."[40]

The Court also prefaced its decision by observing that a hierarchical church was involved, that the controversy was intimately connected with Georgia law, and that "a State may adopt *any* one of various approaches for settling church property disputes so long as it involves no consideration of doctrinal matters . . . ."

Having established these general guidelines, the Court proceeded with an analysis of the methodology applied by the Georgia courts in resolving church property disputes. In essence, the Georgia methodology involved a two-step process. First, the courts determined whether neutral principles of law imposed a trust upon local church property in favor of a parent denomination. If such a trust existed, and its validity was not dependent upon any analysis of religious doctrine or polity, then the courts would give the property in dispute to the parent denomination. If neutral principles of law did not impose such a trust, then the property was subject to control by the local congregation, at least if title to the church property was vested in the local church or church trustees. The second step of the Georgia methodology, employed when neutral principles of law did not impose a trust and the local congregation was divided, permitted courts to award disputed church property to the majority of the church members provided that this presumptive rule of majority representation was not overcome by a showing that neutral principles of law dictated another result.

[39]Note 14, *supra,* at 449.
[40]Note 1, *supra,* at 733-34 (emphasis added).

The Supreme Court approved of this methodology, provided the Georgia courts could demonstrate that Georgia in fact had adopted "a presumptive rule of majority representation, defeasible upon a showing that the identity of the local church is to be determined by some other means." The Court sent the case back to the Georgia courts for proof that Georgia in fact had adopted such a rule.

The Court's decision clarified the scope of the compulsory deference rule, and the rule's relationship to the neutral principles of law approach. The Court ultimately concluded that civil courts are compelled to defer to the rulings of church tribunals only with respect to "issues of religious doctrine or polity," and not with respect to church property disputes: "We cannot agree . . . that the First Amendment requires the States to adopt a rule of compulsory deference to religious authority in resolving church property disputes . . . ."[41] The compulsory deference rule was accordingly limited to matters of religious doctrine and polity.

The four dissenting Justices were distressed by the Court's limitation of the compulsory deference rule to matters of religious doctrine and polity. The dissenters argued that "in each case involving an intrachurch dispute—including disputes over church property—the civil court must focus directly on ascertaining, and then following the decision made within the structure of church governance." By doing so, the dissenters concluded,

> the court avoids two equally unacceptable departures from the genuine neutrality mandated by the First Amendment. First, it refrains from direct review and revision of decisions of the church on matters of religious doctrine and practice that underlie the church's determination of intrachurch controversies, including those that relate to control of church property. Equally important, by recognizing the authoritative resolution reached within the religious association, the civil court avoids interfering directly with the religious governance of those who have formed the association and submitted themselves to its authority.[42]

The Court, while emphasizing that the question before it involved a hierarchical church, also stated that the Georgia "neutral principles" methodology was "flexible enough to accommodate all forms of religious organization and polity." The Court also noted that church property disputes, even in Georgia, need not necessarily be resolved by the courts, for

> the parties can ensure, if they so desire, that the faction loyal to the hierarchical church will retain the church property. They can modify the deeds or the corporate

---

[41]443 U.S. 595, 605 (1979).
[42]*Id.* at 618.

charter to include a right of reversion or trust in favor of the general church. Alternatively, the constitution of the general church can be made to recite and express trust in favor of the denominational church. The burden involved in taking such steps will be minimal. And the civil courts will be bound to give effect to the result indicated by the parties, provided it is embodied in some legally cognizable form.[43]

The Supreme Court in *Jones* clarified the law of church property disputes. It affirmed that church property disputes not involving questions of religious doctrine or polity can be resolved on the basis of any doctrinally neutral method, including neutral principles of law or a rule of compulsory deference to the determinations of church tribunals. The Court emphatically declared that no one method is constitutionally required, at least where no question of religious doctrine or polity is involved. Where, as in *Jones*, no question of doctrine is involved and the compulsory deference and neutral principles of law approaches would yield conflicting results, a court or legislature is free to choose either method (or some other doctrinally neutral method). If it chooses the neutral principles of law approach, as did the Georgia courts in the *Jones* case, it is entitled to reach a decision contrary to the decision of a church tribunal, provided that no question of religious doctrine or polity is involved.

*Jones* thus did not alter the methodology set forth on pages 209-210. It merely clarified the relationship between the available methods of resolution.

It is interesting to note that a number of courts have expressly repudiated the Georgia methodology approved by the United States Supreme Court in *Jones,* and have adopted a rule of compulsory deference by the courts to the determinations of ecclesiastical commissions or judicatories in church property disputes, whether or not religious doctrine is implicated.[44] Such cases illustrate that diversity will characterize states' solutions to these intractable problems.

In conclusion, how may a denomination ensure that it will retain the property of an affiliated church that votes to withdraw from the denomination? And how, if at all, may an independent church congregation ensure that its property will remain with a particular faction in the event of a church schism? Conversely, when may a local church seeking to disaffiliate from a particular denomination safely assume that it will retain the church property? And how will a faction (a majority or a minority of church members) in an independent church know

---

[43]*Id.* at 606.

[44]Tea v. Protestant Episcopal Church, 610 P.2d 181 (Nev. 1980); Protestant Episcopal Church v. Graves, 417 A.2d 19 (N.J. 1980), *cert. denied,* 449 U.S. 1131 (1981); Southside Tabernacle v. Pentecostal Church of God, Pacific Northwest District, Inc., 650 P.2d 231 (Wash. 1982). *But see* Antioch Temple, Inc. v. Parekh, 422 N.E.2d 1337 (Mass. 1981).

what its rights are, if any, in church property following a schism? The Supreme Court responded to these concerns in *Jones*:

> [T]he neutral principles analysis shares the peculiar genius of private-law systems in general—flexibility in ordering private rights and obligations to reflect the intentions of the parties. Through appropriate reversionary clauses and trust provisions, religious societies can specify what is to happen to church property in the event of a particular contingency, or what religious body will determine the ownership in the event of a schism or doctrinal controversy. In this manner, a religious organization can insure that a dispute over the ownership of church property will be resolved in accord with the desires of the members.[45]

Private resolution of church property disputes may be facilitated in the following ways:

1. *Deeds.* Deeds to church property can provide for private resolution of church property disputes in a variety of ways.

a. First, a parent denomination can have title to local church property deeded to the parent denomination. This is particularly appropriate when the denomination has contributed toward the purchase or construction of a new church. In such a case, neutral principles of law would ordinarily confirm the denominations's ownership of the property.

b. A deed could specify that a local church holds title in trust for a parent denomination.

c. A deed could vest title in the local church, subject however to a reversion clause or a possibility of reverter stipulating that in the event a stated condition occurs title will vest in a parent denomination or in a particular faction. The condition must be worded in such a way that a court could enforce it without the need for inquiries into religious doctrine or polity. Neutral conditions would probably include disaffiliation or a disagreement about who owns church property. In either case, a court would merely be called upon to determine whether a disaffiliation or a property dispute had in fact occurred. Such a determination would not necessarily involve religious doctrine.

d. A parent denomination could have title deeded to itself and the local church as joint tenants or tenants in common. This would normally not be satisfactory, since a majority faction voting to disassociate itself from the denomination could have the property partitioned (the denomination and the local church would each be declared absolute owner of a fraction of the whole).

2. *Trusts.* The parent denomination could declare that all affiliated churches hold property "in trust" for the denomination. Churches voting to disaffiliate would thereby lose all claim to church property. Such a trust would normally

---

[45]443 U.S. 595, 603 (1979).

be inserted in the parent denomination's constitution or bylaws. As an example, the Supreme Court in *Jones* cited paragraph 1537 of the Methodist *Book of Discipline*:

> [T]itle to all real property now owned or hereafter acquired by an unincorporated local church . . . shall be held by and/or conveyed to its duly elected trustees . . . and their successors in office . . . in trust, nevertheless, for the use and benefit of such local church *and of The United Methodist Church.* Every instrument of conveyance of real estate shall contain the appropriate trust clause as set forth in the Discipline . . . .

The *Book of Discipline* also stipulates that in the absence of a trust clause, a trust in favor of The United Methodist Church would be implied if (1) the conveyance is to the trustees of a local church associated with any predecessor to The United Methodist Church, (2) the local church uses the name of any predecessor to The United Methodist Church and is known to the community as a part of The United Methodist Church, or (3) the local church accepts ministers appointed by any predecessor to The United Methodist Church. The Supreme Court inferred that such "implied trusts" would be deemed valid, since they involved no determinations concerning religious doctrine.

3. *Local church charter or bylaws.* In the event of a church dispute, the local church charter or bylaws may also provide for the disposition of property. Again, to be effective, such a provision must not be made dependent upon any determinations involving religious doctrine or polity. This means of private resolution is of limited value, since most church bylaws can be amended by vote of the church membership.

4. *Constitution or bylaws of a parent denomination.* The constitution or bylaws of a parent denomination could contain a provision vesting title to church property in the denomination in the event of a dispute or disaffiliation. Again, such a provision must be made dependent upon neutral conditions. Thus, a provision mandating reversion of church property to the denomination in the event that a local church "departs" or "deviates" from the doctrine of the denomination would not be recognized by the courts, for enforcement of such a provision would involve a scrutiny of religious doctrine.

5. *State statutes.* State legislatures can enact statutes that provide for the disposition of property in the event of a church dispute. Illustratively, the Georgia legislature has enacted a law which provides that "[t]he majority of those who adhere to its organization and doctrines represent the church. The withdrawal by one part of a congregation from the original body, or uniting

with another church or denomination, is a relinquishment of all rights in the church abandoned."[46]

Such statutes must not involve any determination regarding religious doctrine or polity. The Georgia statute previously quoted involves no doctrinal interpretations. A court has only to determine whether a faction in a particular congregation has withdrawn from the original body or united with another church or denomination. Such determinations normally would involve no interpretation of religious doctrine or polity, and thus would constitute an appropriate means of resolving church property disputes.

If none of these neutral principles of law disposes of church property in the event of a church property dispute, then the courts of a particular jurisdiction will be compelled to apply the methodology of resolution that they have developed.

In the sixth chapter of the apostle Paul's first letter to the church at Corinth, he wrote:

> If any of you has a dispute with another, dare he take it before the ungodly for judgment instead of before the saints? . . . [I]f you have disputes about such matters, appoint as judges even men of little account in the church! I say this to shame you. Is it possible that there is nobody among you wise enough to judge a dispute between believers? But instead one brother goes to law against another— and this in front of unbelievers! The very fact that you have lawsuits among you means you have been completely defeated already. Why not rather be wronged. Why not rather be cheated?[47]

Paul's denunciation of lawsuits involving Christians is clearly based in part upon the fear that such suits will give unbelievers a negative impression of Christianity. This fear is still warranted. In the *Watson* decision, the United States Supreme Court itself remarked:

> [We] have held [the case] under advisement for a year; not uninfluenced by the hope, that . . . charity, which is so large an element in the faith of both parties, and which, by one of the apostles of that religion, is said to be the greatest of all the Christian virtues, would have brought about a reconciliation. But we have been disappointed. It is not for us to determine or apportion the moral responsibility which attaches to the parties for this result.[48]

---

[46]GA. CODE § 22-5504.
[47]1 *Cor.* 6:1, 4-7 (NIV).
[48]Note 1, *supra*, at 735.

The decision to take other Christians to court, like most ethical determinations, is thus not a private decision. It is a decision that also affects outsiders' perceptions of the Christian faith. And, it is a decision that, in many cases, will directly contradict Paul's command in 1 Corinthians 6. Such considerations, at the least, should encourage utilization of the various methods of private resolution promoted by the Supreme Court in *Jones v. Wolf.* In most cases such methods would avoid litigation. Their effect, however, would be cosmetic, covering over real and festering disputes among believers for whom Jesus prayed "that they may be one." Only grace—not courts or neutral principles—can resolve these disputes.

# 10

## THE CHURCH AS EMPLOYER

Many churches are employers. They may employ a secretary, custodian, music director, counselor, or business manager. The relationship between a church and its minister also may constitute an employment relationship. As an employer, a church may be subject to a number of laws pertaining exclusively to employers. The more important of these laws will be reviewed in this chapter.

### §A. Income Taxation

#### 1. WITHHOLDING

Federal law requires every employer, including churches and religious organizations, to withhold federal income taxes from employee wages unless exempted by law.[1] Employers are exempted from the withholding, depositing, and payment requirements for several categories of wages, including wages paid for "services performed by a duly ordained, commissioned, or licensed minister of a church in the exercise of his ministry."[2] The income tax regulations define *services performed by a duly ordained, commissioned, or licensed minister of a church in the exercise of his ministry* to include (1) the ministration of sacerdotal (*i.e.,* religious) functions and the conduct of religious worship, and (2) the control, conduct, and maintenance of religious organizations including the religious boards, societies, and other integral agencies of such organizations under the authority of a religious body constituting a church or

[1]I.R.C. § 3402(a).
[2]I.R.C. § 3401(a)(9).

219

church denomination.[3] The regulations specify that service performed by a minister in the control, conduct, and maintenance of a religious organization relates to directing, managing, or promoting its activities. Therefore a church need not withhold federal income taxes from the wages of its minister if the minister is ordained, commissioned, or licensed and the wages are for services performed in the exercise of ministry.

The IRS maintains that a church and its minister may agree voluntarily that his federal income taxes be withheld from his wages, but this is not required. Some ministers find voluntary withholding attractive since it often reduces the year-end tax liability. A minister who elects to enter into a voluntary withholding arrangement with his church need only file a completed Form W-4 (Employee's Withholding Allowance Certificate) with the church. The filing of this form is deemed to be a request for voluntary withholding. Voluntary withholding arrangements may be terminated by mutual consent of the church and its minister. Alternatively, a minister can stipulate that the voluntary withholding arrangement will terminate on a specified date. In such a case, the minister must give his church a signed statement setting forth the date on which he wishes the arrangement to terminate; his name, address, and social security number; the employer's name and address; and a statement that he wishes to enter into a voluntary withholding arrangement with his employer. This statement must be attached to a completed Form W-4. The voluntary withholding arrangement will terminate automatically on the date specified. Finally, either the church or the minister may terminate a voluntary withholding arrangement before a specified or mutually agreed upon termination date by providing a signed notice to the other. If a church and its minister voluntarily agree that income taxes will be withheld, a minister ordinarily will no longer be subject to the estimated tax requirements.

It must be emphasized that there is no blanket withholding exemption for all of the employees of a church or religious organization. The IRS has stated repeatedly that churches and religious organizations are subject to the withholding requirements for all nonministerial employees.[4] In one case, a church challenged the application of federal withholding laws to wages paid to its

---

[3]Treas. Reg. § 31.3401(a)(9)-1(b). The control, conduct, and maintenance of religious organizations has been construed to include teaching at a religious school under the authority of a church or church denomination. However, the IRS has held that the wages of ordained and licensed ministers who worked as stenographers, mail clerks, file clerks, and janitors for the headquarters office of their religious denomination were not exempt from income tax withholding since such ministers were not engaged in the "control, conduct, and maintenance" of a religious organization. Rev. Rul. 57-129, 1957-1 C.B. 313.

[4]IRS Publication 15 ("Circular E"); IRS Publication 505; IRS Publication 517.

organist, pianist, choir director, janitor, and church clerk. In particular, the church advanced the following arguments:

1. A church cannot be made a trustee or collection agency of the government against its will.
2. The First Amendment prevents the IRS from requiring churches to withhold taxes from the wages of their employees.
3. It is not the intent of Congress to require churches to withhold taxes from the wages of their employees.
4. If withholding laws apply to churches, then churches would become "servants" of the federal government in violation of their constitutional right to freely exercise their religion.
5. Church employees can be classified as members of a "religious order," and thus their wages are exempt from withholding.

A federal court, both initially and on rehearing, summarily rejected the church's contentions. It initially observed that the law specifies that *all* wages are subject to withholding with certain specified exceptions, and therefore one can assume that Congress intended wages of church members to be subject to withholding unless such wages fall within one of the exceptions.[5] The court concluded that the wages of nonministerial church employees are nowhere specifically excluded from the withholding requirements, and therefore must be considered subject to withholding. It rejected the church's contention that its employees were members of a religious order and thus exempt from withholding under another provision of the law. Such a view, noted the court, is incompatible with the plain and ordinary meaning of the term *religious order.*
The court also rejected the church's constitutional arguments:

[A] taxing statute is not contrary to the provisions of the First Amendment unless it directly restricts the free exercise by an individual of his religion. We think it clear that, within the intendment of the First Amendment, the Internal Revenue Code, in imposing the income tax and requiring the filing of returns and the payment of the tax, is not to be considered as restricting an individual's free exercise of his religion.[6]

In summary, the wages of nonministerial church employees are subject to withholding. This obligation cannot be avoided by labeling a church employee an independent contractor. Although churches are not obligated to withhold

---

[5] Eighth Street Baptist Church v. United States, 291 F. Supp. 603 (D. Kan. 1968), aff'd on rehearing, 295 F. Supp. 1400 (D. Kan. 1969), aff'd on other grounds, 431 F.2d 1193 (10th Cir. 1970). See also Rev. Rul. 76-341, 1976-2 C.B. 307.
[6] Id. at 604.

federal income taxes from compensation paid to independent contractors, the term *independent contractor* generally refers to persons in business for themselves who offer their services to the public. Ordinarily the term does not refer to church organists, pianists, choir directors, janitors, secretaries, and business managers, or to teachers in a private school operated by a church. The IRS maintains that if an employer-employee relationship exists, it cannot be affected by what the parties call it. Thus, a church cannot transform an employee into an independent contractor by so labeling him in a contract or elsewhere.[7]

If a church has nonministerial employees to whom it pays wages, the following steps should be taken to comply with the withholding requirements:

1. Obtain an employer identification number from the federal government if this has not been done. This number may be obtained by submitting a Form SS-4 (Application for Employer Identification Number) to the IRS.

2. The amount of tax to be withheld depends on the amount of an employee's wages and the information contained on the employee's Form W-4. The Form W-4 should be filled out by each employee and filed with the employer. It is used to report withholding allowances claimed by an employee. In general, an employee may claim one withholding allowance for each person he expects to claim as an exemption on his federal tax return. This includes the employee, his spouse, and dependents. A withholding allowance is also available to an employee who is blind or at least sixty-five years of age, or whose spouse is blind or at least sixty-five. Employees who expect to itemize deductions during a particular year may claim additional withholding allowances for various estimated deductions. If an employee does not provide his employer with a completed Form W-4, the employer must withhold income taxes from the employee's wages as if he were single and claimed no allowances.

3. Compute each employee's wages. *Wages* are defined as "remuneration for services performed by an employee for his employer." Taxable wages may consist of cash or other forms of compensation. They include salaries, allowances, bonuses, overtime pay, and commissions. Certain payments are not considered in computing wages subject to withholding.

4. The amount of federal income tax the employer should withhold from an employee's wages may be computed in a number of ways. The most common

---

[7]IRS Publication 15. Section 530 of the Revenue Act of 1978 permits an organization to treat a worker as an independent contractor if it has a "reasonable basis for not treating such individual as an employee." A "reasonable basis" includes reliance on judicial precedent, a past IRS audit, or a long-standing recognized practice of a significant segment of the industry in which the person is engaged. Section 530 also prohibits further regulations or Revenue Rulings clarifying the employment status of individuals for purposes of employment taxes. In general, the discussion in chapter 1 regarding the distinction between employees and self-employed persons is relevant here.

methods are the *wage bracket method* and the *percentage method.* Under the wage bracket method, the employer simply locates an employee's taxable wages for the applicable payroll period on the wage bracket withholding tables and determines the tax to be withheld by using the column headed by the number of withholding allowances claimed by the employee. Under the percentage method, the employer multiplies the value of one withholding allowance (derived from a table) by the number of allowances an employee claims on his Form W-4, subtracts the total from the employee's wages, and determines the amount to be withheld from a table provided by the IRS. This method, like the wage bracket method, can be used for any length of payroll period.

5. *Until 1984,* churches that are exempt from social security and that withhold federal income taxes from the wages of any employees must file quarterly returns with the IRS on Form 941E (Quarterly Return of Withheld Federal Income Taxes). Form 941E reports income taxes withheld from employee wages. It is due on April 30, July 31, October 31, and January 31 each year. Churches with less than $500 of withheld income taxes at the end of any calendar quarter simply pay the taxes with their quarterly Form 941E. Employers with withheld taxes of $500 or more but less than $3,000 at the end of any month must deposit the taxes with an authorized financial institution by the fifteenth day of the following month. Employers with withheld taxes of $3,000 or more at the end of any "eighth-monthly" period (eighth-monthly periods end on the 3rd, 7th, 11th, 15th, 19th, 22nd, 25th, and last day of each month) must deposit the taxes with an authorized financial institution within three banking days after the close of the eighth-monthly period. All deposits must be accompanied by a federal tax deposit form. Employers subject to the deposit rules must still file quarterly returns on Form 941E. Churches can waive their exemption from social security coverage by filing a Form SS-15 and a Form SS-15a with the IRS. Churches that inadvertently pay social security taxes for at least three consecutive calendar quarters on any nonministerial employees are deemed to have filed forms SS-15 and SS-15a. Churches that waive their exemption from social security coverage are permitted to revoke their waiver by giving written notice two years in advance of the proposed date of revocation, provided that their waiver certificate was in effect for not less than eight years. Churches that waive their exemption from social security must withhold social security taxes as well as income taxes from nonministerial employee wages. Churches that have waived their exemption must file their quarterly returns on Form 941 rather than on Form 941E.

6. *After 1983,* churches are no longer exempt from social security taxes and therefore they must withhold such taxes as well as federal income taxes from each nonminister employee's wages. The amount of social security tax to be withheld from a particular employee's wages is determined by multiplying the current FICA-Medicare combined tax rate by the employee's taxable wage

base. A maximum taxable wage base is determined each year by the Secretary of the Department of Health and Human Services on the basis of wage indexes. The projected combined FICA-Medicare tax rates based on the 1983 Social Security Act amendments are as follows:

|      | Tax on Employee | Tax on Employer |
|------|-----------------|-----------------|
| 1984 | 7.0%            | 7.0%            |
| 1985 | 7.05%           | 7.05%           |
| 1986 | 7.15%           | 7.15%           |
| 1987 | 7.15%           | 7.15%           |
| 1988 | 7.51%           | 7.51%           |
| 1989 | 7.51%           | 7.51%           |
| 1990 | 7.65%           | 7.65%           |

The church must withhold the employee's social security tax from each wage payment. Since churches are no longer exempt from social security taxes, they must use Form 941 rather than Form 941E in reporting withheld income and social security taxes from employee wages. The pre-1984 deposit rules generally apply after 1984. Congress of course may amend the amount of withheld taxes that will trigger the monthly or eighth-monthly deposit rules, so these rules should be checked at least annually.

7. If a church has no nonministerial employees, it is under no legal obligation to withhold taxes and accordingly is not required to file Form 941. Many smaller churches will fall into this category. Even where a Form 941 is not required, a church that treats its minister as an employee may consider it advantageous to file such a form in order to reconcile the minister's W-2 forms. A church that has filed 941 forms in the past generally must continue to do so even if it temporarily is not withholding taxes on any employee.

There are penalties for failure to withhold taxes subject to withholding, failure to withhold enough taxes, failure to make timely deposits, and failure to file returns. These penalties generally are in the form of fines and additions to tax, but may take the form of imprisonment.

## 2. REPORTING REQUIREMENTS

The IRS maintains that churches must prepare a Form W-2 for every employee. The church reports each employee's wages and withheld income and social security taxes on this form. As has been noted elsewhere, ministers may be considered employees for purposes of federal income taxes.[8] A church should be careful to delete a minister's housing allowance from his Form W-2 or Form 1099, assuming that the housing allowance is available. A church should provide triplicate copies of Form W-2 directly to employees by February 1 of the

---

[8]*See* chapter 1, § B, and chapter 6, § A, *supra.*

following tax year, and submit an additional copy for every employee to the Social Security Administration by March 1. The Social Security Administration's copy is transmitted with a Form W-3 (Transmittal of Income and Tax Statements).

The IRS maintains that churches are required to prepare and submit information returns on the appropriate series of Form 1099 in order to report compensatory payments of $600 or more to persons who are not employees of the church or interest payments of $10 or more to any individual.[9] For example, if a church pays $1,000 to an evangelist or guest speaker, this amount should be reported to the IRS by the church on Form 1099-NEC (Nonemployee Compensation) before March 1 of the following tax year. Similarly, if a church issues bonds or notes to finance construction it must report interest payments exceeding $10 that it makes to any investor on Form 1099-INT (Interest Income). Form 1096 is used to summarize and transmit Forms 1099. Obviously, the purpose of Form 1099 is to ensure that the IRS is notified of all distributions of taxable income.

If a minister does not satisfy the common law definition of an employee discussed in chapter 1, then the appropriate way for his church to report his income would be to use Form 1099 rather than Form W-2.

## §B. Social Security Taxes

The Federal Insurance Contributions Act (FICA) imposes an employment tax on most employers and employees in order to help finance the cost of social security benefits.[10] The Act currently exempts "service performed in the employ of a religious, charitable, educational, or other organization described in section 501(c)(3) which is exempt from income tax under section 501(a)."[11] This exemption was removed, however, by Congress in the 1983 amendments to the Social Security Act for calendar years beginning with 1984. As a result, all nonministerial employees of churches, church schools, and religious organizations will be automatically covered by social security. Ministers are considered self-employed for social security purposes and therefore their wages are not subject to FICA taxes even if they are considered employees for income tax and other purposes.

The procedure that churches should follow in withholding and reporting the social security taxes of nonministerial employees is discussed in detail earlier in this chapter.

[9]I.R.C. §§ 6041 and 6042.
[10]I.R.C. §§ 3101-3126.
[11]I.R.C. § 3121(b)(8)(B).

## §C. Unemployment Taxes

Federal and state laws impose an unemployment tax on most employers in order to finance the costs of unemployment benefits. The Federal Unemployment Tax Act,[12] however, exempts "service performed in the employ of a religious . . . organization described in section 501(c)(3)."[13] Nearly every state unemployment tax law does the same.

## §D. Workmen's Compensation

### 1. IN GENERAL

Workmen's compensation laws have been enacted in all fifty states. Such laws provide compensation to employees for injuries resulting from employment. The amount of compensation payable is determined by law and generally is based upon the nature and extent of the employee's injury. In exchange for such benefits, employees give up their right of suing an employer directly. Fault is irrelevant under workmen's compensation laws. As one court has observed, "workmen's compensation, like the gentle rain from heaven, falls on the just and unjust alike."[14] The only inquiries are

1. Did an employment relationship exist?
2. Did the injury occur during the course of employment?
3. What were the nature and extent of the injuries?

Workmen's compensation laws were enacted to give injured workers a quicker, less costly, and more certain recovery than was possible by suing an employer directly for negligence. Prior to the general acceptance of workmen's compensation statutes in the early part of the twentieth century, injured employees were often unsuccessful in collecting damages from their employers. When they did collect, the awards were sometimes so high that they threatened the solvency of the employer. In every case, the costs to the injured employee of suing an employer were high.

The motivating philosophy behind workmen's compensation laws is that the losses arising from employment-related accidents should be distributed between the employer and the consumer as a cost of business. This is accomplished, in most cases, by the employer purchasing insurance to cover the costs of workmen's compensation benefits, with the cost of such insurance being passed on to the consumer through price adjustments.[15] Thus, the ultimate

[12]I.R.C. §§ 3301-3311.
[13]I.R.C. § 3306(c)(8).
[14]Thomas v. Certified Refrigeration, Inc., 221 N.W.2d 378 (Mich. 1974).
[15]Gunter v. Mersereau, 491 P.2d 1205 (Ore. 1971).

cost of an employee's injuries is borne by the consumers of the product or service that the employee was hired to produce.

## 2. TREATMENT OF CHURCHES

Churches are exempted from workmen's compensation laws in six states.[16] Nine more states exempt activities not carried on for monetary gain.[17] Thirteen other states exempt any employer having fewer than a prescribed number of employees.[18] The crucial inquiry is whether churches are exempt from those workmen's compensation laws that contain no specific exemption of churches, nonprofit organizations, or organizations employing less than a prescribed number of employees.

Although very few courts have considered the question,[19] the prevailing view is that religious organizations are subject to workmen's compensation laws unless specifically exempted. One court stated the rule as follows:

> [T]he fact that [a religious organization] is a purely charitable enterprise does not of itself release [it] from the obligations of our workmen's compensation act, which, unlike the acts of some states, does not except charitable or religious institutions, as such, from its operation, nor exclude their employees from its benefits. Where the relationship of employer and employee actually exists between a charitable institution and an injured workman, the latter is entitled to the benefits of our act, otherwise not.[20]

It has been argued that workmen's compensation laws were intended to apply only to commercial businesses and thus should not be extended to non-business activities such as the operation of a church. Many courts have rejected this reasoning as a basis for exempting charitable organizations from workmen's compensation laws, largely on the ground that the term *business* is so broad

---

[16]Alaska, Arkansas, Georgia, Idaho, Mississippi, North Dakota. *See generally* A. LARSON, THE LAW OF WORKMEN'S COMPENSATION § 50.41 (1982) [hereinafter cited as LARSON].

[17]Alaska, Georgia, Hawaii, Idaho, Maryland, New York, Oklahoma, Vermont, Wyoming. *See* LARSON, *supra* note 16, at § 50.41.

[18]For example, Alabama, Arkansas, Georgia, Virginia, and New Mexico exempt employers having fewer than three employees. North Carolina, Rhode Island, and South Carolina exempt employers having fewer than four employees. *See generally* LARSON, *supra* note 16, at § 52.10.

[19]This is no doubt a result of the infrequency of employee accidents on church premises.

[20]Schneider v. Salvation Army, 14 N.W.2d 467, 468 (Minn. 1944). *See also* Hope v. Barnes Hospital, 55 S.W.2d 319 (Mo. 1932).

that it encompasses charitable activities.[21] One court has observed: "[I]t is well to remember that in His earthly career the Head of the Christian Church seriously declared, 'I must be about my Father's business.' Wherefore does not church activity qualify as business? This term has such recognition apart from pecuniary gain."[22]

If a church is not exempt from workmen's compensation law, what is the effect of its failure to obtain workmen's compensation insurance? First, it should be noted that a few states permit employers to elect coverage under workmen's compensation law. To coerce employers into electing coverage, workmen's compensation laws typically impose various legal disabilities upon employers that do not elect coverage. Most workmen's compensation laws are compulsory, however. The employer has no prerogative to remain outside the system. In a "compulsory" jurisdiction, a covered employer that fails to obtain workmen's compensation insurance will ordinarily be subject to a direct action by an injured employee.[23]

In summary, churches are subject to workmen's compensation laws in many states. Nevertheless, very few churches have obtained workmen's compensation insurance. This will render some churches directly liable to injured employees. Since work-related injuries are rare among church employees, and since churches often have adequate general liability insurance to cover those injuries that do occur, the threat of a direct action by an injured employee is not considered sufficiently serious by most churches to warrant the purchase of workmen's compensation insurance. There nonetheless remains the possibility of a catastrophic injury substantially in excess of a church's general liability insurance, which warrants, at the least, serious consideration of workmen's compensation insurance.

## §E. Labor Laws

Congress has enacted a variety of labor laws that apply to some churches and religious organizations. These include the Age Discrimination in Employment Act, Title VII of the Civil Rights Act of 1964, the National Labor Relations Act, the Fair Labor Standards Act, and the Occupational Safety and Health Act. Before turning to a direct examination of these laws, it is important to recognize that they all were enacted by Congress under its constitutional authority to regulate interstate commerce. As a result, the laws apply only to

---

[21]LARSON, *supra* note 16, at §§ 50.20-50.25.

[22]Tepesch v. Johnson, 296 N.W. 740, 745 (Iowa 1941). *See also* Hope v. Barnes Hospital, 55 S.W.2d 319, 321 (Mo. 1932) ("[T]here is nothing about the act as a whole which discloses a legislative purpose to have limited its application solely to industries and businesses within the ordinary sense of the word.").

[23]LARSON, *supra* note 16, at §§ 67.21-67.29.

employers engaged in a business, industry, or activity "affecting commerce."[24] The National Labor Relations Act defines *affecting commerce* as "in commerce, or burdening or obstructing commerce or the free flow of commerce, or having led to or tending to lead to a labor dispute burdening or obstructing commerce or the free flow of commerce."[25]

Besides being narrowed to those employers affecting commerce, some federal labor laws apply only to employers having more than a prescribed number of employees. For example, Title VII of the Civil Rights Act of 1964 applies only to employers engaged in an industry affecting commerce that have fifteen or more employees for each working day in each of twenty or more calendar weeks in the current or preceding calendar year.[26] And, the Age Discrimination in Employment Act applies only to employers engaged in an industry affecting commerce that have twenty or more employees for each working day in each of twenty or more calendar weeks in the current or preceding tax year.

Is a church engaged in a business, industry, or activity affecting commerce? This is a complex question for which no comprehensive answer can be given. In general, the answer in a particular case will depend upon how narrowly or expansively a court construes the term *affecting commerce,* and upon the size of the church and the nature of its operations. Small churches employing no more than one or two persons ordinarily are not engaged in an activity affecting commerce. Such churches serve primarily the local community and their activities ordinarily are local as well. They typically engage in few if any interstate transactions, and no commercial activities. Congress has observed that nonprofit employers in general are "not engaged in 'commerce' and certainly not in interstate commerce . . . [and] frequently assist local governments in carrying out their essential functions, and for this reason should be subject to exclusively local jurisdiction."[27]

Nevertheless, a church or other religious organization engaged in significant commercial activities may be considered to be affecting commerce.[28] Thus, for example, the publishing and distribution of Sunday school literature by a religious denomination has been deemed to be an activity affecting commerce.[29]

---

[24]29 U.S.C. § 142 (National Labor Relations Act); 29 U.S.C. § 203 (Fair Labor Standards Act); 29 U.S.C. § 630(b) (Age Discrimination in Employment Act); 29 U.S.C. § 652 (Occupational Safety and Health Act); 42 U.S.C. § 2000e(b) (Title VII of the Civil Rights Act of 1964).

[25]29 U.S.C. § 152(7).

[26]42 U.S.C. § 2000e(b).

[27]H.R. Rep. No. 245, 80th Cong., 1st Sess. 12 (1947).

[28]NLRB v. World Evangelism, Inc., 656 F.2d 1349 (9th Cir. 1981).

[29]Sunday School Board of the Southern Baptist Convention, 92 N.L.R.B. 801 (1950). *Compare* Lutheran Church Missouri Synod, 109 N.L.R.B. 859 (1954).

It is also possible that a church that operates a child care facility, an elementary school, a home for the aged, or an orphanage is engaged in an activity affecting commerce.

But most churches are not involved in commercial activities, and the correct view would seem to be that such churches, regardless of size, are not involved in an activity affecting commerce. They sell no product or service, they are financed through voluntary contributions, they exist to fulfill noncommercial purposes, and they function outside the economic marketplace. Further, governmental regulation of churches carries with it the hazard of excessive governmental entanglement with religion, which is prohibited by the First Amendment.[30] Certainly most churches have an insubstantial effect on commerce, and therefore should be beyond the reach of federal labor laws.

### 1. Age Discrimination in Employment Act

In 1967, Congress enacted the Age Discrimination in Employment Act to prohibit employers engaged in an industry affecting commerce and employing at least fifty employees from making employment decisions that discriminate against individuals from forty to sixty-five years old on account of age.[31] Congress later amended the Act to apply to employers employing twenty or more employees for each working day in each of twenty or more calendar weeks in the current or preceding year. Congress also expanded the class of protected employees to include those between sixty-five and seventy years of age.

Most churches employ fewer than twenty individuals and thus are exempt from the age discrimination law. Churches employing twenty or more employees and not engaged in commercial activities may be exempt on the ground that they are not engaged in an activity affecting commerce.[32]

### 2. The Civil Rights Act of 1964

The Civil Rights Act of 1964 is considered in detail in another chapter.[33] For purposes of the present chapter, only Title VII of the Civil Rights Act of 1964 will be discussed, since it is the portion of the Act dealing primarily with discrimination by employers.

Title VII, section 703, of the Civil Rights Acts of 1964 states:

---

[30]NLRB v. Catholic Bishop of Chicago, 440 U.S. 490 (1979).

[31]29 U.S.C. §§ 621-634.

[32]In Usery v. Manchester East Catholic Regional School Board, 430 F. Supp. 188 (D.N.H. 1977), a federal court determined that the Age Discrimination in Employment Act did apply to a parochial school board.

[33]*See* chapter 11, § I, *infra*.

(a) It shall be an unlawful employment practice for an employer
(1) to fail or refuse to hire or to discharge any individual, or otherwise to discriminate against any individual with respect to his compensation, terms, conditions, or privileges of employment, because of such individual's race, color, religion, sex, or national origin; or
(2) to limit, segregate, or classify his employees or applicants for employment in any way which would deprive or tend to deprive any individual of employment opportunities or otherwise adversely affect his status as an employee, because of such individual's race, color, religion, sex, or national origin.

This general ban on discrimination applies to all employers, including any church or religious organization, engaged in any "industry affecting commerce that has fifteen or more employees for each working day in each of twenty or more calendar weeks in the current or preceding calendar year . . . ."[34] The Act defines *industry affecting commerce* as "any activity, business, or industry in commerce or in which a labor dispute would hinder or obstruct commerce or the free flow of commerce . . . ."[35]

The Act exempts religious corporations and associations, including churches, from the portion of section 703 banning religious discrimination in any employment decision by an employer subject to the law.[36] However, churches and religious organizations are not exempted from those portions of section 703 banning discrimination in employment decisions on the basis of race, color, sex, or national origin.[37]

The exemption of churches and religious organizations from religious discrimination is broad, and extends to any employment decision. Some courts have challenged the constitutionality of this exemption. For example, one court has called the exemption "a remarkably clumsy accommodation of religious freedom with the compelling interests of the state, providing . . . far too broad a shield for the secular activities of religiously affiliated entities with not the remotest claim to First Amendment protection."[38] Another court has held that the exemption violates the First Amendment to the extent that it permits religious organizations to discriminate on the basis of religion in employment decisions involving secular positions (*e.g.*, secretary, custodian). The court did acknowledge that the First Amendment requires that religious organizations be free to discriminate on the basis of religion in employment decisions re-

[34]42 U.S.C. § 2000e(b).

[35]42 U.S.C. § 2000e(h).

[36]42 U.S.C. § 2000e-1.

[37]Ritter v. Mount St. Mary's College, 495 F. Supp. 724 (D. Md. 1980).

[38]EEOC v. Southwestern Baptist Theological Seminary, 485 F. Supp. 255, 260 (N.D. Tex. 1980), *rev'd on other grounds,* 651 F.2d 277 (5th Cir. 1981).

garding those "who will advocate, defend, or explain the group's beliefs or way of life."[39]

The Act also permits schools, colleges, and other educational institutions to hire employees of a particular religion if the educational institution is wholly or substantially owned, supported, controlled, or managed by a particular religious corporation, association, or society, or if the educational institution's curriculum is directed toward the propagation of a particular religion.[40]

Finally, the Act permits employers to hire employees on the basis of religion if religion is a "bona fide occupational qualification reasonably necessary to the normal operation of that particular business or enterprise."[41]

Churches employing fewer than fifteen employees are not covered by Title VII of the Civil Rights Act of 1964, and therefore they are not subject to the prohibitions of discrimination in employment based on race, color, religion, sex, or national origin. Churches employing fifteen or more employees are subject to Title VII only if they are engaged in an activity affecting commerce. As was noted earlier in this section, it is very doubtful that a church of any size constitutes an activity affecting commerce, although such a determination ultimately will rest on how narrowly or expansively the courts define the term *affecting commerce* and the extent to which the church is engaged in commercial activities.

### 3. NATIONAL LABOR RELATIONS ACT

In 1935 Congress decided that disturbances in the area of labor relations led to undesirable burdens on and obstructions of interstate commerce, and passed the National Labor Relations Act.[42] That Act, building on the National Industrial Recovery Act (1933), afforded employees a federally protected right to join labor organizations and bargain collectively through their chosen representatives on issues affecting their employment. Congress also created the National Labor Relations Board (NLRB) to supervise the collective bargaining process. The Board was empowered to investigate disputes about which union, if any, represented employees, and to certify the appropriate representatives as the designated collective bargaining agent. The employer was then required to bargain with these representatives, and the Board was authorized to make sure that such bargaining did in fact occur. Without spelling out the details, the Act

[39]King's Garden, Inc. v. F.C.C., 498 F.2d 51, 56 (D.C. Cir. 1974). *Compare* McClure v. Salvation Army, 460 F.2d 553 (5th Cir. 1972) (decided before the Act's exemption provision was amended in 1972 to permit religious organizations to discriminate on the basis of religion in any employment decision).

[40]42 U.S.C. § 2000e-2(e).

[41]*Id.*

[42]29 U.S.C. §§ 151-168.

stipulated that an employer's refusal to bargain was an unfair labor practice. Thus a general process was established that would ensure that employees as a group could express their opinions and exert their influence over the terms and conditions of their employment. The Board would act to see that the process worked.

Congress enacted the Labor Management Relations Act in 1947 to adjust and minimize any differences in the rights granted to unions, employees, and employers.

Does the National Labor Relations Act apply to religious organizations? This question has caused considerable controversy. Initially, it should be noted that the stated purpose of the Act was to

> eliminate the causes of certain substantial obstructions to the free flow of commerce and to mitigate and eliminate these obstructions when they have occurred by encouraging the practice and procedure of collective bargaining and by protecting the exercise by workers of full freedom of association, self-organization, and designation of representatives of their own choosing, for the purpose of negotiating the terms and conditions of their employment or other mutual aid or protection.[43]

Clearly, then, the Act was designed to apply only to those employment relationships that affect commerce. The Act defines the term *affecting commerce* to mean "in commerce, or burdening or obstructing commerce or the free flow of commerce, or having led or tending to lead to a labor dispute burdening or obstructing commerce or the free flow of commerce."[44]

Further, the Act defines *employer* as

> any person acting as an agent of an employer, directly or indirectly, but shall not include the United States or any wholly owned Government corporation, or any Federal Reserve Bank, or any State or political subdivision thereof, or any person subject to the Railway Labor Act, as amended from time to time, or any labor organization (other than when acting as an employer), or anyone acting in the capacity of officer or agent of such labor organization.[45]

Thus the Act covers all employers not within one of the eight express exceptions. Since religious organizations do not fit within any of the eight exempted categories, the National Labor Relations Board has held that such organizations are covered by the Act at least to the extent that they are engaged

[43]29 U.S.C. § 151.
[44]29 U.S.C. § 152(7).
[45]29 U.S.C. § 152(2).

in some proprietary activity affecting commerce.[46] To illustrate, the NLRB has asserted jurisdiction over the Sunday School Board of the Southern Baptist Convention since it was engaged in the sale of literature on a nationwide basis and thus could be viewed as being involved in a proprietary activity affecting commerce. The NLRB observed:

> The employer asserts that as it is a nonprofit organization which is engaged in purely religious activities, it is not engaged in commerce within the meaning of the Act. We find no merit in this contention. . . . As this Board and the courts have held, it is immaterial that the employer may be a nonprofit organization, or that its activities may be motivated by considerations other than those applicable to enterprises which are, in the generally accepted sense, commercial.[47]

Similarly, the Board asserted jurisdiction over an evangelistic organization that was engaged in substantial commercial activities that were unrelated, except as a revenue source, to the organization's religious activities.[48]

A number of religious organizations have challenged the constitutionality of NLRB determinations that they are covered by the Act. In a leading case, the United States Supreme Court was faced with the issue of whether lay teachers in church-operated schools were under the jurisdiction of the NLRB. The Court found that neither the language nor the legislative history of the National Labor Relations Act disclosed "an affirmative intention . . . clearly expressed" that the NLRB have such jurisdiction. Therefore, the Court declined to construe the Act in a manner that would require the resolution of "difficult and sensitive questions arising out of the guarantees of the First Amendment Religion Clauses."[49] The Court's test for determining the validity of an exercise of jurisdiction by the NLRB over a religious organization may be summarized as follows:

[46]First Church of Christ, Scientist, 194 N.L.R.B. 1006 (1972). Although the NLRB has traditionally assumed jurisdiction over all religious organizations, it has, as a matter of discretion, refused to assert jurisdiction over religious organizations not engaged in commercial activities or religious organizations engaged in commercial activities that earn less than prescribed levels of income. This principle is referred to as the worthy cause doctrine. See generally Sherman & Black, The Labor Board and the Private Nonprofit Employer: A Critical Examination of the Board's Worthy Cause Exemption, 83 HARV. L. REV. 1323 (1970).

[47]Sunday School Board of the Southern Baptist Convention, 92 N.L.R.B. 801, 802 (1950).

[48]NLRB v. World Evangelism, Inc., 656 F.2d 1349 (9th Cir. 1981). See also Tressler Lutheran Home for Children v. NLRB, 677 F.2d 302 (3rd Cir. 1982) (NLRB jurisdiction over church-operated children's home upheld); Jacobo Marti & Sons, Inc. v. NLRB, 676 F.2d 975 (3rd Cir. 1982) (NLRB jurisdiction over cheese processing plant having a close connection with the Amish faith upheld).

[49]NLRB v. Catholic Bishop of Chicago, 440 U.S. 490, 507 (1979).

1. Determine if the exercise of jurisdiction by the NLRB over a religious organization would give rise to serious constitutional questions under the First Amendment.

2. If a serious constitutional question would arise, then the NLRB may not exercise jurisdiction over the religious organization without a showing of an "affirmative intention of the Congress clearly expressed" to confer such jurisdiction.

3. If serious constitutional questions are not raised by an exercise of jurisdiction by the NLRB over a religious organization, then no inquiry is necessary as to whether Congress clearly expressed an intention to confer jurisdiction.

In applying this test, one court has upheld an exercise of jurisdiction by the NLRB over a Christian evangelistic organization engaged in substantial commercial activities. The court noted that no serious First Amendment questions were raised since NLRB jurisdiction resulted in only a "minimal infringement" on the organization's constitutional rights.[50] Serious constitutional questions are raised by an NLRB assertion of jurisdiction over church school teachers, concluded the court, but this is not true of an exercise of jurisdiction over lay employees engaged in the commercial activities of a religious organization.

Another court reached the same conclusion with respect to employees of a church-operated home for neglected children.[51] The court agreed with the Supreme Court that an exercise of jurisdiction by the NLRB over church-operated schools raised serious constitutional questions since such schools actively propagate religious faith. However, the court did not believe that serious constitutional questions were raised by an assertion of jurisdiction by the NLRB over church-operated homes for neglected children since such institutions are not devoted to the propagation of religion. Since no serious constitutional question was raised, the court concluded that an "affirmative intention of Congress clearly expressed" to confer jurisdiction over church-operated homes for neglected children was not necessary.

It appears likely that the NLRB will continue to exercise jurisdiction over religious organizations engaged in substantial commercial activities, and that the courts will uphold such exercises of jurisdiction. As one court has observed, when a religious or nonprofit organization operates in the same way as a secular institution, the NLRB may treat such an organization like a secular institution.[52] Nevertheless, NLRB assertions of jurisdiction over religious organizations probably will not be upheld in any of the following contexts:

[50]NLRB v. World Evangelism, Inc., 656 F.2d 1349 (9th Cir. 1981).

[51]NLRB v. St. Louis Christian Home, 663 F.2d 60 (8th Cir. 1981). *See also* Tressler Lutheran Home for Children v. NLRB, 677 F.2d 302 (3rd Cir. 1982).

[52]NLRB v. St. Louis Christian Home, 663 F.2d 60 (8th Cir. 1981).

1. The organization is not involved in substantial commercial activities.[53]

2. The organization is not engaged in a business or activity affecting commerce. *Commerce* is defined by the National Labor Relations Act as trade, traffic, commerce, transportation, or communication among the several states.[54] Thus, to affect commerce, an organization must engage in interstate purchases, sales, communications, or other business transactions of a substantial nature. A religious organization that purchases all of its supplies from local suppliers and sells no product or service to persons residing in other states may not be engaged in any activity affecting commerce. Note, however, that the Act defines *commerce* to include "communication" among the several states. It has been held that the use of a telephone, even for purely local uses, involves an organization in interstate commerce since the telephone company is engaged in interstate commerce. Also, the purchase of electricity and natural gas from a utility company engaged in interstate commerce may involve a religious organization in commerce.[55]

3. An assertion of NLRB jurisdiction inhibits a religious organization's ability to propagate its beliefs.[56]

4. An assertion of NLRB jurisdiction raises serious constitutional questions under the First Amendment and no "affirmative intention of Congress clearly expressed" confers jurisdiction.[57]

### 4. FAIR LABOR STANDARDS ACT

In 1938 Congress enacted the Fair Labor Standards Act to protect employees engaged in interstate commerce from substandard wages and excessive working hours. The Act achieves its purpose by prescribing a maximum workweek of forty hours for an employee engaged in commerce, unless the employee is paid at the rate of one and one-half times the regular rate of compensation for all hours worked over forty, and by prescribing a minimum wage for all employees

---

[53]The NLRB claims to possess jurisdiction over all religious organizations, but it declines to assert jurisdiction over religious organizations not engaged in substantial commercial activities. An assertion of jurisdiction over a religious organization not engaged in substantial commercial activities might violate the First Amendment. NLRB v. Catholic Bishop of Chicago, 440 U.S. 490 (1979).

[54]29 U.S.C. § 152(6).

[55]*See generally* NLRB v. St. Louis Christian Home, 663 F.2d 60 (8th Cir. 1981). The expansive interpretation of the term *commerce* has not gone without objection. One judge has commented that "it is virtually unthinkable that the Founding Fathers could have foreseen the extent to which an increasingly expansive interpretation of the Commerce Clause could so infringe local authority." Godwin v. Occupational Safety and Health Review Commission, 540 F.2d 1013, 1017 (9th Cir. 1976) (Ely, J., concurring).

[56]NLRB v. Catholic Bishop of Chicago, 440 U.S. 490 (1979).

[57]*Id.*

engaged in interstate commerce. The Act defines *commerce* as "trade, commerce, transportation, transmission, or communication among the several states or between any State and any place outside thereof."[58]

The Act does not specifically exempt religious organizations from its provisions and thus it has been held that the Act covers the employees of such organizations to the extent that they are engaged in commerce. To illustrate, one court held that the Act applied to the employees of a religious denomination's publishing plant even though the plant was organized "to glorify God, publish the full Gospel to every nation, and promote the Christian religion by spreading religious knowledge."[59] The court observed that the amount of goods sent outside the state where they are produced does not have to be large in order to subject the producer to the provisions of the Act, since the shipment in commerce of "any" goods produced by employees employed in violation of the Act's overtime and minimum wage requirements is prohibited. The plant's interstate shipments were more than sufficient, concluded the court, to involve its employees in interstate commerce.

In rejecting the plant's claim that it was engaged in religion and that religion is not commerce, the court observed:

> If we grant that religion itself is not commerce, it still does not follow that a corporation organized for religious purposes may not engage in "commerce" as defined in the Fair Labor Standards Act, that is, by engaging in "trade, commerce, transportation, transmission, or communication among the several states." By engaging in the printing business, as this defendant did, we think it was clearly engaged in "commerce" within the meaning of the Act.[60]

The court also rejected the plant's claim that its First Amendment right to freely exercise its religion would be violated by subjecting it to the Act. The court noted that First Amendment rights are not without limit but may be restricted by the state if it has a sufficiently compelling interest. The objectives underlying the Fair Labor Standards Act, concluded the court, were sufficiently compelling to override a religious organization's First Amendment rights under the circumstances of the present case.[61]

In a related case, another court observed that "[o]rganizations affecting commerce may not escape coverage of social legislation by showing that they were created for fraternal or religious purposes."[62]

[58]29 U.S.C. § 203(b).

[59]Mitchell v. Pilgrim Holiness Church Corp., 210 F.2d 879 (7th Cir. 1954).

[60]*Id.* at 882.

[61]*See also* Prince v. Commonwealth of Massachusetts, 321 U.S. 158 (1944).

[62]McClure v. Salvation Army, 460 F.2d 553, 557 (5th Cir. 1972).

Therefore religious organizations, including churches, will be subject to the Fair Labor Standards Act if they are engaged in commerce.[63] Furthermore, the Supreme Court's test for determining the validity of NLRB jurisdiction over religious organizations likely will apply to the question of coverage of such organizations under the Fair Labor Standards Act. Thus, if application of the Act to a particular religious employer would raise serious constitutional questions under the First Amendment and no "affirmative intention of Congress clearly expressed" confers such jurisdiction, the Act will not apply.[64]

The Act does grant a limited exemption in the case of employees of a religious or nonprofit educational conference center if the center does not operate for more than seven months in any calendar year, or if during the preceding calendar year its average receipts for any six months were not more than one-third of its average receipts for the other six months of the year.[65] And, the Act exempts "any employee employed in a bona fide executive, administrative, or professional capacity" from the overtime and minimum wage provisions of the Act if prescribed income tests are satisfied.[66] The clergy constitutes a learned profession and thus a minister is exempt from the overtime and minimum wage provisions of the Act if his annual income exceeds the level prescribed by the government. Larger churches and many religious organizations may have employees who qualify as executives or administrators. To qualify, an employee must meet both income and job function tests.

5. OCCUPATIONAL SAFETY AND HEALTH ACT

In 1970, Congress enacted the Occupational Safety and Health Act "to assure so far as is possible every working man and woman in the Nation safe and healthful working conditions."[67] The Act achieves its aim primarily through imposing various duties upon employers. The Act defines *employer* as any person or organization "engaged in a business affecting commerce who has employees."[68] *Commerce* is defined under the Act as trade, traffic, commerce, transportation, or communication among the several states.[69]

Since religious organizations are not exempted from the Act, they will be

[63]See the introduction to the present section for a discussion of the meaning of commerce.

[64]*See* chapter 10, § E.3, *supra.*

[65]29 U.S.C. § 213(a)(3).

[66]29 U.S.C. § 213(a)(1); 29 C.F.R § 541.

[67]29 U.S.C. § 651(b).

[68]29 U.S.C. § 652(5).

[69]29 U.S.C. § 652(3).

deemed subject to it with the same limitations previously discussed in connection with the Fair Labor Standards Act.

## §F. Vicarious Liability for the Wrongs of Employees

It is a well-established principle of law that an employer is responsible for the civil wrongs committed by an employee in the course of employment. This vicarious or imputed liability of an employer for the misconduct of an employee is based largely on two considerations. First, it is assumed that the damages and injuries inflicted as a result of the operations of a particular enterprise should be borne by the enterprise itself and made a cost of doing business through price adjustments or liability insurance. Second, it is assumed that vicarious liability will tend to make employers more careful in the selection, training, and supervision of employees.[70]

An employer is responsible for the civil wrongs committed by its employees only if (1) an employer-employee relationship existed at the time of the injury, (2) the injury was caused by an employee's negligence or misconduct, and (3) the employee was in the course or scope of his employment at the time of the injury. The criteria to be employed in determining whether an employer-employee relationship exists have been discussed elsewhere.[71]

In summary, an employee is a person "employed to perform services in the affairs of another and who with respect to the physical conduct in the performance of the services is subject to the other's control or right of control."[72] A minister of a church generally is held to be an employee of the church, and thus his misconduct in the course of his employment will be imputed to his church.[73]

It is also generally held that unpaid church volunteers can be considered employees where the church has a right to control their activities. Thus, for example, one court has held that the negligence of a volunteer divinity student acting in the course of church work was attributable to his church since the church had the right to control his conduct.[74] Obviously, church secretaries, custodians, and other individuals who perform routine and continuous services on behalf of a church will almost always be deemed employees regardless of how a church characterizes them.

A church is not responsible, however, for the misconduct of independent contractors. Independent contractors are persons who offer their services to the public and are generally engaged to do some particular project or piece of

[70]See generally W. PROSSER, THE LAW OF TORTS § 69 (4th ed. 1971).

[71]See chapter 1, § B, supra.

[72]RESTATEMENT (SECOND) OF AGENCY § 220(1) (1958).

[73]See chapter 1, § B, supra.

[74]Malloy v. Fong, 232 P.2d 241 (Cal. 1951).

work, usually for a specified sum, and who may perform the task with little or no supervision or control. They are not considered to be employees.

Only those injuries caused by an employee's misconduct in the course of his employment are attributable to the employer. It is often difficult, however, to ascertain whether an employee is "in the course of his employment" at the time he inflicts an injury upon the person or property of another. Nevertheless, conduct of an employee is generally within the scope of employment if (1) it is of the kind he is employed to perform, (2) it occurs during the hours and within the geographical area authorized by the employment relationship, and (3) it is motivated, at least in part, by a desire to serve the employer.[75] Thus, an employer generally will not be responsible for the misconduct of an employee that occurs before or after working hours, that occurs an unreasonable distance from an authorized work area, or that occurs while the employee is on solely personal business.

It is the prevailing view that an employee's intentional misconduct, criminal acts, or unauthorized acts are not attributable to his employer so long as such acts are inappropriate and unforeseeable in the accomplishment of an authorized result.

A number of courts have held that the members of an unincorporated association are personally liable for the misconduct of agents and employees of the association occurring in the course of employment.[76] Some courts impute liability only to those members of an unincorporated association who took an active part in or affirmatively condoned an employee's misconduct.[77]

### §G. Termination of Employees

It is the prevailing rule that an employee hired for an indefinite term may be discharged by the employer at any time with or without cause, subject to the following limitations:

1. The National Labor Relations Act makes it unlawful for an employer engaged in a business or activity affecting commerce to discharge an employee on the basis of union activities.[78]

2. The Civil Rights Act of 1964 makes it unlawful for an employer that is engaged in a business or activity affecting commerce and that employs fifteen or more employees for each working day in each of twenty or more calendar weeks in a year to discharge any individual on the basis of race, color, religion,

---

[75]RESTATEMENT (SECOND) OF AGENCY § 228 (1958).

[76]See generally Annot., 62 A.L.R.3rd 1165 (1975).

[77]Id.

[78]See chapter 10, § E, supra, for a discussion of the meaning of the term affecting commerce.

sex, or national origin. The Act does permit religious organizations to discharge or otherwise discriminate against employees on the basis of religion. The constitutionality of this exemption provision has been questioned with respect to the secular employees (*e.g.*, secretaries, custodians) of religious organizations.[79]

3. Although not directly limiting an employer's right to discharge an employee engaged for an indefinite term, some states have enacted laws requiring employers to provide discharged employees with a letter setting forth the "true cause" of the discharge.[80] Ordinarily, however, the employer is not obligated to provide such a letter unless it receives a written request from a discharged employee.

4. A few courts have "implied" a condition in employment contracts that an employee be discharged only in good faith, or have protected employees by granting them the right to sue their employer for wrongful or retaliatory discharge.[81] Thus, for example, employees who were discharged for refusing to commit perjury or a crime, or for filing a workmen's compensation claim against their employer have been able to sue their employer for retaliatory discharge.[82] This exception to the employer's right to discharge employees engaged for indefinite terms of employment has been narrowly construed, and is rejected altogether by a majority of jurisdictions.

The courts generally hold that an employee hired for a definite term may not be discharged before the end of his employment term unless good cause exists or the employer reserves the right in a written contract to discharge the employee before the expiration of the term "without cause." An employer need not demonstrate good cause to justify a failure to rehire an employee upon the expiration of a definite term of employment.

*Good cause* has been held to include the death, serious illness, or disability of an employee; abandonment of employment by an employee; breach of contract; refusal to perform duties; incompetency; neglect of duties; misconduct; insubordination; intoxication; and intemperance.

An employee who is discharged without good cause before the end of a specified term of employment generally is entitled to recover as damages the salary and other benefits agreed upon for the remainder of the employment term less the amount the employee earned, or with reasonable diligence might have earned, from other employment of the same or a similar nature during the period.

---

[79] *See* chapter 10, § E, *supra*.

[80] MO. REV. STAT. § 290.140.

[81] *See generally* Note, *Protecting At Will Employees Against Wrongful Discharge: The Duty to Terminate Only in Good Faith*, 93 HARV. L. REV. 1816 (1980).

[82] *Id.*

# 11

# GOVERNMENT REGULATION OF CHURCHES

Churches are not immune from governmental regulation. Regulations affecting churches consistently are upheld if they (1) avoid excessive governmental entanglement with religion, (2) are supported by a compelling governmental interest, (3) are reasonably related to the accomplishment of a legitimate governmental objective, (4) are the least restrictive means of accomplishing the intended result, and (5) require no judicial determination of the validity of religious belief. Such regulations do not violate the First Amendment or any other legal right of religious organizations. One court, in rejecting a religious organization's claim to immunity from governmental regulation on the ground that it was engaged in "God's work," observed that "[n]o court has ever found that conduct, by being so described, is automatically immunized from all regulation in the public interest."[1] Thus, for example, courts have upheld reasonable governmental regulation of securities offerings, labor practices, construction projects, fundraising schemes, child-care and nursing-care facilities, and private schools of churches and religious organizations. The more significant forms of governmental regulation of churches and religious organizations will be summarized in this chapter.

## §A. Regulation of Charitable Solicitations

Many states have enacted laws regulating the solicitation of contributions by charitable organizations. Such laws have been enacted to assure contributors that funds solicited for a specified charitable purpose will be used substantially for that purpose and not diverted to some other activity or dissipated through administrative expenses.

---

[1]Securities and Exchange Commission v. World Radio Mission, Inc., 544 F.2d 535, 539 n.7 (1st Cir. 1976).

Most charitable solicitation laws require charities that solicit funds to register with the state. Registration typically involves filing with the state attorney general a registration statement setting forth the name of the charity, the names and addresses of officers and directors, the purposes of the charity, the purposes for which contributions will be used, the period of time during which the solicitation will be conducted, the methods by which solicitations will be made, and the names and addresses of any professional fundraisers. In addition to the filing of a registration statement, charitable organizations generally are required to file annual reports setting forth financial statements, a schedule of charitable activities, and amounts expended on such activities during the year.

Religious organizations, including churches, are insulated from regulation in many states either because of an exemption[2] or because no charitable solicitation law has been enacted.[3] Many charitable solicitation laws exempt only some religious organizations. To illustrate, some laws exempt only those religious organizations (1) that are bona fide religious institutions,[4] (2) that solicit funds solely by means of members acting without compensation,[5] (3) that solicit funds only within the county where the religious organization is located or within an adjoining county that is less than six miles away,[6] (4) that do not employ professional fundraisers,[7] (5) that do not receive their financial support primarily from persons other than members,[8] (6) that have received a declaration of current tax-exempt status from the government of the United States,[9] or (7) that are entitled to receive a declaration of current tax-exempt status from the government of the United States.[10]

The applicability of charitable solicitation laws to religious organizations has been challenged in a number of cases. To illustrate, a religious group that

[2]*See, e.g.,* GA. CODE § 35-1003(a); ILL. REV. STAT. ch. 23, § 5103; N.J. REV. STAT. § 45:17A-5(a).

[3]For example, Louisiana, Montana, and Missouri have not enacted charitable solicitation laws.

[4]FLA. STAT. § 496.02(b).

[5]CONN. GEN. STAT. § 19-3231.

[6]IOWA CODE § 122.4

[7]MD. CORPS. & ASS'NS CODE ANN. § 103C.

[8]S.C. CODE § 33-55-60(1).

[9]PA. STAT. ANN. § 160-2(1); R.I. GEN. LAWS § 5-52-1(a); W. VA. CODE § 29-19-2(1).

[10]WASH. REV. CODE § 19.09.030. The exemption of religious organizations recognized by the Washington Code takes into account the fact that churches, conventions and associations of churches, and integrated auxiliaries of churches are automatically entitled to tax-exempt status without any formal recognition by the government. The exemption provisions found in the charitable solicitation laws of Pennsylvania, Rhode Island, and West Virginia unfortunately overlook this fact.

received more than half of its support from nonmembers challenged the constitutionality of a state charitable solicitation law that exempted only those religious organizations receiving more than half of their support from members.[11] The United States Supreme Court concluded that the law violated the nonestablishment of religion clause of the First Amendment since it constituted an impermissible governmental preference of some religious sects over others. The Court did hold, however, that each state "has a significant interest in protecting its citizens from abusive practices in the solicitation of funds for charity, and that this interest retains importance when the solicitation is conducted by a religious organization."[12] The Court refrained from deciding whether a state charitable solicitation law requiring all religious organizations to register and file annual reports would be permissible.[13]

Another court, in striking down a state charitable solicitation law exempting all religious organizations except those whose financial support came primarily from nonmembers, concluded that the First Amendment prohibits any state from subjecting religious organizations to the administrative requirements of a charitable solicitation law.[14] The court noted:

[F]or a statute to pass muster under the strict test of Establishment Clause neutrality, it must pass the three-prong review distilled by the Supreme Court from "the cumulative criteria developed over many years": "First, the statute must have a secular purpose; second, its principal or primary effect must be one that neither advances nor inhibits religion . . . ; finally the statute must not foster an excessive government entanglement with religion."[15]

The court concluded that the first part of the Supreme Court's three-prong test was satisfied, since the Act had a valid secular purpose of protecting the public from fraud. It found, however, that the Act violated both the second and third elements since it inhibited certain religious groups and constituted an impermissible governmental entanglement with religion:

As applied to religious organizations, the enforcement of these provisions inevitably entangles the state and its agencies in a persistent inquiry into whether

---

[11]Larson v. Valente, 102 S. Ct. 1673 (1982).

[12]*Id.* at 1685.

[13]The Court observed: "We do not suggest that the burdens of compliance with the Act would be intrinsically impermissible if they were imposed evenhandedly." *Id.* at 1688.

[14]Heritage Village Church and Missionary Fellowship, Inc. v. State, 263 S.E.2d 726 (N.C. 1980).

[15]*Id.* at 731.

particular expenditures of a religious organization are secular or religious in nature, or whether the religious expenditures support the same religious purposes represented in the organization's license application.[16]

## §B. Limitations on Charitable Giving

A number of states have enacted statutes limiting the right of religious organizations to receive gifts by will or by any other instrument designed to take effect at a donor's death. The purpose of such laws is to prevent "deathbed" gifts to religious organizations by persons who might be unduly influenced by religious considerations. More generally, such laws are intended to protect a donor's family from disinheritance due to charitable gifts made either without proper deliberation or as a result of the recipient's undue influence.

A number of these statutes invalidate any gift to a religious organization made in a will executed within a prescribed period before the donor's death. For example, one state law invalidates any gift to a religious organization contained in a will executed within eight months before a donor's death.[17] Other laws invalidate any testamentary gift[18] made by a donor within thirty[19] or ninety days[20] of death.

A number of statutes invalidate in whole or in part testamentary gifts made within a prescribed period before the donor's death if the donor left a surviving spouse or descendants. For example, one state law invalidates any testamentary gift to charity made within thirty days of the donor's death if the donor left a surviving spouse, brother, sister, nephew, niece, descendant, or ancestor.[21] Another state law invalidates any testamentary gift to charity made within six months of the donor's death if the donor left a surviving spouse or descendant who contests the gift within eight months of the donor's death.[22] Other states invalidate testamentary gifts to charity that exceed one-third of the value of the estate of a donor survived by descendants,[23] that exceed one-third of the value of the estate of a donor survived by a spouse or descendants,[24] that exceed

---

[16]*Id.* at 735. The *Heritage Village* decision was rejected by three dissenting judges in a well-reasoned and articulate opinion.

[17]FLA. STAT. § 731.19.

[18]The term *testamentary gift* refers generally to any gift made in a will or other instrument designed to take effect at the donor's death.

[19]IDAHO CODE § 14-326.

[20]GA. CODE § 113-107; MISS. CODE ANN. § 671.

[21]CAL. PROBATE CODE §§ 41-43.

[22]FLA. STAT. § 731.19.

[23]IDAHO CODE § 14-326.

[24]GA. CODE § 113-107; MISS. CODE ANN. § 3565.

one-fourth of the value of the estate of a donor survived by descendants,[25] or that exceed one-half of the value of the estate of a donor survived by descendants or parents.[26] In some states the invalidity is automatic, while in others the charitable gift must be contested or it will stand.

The validity of statutes limiting the right of religious organizations to receive gifts under the will of a donor has been questioned in a number of cases. In a leading case, the Supreme Court of Pennsylvania struck down a state law invalidating any testamentary gift for religious or charitable purposes included in a will executed within thirty days of the death of the donor.[27] The court reasoned that the Fourteenth Amendment to the United States Constitution, which prohibits states from denying to any persons the "equal protection of the laws," requires that statutory classifications must be "reasonable, not arbitrary, and must rest upon some ground of difference having a fair and substantial relation to the object of the legislation, so that all persons similarly circumstanced shall be treated alike."[28] The Pennsylvania statute, concluded the court, divided donors into two classes, one class being composed of donors whose wills provided for charitable gifts and who died within thirty days of executing their wills, and the other of donors who either made no charitable gifts in their wills or who survived the execution of their wills by at least thirty days. Gifts made by a donor in the first class were nullified by the statute, while gifts made by donors in the second class were permitted.

Such a classification, concluded the court, violated the Fourteenth Amendment's equal protection clause and therefore was impermissible:

> Clearly, the statutory classification bears only the most tenuous relation to the legislative purpose. The statute strikes down the charitable gifts of one in the best of health at the time of the execution of his will and regardless of age if he chances to die in an accident 29 days later. On the other hand, it leaves untouched the charitable bequests of another, aged and suffering from a terminal disease, who survives the execution of his will by 31 days. Such a combination of results can only be characterized as arbitrary.[29]

The court also observed that although the legislative purpose was to protect a donor's immediate family, the statute sought to nullify testamentary gifts to charity even where the donor left no immediate family. Protection of distant

[25]Ohio Rev. Code Ann. § 2107.06.

[26]N.Y. Estates, Powers & Trusts Law § 5-3.3.

[27]In re Estate of Cavill, 329 A.2d 503 (Pa. 1974). *See generally* Annot., 6 A.L.R.4th 603 (1981).

[28]*Id.* at 505.

[29]*Id.* at 505-06.

relatives with whom a donor may have had little if any contact during his life was not consistent with the statute's purpose, the court concluded.

Other courts have reached similar results. Thus, for example, a District of Columbia statute invalidating any gift to a clergyman or religious organization made in a will executed less than thirty days prior to a donor's death was struck down on the ground that it arbitrarily discriminated against clergymen and religious organizations. A court emphasized that the law did not invalidate gifts to nonreligious charitable organizations that were in an equal position with religious organizations to influence a donor.[30]

One judge has observed that laws limiting the right of religious organizations to receive testamentary gifts are invalid if they are based on a desire to prevent clergymen from influencing the dying by holding out "hopes of salvation or avoidance of damnation" in return for generous gifts to further the practice of religion. Such an objective "is precisely what the 'free exercise' of religion clause of the First Amendment forbids, for it is premised upon the assumption that such representations are false and hence Congress can enact safeguards against their effect."[31]

Another court held that a state's adoption of the Uniform Probate Code by implication repealed a law limiting testamentary gifts to charity.[32]

Although a few courts have upheld the constitutionality of such laws,[33] it seems likely that statutory limitations on the right of charitable organizations to receive testamentary gifts will generally be viewed with disfavor by the courts. The repeal of such statutes ordinarily would have the salutary effect of abolishing the irrebuttable presumption that certain gifts to charity are the product of undue influence, and of compelling disinherited heirs to prove undue influence in order to invalidate testamentary gifts to charity.

## §C. Federal and State Securities Laws

Laws regulating the sale of securities have been enacted by the federal government[34] and by all fifty states.[35] The term *security* is defined very broadly by such laws. The Uniform Securities Act, which has been adopted by a majority of the fifty states, defines a *security* as

---

[30]Estate of French, 365 A.2d 621 (D.C. 1976), *appeal dismissed,* 434 U.S. 59 (1977).

[31]*Id.* at 625 (Reilly, C.J., concurring).

[32]Matter of Estate of Holmes, 599 P.2d 344 (Mont. 1979).

[33]In re Will of Kruger, 257 N.Y.S.2d 232 (1965), *aff'd,* 267 N.Y.S.2d 215 (1966).

[34]Securities Act of 1933, 15 U.S.C. §§ 77a-77aa.

[35]Nearly forty states have enacted all or significant portions of the Uniform Securities Act.

any note; stock; treasury stock; bond; debenture; evidence of indebtedness; certificate of interest or participation in any profit-sharing agreement; collateral trust certificate; preorganization certificate or subscription; transferable share; investment contract; voting trust certificate; certificate of deposit for a security; certificate of interest or participation in an oil, gas, or mining title or lease or in payments out of production under such a title or lease; or in general any interest or instrument commonly known as a "security" . . . .[36]

This definition is broad enough to include many instruments utilized in church fundraising efforts.

Securities laws were enacted to protect the public against fraudulent and deceptive practices in the sale of securities and to provide full and fair disclosure to prospective investors. To achieve these purposes, most securities laws impose the following conditions on the sale of securities:

1. registration of proposed securities with the federal or state government in advance of sale
2. filing of sales and advertising literature with the federal or state government
3. registration of agents and broker-dealers who will be selling the securities
4. prohibition of fraudulent practices

Although the federal government and most states exempt securities offered by any organization "organized and operated not for private profit but exclusively for religious . . . purposes" from registration,[37] it is important to note that some states do not exempt the securities of religious organizations from registration;[38] others impose conditions on the exemption;[39] many require that an application for exemption be submitted and approved before a claim of

[36]UNIFORM SECURITIES ACT § 401 (l).

[37]Section 3(a)(4) of the federal Securities Act of 1933 and section 402 of the Uniform Securities Act exempt the securities of nonprofit religious organizations from registration.

[38]For example, the securities laws of Indiana, Louisiana, Minnesota, Nevada, Ohio, and Pennsylvania do not exempt the securities of religious organizations from registration.

[39]For example, § 451.802(a)(8) of the Michigan Securities Act exempts the securities of nonprofit organizations from registration only if an offering circular is submitted and approved, no commissions are paid to any person other than a registered broker-dealer, and sales are made only through registered broker-dealers or persons exempted from the term *agent*. These conditions apply only to offerings with an aggregate sales price of $50,000 or more. The South Dakota Securities Act exempts only those religious organizations that are organized under South Dakota law. North Carolina has a similar provision. A wide variety of other "conditions" exist in other states.

exemption will be recognized; and all securities laws subject churches and other religious organizations to the antifraud requirements. Churches therefore must not assume that any securities that they may offer are automatically exempt from registration or regulation. In the minority of jurisdictions in which a church must register its securities, registration is accomplished by filing a registration statement with the state securities commission setting forth the following information: the name and address of the church; the date of incorporation; a description of the general character of the church's operations; a description of the church's properties; the name, address, and occupation of each director, and the compensation, if any, that each receives from the church; the kind and amount of securities to be offered; the proposed offering price for each security; estimated commissions and finding fees; and estimated cash proceeds to the church from the sale of registered securities. In addition, the following materials must accompany the registration statement: a copy of any prospectus, offering circular, or other sales literature; a specimen copy of the securities being registered; a copy of the church's articles of incorporation and bylaws; a copy of any trust indenture under which the securities are being offered; a signed opinion of legal counsel as to the legality of the security being registered; a written consent of any accountant having prepared or certified a report or valuation which is used in connection with the registration statement; a balance sheet; profit and loss statements for each of the preceding three fiscal years; a check to cover the filing fee; and such other material as the securities commission may require.[40]

The method of registration described above is referred to as registration by qualification. Most states provide for two other methods of registration: registration by coordination and registration by notification. Churches will rarely if ever utilize registration by coordination, since this method assumes registration of an issuer's securities under the federal Securities Act of 1933 and churches are exempt from registration under this Act. Registration by notification is available to securities issued by a corporation that has been in continuous operation for at least five years if the corporation satisfies a minimum net earnings test. A registration statement similar to that described in connection with registration by qualification must be filed for a registration by notification.

The registration statement ordinarily is prepared on a form provided by the state securities commission. Considerable effort has been expended to standardize securities laws and related forms among the fifty states. Most states now permit issuers to register their securities on a uniform application developed by the American Bar Association. This uniform application is called Form U-1.

[40]UNIFORM SECURITIES ACT § 304.

Generally, the filing of a registration statement with a state securities commission constitutes registration of the security unless the commission objects to the registration statement within a prescribed period. A state securities commission retains the authority to suspend or revoke a registration of securities on the basis of a variety of grounds, including fraud, unreasonable commissions, illegality, omission of a material fact in the registration statement, and willful violation of any rule, order, or condition imposed by the securities commission.[41] Registration of securities generally is effective for one year, although some state laws stipulate that a registration will expire when the securities described in the registration statement have been sold.

Most securities laws that exempt church securities from registration also exempt churches from the requirement of filing sales and advertising literature with the securities commission. Again, churches must not assume that they are exempt from the filing requirement, since some state securities laws contain no such exemption. Furthermore, even if a church is exempt from the requirement of filing its sales and advertising literature with a state securities commission, it may be deemed to have entered into fraudulent transactions with investors if at or before the time of a sale or an offer to sell it does not provide each investor with a prospectus or offering circular containing sufficient information about the securities to enable an investor to make an informed investment decision.

The North American Securities Administrators Association has developed guidelines for a church to follow in drafting a prospectus or offering circular. In general, these guidelines require certain basic information on the cover page, and in addition require a full description of the history and operations of the church; the church's prior borrowing experience; risk factors associated with investment in the church's securities; how funds will be held during the offering period; anticipated use of proceeds; current financial condition of the church, accompanied by financial statements for the past three years; the church's properties; the type and amount of the securities to be offered, including interest rates, maturity dates, payment dates, and paying agent; the plan of distribution; pending or threatened legal proceedings against the church; tax aspects of ownership of the church's securities; and the church's leadership.

It is important to observe that most states require that persons who sell or offer to sell securities be registered with the state securities commission. Registration involves submitting a detailed application[42] and, in most cases, the successful completion of a securities law examination. Many states that exempt the securities of religious organizations from registration do not exempt persons

---

[41]*Id.* at § 306.

[42]Most states accept the uniform Form U-4 prepared by the National Association of Securities Dealers. *See generally* chapter 4, § G, *supra.*

selling or offering to sell such securities from the salesman registration requirements.

No state securities law exempts religious organizations from the antifraud provisions. The antifraud provisions of the Uniform Securities Act are set forth in section 101:

> It is unlawful for any person, in connection with the offer, sale or purchase of any security, directly or indirectly
>
> (1) to employ any device, scheme, or artifice to defraud;
>
> (2) to make any untrue statement of a material fact or to omit to state a material fact necessary in order to make the statements made, in the light of the circumstances under which they are made, not misleading; or
>
> (3) to engage in any act, practice, or course of business which operates or would operate as a fraud or deceit upon any person.

This section is substantially the same as section 17(a) of the federal Securities Act of 1933. Section 17 expressly states that the Act's exemption of nonprofit organizations from the registration requirements does not apply to the antifraud provisions.

The antifraud provisions of federal and state securities laws are very broad. They have been construed to prohibit a wide variety of activities, including making false or misleading statements about church securities; failing to disclose material risks associated with securities; manipulating the church's financial records in order to facilitate the sale of securities; failing to establish a debt service or sinking fund reserve out of which church securities will be retired; making false predictions; recommending the sale of securities to investors without regard to their financial condition; inducing transactions that are excessive in view of an investor's financial resources; borrowing money from an investor; commingling investors' funds with the personal funds of another, such as a salesman; deliberately failing to follow an investor's instructions; making unfounded guarantees; misrepresenting to investors the true status of their funds; representing that funds of investors are insured or secure when in fact they are not; representing that investments are as safe as if they had been made in a bank, when this is not the case; and representing that securities have been approved of or recommended by the state securities commission or that the commission has passed in any way on the merits or qualifications of the securities or of any agent or salesman.

In a leading case, the federal Securities and Exchange Commission brought an action in federal court seeking to enjoin a church and its leader from violating the antifraud provisions of the Securities Act of 1933.[43] The church had solicited funds through investment plans consisting essentially of the sale of interest-

---

[43]Securities and Exchange Commission v. World Radio Mission, Inc., 544 F.2d 535 (1st Cir. 1976).

bearing notes to the general public. The notes were promoted through advertising literature extolling the security of the investment. For example, one
advertisement stated in part:

> You may be a Christian who has committed his life into the hands of God, but
> left his funds in the hands of a floundering world economy. Financial experts
> everywhere are predicting a disaster in the economy. They say it is only a matter
> of time. . . . God's economy does not sink when the world's economy hits a reef
> and submerges! Wouldn't it be wise to invest in His economy?

The Securities and Exchange Commission argued that the church had defrauded investors by such representations when in fact it had a substantially
increasing operating deficit that had jumped from $42,349 to $203,776 in the
preceding three years. This fact was not disclosed to investors.

The church argued that religious organizations are protected by the First
Amendment from the reach of securities laws. In rejecting this contention, the
court observed: "Defendants constantly emphasize that they are engaged in
'God's work.' No court has ever found that conduct, by being so described, is
automatically immunized from all regulation in the public interest."[44] The court
quoted with approval the United States Supreme Court's earlier observation
that "[n]othing we have said is intended even remotely to imply that, under
the cloak of religion, persons may, with impunity, commit frauds upon the
public."[45] The court found it irrelevant that investors had a "religious" motivation, that most investors were "believers," and that the church did not intend
to defraud or deceive anyone.

In another case, a minister was found guilty of engaging in fraudulent practices through failing to disclose to investors of church securities that he had
$116,000 in unsatisfied debts, that he had incurred $700,000 in unsatisfied
debts on behalf of a previous church through the sale of securities, and that
the church's financial statements were in error.[46]

A church engaged in a chain distributor scheme of marketing ministerial
credentials was found guilty of a fraudulent practice.[47] The church, whose

---

[44]*Id.* at 539 n.7.

[45]*Id.* at 537 n.3, quoting Cantwell v. Connecticut, 310 U.S. 296, 306 (1940). The
court was "surprised . . . by defendants' recitation of the parable of the servants en-
trusted with their master's talents. We do not question the parable, but insofar as it
indicates a duty to make loans, it is to make profitable ones. A servant contemplating
lending to a possibly shaky enterprise would do well to note the final verse." *Id.* at 538
n.6.

[46]Order of Florida Comptroller No. 78-1-DOS (February 17, 1978).

[47]People v. Life Science Church, 450 N.Y.S.2d 664 (1982).

archbishop was an attorney who had been disbarred for tax fraud in connection with the activities of the church, encouraged persons to become members by purchasing ministerial credentials for $3,500. Once the fee was paid, the minister would name and establish his own church chartered by the parent church. He could then either make donations to his church or take a vow of poverty placing all his property in the name of his church and then pay all personal and family expenses through the church's account, thereby avoiding all taxes. Each minister was given the right to act as a "missionary representative" and was entitled to a ten percent commission for each new member he recruited into the church. After recruiting two fully paid members in one month, the missionary representative was granted advancement to the "missionary supervisor" level and thereby became eligible to receive a special bonus of $500 for each new fully paid minister recruited. After the missionary supervisor level, one could become a "director" and receive a forty percent commission. Ministers were enticed through a demonstration of number doubling. Two became four, eight became sixteen, thirty-two became sixty-four, and commissions mounted from $350 to a total of $1,023,500 when 2,047 new recruits were added. A chart was prepared to give dramatic visual impact on how to become a millionaire. A court summarily concluded that such a scheme was fraudulent, and that application of state securities law to the church did not violate the First Amendment.

Many other churches have been investigated by the federal Securities and Exchange Commission and by state securities commissions. In most cases, the investigation was prompted by the complaint of an investor.

Churches that violate state securities laws face a variety of potential consequences under state and federal securities laws. These include investigations, hearings, subpoenas, injunctions, criminal actions, cancellation of sales, suits for monetary damages by aggrieved investors, monetary fines, and revocation of an exemption, or registration, of securities.

Finally, it is important to recognize that "good faith," lack of an intention to deceive, or lack of knowledge that a particular transaction is either fraudulent or otherwise in violation of securities law does not necessarily insulate one from liability. One court has held, for example, that the sale of unregistered securities in violation of state securities law is punishable despite the innocent intentions of the seller.[48] It is the prevailing rule of law, however, that private actions by

---

[48]Moerman v. Zipco, Inc., 302 F. Supp. 439 (E.D.N.Y. 1969), aff'd, 422 F.2d 871 (2nd Cir. 1970); Trump v. Badet, 327 P.2d 1001 (Ariz. 1958).

aggrieved investors alleging fraud in the sale of securities must demonstrate an actual intent to deceive or defraud.[49]

## §D. Copyright Law

### 1. IN GENERAL

The United States Constitution gives Congress the power to enact laws that "promote the progress of . . . [the] useful arts, by securing for limited times to authors . . . the exclusive right to their respective writings." In 1790, under the power granted by the new Constitution, Congress enacted the first copyright law. Congress enacted several other copyright laws in the ensuing years, and in 1870 enacted the first comprehensive copyright statute. This law was substantially revised in 1909. In 1976, Congress enacted a newly revised copyright act, which became effective on January 1, 1978. The new law is known as the Copyright Act of 1976.

In commenting on the purpose of the original constitutional provision, the United States Supreme Court has observed:

> [The Constitution] describes both the objective which Congress may seek and the means to achieve it. The objective is to promote the progress of . . . the arts. . . . To accomplish its purpose, Congress may grant to authors the exclusive right to the fruits of their respective works. An author who possesses an unlimited copyright may preclude others from copying his creation for commercial purposes without permission. In other words, to encourage people to devote themselves to intellectual and artistic creation, Congress may guarantee to authors . . . a reward in the form of control over the sale or commercial use of copies of their works.[50]

Compensation of authors is thus a secondary purpose of the copyright law.

### 2. SECURING COPYRIGHT PROTECTION

The objective of copyright law is to promote the progress of the useful arts by granting authors certain exclusive rights in their works. Under the Copyright Act of 1976, an author receives initial copyright protection as soon as he creates an original work of authorship and fixes it in any tangible medium of expres-

---

[49]The United States Supreme Court so held in Ernst & Ernst v. Hochfelder, 425 U.S. 185 (1976). While the *Ernst* decision dealt only with proof of an intent to deceive under the antifraud provisions of federal securities law, the decision has been held to apply by implication to private actions under the antifraud provisions of state securities laws. *See, e.g.,* Greenfield v. Cheek, 593 P.2d 293 (Ariz. 1978).

[50]Goldstein v. California, 412 U.S. 546, 555 (1973).

sion.[51] There are thus three prerequisites to initial copyright protection in a work: (1) the work must be original, (2) it must be a work of authorship, and (3) it must be fixed in a tangible medium of expression.

A work is *original* if an author created it by his own skill, labor, and judgment, and not by directly copying or evasively imitating the work of another. One court has stated that "[o]riginality means that the work owes its creation to the author and thus in turn means that the work must not consist of actual copying."[52] It is therefore clear that originality connotes independent creation.

It has been held consistently that originality does not necessarily mean novelty or creativity. One court has observed that "there must be independent creation, but it need not be invention in the sense of striking uniqueness, ingeniousness, or novelty," and that the test of originality "is concededly one with a low threshold in that 'all that is needed . . . is that the author contributed something more than a merely trivial variation, something recognizably his own.' "[53]

For a work to be entitled to initial copyright protection, it must constitute a *work of authorship* as defined by the Copyright Act. Section 102 of the Act provides that works of authorship include

1. literary works, such as books, periodicals, and manuscripts
2. musical works, including any accompanying words
3. dramatic works, including any accompanying music
4. pantomimes and choreographic works
5. pictorial, graphic, and sculptural works
6. motion pictures and other audiovisual works
7. sound recordings

Section 103 stipulates that compilations and derivative works are also entitled to copyright protection. *Compilation* is defined as "a work formed by the collection and assembling of pre-existing materials . . . that are selected, coordinated, or arranged in such a way that the resulting work as a whole constitutes an original work of authorship." *Derivative work* is defined as "a work based upon one or more pre-existing works, such as a translation, musical arrangement, dramatization, fictionalization, abridgement, condensation, or any other form in which a work may be recast, transformed, or adapted."

It is important to recognize that names and titles are not subject to copyright protection. They may be entitled to protection under federal trademark law if

[51]17 U.S.C. § 102(a).

[52]L. Batlin & Son, Inc. v. Snyder, 536 F.2d 486, 490 (2nd Cir. 1976), *cert. denied,* 429 U.S. 857 (1976).

[53]*Id.*

they are affixed to or associated with products or services and serve to identify the source of the products or services in a unique way.

For a work to be entitled to initial copyright protection, it must be fixed in some tangible medium of expression. Ideas, concepts, and discoveries therefore are not eligible for copyright protection until they are reduced to a tangible form.

The initial copyright protection that an author receives under the Copyright Act persists until the author publishes his work. The Act defines *publication* as "the distribution of copies . . . of a work to the public by sale or other transfer of ownership, or by rental, lease, or lending."[54] If an author wishes to perpetuate his copyright protection in a work after its publication, he generally must comply with the Act's notice requirements. Section 401 states:

> Whenever a work protected under this [Act] is published in the United States or elsewhere by authority of the copyright owner, a notice of copyright as provided by this section shall be placed on all publicly distributed copies from which the work can be visually perceived . . . .

Section 401 further specifies that the copyright notice must consist of the following three elements: (1) the symbol © or the word *copyright* or the abbreviation *copr.*, or, in the case of a sound recording, the symbol ℗; (2) the year of the first publication of the work; and (3) the name of the owner of the copyright or an abbreviation by which the name can be recognized. Section 401 also requires the copyright notice to be affixed to copies in such manner and location as to give reasonable notice of the claim of copyright.

Common defects in copyright notices include omission of one of the three essential elements; the elements of the notice are so dispersed that a necessary element is not identifiable as a part of the notice; the notice is not affixed to copies in such manner and location as to give reasonable notice of the claim of copyright;[55] the notice is in a foreign language; the name in the notice is that

---

[54]17 U.S.C. § 101.

[55]Copyright Office regulations set forth examples of acceptable locations for copyright notices. For example, in the case of works published in book form, the regulations provide that notices located in the following positions are acceptable: the title page; the page immediately following the title page, if any; either side of the front cover, if any; either side of the front leaf if there is no front cover; either side of the back cover, if any; either side of the back leaf if there is no back cover; the first page of the main body of the work; the last page of the main body of the work; any page between the front page and the first page of the main body of the work if there are no more than 10 pages between the front page and the first page of the main body of the work and the notice is reproduced prominently and is set apart from other matter on the page where it appears; any page between the last page of the main body of the work and the back page if there are no more than 10 pages between the last page of the main body of the work and the back page and the notice is reproduced prominently and is set apart from

of someone who had no authority to secure the copyright in his name; the year date in the copyright notice is later than the date of the year in which the copyright was actually secured; a notice is so permanently covered that it cannot be seen without tearing the work apart; a notice is so illegible or so small that it cannot be read without magnification; a notice is on a detachable tag and will eventually be detached and discarded when the work is put into use; or a notice is on a wrapper or container which is not a part of the work and which will eventually be removed and discarded when the work is put to use.

Certain defects in notice will not invalidate a copyright. For example, section 406 states that a copyright notice that lists the name of someone other than the copyright owner will not invalidate the copyright. The same section further states that a copyright notice that lists a year date earlier than the year in which publication first occurred will not invalidate the copyright, though it may affect the copyright term. If the year date is more than one year later than the year of publication, the work is considered to have been published without any notice.

The omission of a valid copyright notice from publicly distributed copies of a work will invalidate the author's copyright protection, unless (1) the notice was omitted from only a relatively small number of copies; (2) the work is registered with the Copyright Office within five years of publication without the notice, and a reasonable effort is made to add the notice to all copies distributed after the omission is discovered; or (3) the notice is omitted in violation of an express requirement in writing that, as a condition of the copyright owner's authorization of the public distribution of copies, they bear the prescribed notice. Of course, an author's copyright protection is not affected by the unauthorized removal, destruction, or obliteration of a valid notice from any publicly distributed copies.[56]

Section 407 of the Copyright Act provides that "the owner of copyright or of the exclusive right of publication in a work published with notice of copyright in the United States shall deposit, within three months after the date of such publication . . . two complete copies of the best edition" with the Copyright Office in Washington, D.C. Deposit of copyrighted works is a legal requirement. If no deposit is made, the Copyright Office may demand that the owner

---

other matter on the page where it appears; in the case of a work published as an issue of a periodical, in addition to any of the locations listed above, a notice is acceptable if located as part of or adjacent to a masthead, on the page containing the masthead if the notice is reproduced prominently and is set apart from other matter appearing on the page, or adjacent to a prominent heading appearing at or near the front of the issue containing the title of the periodical and any combination of the volume and issue number and date of the issue. See 37 C.F.R. § 201.20(d).

[56]17 U.S.C. § 405(c).

comply with the deposit requirement. If the owner does not comply with such a demand within three months, he will be assessed a fine of not more than $250 for each work, plus the cost to the Copyright Office of independently procuring two copies of the work, plus a penalty of $2,500 if noncompliance is willful.

Copyright Office regulations exempt various categories of materials from the deposit requirement of Section 407. Such categories include (1) greeting cards, picture postcards, and stationery; (2) lectures, sermons, speeches, and addresses when published individually and not as a collection of the works of one or more authors; (3) computer programs published only in machine readable copies; and (4) prints, labels, and other advertising matter published in connection with the lease or sale of articles of merchandise or works of authorship.

There is presently no fee for depositing copies with the Copyright Office. The Copyright Office does charge a nominal fee for the issuance of a receipt of deposit, but such a receipt is not necessary. It is important to note that Section 407 provides that the deposit requirement—regardless of fines and penalties—is not a condition of copyright protection.

The owner of a copyright in a work may register the copyright claim by delivering two complete copies of the best edition of a published work or one complete copy of an unpublished work, along with an application form and the application fee (currently ten dollars) to the Copyright Office. Deposits made to fulfill the deposit requirements of Section 407 may be used to satisfy the deposit requirements for registration if they are accompanied by the appropriate application form and the prescribed fee. Section 408(a) unequivocally states that "registration is not a condition of copyright protection." While registration is not necessary to secure copyright protection, it is nevertheless advisable in many contexts for a variety of reasons, including the following:

1. It is an inexpensive and simple procedure.

2. Section 410(c) provides that "[i]n any judicial proceedings the certificate of a registration made before or within five years after first publication of the work shall constitute prima facie evidence of the validity of the copyright and of the facts stated in the certificate." This advantage could save considerable time and expense if an infringement suit is ever filed, particularly when the infringement occurs several years after publication.

3. Registration entitles the copyright owner to broader rights. Section 412 provides that registration in advance of infringement or at any time within three months of initial publication entitles the copyright owner to statutory damages and attorneys fees in any infringement action. Statutory damages, which range from $250 to $10,000, are especially desirable when the amount of actual damages is difficult to ascertain.

4. Registration puts the public on constructive (*i.e.*, implied) notice that

copyright protection is claimed in a particular work. This is helpful in infringement actions.

5. Registration may compensate for the omission of a proper copyright notice. Section 405(a)(2) states that omission of a valid copyright notice does not invalidate the copyright in a work if "registration for the work has been made before or is made within five years after publication without notice, and a reasonable effort is made to add notice to all copies . . . that are distributed to the public . . . after the omission has been discovered . . . ."

A copyright is not of unlimited duration. The following table summarizes the duration of copyright protection in a variety of circumstances.

### Duration of Copyright Protection

| Work | Duration |
|---|---|
| Works created after January 1, 1978 | Life of author plus 50 years |
| Joint works created after January 1, 1978 | Life of last surviving author plus 50 years |
| Anonymous and pseudonymous works and works made for hire created after January 1, 1978 | 75 years from date of first publication, or 100 years from date of creation, whichever is earlier |
| Works created but not published or copyrighted before January 1, 1978 | From January 1, 1978, in accordance with above rules |
| Copyrights in first term on January 1, 1978 | 28 years from date of copyright, plus 47 years if application is made within 1 year of expiration of 28-year term |
| Copyrights in their renewal term before January 1, 1978 | 75 years from date of copyright |

### 3. Copyright Ownership and Transfer

Section 201 of the Copyright Act states that copyright protection initially vests in the author or authors of a work. Thus, as soon as an author creates an original work in a tangible form, he becomes the owner of the copyright interest in that work. The copyright ownership remains with the author until he effectively transfers it.

A work prepared by an employee within the scope of his employment is a "work made for hire." The employer is considered to be the author of such a work and the owner of the copyright unless it is expressly agreed otherwise in a written instrument signed by both employer and employee. Whether a particular work was created in the course of employment involves an inquiry into the nature of the relationship between the writer and his employer. The following factors suggest that a work was made by an employee in the course of his employment and thus is a work made for hire: the payment of wages or other remuneration; the right of the employer to direct and supervise the manner in which the work is performed; the existence of an employment contract; regular working hours; and the fact that the work was created in whole or in part at the employer's place of business.[57]

Section 201(d) states that the ownership of a copyright may be transferred in whole or in part by any means of conveyance or by operation of law and may be bequeathed by will or pass as personal property by the applicable laws of intestate succession. The same section specifies that a copyright owner may transfer any of the "exclusive rights" associated with a valid copyright.

### 4. INFRINGEMENT

A copyright owner has the exclusive right to reproduce the copyrighted work in copies; prepare derivative works based upon the copyrighted work, such as translations, musical arrangements, and abridgments; distribute copies of the work to the public by sale; and perform the work publicly.[58] Anyone who violates any of these exclusive rights ordinarily is an infringer of the copyright. The Copyright Act specifies, however, that the following categories of conduct do not constitute infringement:

1. The fair use of a copyrighted work for purposes such as criticism, comment, news reporting, teaching, scholarship, or research. In determining "fair use," courts will consider (a) the purpose and character of the use, (b) the nature of the copyrighted work, (c) the amount and substantiality of the portion used in relation to the copyrighted work as a whole, and (d) the effect of the use upon the potential market for or value of the copyrighted work.

2. Certain reproductions of copyrighted works by libraries or archives if the reproductions are made without commercial motivation, the library or archives is open to the public, and reproductions contain the original copyright notice.

3. The performance or display of a work by instructors or pupils in the course of face-to-face teaching activities of a nonprofit educational institution in a classroom setting.

4. The performance of a nondramatic literary or musical work or of a dra-

---

[57]Picture Music, Inc. v. Bourne, Inc., 314 F. Supp. 640 (S.D.N.Y. 1970), aff'd, 457 F.2d 1213 (2nd Cir. 1972), cert. denied, 409 U.S. 997 (1972).

[58]17 U.S.C. § 106.

matico-musical work of a religious nature, or display of a work, in the course of services at a place of worship or other religious assembly.

5. The performance of a nondramatic literary or musical work in the course of a transmission, if the performance is a regular part of the instructional activities of a nonprofit educational institution and the transmission is made primarily for reception in classrooms or by disabled persons unable to attend classrooms.

6. The performance of a nondramatic literary or musical work otherwise than in a transmission to the public, without commercial motivation and without payment of any fee or other compensation to the performer or organizer, so long as there is no admissions charge or the proceeds from any admissions charge are used exclusively (less reasonable costs of production) for education, religion, or charitable purposes and not for private gain, unless the copyright owner has served written notice of objection to the performance to the person responsible for the performance at least seven days prior thereto.

Even if none of the exceptions to copyright infringement recited above is applicable, an alleged infringer has a variety of defenses available to him, including the following: the infringed work does not have a valid copyright because it was not original, it was not a "work of authorship," or it was not fixed in a tangible medium of expression; the copyright owner consented to the infringement; the copyright owner did not file an infringement suit within three years after the infringement occurred; the copyright notice was either defective or omitted; or the copyright term has expired.

A copyright owner who demonstrates that another has infringed upon his copyright has a variety of remedies available to him, including court injunctions prohibiting further infringement, impoundment of infringing articles, actual monetary damages, statutory damages, costs, and legal expenses.

### 5. Application of Copyright Law to the Church

Section 110(3) of the Copyright Act specifies that the "performance of a nondramatic literary or musical work or of a dramatico-musical work of a religious nature, or display of a work, in the course of services at a place of worship or other religious assembly" is not an infringement of copyright. *Performance of a nondramatic literary work* means reading from a book or periodical in a nondramatic manner. Thus, for example, a copyrighted translation of the Bible can be quoted publicly in the course of religious services, as can any book or periodical of a religious nature. Without the exception contained in section 110, such readings might constitute copyright infringement since one of a copyright owner's exclusive rights is the right to perform his work publicly. Similarly, a copyrighted musical work of a religious nature can be performed in the course of services at a place of worship or other religious assembly. Therefore copyrighted hymns, solo materials, orchestrations, and choral arrangements of a religious nature may be performed in religious services. Without the exception contained in section 110, such performances might constitute copyright infringements. Dramatico-musical works of a religious nature may also be performed in the course of religious services. Such works include certain performances of sacred music that may be regarded as dramatic, such as oratorios and cantatas. Also exempted from copyright infringement are displays of works of all kinds in the course of religious services.

The exemption is not intended to cover performances of secular operas, musical plays, motion pictures, and the like, even if they have an underlying religious or philosophical theme and take place in the course of religious services.

To be exempted under section 110, a performance or display must be "in the course of services," and thus activities at a place of worship that are for social, educational, fundraising, or entertainment purposes are excluded. Some performances of these kinds may be exempted under section 110(4). This section exempts from copyright infringement certain performances of nondramatic literary or musical works that are performed without admissions charge or that are performed with an admissions charge if the proceeds are used exclusively for educational, religious, or charitable purposes and not for private financial gain, unless the copyright owner has served notice of objection to the performance at least seven days before the performance.

Since the performance or display must also occur "at a place of worship or other religious assembly" the exemption would not extend to religious broadcasts or other transmissions to the public at large, even where the transmissions were sent from a place of worship. Nor would the exemption apply to the public distribution of tape recordings of religious services containing any copyrighted materials. Thus, while a copyrighted religious musical work may be performed at a religious service, publicly distributed tape recordings of the service that reproduce the copyrighted work do not constitute a performance of the work in the course of services at a place of worship and, accordingly, such recordings are not exempt under section 110. On the other hand, as long as services are being conducted before a religious assembly, the exemption would apply even if they were conducted in such places as auditoriums and outdoor theaters.

The exemption provided by section 110 exempts only religious performances in the course of religious services from copyright infringement. The Act states that to *perform* a work means to recite or render it. Performance of a copyrighted hymn or choral arrangement thus means to sing it, and performance of a copyrighted cantata means to present it. There is therefore no license to copy a copyrighted work, such as by duplicating a single piece of music for all of the members of a choir, since duplication does not constitute a performance even though the duplicated copies may eventually be used in a performance. Only the copyright owner has the right to reproduce a copyrighted work by making copies. Similarly, a church may not assemble a booklet of copyrighted hymns or choruses (lyrics or music) for use by its members in the course of religious services since this would necessitate copying the protected works. Of course, a church can duplicate a musical work or lyrics whose copyright term has expired or that never was subject to copyright protection since such works are considered to be in the public domain.

Often overlooked is the fact that both the musical score and lyrics of a hymn or chorus are eligible for copyright protection. Section 102(a) of the Copyright Act states that copyright protection subsists in original "musical works, including any accompanying words," that are reduced to a tangible form. Thus, if an individual composes both the music and lyrics of an original hymn, he is entitled to copyright protection for both. This has important consequences. It means, primarily, that no one can make copies of either the music or lyrics without authorization. A church will infringe upon this copyright protection if it, for example, inserts only the words of a particular song in a booklet or on a songsheet, or types them on a piece of paper and projects them onto a screen.

It is also important to recognize that one of the copyright owner's exclusive rights is the right to prepare derivative works based upon the copyrighted work. Derivative works include musical arrangements. Therefore, it is not permissible for anyone other than the copyright owner or one whom the copyright owner has authorized to create an arrangement of a copyrighted musical work. To illustrate, one church choir director who made a choral arrangement of a copyrighted hymn without authorization was found to be guilty of copyright infringement.[59] The director's arrangement consisted of the entire score of the copyrighted hymn plus the insertion of a four-measure introduction. The director made several copies of his arrangement on the church's duplicating machine. Each copy contained the director's name and identified him as the arranger. The copyright owner brought a lawsuit against the director and his church, alleging copyright infringement. A federal appeals court found the director and his employing church jointly liable for copyright infringement. The court found the director's lack of intent to infringe to be irrelevant, and concluded that the copying of all or substantially all of a copyrighted musical work could not be considered "fair use."

It is permissible to make arrangements of preexisting musical works if the preexisting work is in the public domain or if the copyright owner of the preexisting work grants permission. Section 103 of the Act states that lawfully made derivative works are entitled to copyright protection if they otherwise qualify. Section 103 also stipulates that copyright protection in a derivative

---

[59]Wihtol v. Crow, 309 F.2d 777 (8th Cir. 1962).

work extends only to the material contributed by the author of such work as distinguished from the preexisting material employed in the work. Thus, although a musical arrangement of a public domain song is subject to copyright protection, the copyright protection extends only to the new musical score and not to the lyrics of the preexisting work. As a result, churches can copy the lyrics of such arrangements without infringing the arranger's copyright.

Another court rejected the claim that the First Amendment right to freely exercise one's religion immunized from liability for copyright infringement a group of priests who toured the country giving unauthorized performances of the rock opera *Jesus Christ Superstar.*[60]

Some churches use transparencies or opaque projectors to display a copy of a hymn or other musical work in order to teach a choir or congregation the words and music. Is this practice permissible? Initially, it should be recalled that one of a copyright owner's "exclusive rights" is the right to display a copyrighted work publicly. Section 109(b) of the Copyright Act limits this exclusive right by stipulating that

> the owner of a particular copy lawfully made under this title, or any person authorized by such owner, is entitled, without the authorization of the copyright owner, to display that copy publicly, either directly or by the projection of no more than one image at a time, to viewers present at the place where the copy is located.

Congress, in commenting on this provision, observed that "[w]here the copy itself is intended for projection, as in the case of a photographic slide, negative, or transparency, the public projection of a single image would be permitted as long as the viewers are 'present at the place where the copy is located.' "[61] The projection of multiple images of a work would not be protected, as when the same work is displayed simultaneously on more than one screen.

Section 109(b) would authorize the use of an opaque projector to display a copy of a musical work in the course of choir rehearsals or church services since the opaque projector displays an image of a lawfully made copy consisting ordinarily of either sheet music or a page in a hymnal. But if a church makes a transparency of an existing copyrighted musical work without authorization, such a transparency would not be a lawfully made copy and thus could not be displayed without infringing the owner's copyright. Section 109(b) would authorize the display of a transparency in the course of choir rehearsals or church

---

[60]Robert Stigwood Group Limited v. O'Reilly, 346 F. Supp. 376 (D. Conn. 1972), *rev'd on other grounds,* 530 F.2d 1096 (2nd Cir. 1976), *cert. denied,* 429 U.S. 848 (1976).

[61]H.R. Rep. No. 94-1476, 94th Cong., 2d Sess. 79-80 (1976).

services if the transparency constituted a lawfully made copy. This could occur in two ways. First, a transparency purchased from an authorized vendor would be a lawful copy and could be displayed publicly. Second, a transparency of a public domain work could be fabricated and displayed.

Congress has stated that the purpose of section 109(b) is not only to preserve the traditional privilege of the owner of a copy to display it directly, but also to place reasonable restrictions on the ability of others to display it indirectly in such a way that the copyright owner's market for reproduction and distribution of copies would be affected.[62] Accordingly, it is likely that continued public display of a copyrighted work by a church would tend to result in a loss of the protection afforded by section 109(b). For example, if a church choir director projected a copyrighted musical arrangement on a screen for several weeks in succession in an effort to have his choir memorize the work, the repetitive display of the work might not be eligible for protection under section 109(b).

Finally, considerable confusion surrounds the application of section 110(1) of the Copyright Act to churches. Section 110(1) states that the "performance or display of a work by instructors or pupils in the course of face-to-face teaching activities of a nonprofit educational institution, in a classroom or similar place devoted to instruction" is not an infringement of copyright. This section permits the performance or display of copyrighted works, and thus the following activities are authorized: reading aloud from a copyrighted text, performing or singing a musical work, displaying a filmstrip or movie, or displaying text or pictorial material by means of an opaque projector. Nothing in section 110(1) is intended to sanction the unauthorized reproduction of copies. And, it is unlikely that section 110(1) will be interpreted to apply to educational instruction within churches, since churches probably will be construed to be religious and not educational institutions. Furthermore, the exemption applies only to teaching activities in a classroom or similar place devoted to systematic instructional activities. Thus, performance in an auditorium or sanctuary where the audience is not confined to the members of a particular class would not be exempted.

## §E. Zoning Law

The vast majority of municipalities in the United States have enacted zoning laws. The purpose of a municipal zoning law

is to regulate the growth and development of the city in an orderly manner. Among the objectives to be served is to avoid mixing together of industrial,

---

[62]*Id.* at 80.

commercial, business and residential uses; the prevention of undue concentrations of people in certain areas under undesirable conditions; making provisions for safe and efficient transportation; for recreational needs; and for the enhancement of aesthetic values, all in order to best serve the purpose of promoting the health, safety, morals and general welfare of the city and its inhabitants.[63]

It is important to recognize that municipalities have no inherent authority to enact zoning laws. Zoning laws constitute an exercise of the police power—that is, the authority inherent in state governments to enact laws in furtherance of the public health, safety, morals, and general welfare. Unless a state specifically delegates such authority to a municipality, the municipality will have no authority to enact a zoning ordinance. Most states, however, have adopted "enabling acts" which delegate such authority to designated municipalities. The authority of a municipality to enact a zoning ordinance therefore is limited by the terms of the enabling statute. It is also limited by constitutional considerations, for it is a well-settled legal principle that the United States Constitution prohibits the enactment of zoning ordinances that are unreasonable, discriminatory, or arbitrary. And since a state's delegation of zoning power to a municipality constitutes a delegation of state "police power," a municipal zoning ordinance to be valid must in fact further the public health, safety, morals, or general welfare.

The typical zoning ordinance divides a municipality into zones or districts in which only certain activities or uses are permitted. For example, it is common for a municipal zoning ordinance to divide a municipality into residential, commercial, and industrial districts, with the activities and uses permitted in each district described in the ordinance. Nonconforming uses and activities may be authorized in some cases through variances, special use permits, or by the fact that the nonconforming use preceded the enactment of the zoning ordinance.

The zoning laws of most municipalities permit churches in residential districts. This principle is a vestige of the pre-automobile era when churches located themselves within walking distance of private residences. With the advent of the automobile, churches became more incompatible with residential districts because of the increase in noise, pollution, traffic congestion, and danger created by the automobiles of church members. Accordingly, many municipalities have attempted to exclude churches from residential districts. To illustrate, one municipality denied a congregation permission to construct a church on a two-acre tract of undeveloped property in a residential district on the grounds that the presence of a church and its associated traffic would devalue the adjoining properties, create a fire hazard, and adversely affect the health,

[63]Naylor v. Salt Lake City Corporation, 410 P.2d 764, 765 (Utah 1966).

safety, and welfare of neighborhood residents. A court, in overruling the action of the municipality, held that the potential traffic and safety hazards and property devaluation were outweighed by "the constitutional prohibition against the abridgement of the free exercise of religion and by the public benefit and welfare which is itself an attribute of religious worship in a community."[64]

Another court, in striking down a municipal ordinance that prohibited churches in residential areas, held that the ordinance constituted "a violation of the fundamental right of freedom to worship protected by the First and Fourteenth Amendments to the United States Constitution . . . ."[65] The court observed that "[e]arly and modern case law alike has not countenanced the exclusion of churches from residential districts, even though inconveniences may be caused by the influx into a neighborhood of vehicular or pedestrian traffic."[66] The court also acknowledged that churches are subject to such reasonable regulations as may be necessary to promote the public health, safety, and general welfare, but insisted that "[r]easonable restrictions . . . are not tantamount to exclusion."[67]

Such cases reflect the view of "the long line of cases"[68] or the "wide majority of courts"[69] that churches may not be excluded from residential districts. This conclusion generally rests upon one of two grounds: first, that the exclusion of churches from residential districts infringes upon the freedom of religion guaranteed by the First Amendment, and second, that a total exclusion of churches is an invalid and impermissible exercise of the police power since it cannot be said to further the public health, safety, morals, or general welfare.[70] Obviously, any attempt by a municipality to totally exclude churches from all districts, whether residential, commercial, or industrial, would be unconstitutional.[71]

A small minority of jurisdictions have held that churches may be excluded from residential districts if neighboring landowners can demonstrate an ad-

---

[64]American Friends of the Society of St. Pius, Inc. v. Schwab, 417 N.Y.S.2d 991, 993 (1979), *appeal denied*, 425 N.Y.S.2d 1027 (1980).

[65]Church of Christ v. Metropolitan Board of Zoning, 371 N.E.2d 1331, 1333-34 (Ind. 1978).

[66]*Id.* at 1334.

[67]*Id.*

[68]5 E. YOKLEY, ZONING LAW AND PRACTICE § 35-14 (4th ed. 1980).

[69]State v. Maxwell, 617 P.2d 816, 820 (Ha. 1980).

[70]*See generally* A. RATHKOPF, THE LAW OF ZONING AND PLANNING § 20.01 (1982) [hereinafter cited as RATHKOPF]; Comment, *Zoning the Church: Toward a Concept of Reasonableness,* 12 CONN. L. REV. 571 (1980); Note, *Zoning Ordinances, Private Religious Conduct, and the Free Exercise of Religion,* 76 NW. L. REV. 786 (1981); Note, *Churches and Zoning,* 70 HARV. L. REV. 1428 (1957).

[71]*See* RATHKOPF, *supra* note 70, at section 20.01.

verse impact upon the public health, safety, morals, or welfare. Thus, in one case, a church was held to have been properly excluded from a residential district where there was evidence that the presence of a church would create traffic congestion with associated noise, fumes, intrusion of automobile lights, blocking of private driveways by parked cars, and delays in normal travel for residents using nearby streets.[72] The court concluded that exclusion of churches from residential districts did not violate the First Amendment guaranty of freedom of religion. Another court upheld the validity of a zoning ordinance that permitted churches to be constructed in residential districts only upon the issuance of a special use exception following a hearing and a finding that the church would not adversely affect the value of surrounding lands and that adequate parking would be available.[73]

One court, in upholding a city's exclusion of a church from a residential area, rejected the claim that the church's freedom of religion had been abridged: "The denial of a building permit did not prohibit any one from religious worship and there is nothing in the record before us to indicate that the church building could not be erected if located in the area zoned for that purpose."[74] It is a fairly common practice for municipalities to require churches to apply for a special use permit prior to construction of a sanctuary in a residential district. This procedure ordinarily involves submission of detailed building and site plans to the municipality. The municipality, while incapable of completely excluding churches from residential districts, can determine those sites within a residential district that are best suited to church use. This procedure has been sanctioned by a number of courts as a proper accommodation of freedom of worship with the legitimate interests of residential property owners.[75] A municipality has the burden of justifying the denial of a permit. One court has observed:

Since a city cannot legally exclude a church from a residential district by a zoning ordinance, it cannot legally accomplish the same result by denying permits unless the reasons for refusing the permits are based on valid evidence showing that the existence of a church in this area would be detrimental to the health, the safety, the morals or the general welfare of the community.[76]

[72]Milwaukie Co. of Jehovah's Witnesses v. Mullen, 330 P.2d 5 (Ore. 1958).

[73]Plyant v. Orange County, 328 So.2d 199 (Fla. 1976).

[74]Corporation of Presiding Bishop v. City of Porterville, 203 P.2d 823, 825-26 (Cal. 1949), *appeal dismissed,* 338 U.S. 805 (1949). *Accord* Matthews v. Board of Supervisors, 21 Cal. Rptr. 914 (Cal. 1962).

[75]*See* RATHKOPF, *supra* note 70 at § 20.01.

[76]Congregation Committee v. City Council, 287 S.W.2d 700 (Tex. 1956).

Some courts, while recognizing the right of churches to exist in residential districts, have upheld the application of reasonable municipal regulations to churches. To illustrate, it has been held that a local ordinance requiring churches to provide one usable off-street parking place for each three sanctuary seats did not abridge a church's freedom of religion.[77] And, it has been held that a local ordinance prohibiting off-street parking of trucks and buses in residential districts could be applied to churches located in such districts.[78]

As has been noted elsewhere,[79] it is occasionally difficult to determine whether a particular use or activity constitutes a church. For example, the following uses have been deemed to constitute churches and thus their location within a residential district was upheld: use of a home across the street from a church for women's fellowship meetings and religious education classes,[80] a single-family residence used by the United Presbyterian Church as a religious coffeehouse for university students,[81] a twenty-four-acre tract of land containing a large mansion which was used as a synagogue and a meeting place for the congregation's social groups and youth activities,[82] and a thirty-seven-acre estate used by an Episcopal church as a religious retreat and center for religious instruction.[83]

The term *church* has been held not to include camp meetings;[84] a parish house used for Sunday school, choir practice, and church committee meetings;[85] a religious retreat house;[86] a dwelling of sixteen bedrooms and twelve bathrooms occupied by twenty-five persons comprising four different families, all members of the American Orthodox Catholic church;[87] a child-care center operated in a minister's residence;[88] and a twenty-eight-acre tract used by a Jewish foundation as a conference center, leadership training center, and children's retreat.[89]

---

[77]Allendale Congregation of Jehovah's Witnesses v. Grosman, 152 A.2d 569 (N.J. 1959).

[78]East Side Baptist Church v. Klein, 487 P.2d 549 (Colo. 1971).

[79]*See* chapter 7, *supra.*

[80]Twin-City Bible Church v. Zoning Board of Appeals, 365 N.E.2d 1381 (Ill. 1977).

[81]Synod of Chesapeake, Inc. v. Newark, 254 A.2d 611 (Del. 1969).

[82]Community Synagogue v. Bates, 154 N.Y.S.2d 15 (1956).

[83]Diocese of Rochester v. Planning Board, 154 N.Y.S.2d 849 (1956).

[84]Portage Township v. Full Salvation Union, 29 N.W.2d 297 (Mich. 1947).

[85]Newark Athletic Club v. Board of Adjustment, 144 A. 167 (N.J. 1928).

[86]Independent Church of the Realization of the Word of God, Inc. v. Board of Zoning Appeals, 437 N.Y.S.2d 443 (1981).

[87]People v. Kalayjian, 352 N.Y.S.2d 115 (1973).

[88]Heard v. Dallas, 456 S.W.2d 440 (Tex. 1970).

[89]State ex rel. B'nai B'rith Foundation v. Walworth County, 208 N.W.2d 113 (Wis. 1973).

Many zoning laws permit uses that are "accessory" to a permitted use. To illustrate, one court upheld a church's right to construct a recreational complex on property adjacent to its sanctuary despite the claim of neighboring land-owners that the complex was not a church and thus should not be permitted in a residential district.[90] The court concluded that "the term 'church' is broader than the church building itself" and must be interpreted to include "uses customarily incidental or accessory to church uses . . . if reasonably closely related, both in distance and space, to the main church purpose."[91] The court upheld the use of the recreational complex since the activities conducted on the field were an integral part of the church's overall program.

Other courts have found that the following uses were accessory to a permitted church use and therefore were appropriate in a residential district: a church activities building and playground,[92] a kindergarten play area,[93] a parking lot,[94] residential use of church buildings by members,[95] a home for parochial school teachers,[96] a school,[97] and a neon sign constructed on church property to inform the public as to the time of worship services.[98]

Not every use of church property, however, will be so approved. The fol-lowing uses of church property have been disallowed on the ground that they were not accessory to permitted church use: parking of a church bus on church property,[99] a ritualarium constructed by a Jewish synagogue,[100] a 301-foot radio transmission tower that was more than ten times higher than neighboring residences,[101] and a school.[102]

---

[90]Corporation of the Presiding Bishop v. Ashton, 448 P.2d 185 (Ida. 1968).

[91]*Id.* at 188.

[92]Board of Zoning Appeals v. New Testament Bible Church, Inc., 411 N.E.2d 681 (Ind. 1980).

[93]Diocese of Rochester v. Planning Board, 154 N.Y.S.2d 849 (1956).

[94]Mahrt v. First Church of Christ, Scientist, 142 N.E.2d 567 (Ohio 1955), *aff'd*, 142 N.E.2d 678 (Ohio 1955).

[95]Havurah v. Zoning Board of Appeals, 418 A.2d 82 (Conn. 1979).

[96]Board of Zoning Appeals v. New Testament Bible Church, Inc., 411 N.E.2d 681 (Ind. 1980).

[97]City of Concord v. New Testament Baptist Church, 382 A.2d 377 (N.H. 1978); Westbury Hebrew Congregation, Inc. v. Downer, 302 N.Y.S.2d 923 (1969); Diocese of Rochester v. Planning Board, 154 N.Y.S.2d 849 (1956).

[98]Parkview Baptist Church v. Pueblo, 336 P.2d 310 (Colo. 1959).

[99]East Side Baptist Church v. Klein, 487 P.2d 549 (Colo. 1971).

[100]Sexton v. Bates, 85 A.2d 833 (N.J. 1951), *aff'd*, 91 A.2d 162 (N.J. 1952).

[101]Gallagher v. Zoning Board of Adjustment, 32 Pa. D. & C.2d 669 (Pa. 1963).

[102]Damascus Community Church v. Clackamas County, 610 P.2d 273 (Ore. 1980), *appeal dismissed*, 450 U.S. 902 (1981).

## §F. Building Codes

Many municipalities have enacted building codes prescribing minimum standards in the construction of buildings. Such codes typically regulate building materials, construction methods, building design, fire safety, and sanitation. The validity of such codes has consistently been upheld by the courts.[103]

The courts consistently hold that churches must comply with municipal building codes that are reasonably related to the legitimate governmental purpose of promoting the public health, safety, morals, or general welfare. Thus it has been held that "the building of churches is subject to such reasonable regulations as may be necessary to promote the public health, safety, or general welfare."[104] In one case, a municipality brought an action against a church in order to prevent the continued use of a church school that did not comply with the building code.[105] The church school was allegedly deficient in several respects, including inadequate floor space, inadequate ventilation, no approved fire alarm system, no fire extinguishers, no fire detectors, no sprinkler system, no fire-retardant walls, no exit signs, uneven stairs, and doors that did not open outward. The Supreme Court of Washington State acknowledged that application of the building code to the church school would result in a closing of the school, and that this in turn would impair the church members' constitutional right to guide the education of their children by sending them to a church-operated school. However, the court observed that this constitutional right was not absolute, but could be limited by a showing that the building code was supported by a "compelling state interest" and that it was the least restrictive means of accomplishing the state's interest.

Similarly, another court upheld the action of a municipality in ordering substantial renovations in a church-operated school to bring it into compliance with the building code.[106] The court rejected the church's claims that the less stringent building code provisions applicable to church buildings should apply to the school, and that application of the more stringent building code provisions applicable to schools would infringe upon the church's right to freely exercise its religion. The court observed:

This is not a case where application of the Code forces a choice between aban-

---

[103]5 E. YOKLEY, ZONING LAW AND PRACTICE § 31-2 (1980).

[104]Board of Zoning v. Decatur, Ind. Co. of Jehovah's Witnesses, 117 N.E.2d 115, 118 (Ind. 1954). Accord City of Sherman v. Simms, 183 S.W.2d 415 (Tex. 1944); Wojtanowski v. Franciscan Fathers Minor Conventuals, 148 N.W.2d 54 (Wis. 1967); Hintz v. Zion Evangelical United Brethren Church, 109 N.W.2d 61 (Wis. 1961).

[105]City of Sumner v. First Baptist Church, 639 P.2d 1358 (Wash. 1982).

[106]Faith Assembly of God v. State Building Code Commission, 416 N.E.2d 228 (Mass. 1981).

doning one's religious principles and facing criminal charges. . . . The Code does not restrict or make unlawful any religious practice of the plaintiff; the Code simply regulates the condition of the physical facility if it functions as a school . . . .[107]

It has also been held that a state law establishing minimum standards for the safety of children in child-care facilities and enforcing such standards through inspections and licensing did not violate the religious freedom of a children's home administered by a religious organization.[108]

## §G. Nuisance

In general, the term *nuisance* refers to an activity or use of property that results in material annoyance, inconvenience, discomfort, or harm to others. It is, for example, a nuisance to use one's property in such a way as to cause excessive noise, odor, smoke, vibration, debris, drainage, obstruction, or injury to neighboring landowners. It ordinarily is not a defense that the condition constituting a nuisance existed before the arrival of neighboring residents.

An activity or condition permitted on church property can constitute a nuisance. One court has held:

A church building is as lawful as any other structure. It is not only lawful, but essential to our Christian civilization . . . . It is not, however, above the law. Like any other edifice or structure, however lawful in purpose and use ordinarily, it may become unlawful. The place of its location, and the time and manner of its use, may be such, under the circumstances, as to constitute that interference with the rights of others as to become in law a nuisance . . . .[109]

To illustrate, a church that conducted lengthy revival services punctuated by shouting and singing that could be heard more than a mile away was found guilty of permitting a nuisance.[110]

Another court refused to prevent the construction of a church in a residential district despite the allegations of neighboring landowners that the church consisted of "holy rollers" who would conduct boisterous services until the late

---

[107]*Id.* at 230.

[108]Roloff Evangelistic Enterprises, Inc. v. State, 556 S.W.2d 856 (Tex. 1977), *appeal denied,* 439 U.S. 803 (1978). *See also* Corpus Christi Peoples' Baptist Church, Inc. v. Texas Department of Human Resources, 481 F. Supp. 1101 (S.D. Tex. 1979), *aff'd,* 621 F.2d 638 (5th Cir. 1980); State Fire Marshall v. Lee, 300 N.W.2d 748 (Mich. 1980); State v. Fayetteville Street Christian School, 258 S.E.2d 459 (N.C. 1979), *vacated,* 261 S.E.2d 908 (N.C. 1980), *appeal dismissed,* 449 U.S. 808 (1980).

[109]Waggoner v. Floral Heights Baptist Church, 288 S.W. 129, 131 (Tex. 1926).

[110]Assembly of God Church v. Bradley, 196 S.W.2d 696 (Tex. 1946).

hours of the evening, making neighboring homes unfit for habitation.[111] The court reasoned that the existence of a church building close to the homes of neighboring landowners, as well as the noise that might result from an "orderly and properly conducted Christian service therein," were not matters that would constitute a nuisance. The court did acknowledge that it was possible for a church to conduct services with sufficient noise to constitute a nuisance. Nevertheless, the court concluded that it could not prevent the construction of a church in a residential neighborhood based on the mere conjecture of neighboring landowners that the church ultimately would constitute a nuisance.

Another court, in a similar case concluded that "[s]omething more than the threatened commission of an offense against the law of the land is necessary to call into exercise the injunctive powers of the court."[112] The court also held that a church building itself is not a nuisance, and therefore its construction cannot be enjoined on the ground that it will be the source of unreasonably loud worship services. The proper remedy for unreasonably loud services, concluded the court, would be to halt or abate the excessive noise, and not to prevent the construction of the church.

The playing of church bells three times a day and four times on Sundays at regular hours for a period of approximately four minutes has been held not to constitute a nuisance despite the contention of neighboring landowners that the volume of the bells adversely affected their health and serenity. The court held that a material interference with physical comfort must occur before a nuisance can exist, and that the ringing of church bells simply did not constitute a material interference:

> Bells in one form or another are a tradition throughout the world. . . . In the Christian world, every church is proud of its bells. The bells are rung for joy, for sadness, for warnings and for worship. There are people who find total beauty in the . . . daily ritual ringing at the Cathedral of Notre Dame in Paris. There is little question that the sound is often deadening when these bells start to ring, but for the general enjoyment of the public, it is considered acceptable.[113]

Finally, it has been held that the use of church property for school purposes does not amount to a nuisance.[114]

---

[111]Dorsett v. Nunis, 13 S.E.2d 371 (Ga. 1941).

[112]Murphy v. Cupp, 31 S.W.2d 396, 399 (Ark. 1930).

[113]Impellizerri v. Jamesville Federated Church, 428 N.Y.S.2d 550 (1979).

[114]Mooney v. Village of Orchard Lake, 53 N.W.2d 308 (Mich. 1952).

## §H. Government Investigations

As has been noted elsewhere,[115] the IRS possesses broad authority to inspect church records. This authority has been upheld on numerous occasions. Government investigations may be initiated by other federal agencies as well. For example, the Postal Service has broad authority to investigate "any scheme or artifice to defraud, or . . . obtaining money or property by means of false or fraudulent pretenses, representations, or promises" in connection with the use of the mail.[116] The Federal Communications Commission is given broad authority to investigate complaints regarding a broadcast licensee's performance. And the Equal Employment Opportunity Commission is invested with authority to investigate the compliance of religious organizations with the Civil Rights Act of 1964.

## §I. The Civil Rights Act of 1964

The Civil Rights Act of 1964 was enacted by Congress "to achieve a peaceful and voluntary settlement of the persistent problem of racial and religious discrimination. . . ."[117] Title II of the Act prohibited discrimination in "places of public accommodation" on account of religion or race; Titles III and IV ordered an end to all racial and religious segregation in "public facilities" and in public education; Title VI mandated that no recipient of federal assistance discriminate on racial grounds; and Title VII mandated nondiscrimination in employment. The other Titles of the Act are of no direct relevance to religious organizations. Titles VI and VII are of the greatest significance to religious organizations, and they shall be considered in turn.

### 1. TITLE VI OF THE CIVIL RIGHTS ACT OF 1964

Title VI of the Civil Rights Act of 1964 currently states:

> No person in the United States shall, on the ground of race, color, or national origin, be excluded from participation in, be denied the benefits of, or be subjected to discrimination under any program or activity receiving Federal financial assistance.

Since the term *person* is defined elsewhere in the Act to include individuals, corporations, and unincorporated associations,[118] it is safe to assume that Title

---

[115]*See* chapter 8, § C, *supra*.
[116]18 U.S.C. § 1341.
[117]SEN. REPORT No. 872, 88th Cong., 2nd Sess. (1964).
[118]Section 701(a).

VI applies to churches, religious schools, and all other religious institutions and organizations. Accordingly, if any religious institution or organization receives any form of federal financial assistance, it may not discriminate on the basis of "race, color, or national origin" in expending such funds. Schools, child-care centers, orphanages, and nursing homes operated by or affiliated with religious organizations are the types of institutions most likely to receive direct federal financial assistance.[119]

Indirect forms of federal financial assistance will also trigger the application of Title VI. To illustrate, a federal court has ruled that a religious college receives federal financial assistance when some of its students receive veterans' benefits.[120] Another court has concluded that "a tax deduction for charitable contributions is a grant of Federal financial assistance within the scope of the 1964 Civil Rights Act."[121] This reasoning would subject virtually every tax-exempt religious organization to the provisions of Title VI. This decision has been questioned,[122] and no other court seems to have applied its radical conclusion. Something more than a government-granted exemption from taxation will thus be necessary for Title VI to apply to religious organizations, but something less than direct payments will suffice. One court has observed: "The method of payment does not determine the result; the literal language of Section 601 requires only federal assistance—not payment—to a program or activity for Title VI to attach."[123]

## 2. Title VII of the Civil Rights Act of 1964

Title VII, Section 703(a), of the Civil Rights Act of 1964 presently specifies:

(a) It shall be an unlawful employment practice for an employer
(1) to fail or refuse to hire or to discharge any individual, or otherwise to discriminate against any individual with respect to his compensation, terms, conditions, or privileges of employment, because of such individual's race, color, religion, sex, or national origin; or
(2) to limit, segregate, or classify his employees or applicants for employment in any way which would deprive or tend to deprive any individual of employment

---

[119]Examples of direct federal financial aid would include medicaid funds to nursing care providers connected or affiliated with a religious organization, and funds received by religiously affiliated schools under federal food and service reimbursement programs.

[120]Bob Jones University v. Johnson, 396 F. Supp. 597 (D.S.C. 1974), aff'd, 529 F.2d 514 (4th Cir. 1975).

[121]McGlotten v. Connally, 338 F. Supp. 448, 462 (D.D.C. 1972).

[122]Bob Jones University v. Simon, 416 U.S. 725, 731-32 n.6 (1974).

[123]Bob Jones University v. Johnson, 396 F. Supp. 597, 602 (D.S.C. 1974), aff'd, 529 F.2d 514 (4th Cir. 1975).

opportunities or otherwise adversely affect his status as an employee, because of such individual's race, color, religion, sex, or national origin.

This general ban on discrimination applies to all employers, including religious organizations, engaged in an industry or activity "affecting commerce," unless one of the following exceptions is applicable.[124]

a. *Less Than Fifteen Employees*

Since congressional authority to enact the Civil Rights Act of 1964 was based upon congressional power to regulate interstate commerce,[125] Congress had constitutional authority to prohibit only discrimination by employers actually engaged in some activity or business affecting commerce. Congress has conclusively presumed that organizations employing less than fifteen employees cannot be deemed to be engaged in interstate commerce.[126] This limitation has been held to be jurisdictional.[127] Part-time employees can be counted in computing an organization's total number of employees.[128] Accordingly, organizations that have not employed "fifteen or more employees for each working day in each of twenty or more calendar weeks in the current or preceding calendar year" are not subject to the prohibition of employment discrimination contained in Title VII of the Civil Rights Act of 1964. A church employing more than fifteen persons can also establish that it is exempt by demonstrating that it is not engaged in a business or activity "affecting commerce." In general, churches that are not engaged in commercial enterprises and that engage in few if any interstate business transactions arguably are not engaged in an activity affecting commerce and thus are not covered by the Act. Unfortunately, such a deter-

---

[124]Illustratively, the Salvation Army has been held to be an employer subject to Title VII. McClure v. Salvation Army, 460 F.2d 553 (5th Cir. 1972), *cert. denied*, 409 U.S. 896 (1972).

[125]Article I, § 8, Clause 3 of the United States Constitution provides that Congress shall have power to "regulate commerce with foreign nations, and among the several states, and with the Indian tribes."

[126]The Act provides that "[t]he term 'employer' means a person engaged in an industry affecting commerce who has fifteen or more employees for each working day in each of twenty or more calendar weeks in the current or preceding calendar year. . . ." 42 U.S.C. § 2000e.

[127]Bonomo v. National Duck Pin Bowling Congress, Inc., 469 F. Supp. 467 (D. Md. 1979). The courts are without authority to entertain employment discrimination suits against employers having less than fifteen employees.

[128]Pedreyra v. Cornell Prescription Pharmacies, Inc., 465 F. Supp. 936 (D. Colo. 1979).

mination is based entirely on how narrowly or expansively a particular judge wants to construe the phrase *affecting commerce.*

b. *Religious Educational Institutions*

Title VII, Section 703(e)(2) of the Civil Rights Act of 1964 specifies:

> [I]t shall not be an unlawful employment practice for a school, college, university, or other educational institution or institution of learning to hire and employ employees of a particular religion if such school, college, university, or other educational institution or institution of learning is, in whole or in substantial part, owned, supported, controlled, or managed by a particular religion or by a particular religious corporation, association, or society, or if the curriculum of such school, college, university, or other educational institution or institution of learning is directed toward the propagation of a particular religion.

This provision exempts religious educational institutions, whether at the primary, secondary, or college level, from the prohibition of religious discrimination contained in Title VII of the Civil Rights Act of 1964. Significantly, this provision speaks generally of the right of religious educational institutions to discriminate on the basis of religion in the hiring of employees who will directly promote religious belief, such as teachers, as well as those who will not, such as clerical, custodial, and administrative personnel. The constitutionality of this provision—insofar as it permits religious schools to discriminate in employment decisions with regard to "secular" positions—is uncertain.[129]

c. *Religion as a "Bona Fide Occupational Qualification"*

Title VII, Section 703(e)(1) of the Civil Rights Act of 1964 states:

> Notwithstanding any other provision of this title . . . it shall not be an unlawful employment practice for an employer . . . to hire and employ employees . . . on the basis of his religion, sex, or national origin in those certain instances where religion, sex, or national origin is a bona fide occupational qualification reasonably necessary to the normal operation of that particular business or enterprise . . . .

If an employer otherwise subject to the Civil Rights Act of 1964 can demonstrate that religion is a bona fide occupational qualification for a particular

---

[129]*See, e.g.,* King's Garden, Inc. v. Federal Communications Commission, 498 F.2d 51 (D.C. Cir. 1974), *cert. denied,* 419 U.S. 996 (1974). *But cf.* Equal Employment Opportunity Commission v. Southwestern Baptist Theological Seminary, 651 F.2d 277 (5th Cir. 1981); Equal Employment Opportunity Commission v. Mississippi College, 626 F.2d 477 (5th Cir. 1980), *cert. denied,* 453 U.S. 912 (1981); Ritter v. Mount St. Mary's College, 495 F. Supp. 724 (D. Md. 1980).

position, then the employer may lawfully discriminate on the basis of religion in filling the position.

Parenthetically, it should be noted that a guideline promulgated by the Equal Employment Opportunity Commission provides that secular employers have an obligation to "make reasonable accommodations to the religious needs of employees and prospective employees where such accommodations can be made without undue hardship on the conduct of the employer's business."[130] The essence of this guideline is reproduced in Title VII of the Civil Rights Act of 1964, which prohibits religion-based discrimination in most employment decisions and which defines religion to include "all aspects of religious observance and practice, as well as belief, unless an employer demonstrates that he is unable to reasonably accommodate to an employee's or prospective employee's religious observance or practice without undue hardship on the conduct of the employer's business."[131]

In several decisions, the courts have ordered employers to make "reasonable accommodation" of the religious needs of employees whose religious beliefs prevented them from working on certain days of the week. Most courts have required employers to attempt scheduling adjustments or reassignments prior to terminating such employees.[132] If rescheduling, reassignments, or other accommodative action would impose an undue hardship upon an employer, accommodation of religious belief is not necessary. Similarly, courts have held that employers cannot summarily discharge employees whose religious beliefs preclude them from joining labor unions.[133]

Some courts have maintained that the requirement that employers take reasonable action to accommodate the religious beliefs of employees is an unconstitutional establishment of religion, and thus the present viability of the religious accommodation mandate is unclear.[134]

---

[130]29 C.F.R. § 1605.1.

[131]Section 701(j).

[132]Reid v. Memphis Publishing Company, 369 F. Supp. 684 (W.D. Tenn. 1973), aff'd, 521 F.2d 512 (6th Cir. 1975), cert. denied, 429 U.S. 964 (1976); Claybaugh v. Pacific Northwestern Bell Telephone Company, 355 F. Supp. 1 (D. Ore. 1973).

[133]Yott v. North American Rockwell Corporation, 602 F.2d 904 (9th Cir. 1979), cert. denied, 445 U.S. 928 (1980); Nottelson v. A. O. Smith, Corp., 489 F. Supp. 94 (E.D. Wis. 1980), aff'd, 643 F.2d 445 (7th Cir. 1981), cert. denied, 102 S. Ct. 587 (1981).

[134]Cummins v. Parker Seal Co., 516 F.2d 544 (6th Cir. 1975) (Celebrezze, J., dissenting), aff'd, 429 U.S. 65 (1976); Anderson v. General Dynamics Convair Aerospace Division, 489 F. Supp. 782 (S.D. Cal. 1980), rev'd, 648 F.2d 1247 (9th Cir. 1981), cert. denied, 102 S. Ct. 1006 (1982).

d. *Employment Decisions of Religious Corporations*

Finally, Title VII, section 702, of the Civil Rights Act of 1964 states:

This title shall not apply to . . . a religious corporation, association, educational institution, or society with respect to the employment of individuals of a particular religion to perform work connected with the carrying on by such corporation, association, educational institution, or society of its activities.

This provision permits religious corporations, associations, and educational institutions to discriminate on the basis of religion in the employment of any person for any position. As originally enacted, section 702 permitted religious employers to discriminate on the basis of religion only in employment decisions pertaining to their "religious activities." Congress amended section 702 in 1972 to enable religious organizations to discriminate on the basis of religion in all employment decisions. In 1974, a federal appeals court concluded that "it is reasonably clear that the 1972 exemption violates the Establishment Clause."[135] The court added that "the 1972 exemption appears unconstitutional on Fifth Amendment grounds as well" since it "violates the equal protection of the laws guaranteed by the Due Process Clause."[136]

Another court has characterized section 702 as "a remarkably clumsy accommodation of religious freedom with the compelling interests of the state, providing . . . far too broad a shield for the secular activities of religiously affiliated entities with not the remotest claim to first amendment protection . . . ."[137] This court thus intimated that the 1972 amendment to section 702, which permits religious discrimination in all employment decisions of religious employers and not just those involving "religious activities," is unconstitutionally broad. The court did concede that it would be unconstitutional not to allow religious organizations to discriminate on the basis of religion in employment decisions pertaining to religious activities.

Finally, it should be noted that the relationship between a church and its minister is accorded preferential treatment under the law. In one case, a minister-employee of the Salvation Army alleged that her employer had violated

---

[135]King's Garden, Inc. v. Federal Communications Commission, 498 F.2d 51, 54 n.7 (D.C. Cir. 1974), *cert. denied,* 419 U.S. 996 (1974).

[136]*Id.* at 57.

[137]Equal Employment Opportunity Commission v. Southwestern Baptist Theological Seminary, 485 F. Supp. 255, 260 (N.D. Tex. 1980), *rev'd on other grounds,* 651 F.2d 277 (5th Cir. 1981), *cert. denied,* 102 S. Ct. 1749 (1982). *See also* Feldstein v. Christian Science Monitor, 555 F. Supp. 974 (D. Mass. 1983) (Christian Science Monitor held to be a religious activity of the First Church of Christ, Scientist, a religious organization, and thus it could discriminate in employment decisions on the basis of religion).

the Civil Rights Act of 1964 by paying female officers smaller salaries than similarly situated males. A federal appeals court concluded that the relationship of the Salvation Army to its officers was a church-minister relationship, and that the application of the provisions of Title VII to the employment relationship existing between a church and its minister would result in an impermissible encroachment by the government into an area of purely ecclesiastical concern.[138]

Three principles may be derived from the cited cases. First, religious organizations can presently discriminate on the basis of religion in employment decisions involving "religious activities." This exemption from the antidiscrimination provisions of Title VII undoubtedly will continue to be considered constitutional. Second, the 1972 amendment to section 702, insofar as it permits religious organizations to discriminate on the basis of religion in employment decisions involving secular skills and positions, probably will be declared unconstitutional. Third, the relationship between a church and its minister or ministers is a matter of purely ecclesiastical concern, and accordingly is beyond the reach of the Civil Rights Act.

[138]McClure v. Salvation Army, 460 F.2d 553 (5th Cir. 1972), *cert. denied,* 409 U.S. 896 (1972).

# 12

# NEGLIGENCE AND PREMISES LIABILITY

The two primary bases of church legal liability are vicarious liability for the negligence of employees and liability for injuries occurring on church-owned property. Both bases will be considered in the present chapter, in addition to a review of the question of denominational liability.

## §A. Negligence

### 1. In General

Negligence consists of conduct that creates an unreasonable risk of foreseeable harm to others. It connotes carelessness, heedlessness, inattention, or inadvertence. Church liability most often arises in the context of a church employee's negligent use of a church-owned or privately owned vehicle in the course of church business. As has been noted elsewhere,[1] if an employee was in the course of his employment at the time of his negligent conduct, any resulting injuries or damages are attributable to his employing church. To illustrate, courts have imputed to churches the following negligent activities of church employees: a minister participated in a race between his automobile and another driven by his assistant, causing both vehicles to travel at an excessive speed and forcing the assistant's vehicle to enter an intersection on the wrong side of the road, causing an accident;[2] a minister drove his vehicle across the center line of a highway and collided with an oncoming vehicle;[3] and a minister's reckless driving resulted in injuries to the occupant of another ve-

---

[1]*See* chapter 1, § B, *supra.*
[2]Malloy v. Fong, 232 P.2d 241 (Cal. 1951).
[3]Vind v. Asamblea Apostolica de La Feen Christo Jesus, 307 P.2d 85 (Cal. 1957).

hicle.[4] A church of course will not be liable for the negligence of an employee acting on his own time in the pursuit of purely personal business. Thus, a Catholic church was not liable for the negligence of a priest while driving an automobile en route to a purely social visit with some friends.[5]

Other examples of negligence in the operation of a motor vehicle include driving a vehicle in darkness or fog without lights, passing another vehicle in a no-passing zone, operating a vehicle with a safety defect, failing to yield the right of way, failing to stop at a stop sign or red light, failing to reduce speed in a residential neighborhood when children are present, making a turn without signaling or from an improper lane, or operating a vehicle while under a physical disability.

A church can be liable for the negligence of employees in other contexts as well. For example, churches have been held liable for the negligence of their employees in failing to adequately supervise the conduct of children at a church picnic at which a child drowned;[6] in allowing a dangerous condition to continue in a crowded church service, which resulted in injury to a member;[7] in permitting a snowmobile party on farmland without making an adequate inspection for dangerous conditions;[8] and in failing to adequately supervise the activities of a church-sponsored scout troop.[9]

## 2. Defenses

A church has a variety of potential defenses against alleged liability for the negligence of employees, including (1) assertion that the person inflicting the injury or damage was not in the course of his employment at the time of the injury or damage, (2) charitable immunity, (3) contributory negligence, (4) assumption of risk, (5) intervening cause, and (6) liability insurance. These defenses will be considered in turn.

[4]Miller v. International Church of the Foursquare Gospel, Inc., 37 Cal. Rptr. 309 (Cal. 1964) (negligence imputed to religious denomination).

[5]Ambrosio v. Price, 495 F. Supp. 381 (D. Nebr. 1979).

[6]Herring v. R.L. Mathis Certified Dairy Co., 162 S.E.2d 863 (Ga. 1968), aff'd in part and rev'd in part, Bourn v. Herring, 166 S.E.2d 89 (Ga. 1969). See also L.M. Jeffords v. Atlanta Presbytery, Inc., 231 S.E.2d 355 (Ga. 1976); Brown v. Church of Holy Name of Jesus, 252 A.2d 176 (R.I. 1969).

[7]Bass v. Aetna Insurance Co., 370 So.2d 511 (La. 1979).

[8]Sullivan v. Birmingham Fire Insurance Co., 185 So.2d 336 (La. 1966), cert. denied, 186 So.2d 632 (La. 1966).

[9]Kearney v. Roman Catholic Church, 295 N.Y.S.2d 186 (N.Y. 1968).

### a. *Status of Person Causing Injury*

Since a church is liable only for the injuries caused by employees acting in the course of employment, a church generally will not be liable for injuries inflicted by nonemployees or by employees not acting in the course of their employment. The meaning of the terms *employee* and *in the course of employment* have been discussed fully elsewhere.[10]

### b. *Charitable Immunity*

In a majority of states, religious organizations are subject to being sued for the negligence of their employees just as any commercial organization.[11] In two states, however, religious organizations are granted complete immunity.[12] The view that religious organizations should be completely immune from liability for the negligence of their employees was once common. It gradually was rejected by the great majority of states, and likely will be completely discarded in the future. The principle of total immunity was frequently criticized. One court observed: "Even the most cursory research makes it apparent that there is no ground upon which this doctrine of nonliability has rested . . . that has not been assailed and criticized at length by some other court . . . ."[13]

In a large minority of states, religious organizations are granted qualified immunity, depending on the status of the victim.[14] For example, some states immunize religious organizations from liability for the negligence of agents and employees committed against "beneficiaries" of the organization. This view ordinarily is based upon one of the following grounds: the funds of religious organizations are held in trust for charitable purposes and may not be diverted to the payment of damages; the misconduct of an employee should not be imputed to a religious organization when the service of the employee is for the benefit of humanity and not for the economic gain of the organization that employs him; a religious organization is engaged in work highly beneficial to the state and to humanity, and its funds should not be diverted from this important purpose to the payment of damages; and one accepting the benefits of a religious organization implicitly agrees not to hold it liable for injuries that

---

[10]*See* chapter 10, § F, *supra.*

[11]*See generally* E. FISCH, D. FREED, & E. SCHACHTER, CHARITIES AND CHARITABLE FOUNDATIONS ch. 25 (1974 and Suppl. 1982-83), hereinafter cited as CHARITIES AND CHARITABLE FOUNDATIONS.

[12]Arkansas and Maine are the two states that presently grant complete charitable immunity. *See* CHARITIES AND CHARITABLE FOUNDATIONS, *supra* note 11, at § 622.

[13]Gable v. Salvation Army, 100 P.2d 244, 246 (Okla. 1940).

[14]*See generally* CHARITIES AND CHARITABLE FOUNDATIONS, *supra* note 11, at ch. 25; Annot., 25 A.L.R.2d 29 (1952).

he may receive at the hands of its employees.[15] To illustrate, a woman who visited a church to view the sanctuary and its stained-glass windows was deemed to be a beneficiary of the church and hence incapable of recovering for injuries she suffered in the church.[16] Other examples of beneficiaries include a church Sunday school teacher,[17] a nonmember who attended a church social,[18] a member of a Girl Scout troop that met on church property,[19] a person attending a religious service,[20] and a guest at a church wedding.[21]

Some states that grant religious organizations a qualified immunity from the negligence of employees permit an injured beneficiary to sue the organization directly if it was negligent in hiring the employee who inflicted the injury.[22] Other qualified immunity states permit a religious organization to be sued by an injured beneficiary if the organization was engaged in a commercial enterprise at the time of the injury.[23] A few states impose monetary limits on the size of judgments that can be rendered against religious organizations, and some permit injured beneficiaries to sue a religious organization's liability insurer directly.[24]

### c. Contributory Negligence

Contributory negligence is conduct on the part of a person injured through the negligence of another that itself falls below the standard to which a reasonable person would conform for his own safety and protection. In many states, the contributory negligence of an accident victim operates as a complete defense to negligence. Thus, if the victim of another's negligence was himself negligent, and his own negligence contributed materially to the accident, he may be barred from recovery. To illustrate, the driver of a motor vehicle who is injured when struck by another vehicle being operated in a negligent manner may be barred from recovering if he himself was driving in excess of the speed limit, if he was operating his vehicle in violation of a traffic law or regulation, if he suddenly

---

[15]Egerton v. R.E. Lee Memorial Church, 273 F. Supp. 834 (W.D. Va. 1967), aff'd, 395 F.2d 381 (4th Cir. 1968).

[16]Id.

[17]Wiklund v. Presbyterian Church, 217 A.2d 463 (N.J. 1966).

[18]Burgie v. Muench, 29 N.E.2d 439 (Ohio 1940).

[19]Bianchi v. South Park Presbyterian Church, 8 A.2d 567 (N.J. 1939).

[20]Cullen v. Schmit, 39 N.E.2d 146 (Ohio 1942).

[21]Anasiewicz v. Sacred Heart Church, 181 A.2d 787 (N.J. 1962), appeal denied, 184 A.2d 419 (1962).

[22]See CHARITIES AND CHARITABLE FOUNDATIONS, supra note 11, at § 624.

[23]Id. at § 628.

[24]Id. at § 624.

and without justification stopped his vehicle, if he failed to indicate an intention to turn by use of a turn signal, if he was operating his vehicle under dark or foggy conditions without lights, or if he was operating his vehicle with a known safety defect. Similarly, a pedestrian or bicyclist who is injured by the negligence of a motor vehicle operator may be barred from recovery by his own negligence, such as when a bicyclist unexpectedly turns into the path of an oncoming vehicle or travels on a darkened street at night without lights or reflective devices, or when a pedestrian attempts to cross a busy street at night at a point other than a crosswalk.

Of course, contributory negligence is a defense to another's negligence only if it in fact *contributed* to the accident.

Many states have attempted to lessen the severity of the rule denying any recovery to an accident victim who himself was contributorily negligent through the adoption of comparative negligence statutes. Under the so-called pure comparative negligence statutes, an accident victim whose contributory negligence was not the sole cause of his injuries may recover against another whose negligence was the primary cause of the accident, but his monetary damages are diminished in proportion to the amount of his own negligence. Under a pure comparative negligence statute, a plaintiff may recover against a negligent defendant even though his own contributory negligence was equal to or greater than the defendant's negligence.

Many other states have adopted the "equal to or greater than" rule or the "fifty percent" rule. Under these statutes, a plaintiff whose contributory negligence is equal to or greater than the defendant's negligence is totally barred from recovery. But, if the plaintiff's contributory negligence is less than the defendant's negligence, he may recover damages, although his damages are diminished in proportion to the amount of his own negligence.

Other states permit a plaintiff to recover for the injuries caused by a negligent defendant if his own contributory negligence was slight in comparison to the negligence of the defendant.

### d. *Assumption of Risk*

A person who voluntarily exposes himself to a known danger or to a danger that was so obvious that it should have been recognized will be deemed to have assumed the risks of his conduct. As a result, a plaintiff who voluntarily exposes himself to the negligent conduct of a defendant with full knowledge of the danger will be barred from recovery for any injuries resulting from the defendant's negligence. Assumption of risk is closely related to contributory negligence. One court has distinguished the two by noting that assumption of risk connotes "venturousness," whereas contributory negligence connotes a state of carelessness.[25] To illustrate, a pedestrian walking down the middle of a public highway at night or a guest riding with a drowsy or intoxicated driver without objection ordinarily will be deemed to have assumed the risks of his conduct.

### e. Intervening Cause

It is generally held that a person's negligence is not the legal cause of an injury that results from the intervention of a new and independent cause that is (1) neither anticipated nor reasonably foreseeable by him, (2) not a consequence of his negligence, (3) not controlled by him, and (4) the actual cause of the injury in the sense that the injury would not have occurred without it. If an intervening cause meets these conditions, it is considered a "superseding" cause that terminates the original wrongdoer's liability. For example, a superseding, intervening cause was found to have insulated the original wrongdoer from liability for his negligence in the following situations: a bus driver ran a stop sign, causing a car approaching from an intersecting street to abruptly stop, resulting in the car being struck by another car that had been following it too closely;[26] a motorist's negligent driving resulted in a collision with a second vehicle, and a third motorist, whose attention was distracted by the scene of the accident, struck a pedestrian;[27] and a motorist's negligent operation of his automobile caused an accident, and a police officer investigating the scene of the accident was injured when struck by another vehicle being operated in a negligent manner.[28]

### f. Liability Insurance

Although technically not a defense to the negligence of employees, a general liability insurance policy may protect a church against liability, since the insurer ordinarily is under a duty to defend the insured against claims of negligence and to pay any resulting damages up to the policy limits. In some cases, even though a church has a general liability policy, it may be liable for the negligence of its employees, such as when the amount of damages exceeds the policy limits; the policy has lapsed because of nonpayment of premiums; failure to notify the insurer and provide a proof of loss within the time limits prescribed by the policy or by state law; failure to promptly forward a summons or lawsuit to the insurer; misrepresentations contained in the church's insurance application; failure to cooperate with the insurer; or the loss is not covered by the terms

[25]Cross v. Noland, 190 S.E.2d 18 (W. Va. 1972).
[26]Seeger v. Weber, 113 N.W.2d 566 (Wis. 1962).
[27]Lewis v. Esselman, 539 S.W.2d 581 (Mo. 1976).
[28]Schrimsher v. Bryson, 130 Cal. Rptr. 125 (1976).

of the policy. In addition, an insurer may not be liable for punitive damages or for interest and costs.

## §B. Premises Liability

### 1. IN GENERAL

It is not uncommon for injuries to occur on church premises. Many parishioners have slipped on icy sidewalks or parking lots, fallen down stairs, tripped on slippery floors, or walked through plate glass doors. What is a church's liability in such cases?

In most states, the liability of a church for injuries caused on its premises depends upon the status of the victim. Most courts hold that a person may be on another's property as an *invitee,* a *licensee,* or a *trespasser.* An *invitee* may be either a public invitee or a business visitor. A public invitee is a person who is invited to enter or remain on land as a member of the public for a purpose for which the land is held open to the public. A business visitor is a person who is invited to enter or remain on land for a purpose directly or indirectly connected with business dealings with the owner of the land.

Landowners owe the greatest duty of care (*i.e.,* legal obligation) to invitees, since invitees by definition are on a landowner's property at his express or implied invitation. Most courts hold that a landowner owes invitees a duty to use reasonable and ordinary care to keep the premises safe, including the responsibility of correcting those concealed hazards of which he knows or reasonably should know, or at least warning invitees of such hazards. Even so, a landowner is not a guarantor of the safety of invitees. Thus, if a landowner exercises reasonable care in making the premises safe for invitees or if adequate warning is given about concealed perils, a landowner will not be responsible for injuries that occur. Many courts have refused to hold landowners responsible for an invitee's injuries caused by an obvious hazard or by a concealed hazard of which the invitee was aware. Some courts have concluded that church members attending church services or activities are invitees because they satisfy the definition of *public invitee.* Thus, one court concluded that a church member who was injured when she tripped and fell over a wooden cross that had been used in a skit presented at a church meeting was a public invitee since she had been invited to enter the premises as a member of the public for a purpose for which the property was held open to the public.[29]

A *licensee* generally is defined as one who is privileged to enter or remain on property because of the owner's express or implied consent. It is often said that invitees enter one's property by invitation, either express or implied, and

---

[29]Stevens v. Bow Mills Methodist Church, 283 A.2d 488 (N.H. 1971). *See also* Hedglin v. Church of St. Paul, 158 N.W.2d 269 (Minn. 1968).

that licensees are not invited but their presence is tolerated or merely permitted. In most states a landowner is responsible for warning licensees of hidden dangers of which the landowner is actually aware and to refrain from willfully or wantonly injuring them or recklessly exposing them to danger. The landowner has no duty to protect a licensee against hidden dangers of which the landowner is unaware. Thus, a landowner is under no duty to make his premises safe by inspecting for and correcting hidden conditions that may cause injury.

A *trespasser* is a person who enters another's property without invitation or consent. In general, a landowner owes no duty to an undisclosed trespasser, and thus a trespasser has no legal remedy if he is injured by a dangerous condition on another's property. If a landowner is reasonably apprised of the presence of a trespasser, he must refrain from willfully or wantonly injuring him, and, according to some courts, must warn him of concealed hazards of which the owner is actually aware.

A few states in recent years have abandoned the prevailing view of assessing a landowner's liability for injuries occurring on his premises by focusing on the status of the victim. These states have substituted a simple standard of reasonable care that a landowner owes to all lawful visitors. In determining a landowner's liability, the status of a victim is still relevant but not controlling. Thus, for example, the fact that an injured victim was a trespasser will reduce the landowner's duty of care since a reasonable person would not take the same steps to ensure the safety of trespassers that he would for invitees.

The great majority of cases involving accidents on church property have determined the church's liability on the basis of the status of the victim. Many courts have concluded that certain classes of persons are business invitees of a church because the business or purpose for which they come onto a church's premises are of material or monetary benefit, either actual or potential, to the church. To illustrate, the president of a state organization of church women who was injured when she fell down a darkened church stairway was held to be an invitee of the church because she had been expressly invited to appear and preside over a women's meeting and her presence was of mutual benefit to herself and the church.[30] Since she was an invitee, the court concluded that the church owned her a duty to exercise ordinary care to keep the premises in reasonably safe condition and that this duty had been breached. In another case, a woman who was injured when she slipped and fell on a freshly waxed floor inside a church while on a tour at the invitation of her son was held to be an invitee to whom the church was liable because of its failure to remedy the dangerous condition.[31] The church's contention that the victim was not an

[30]Sullivan v. First Presbyterian Church, 152 N.W.2d 628 (Iowa 1967).
[31]Claridge v. Watson Terrace Christian Church, 457 S.W.2d 785 (Mo. 1970).

NEGLIGENCE AND PREMISES LIABILITY / 291

invitee because the church received no benefit from her presence was rejected by the court:

> Not only was she welcome, but her status as a potential member and future contributor provided a benefit to the church in an economic sense. That benefit so derived is not speculative but is comparable to, and no less than, that where the customer shops but does not buy. This was sufficient to give her all the required attributes of an "invitee."[32]

Another court rejected a church's claim that a Sunday school teacher who was injured when she slipped and fell on an icy sidewalk in front of the church was not entitled to recovery as an invitee since she was a mere social guest.[33] The court acknowledged that those who enter another's property as guests, whether for benevolent or social reasons, are licensees to whom the landowner owes a very minimal duty of care. The court concluded that the operation of a church is more than a mere social gathering: "To very many people it concerns a business of extreme moment, however unworldly."[34] The court also insisted that the injured teacher's presence on church property was primarily for the benefit of the church, for "despite the voluntary and unrecompensed status of the plaintiff, she entered these premises as a matter of duty to the [church], and for the furtherance of the important interest, albeit a spiritual one, of the church, as distinguished from her own."[35] The court accordingly held that the teacher was a business invitee to whom the church had breached its duty of reasonable care.

Another court concluded that a church member who was injured in a fall from a negligently assembled scaffolding while donating his labor in the construction of a church building was an invitee of the church since the business or purpose for which he had come upon the premises was of economic benefit to the church.[36] Accordingly, the church was found liable for breaching its duty of exercising reasonable care to render its premises safe from, or at least warn of, dangerous conditions of which the church knew or could discover with reasonable diligence.

In many cases, the courts have concluded that a particular accident victim was present on church premises as a licensee. In most cases, a finding that an accident victim is a licensee will insulate the church from liability, since the only duty that a church owes to a licensee in most states is the duty to refrain

---

[32]*Id.* at 788.

[33]Atwood v. Board of Trustees, 98 A.2d 348 (N.J. 1953).

[34]*Id.* at 350.

[35]*Id.*

[36]Haugen v. Central Lutheran Church, 361 P.2d 637 (Wash. 1961).

from injuring a licensee willfully or wantonly and to exercise ordinary care to avoid imperiling him by any active conduct. In some states, a church also owes a licensee a duty to correct concealed hazards of which it is actually aware or at least to warn a licensee of such hazards. But a church does not owe a licensee a duty to exercise reasonable care in maintaining church premises in a reasonably safe condition, and it does not have a duty to make inspections for dangerous conditions. This latter duty is owed only to invitees.

To illustrate, some courts take the position that those attending religious services are mere licensees. In a leading case, a court denied recovery to a church member who was injured when she was pushed by a crowd of departing members down the front steps of her church.[37] The victim contended that she was entitled to recover because she was an invitee to whom the church owed a high degree of care. In particular, she alleged that she was on the church premises because the church had "importuned" her to come, and that she attended mass for the benefit of Jesus Christ and her church. In rejecting these contentions, the court observed:

> [A]n invitation to enter and worship, whether it be either express or implied, does not constitute one who accepts the invitation an invitee in the legal sense. In order for such a relationship to arise the person entering onto the premises, i.e. the invitee, must have done so for purposes which would have benefited the owner or occupant of the premises, i.e. the invitor, or have been of mutual benefit to the invitee and the invitor. And as we view it, this benefit must be of a material or commercial rather than of a spiritual, religious, or social nature. . . . It cannot be successfully or logically argued that a person enters a place of worship, call it by any name, and participates in worship and prayer to the God or Supreme Being of his choice for the benefit of the body or organization which owns the church, the religious or lay readers who conduct the services, or the God or Supreme Being whom he worships and asks for guidance, help or forgiveness. One of the concepts of all religious beliefs known to us is that participation in religious activities is for the benefit of the mortals who participate therein. Places of worship exist as symbols and reminders of the existence of a greater and higher force and as places set apart from the material phases of our lives where we can for our convenience together practice and give overt evidence of our adherence to our religious beliefs. If it were not true that participation in religious services, proceedings and ceremonies is for the benefit of the individuals who gather to do so, it would be impossible to explain their presence at such activities.[38]

The court also rejected the victim's contention that she should be classified

---

[37]McNulty v. Hurley, 97 So.2d 185 (Fla. 1957). *Accord* Autry v. Roebuck Park Baptist Church, 229 So.2d 469 (Ala. 1969).

[38]*Id.* at 188.

as an invitee because the church benefited when she made a contribution into the collection plate: "As it is that we who serve our God gain in so doing, so it is that we who give material things to assist in the work of our chosen religious belief receive by so doing. We are the recipients, not the benefactors."[39] The court concluded that since the victim was a mere licensee, the church owed her only a duty to refrain from wanton negligence and willful misconduct, and to warn her of any hidden defect or condition known to it to be dangerous. This minimal duty, observed the court, was not breached.

In another case, a court concluded that a woman who was injured when she slipped and fell on a slippery church floor while attending the ordination of her grandson was a mere licensee to whom the church owed a minimal duty of care.[40] In rejecting the victim's claim that she was an invitee to whom the church owed a high degree of care because her presence benefited the church, the court observed: "To the extent that the church benefited at all, such benefit was not a material or commercial one, as it must be in order to raise a licensee's status to an 'invitee' and to impose the greater degree of care for his safety."[41]

Other courts have found the following persons to be licensees and accordingly have denied a legal remedy for injuries suffered on church premises: a member of an industrial basketball league that played its games in a church gymnasium,[42] a five-year-old girl who was visiting a church at which her grandmother was employed,[43] a church member who was injured while walking across a church lawn seeking entrance into a church to light a candle for her daughter,[44] a policeman who was investigating a complaint that a church was being broken into,[45] and a child who was burned by a fire while playing on church property.[46]

Ultimately, the liability of a church for injuries suffered on its premises depends upon how narrowly or expansively the courts of a particular state define the term *invitee*. As the cases previously discussed illustrate, there is considerable difference of opinion regarding the definition of this term. The United States Supreme Court has observed:

In an effort to do justice in an industrialized urban society, with its complex economic and individual relationships, modern common-law courts have found it

---

[39]*Id.* at 189.

[40]Broad Street Christian Church v. Carrington, 234 So.2d 732 (Fla. 1970), *cert. denied,* 238 So.2d 427 (Fla. 1970).

[41]*Id.* at 733.

[42]Turpin v. Our Lady of Mercy Catholic Church, 202 S.E.2d 351 (N.C. 1974).

[43]Lemon v. Busey, 461 P.2d 145 (Kan. 1969).

[44]Coolbaugh v. St. Peter's Roman Catholic Church, 115 A.2d 662 (Conn. 1955).

[45]Scheurer v. Trustees of Open Bible Church, 192 N.E.2d 38 (Ohio 1963).

[46]Wozniczka v. McKean, 247 N.E.2d 215 (Ind. 1969).

necessary to formulate increasingly subtle verbal refinements, to create subclassifications among traditional common-law categories, and to delineate fine gradations in the standards of care which the landowner owes to each. Yet even within a single jurisdiction, the classifications and subclassifications bred by the common law have produced confusion and conflict. . . . Through this semantic morass the common law has moved, unevenly and with hesitation, towards "imposing on owners and occupiers a single duty of reasonable care in all the circumstances."[47]

Churches have been found innocent of wrongdoing in several cases irrespective of the status of the person injured on their property because the condition or activity that caused the injury could not under any circumstances serve as a basis for legal liability. For example, it has been held that a church is under no duty to illuminate its parking lot when no church activities are in process;[48] to remove oil and grease from its parking lot;[49] to place markings on a sliding glass door;[50] to begin removing snow from church stairways before the end of a snowstorm;[51] or to remove every square inch of snow and ice from its parking lot following a storm.[52]

## 2. DEFENSES

Most of the defenses discussed in the preceding section in connection with the negligence of church employees are available to a church that is sued for injuries occurring on its premises. Thus, for example, in those states that provide immunity to charitable organizations for injuries suffered by "beneficiaries," it has been held that if a person injured on church property was a beneficiary of the church's activities, then no action can be maintained against the church.[53]

The contributory negligence of a person injured on church property may also insulate the church from liability. Thus, it has been held that a church member who was injured when she fell while walking in a dark hallway connecting the sanctuary with a social hall was precluded from suing the church by her own contributory negligence.[54] The court observed that darkness is in

[47]Kermarec v. Compagnie Generale, 358 U.S. 625, 630-31 (1959).

[48]Huselton v. Underhill, 28 Cal. Rptr. 822 (1963).

[49]Goard v. Branscom, 189 S.E.2d 667 (N.C. 1972), cert. denied, 191 S.E.2d 354 (N.C. 1972).

[50]Sullivan v. Birmingham Fire Insurance Co., 185 So.2d 336 (La. 1966), cert. denied, 186 So.2d 632 (La. 1966).

[51]Hedglin v. Church of St. Paul, 158 N.W.2d 269 (Minn. 1968).

[52]Byrne v. Catholic Bishop, 266 N.E.2d 708 (Ill. 1971).

[53]See chapter 12, § A, supra.

[54]Trinity Episcopal Church v. Hoglund, 222 So.2d 781 (Fla. 1969).

itself sufficient warning to signal caution to one entering an unfamiliar situation, and that if one fails to heed the signal, he is guilty of contributory negligence. Similarly, a church member who slipped and fell on an icy stairway while leaving a church service was found to have been contributorily negligent because she failed to use an available handrail.[55]

Intervening, superseding causes, assumption of risk, and general liability insurance may also reduce or eliminate a church's liability for injuries occurring on its premises.

## §C. Denominational Liability

In recent years, a few religious denominations have been sued for the alleged misconduct of affiliated churches. In one of the earliest cases, the national conference of the Pentecostal Holiness Church was sued for breach of contract when its Florida regional conference defaulted on a life-care contract with two elderly church members who resided in a nursing home owned by the conference.[56] A state appeals court concluded that the national conference could not be sued for the financial improprieties of a local church or regional conference since local churches and regional conferences were totally independent of the national conference with respect to financial matters.

In a similar case, the United Methodist Church (UMC) was sued for the alleged improprieties of a subsidiary corporation that operated fourteen nursing homes in California, Arizona, and Hawaii. When the subsidiary encountered financial difficulties, it raised the monthly payments of residents in violation of the terms of their "continuing care agreements" that guaranteed lifetime nursing and medical care for a fixed price. The subsidiary went bankrupt, and a class of nearly 2,000 residents sued the UMC for fraud and breach of contract. Although the case eventually was settled out of court, a California appeals court did rule that the UMC could be sued for the misconduct of its subsidiary.[57] The court emphasized that the UMC was a hierarchical denomination with control over local churches and subsidiary institutions, ranging from restrictions on the purchase or sale of property to the selection of local church pastors. Such control, observed the court, made the UMC responsible for the liabilities of its affiliated churches and subsidiary institutions. The court also found it relevant that the subsidiary organization that operated the nursing homes was engaged in a commercial enterprise.

[55]Hedglin v. Church of St. Paul, 158 N.W.2d 269 (Minn. 1968).

[56]Pentecostal Holiness Church, Inc. v. Mauney, 270 So.2d 762 (Fla. 1972), *cert. denied,* 276 So.2d 51 (Fla. 1973). *See also* Kersch v. The General Council of the Assemblies of God, 535 F. Supp. 494 (N.D. Cal. 1982).

[57]Barr v. United Methodist Church, 153 Cal. Rptr. 322 (1979), *cert. denied,* 444 U.S. 973 (1979).

The court suggested that the First Amendment might prohibit direct actions against the UMC on account of the actions of subsidiary organizations if the allowance of such actions "would affect the distribution of power or property within the denomination, would modify or interfere with modes of worship affected by Methodists or would have any effect other than to oblige UMC to defend itself when sued upon civil obligations it is alleged to have incurred."[58]

In summary, these cases suggest that a regional or national religious organization will be responsible for the improprieties of a local affiliated church or other charitable institution only if all of the following conditions are satisfied:

1. The local church or charitable institution is actually affiliated with the parent organization.

2. The parent organization exercises or has the authority to exercise control over that activity of the affiliate that caused the damage or injury.

3. Liability of the parent organization for the actions of an affiliate will not alter the polity or government of the parent body.

4. The controversy is not a purely ecclesiastical dispute concerning religious doctrine or practice.

In determining whether a parent religious organization exercises sufficient control over an affiliate to make the parent organization responsible for the affiliate's actions, a court will primarily review the charter and bylaws of the parent organization and its affiliate. Other documents, practices, or representations that demonstrate control are also relevant and will be considered.

[58] *Id.* at 332.

# 13

---

# ADMINISTRATION OF PRIVATE SCHOOLS

The American educational system was created primarily to facilitate the establishment and propagation of the Christian faith. The express purpose of one of the very earliest American common school systems was to defeat "one chief project of that old deluder, Satan, to keep men from the knowledge of the Scriptures."[1] A Supreme Court Justice has observed:

> Traditionally, organized education in the Western world was church education. It could hardly be otherwise when the education of children was primarily study of the Word and ways of God. Even in the Protestant countries, where there was a less close identification of Church and State, the basis of education was largely the Bible, and its chief purpose inculcation of piety. . . . The emigrants who came to these shores brought this view of education with them. Colonial schools were certainly started with a religious orientation.[2]

During the nineteenth century, religious teaching and indoctrination were largely removed from the public educational system. It has been noted that "by 1875 the separation of public education from Church entanglements, of the State from the teaching of religion, was firmly established in the consciousness of the nation."[3] Yet, this separation was not so rigid as to preclude the accommodation of numerous religious practices, including Bible study clubs, distribution of Bibles and religious literature, readings from the Bible and recitation of prayers, "released time" programs during which public school

---

[1]THE LAWS AND LIBERTIES OF MASSACHUSETTS (1648).

[2]People of State of Illinois ex rel. McCollum v. Board of Education, 333 U.S. 203, 213-14 (1948) (Frankfurter, J., concurring).

[3]*Id.* at 217.

students were periodically released from class to attend voluntary religious instruction in classrooms set aside for such use, and utilization of school facilities after hours for religious worship. Throughout the nineteenth century all of these practices were deemed consistent with the First Amendment's establishment clause despite the increasing differentiation between religious and secular instruction.

Beginning in 1948, however, the United States Supreme Court embarked upon a course of radical disestablishment that was soon reflected in its aversion to nearly all vestiges of religion in the public school system. Suddenly, after having been accepted as constitutionally permissible for over a century and a half, Bible readings and the recitation of nonsectarian prayers at the beginning of each school day and released time programs that utilized school property for voluntary religious instruction were outlawed by the Court. In time it also banned the Ten Commandments from public school classrooms. And it refused to review state and lower federal court decisions forbidding all forms of group religious expression in public secondary schools. The Supreme Court's sudden aversion to religion in the public school system was soon mirrored by lower federal courts, state courts, and local school boards.[4]

[4]*See, e.g.,* Epperson v. Arkansas, 393 U.S. 97 (1968) (state law prohibiting the teaching of evolution in public schools held unconstitutional); Meltzer v. Board of Public Instruction, 548 F.2d 559 (5th Cir. 1977), *cert. denied,* 439 U.S. 1089 (1979) (school board regulation mandating daily Bible readings in public schools and permitting distribution of Gideon Bibles to public school students held unconstitutional); Daniel v. Waters, 515 F.2d 485 (6th Cir. 1975) (state law requiring that the Genesis account of creation be contained in biology textbooks used in public schools held unconstitutional); DeSpain v. DeKalb County Community School District, 384 F.2d 836 (7th Cir. 1967), *cert. denied,* 390 U.S. 906 (1968) (public kindergarten teacher could not constitutionally request students to recite grace before morning refreshments); Stein v. Oshinsky, 348 F.2d 999 (2nd Cir. 1965) (public school's refusal to allow kindergarten students to say grace before refreshments held constitutional); Collins v. Chandler Unified School District, 470 F. Supp. 959 (D. Ariz. 1979), *rev'd on other grounds,* 644 F.2d 759 (9th Cir. 1981), *cert. denied,* 454 U.S. 863 (1981) (voluntary, student-initiated prayer prior to public high school student body assemblies ruled unconstitutional); Goodwin v. Cross County School District, 394 F. Supp. 417 (E.D. Ark. 1973) (school board policy which allowed persons to come onto public school property to distribute Bibles to elementary school children held unconstitutional); Hunt v. Board of Education, 321 F. Supp. 1263 (S.D. W.Va. 1971) (school board could constitutionally prohibit public high school students from engaging in voluntary prayer on school premises before the commencement of classes); American Civil Liberties Union v. Albert Gallatin Area School District, 307 F. Supp. 637 (W.D. Pa. 1969) (school board policy encouraging recitation of the Lord's Prayer on public school premises during school sessions violates the Constitution); Johnson v. Huntington Beach Union High School District, 137 Cal. Rptr. 43 (Cal. 1977), *cert. denied,* 434 U.S. 877 (1977) (permitting voluntary Bible study club to meet and conduct its activities on public school property during the school day violates the Constitution); Commissioner of Education v. School Committee of Leyden, 267 N.E.2d 226

By 1980, the process of eliminating religion from the public schools was nearly complete. School children could no longer collectively pray or read their Bibles during school hours or before or after school on school property even on a purely voluntary basis. Bible clubs, once popular in many schools, were banned. The Ten Commandments could not be posted in public school classrooms. The right to teach the Genesis account of creation was under concerted attack. Kindergarten students could no longer collectively say grace before refreshments. No material having any religious significance could be taught in the classroom. The Gideons were banned from many school districts. The constitutionality of Christmas programs, Christmas decorations, and vacations associated with religious holidays was being challenged with some success. In a few isolated school districts one pathetic vestige of religion remained: the school day opened with a minute of silence during which students could pray, meditate, or occupy themselves in any other manner they chose. Even this practice was vigorously challenged.[5] Some of these practices persisted in isolated schools and school districts because they had not been challenged.

Ironically, in its decision outlawing Bible readings in public schools, the Supreme Court observed:

> It is insisted that unless these religious exercises are permitted a "religion of secularism" is established in the schools. We agree, of course, that the State may not establish a "religion of secularism" in the sense of affirmatively opposing or showing hostility to religion, thus "preferring those who believe in no religion over those who do believe."[6]

For growing numbers of parents, these words were a mockery. Many parents removed their children from the public schools and enrolled them in private schools in protest against the secularism that pervaded public education. Countless others, appalled by the moral deterioration and lawlessness that seemed

---

(Mass. 1971), *cert. denied,* 404 U.S. 849 (1971) (school-committee-sanctioned voluntary religious exercises, held on public school property at start of school day, held unconstitutional); Opinion of the Justices, 307 A.2d 558 (N.H. 1973) (state law which would authorize recitation of Lord's Prayer in public schools held unconstitutional); State Board of Education v. Board of Education of Netcong, 262 A.2d 21 (N.J. 1970), *aff'd,* 270 A.2d 412 (N.J. 1970), *cert. denied,* 401 U.S. 1013 (1971) (school board policy permitting use of public school gymnasium prior to start of school day for voluntary religious exercises held unconstitutional); Trietley v. Board of Education, 409 N.Y.S.2d 912 (1978) (school board's refusal to permit students to conduct Bible studies on public school property before or after school hours did not constitute an unconstitutional abridgement of the right to freely exercise one's religion).

[5]Kent v. Commissioner of Education, 402 N.E.2d 1340 (Mass. 1980). *But see* Gaines v. Anderson, 421 F. Supp. 337 (D. Mass. 1976).

[6]School District of Abington v. Schempp, 374 U.S. 203, 225 (1963).

rampant in many public schools transferred their children to private schools. Many parents fled the public schools to avoid racial desegregation. Others sought higher quality instruction. Whatever the cause, the exodus of students out of the public schools and into private schools constitutes one of the most notable social phenomena of the last half of this century. The corresponding proliferation of private schools, and church-related ones in particular, has generated many novel problems. In the pages that follow, the more significant of such questions will be analyzed in light of the most recent judicial and legislative precedent.

## §A. Incorporation and Tax Exemption

Should a private religious school incorporate? Should it seek exemption from federal income taxes? These are questions of fundamental importance for private religious schools. The answers depend primarily upon the relationship if any that a particular school has with a church. As a general rule, it would be advantageous for a religious school operating independently of any control or supervision by a church or other religious organization to be incorporated.[7] Such a school must also separately apply for recognition of tax-exempt status. This procedure is discussed in detail elsewhere.[8]

Most private schools are connected with a particular church congregation and are subject to the direct supervision and control of the church. Most courts have held that such a school constitutes an integral part of the church and therefore shares the church's corporate status as does any other department or ministry of the church. To illustrate, one court has observed that "a school may be considered as an integral and inseparable part of a church" even though not every church has a full-time school associated with it.[9] Accordingly, the court held that a church school was a proper use of property zoned for church uses. Other courts have concluded that a private religious school controlled by a church is an integral part of the parent church and hence shares the church's exemption from state unemployment taxes.[10] A federal judge has observed that a private religious school is a "direct, intimate adjunct of church activities conducted in the house of worship. From the earliest days, when governments

[7]See chapter 8, § B, *supra.*

[8]See chapter 14, § B, *infra.*

[9]Concord v. New Testment Baptist Church, 382 A.2d 377, 380 (N.H. 1978). *Accord* Employment Division v. Archdiocese of Portland, 600 P.2d 926 (Ore. 1979).

[10]*See, e.g.,* St. Martin Evangelical Lutheran Church v. South Dakota, 101 S. Ct. 2142, 2147 n.10 (1981).

were doing absolutely nothing about it, nearly all religious denominations have conducted school, including colleges, as an integral part of their activities."[11]

Since under the prevailing view a church-operated school is considered to be an integral part of the church, the school will share the church's corporate status and need not be separately incorporated. It will derivatively enjoy all the advantages of the corporation form of organization because of its relationship with the church. Of course, this discussion assumes that the church itself is incorporated and exercises sufficient control over the school to support the conclusion that the school is in fact an integral part of the church. If the church with which a school is connected is not incorporated, the proper procedure would be to incorporate the church and not the school.

Some churches have separately incorporated their schools to insulate themselves from any legal liability that might arise from such operations. This tactic will fail in most cases if a church continues to exert control over the new "corporation," since it is well-established that the misconduct of a wholly owned subsidiary corporation is attributable to the parent corporation if the latter exercises control over the subsidiary. Thus, for example, if the directors, administration, and staff of a separately incorporated church school are selected by or subject to the approval of the parent church, and if title to the school property is in the name of the church, the fact that the school is a separate corporation will not insulate the church from liability for injuries or damages that occur in the course of school operations.

Separate incorporation of a church-operated school will also suggest that the school is not in fact an integral part of the church. This obviously could have adverse consequences since the school's tax-exempt status typically derives from its integral relationship with its parent church. It might also prevent the school from being operated on land zoned for church use.

In most cases a church-operated school will share the parent church's exemption from federal and state income taxes, local property taxes, and unemployment taxes. This conclusion assumes that the school is controlled by a church to such a degree that it can be said to be an integral part of the church. If a church-operated school is separately incorporated, it may not be deemed to be an integral part of the church and thus its exemption from various federal, state, and local taxes may be jeopardized. To illustrate, the United States Supreme Court, in ruling that church-operated schools share a parent church's exemption from unemployment taxes, specifically limited its ruling to unincorporated church-operated schools having "no separate legal existence from

[11]Brown v. Dade Christian Schools, Inc., 556 F.2d 310, 326 (5th Cir. 1977) (Coleman, J., dissenting).

a church."[12] The Court concluded that the section of the federal unemployment tax law exempting service performed in the employ of a church was meant to apply to unincorporated church-operated schools.

Finally, it should be noted that the income tax regulations specify that a separately incorporated church school is not entitled to tax exemption as an "integrated auxiliary" of a church.[13] The implication of this regulation is that unincorporated church-operated schools do share the tax-exempt status of their parent church, that separately incorporated schools do not, and that separately incorporated schools are not eligible for exemption as "integrated auxiliaries" of tax-exempt churches. In summary, it would appear to be the view of the IRS that a separately incorporated church school must independently apply for and obtain tax-exempt status.

## §B. Proof of Nondiscrimination

In 1971, a federal district court in the District of Columbia ruled that the Internal Revenue Code "does not contemplate the granting of special Federal tax benefits to . . . organizations . . . whose organization or operation contravene Federal public policy."[14] The court claimed to have discovered a "Federal public policy against support for racial segregation of schools, public or private,"[15] and accordingly concluded that the provisions of the Code granting federal tax exemptions to charitable organizations "can no longer be construed so as to provide to private schools operating on a racially discriminatory premise the support of the exemptions and deductions which Federal tax law affords to charitable organizations and their sponsors."[16]

In 1971, the IRS ruled that a private school "not having a racially nondiscriminatory policy as to students is not 'charitable' . . . and accordingly does not qualify as an organization exempt from Federal income tax."[17] The IRS subsequently issued two revenue procedures that gave detailed guidelines for determining whether a particular private school is in fact engaged in racial

[12]St. Martin Evangelical Lutheran Church v. South Dakota, 101 S. Ct. 2142, 2148 n.12 (1981).

[13]Treas. Reg. § 1.6033-2(g)(5)(iv).

[14]Green v. Connally, 330 F. Supp. 1150, 1162 (D.D.C. 1971), aff'd sub nom., Coit v. Green, 404 U.S. 997 (1971).

[15]Id. at 1163.

[16]Id. at 1164. This ruling technically applied only to independent or separately incorporated private schools whose exempt status derived from a charitable purpose, not to those private schools whose exemption derived from their relationship with a particular church. This important distinction, however, was soon forgotten.

[17]Rev. Rul. 71-447, 1971-2 C.B. 230.

discrimination.[18] Revenue Procedure 75-50 stipulates that "[a] school must show affirmatively both that it has adopted a racially nondiscriminatory policy as to students that is made known to the general public and that since the adoption of that policy it has operated in a bona fide manner in accordance therewith." Specifically, Revenue Procedure 75-50 states that a private school must

1. Include a statement in its charter, bylaws, or other governing instrument, or in a resolution of its governing body, that it has a racially nondiscriminatory policy toward students.

2. Include a statement of its racially nondiscriminatory policy toward students in all its brochures and catalogs dealing with student admissions, programs, and scholarships.

3. Make its racially nondiscriminatory policy known to all segments of the general community served by the school through the publication of a notice of its racially nondiscriminatory policy at least annually in a newspaper of general circulation serving all racial segments of the community,[19] or through utilization of the broadcast media to publicize its nondiscriminatory policy if this use makes such nondiscriminatory policy known to all segments of the general community.[20] However, such notice is not required if one or more of the following conditions is satisfied:

[18]Rev. Proc. 72-54, 1972-2 C.B. 834; Rev. Proc. 75-50, 1975-2 C.B. 587.

[19]This publication must be repeated at least once annually during the period of the school's solicitation of students, or in the absence of a solicitation program, during the school's registration period. The notice must appear in a section of the newspaper likely to be read by prospective students and their families and it must occupy at least three column inches. It must be captioned in at least 12-point boldface type as a notice of nondiscriminatory policy toward students, and its text must be printed in at least 8-point type. The IRS has stated that the following notice is acceptable if it meets the typeface requirements:

### NOTICE OF
### NONDISCRIMINATORY POLICY
### AS TO STUDENTS

The "M School" admits students of any race, color, national and ethnic origin to all the rights, privileges, programs, and activities generally accorded or made available to students at the school. It does not discriminate on the basis of race, color, national and ethnic origin in administration of its educational policies, admissions policies, scholarship and loan programs, and athletic and other school-administered programs.

[20]If a school chooses to use the broadcast media to publicize its policy of racial non-discrimination, it must provide documentation that the means by which the policy was communicated to all segments of the general community was reasonably expected to be effective. Appropriate documentation includes copies of the tapes or script used and records showing that there was an adequate number of announcements, that they were made during hours when the announcements were likely to be communicated to all segments of the general community, that they were of sufficient duration to convey the

a. During the preceding three years the enrollment consists of students at least seventy-five percent of whom are members of the sponsoring religious denomination or unit and the school publicizes its nondiscriminatory policy in religious periodicals distributed in the community, provided that if the school chooses to advertise in newspapers of general circulation, then it must comply with the notice requirements for newspapers.

b. The school customarily draws a substantial percentage of its students from around the world, across the nation, or throughout a large geographic section or sections of the United States and follows a racially nondiscriminatory policy toward students that is published in all brochures and catalogs dealing with student admissions, programs, and scholarships.

c. The school draws its students from local communities and follows a racially nondiscriminatory policy toward students and demonstrates that it follows a racially nondiscriminatory policy by showing that it currently enrolls students of racial minority groups in meaningful numbers.

4. Be able to show that all of its programs and facilities are operated in a racially nondiscriminatory manner.

5. Be able to show that all scholarships or other comparable benefits are offered on a racially nondiscriminatory basis. Their availability on this basis must be known throughout the general community being served by the school and should be referred to in the published or broadcast notices of nondiscriminatory policy.

6. Certify annually to the IRS that it has satisfied all the preceding requirements. The annual certification is accomplished by filing a Form 5578 with the IRS. A Form 5578 is reproduced at the end of this chapter.

The United States Supreme Court has held that private schools may not employ racially discriminatory admissions criteria.[21] In so holding the Court relied upon a federal statute[22] stipulating that "[a]ll persons within the jurisdiction of the United States shall have the same right . . . to make and enforce contracts . . . as is enjoyed by white citizens . . . ." The Court acknowledged that it was not deciding the issue of the legality of racially discriminatory admissions policies based upon religious beliefs. This narrower question has been considered by other courts. To illustrate, a federal appeals court has upheld the authority of the IRS to revoke the tax-exempt status of Bob Jones

---

message clearly, and that they were broadcast on radio or television stations likely to be listened to by substantial numbers of all racial segments of the general community. Announcements must be made during the period of the school's solicitation for students, or in the absence of a solicitation program, during the school's registration period.

[21]Runyon v. McCrary, 427 U.S. 160 (1976).

[22]42 U.S.C. § 1981.

University on the basis of the school's prohibition of interracial dating and marriage, despite the school's claim that its policies were founded on Biblical principles.[23] The court initially observed that the First Amendment principle of free exercise of religion "cannot be invoked to justify exemption from a law of general applicability grounded on a compelling state interest," and it concluded that "[t]he government interest in this case is compelling."[24] The court emphasized that the revocation of exempt status did not prohibit the school or any student from adhering to the policy against interracial dating or marriage. This decision was affirmed by the United States Supreme Court in 1983.

In 1978, the IRS proposed a set of controversial guidelines to be used in determining whether a private school was guilty of racial discrimination. These guidelines proposed various "presumptions" and met with widespread criticism. Congress has since taken action prohibiting the IRS from using any funds to implement the guidelines.

## §C. Right to Attend

The courts have consistently recognized the right of parents to send their children to nonpublic schools. The United States Supreme Court many years ago struck down an Oregon law requiring children between the ages of eight and sixteen to attend public schools.[25] The Court observed:

> [W]e think it entirely plain that the Act of 1922 unreasonably interferes with the liberty of parents and guardians to direct the upbringing and education of children under their control. As often heretofore pointed out, rights guaranteed by the Constitution may not be abridged by legislation which has no reasonable relation to some purpose within the competency of the state. The fundamental theory of liberty upon which all governments in this Union repose excludes any general power of the state to standardize its children by forcing them to accept instruction from public teachers only. The child is not the mere creature of the state; those who nurture him and direct his destiny have the right, coupled with the high duty, to recognize and prepare him for additional obligations.[26]

The right of parents to send their children to private schools has been re-

[23]Bob Jones University v. United States, 639 F.2d 147 (4th Cir. 1980), aff'd, ___ S. Ct. ___ (1983). See also Goldsboro Christian Schools, Inc. v. United States, 644 F.2d 879 (4th Cir. 1981), aff'd, ___ S. Ct. ___ (1983); Brown v. Dade Christian Schools, Inc., 556 F.2d 310 (5th Cir. 1977); Goldsboro Christian Schools, Inc. v. United States, 436 F. Supp. 1314 (D.S.C. 1977).

[24]Id. at 153.

[25]Pierce v. Society of Sisters, 268 U.S. 510 (1925).

[26]Id. at 534-35.

peatedly affirmed.[27] In recent years the courts have recognized that states may impermissibly interfere with a parent's right to direct the upbringing and education of his children by imposing excessive and unreasonable regulatory burdens upon private schools.[28]

## §D. The Distinction Between Public and Private Education

It is often crucial to ascertain whether a particular school is a public or private institution since the applicability of several constitutional and statutory provisions turns upon this distinction. To illustrate, the due process clause of the Fourteenth Amendment to the United States Constitution provides that no state or state instrumentality shall deprive any person of life, liberty, or property without the procedural safeguards implicit in the notion of due process. Public schools are state instrumentalities, and hence they are subject to the due process clause. Thus public schools may not, for example, discipline or discharge students without following the procedures mandated by the courts, for to do so would be to deprive such students of liberty without due process. Such procedures typically include an evidentiary hearing, an impartial arbiter, the right to confront opposing witnesses, the right to counsel, and the opportunity to present evidence. Similarly, public schools may not discharge tenured schoolteachers without due process. Private schools that are not state instrumentalities are not subject to the due process clause.

Many other constitutional limitations are imposed on state instrumentalities. Virtually the entire Bill of Rights has been judicially "incorporated" into the due process clause of the Fourteenth Amendment and thereby made applicable to states and state instrumentalities. As a result, public schools and other state institutions may not impair such rights as speech, press, assembly, association, free exercise and nonestablishment of religion, freedom from unreasonable searches and seizures, and protection from cruel and unusual punishment without following judicially mandated procedural safeguards. Several state and federal statutes contain provisions incorporating the public-private distinction.

In summary, the characterization of a religious school as being either public or private is of fundamental importance. But how is such a school to be characterized? It can safely be said that most if not all religious schools are private institutions beyond the reach of the kinds of constitutional and legislative provisions summarized above. To illustrate, in one case a court rejected the

---

[27]*See, e.g.,* Parham v. J.R., 442 U.S. 584 (1979); Zablocki v. Redhail, 434 U.S. 374 (1978); Wolman v. Walter, 433 U.S. 229 (1977); Maher v. Roe, 432 U.S. 464 (1977); Smith v. Organization of Foster Families, 431 U.S. 816 (1977); Carey v. Population Services, International, 431 U.S. 678 (1977); Whalen v. Roe, 429 U.S. 589 (1977); Cook v. Hudson, 429 U.S. 165 (1976).

[28]State of Ohio v. Whisner, 351 N.E.2d 750 (Ohio 1976).

claim of a student who had been discharged from a private religious school that his constitutional right to due process had been violated by the school's summary expulsion procedure.[29] The court concluded that the requirements of due process did not apply since the school was a private and not a public or state institution. This conclusion was not affected by the fact that the school received governmental aid:

> The federal judiciary is nearly unanimous in holding that financial assistance to a private university or professional school, without more, does not render the actions of the educational institution state action . . . . In several of these cases, the governmental contribution was quite substantial. For example, in [one case] federal aid constituted 25% of the school's budget; in [another case] public funds contributed to 40% of . . . total revenues. Yet despite the significant input of governmental aid, state action was not present. The percentage contribution in the instant case is but a fraction of those indicated above.[30]

The court also rejected the student's claim that regulatory oversight of private schools by the state transformed them into state entities since "the state has minimal control over private educational facilities" and is concerned "only with sanitation, qualifications of teachers and minimum course requirements."[31]

In another case, the expulsion of two pupils for violation of a school disciplinary rule regarding absence was held not to be governed by the due process clause despite the fact that the state regulated course and curriculum materials in private schools to a limited extent, private schools were exempt from property taxes, students of private schools could use public transportation, most private schools participated in the school lunch program, and a private school desiring to obtain a certificate from the state board of education had to meet more extensive state requirements.[32]

## §E. Discharge and Discipline of Students

The public schools, being state instrumentalities, may not deprive students of liberty or property without the procedural safeguards mandated by the Fourteenth Amendment's due process clause. Discipline, suspension, and discharge each obviously involves abridgement of liberty, and hence the public schools may not impose such sanctions without providing a fair and reasonable procedure.

[29]Huff v. Notre Dame High School, 456 F. Supp. 1145 (D. Conn. 1978).

[30]*Id.* at 1148.

[31]*Id.*

[32]Bright v. Isenbarger, 314 F. Supp. 1382 (N.D. Ind. 1970), *aff'd*, 445 F.2d 412 (7th Cir. 1971).

As has been demonstrated in the preceding section, private religious schools are not instrumentalities of the state and hence they are exempted from the requirements imposed upon public schools by the due process clause. This means that a private school is virtually unconstrained by law in the discipline, suspension, and discharge of students. This conclusion has been affirmed by many courts. For example, one court upheld the constitutionality of the summary discharge of a student by a nonpublic secondary school over her objection that she had been denied due process. The court concluded that the school was a private and not a public institution and hence the protections of due process were simply not available.[33] Another court concluded that a Catholic high school is not a state instrumentality, and thus the school did not violate the due process clause in the manner in which it expelled two students. The court observed:

> [P]rivate schools may discourage criticism and irreverence toward existing institutions or policies while public schools may not. Private schools may emphasize moral development and strict discipline in ways which public schools may not employ. Private schools may impose disciplined conformity of dress, speech and action, such as found in military schools and to a lesser extent in most private schools, which public schools may not.[34]

Of course, a school may be liable to a student for monetary damages if it discharges him in violation of the terms of its own contract. In addition, some states have enacted laws banning the use of corporal punishment in private as well as public schools.

### §F. Discharge and Discipline of Teachers

In general, if a teacher has contracted to work for a definite term, a school may not terminate such employment without breaching the contract. Breach of contract will render the school liable for money damages, which may be the balance due under the contract. To illustrate, it has been held that when teachers are discharged by a private school before the end of their contractual term, the school "is legally required to pay to them the salaries which they would have been entitled to had they been permitted to render services for the full term stipulated by the agreement."[35] Since the teacher is employed by a private institution, no procedural due process requirements need attend

[33]Wisch v. Sanford School, Inc., 420 F. Supp. 1310 (D. Del. 1976).

[34]Bright v. Isenbarger, 314 F. Supp. 1382, 1391-92 (N.D. Ind. 1970) (citations omitted), aff'd, 445 F.2d 412 (7th Cir. 1971).

[35]Dunn v. Bessie F. Hiern School, Inc., 209 So.2d 538, 542 (La. 1968), cert. denied, 211 So.2d 331 (La. 1968).

the discharge determination. Of course, a school can discharge a teacher before the end of a term specified in an employment contract if the contract specifies grounds for early dismissal. For example, a teacher employed by a private school for a full school year and discharged two months prior to the end of the term was found to have been properly discharged since her contract stipulated discharge before the end of the term upon the occurrence of a "serious ground of complaint"—which did occur.[36] It has also been held that a teacher hired for a full school year was properly dismissed before the end of her term since she had fraudulently concealed from her employer her dismissal from another school during the previous school year.[37] The court held that a false representation of a material fact by a teacher, with full knowledge of its falsity and with an intent to induce a school to enter into a contract of employment to teach, constitutes fraud sufficient to entitle the school to disregard the contract.[38]

Teachers employed for definite terms can be discharged at the conclusion of such terms without a hearing or other procedure since they have no right to be rehired beyond the term of their current employment without some contractual provision to the contrary. One court has noted that a

> non-tenured teacher at a private school operating on a one academic year contract [has] no right to renewal of her contract and [is] not entitled either by law or by contract to a hearing upon renewal . . . . There is no due process guarantee of the procedural rights of a hearing and a statement of reasons for nonrenewal . . . .[39]

Private schools are under no obligation to create a tenure policy. If they choose to do so, the discharge of a tenured teacher will be subject to the procedures and standards mandated by the tenure policy. Typically, the school will have to establish incompetency or unfitness, or some related ground. Tenured private school teachers are still not entitled to procedural due process protections, and thus they ordinarily must be content with whatever procedures are afforded them by the school tenure policy.

If a teacher is employed for an indefinite term he may be discharged at any time, with or without cause. Again, procedural due process requirements are inapplicable.[40]

[36]Martin v. Coral Gables Academy, 369 So.2d 255 (La. 1979), *cert. denied*, 371 So.2d 1344 (La. 1979). *Accord* Pfendler v. Anshe Emet Day School, 401 N.E.2d 1094 (Ill. 1980).

[37]Ostrolenk v. Louise S. McGehee School, 402 So.2d 237 (La. 1981), *cert. denied*, 404 So.2d 1259 (La. 1981).

[38]*Id.* at 240.

[39]Titchener v. Avery Coonley School, 350 N.E.2d 502, 508 (Ill. 1976).

[40]Lillie v. Commerce City Kindergarten, Inc., 487 P.2d 605 (Colo. 1971); Borne v. Magnolia School, 277 So.2d 642 (La. 1973).

Under Title VII of the Civil Rights Acts of 1964, a teacher employed by a school that employs at least fifteen persons may not be disciplined or discharged because of his race, color, sex, or national origin.[41] Title VII was amended in 1978 to emphasize that the ban on sex discrimination in employment was to be interpreted to include discrimination on the basis of pregnancy and childbirth. In commenting on the purposes of the amendment Congress noted:

> In addition to the impact of this bill on fringe benefit programs, other employment policies which adversely affect pregnant workers are also covered. These policies include: refusal to hire or promote pregnant women; termination of pregnant women; mandatory leave for pregnant women arbitrarily established at a certain time during their pregnancy and not based on their inability to work; reinstatement rights, including credit for previous service and accrued retirement benefits; and accumulated seniority.[42]

Title VII is directed at discriminatory treatment of employees by employers who have a minimum of fifteen employees. Title VII is violated only if a private religious school treats one employee or class of employees differently from another on the basis of race, color, sex, or national origin. Thus, for example, Title VII's prohibition of sex discrimination will be violated only if pregnancy is the basis for treating female employees less favorably than nonpregnant employees. For example, refusal to hire or promote a woman solely because of pregnancy violates Title VII. Discharging a female employee solely because of pregnancy is a violation of Title VII. Mandatory leave for pregnant women arbitrarily established at a certain time during pregnancy and not based on inability to work is also discrimination based upon the condition of pregnancy and as such violates Title VII. Similarly, a refusal to grant accumulated seniority or retirement benefits to women who seek to return to work following maternity leave is also a violation of Title VII, at least when employees who are temporarily absent from work because of other disabilities are granted accumulated seniority or retirement benefits.

A policy of denying a pregnant woman her old job or an equivalent position upon her return to work following maternity leave obviously would violate Title VII if other disabled employees are not similarly treated. But a general policy that guarantees no employee his or her old job back following an extended leave would seem perfectly consistent with Title VII. The mere existence of an apparently nondiscriminatory reinstatement policy does not end the inquiry, however, since the Supreme Court has held that "both intentional discrimi-

---

[41]See chapter 11, § I, supra. Title VII also prohibits religious discrimination in employment decisions, but church-operated schools are exempted from this prohibition.

[42]H.R. Rep. No. 95-948, 95th Cong., 2nd Sess. 6 (1978).

nation and policies neutral on their face but having a discriminatory effect may run afoul of [Title VII]."[43]

However, as has been noted elsewhere,[44] private religious schools may discriminate in most employment decisions on the basis of religion.

## §G. Tuition Refunds

If a student withdraws from or is discharged by a religious school during the school term, is he entitled to a pro rata refund of prepaid tuition? One court has held:

> Where a contract for schooling is for an entire specified term and a pupil withdraws for reasons of her own, without fault on the part of the school, it is the general rule that the school is entitled to the agreed tuition for the entire term.[45]

Another court has defended this view on the ground that a tuition forfeiture is a reasonable means of compensating a school for the expenses it incurs in preparing for a child and holding a place for him.[46] This assumes of course that the tuition forfeiture was expressly stipulated in the enrollment contract or in some other document incorporated by reference in the contract.

Other courts reject the legal validity of tuition forfeitures. To illustrate, one court has held that when a private school charged tuition of $2,400 payable in full upon enrollment, and the enrollment agreement specified that students who withdrew before the end of the academic year were entitled to a pro rata refund less a nonrefundable enrollment fee of $600, such an agreement was "unconscionable" and unenforceable since the nonrefundable enrollment fee amounted to a penalty and was not a valid liquidated damages provision.[47] It would appear that most courts would uphold the validity of nonrefundable amounts that can be justified on the basis of actual cost or expense. For example, one court concluded that forfeiture of tuition by a student who voluntarily withdrew from a private academy was justified since the academy had dem-

---

[43]Nashville Gas Co. v. Satty, 434 U.S. 136, 141 (1977).

[44]See chapter 11, § I, *supra. See also* Larsen v. Kirkham, 499 F. Supp. 960 (D. Utah 1980).

[45]J J & L Investment Co. v. Minaga, 487 P.2d 561, 562 (Colo. 1971); King v. American Academy of Dramatic Arts, 425 N.Y.S.2d 505 (1980); Brenner v. Little Red School House, Ltd., 266 S.E.2d 728 (N.C. 1980), *rev'd on other grounds*, 274 S.E.2d 206 (N.C. 1981); Albermarle Educational Foundation, Inc., Basnight, 167 S.E.2d 486 (N.C. 1969).

[46]Brenner v. Little Red School House, Ltd., 266 S.E.2d 728 (N.C. 1980), *rev'd on other grounds*, 274 S.E.2d 206 (N.C. 1981).

[47]Educational Beneficial, Inc. v. Reynolds, 324 N.Y.S.2d 813 (1971).

onstrated that it had purchased supplies and employed teachers based upon the expectation of receiving tuition from the student.[48]

## §H. Government Regulation of Private Schools

Many courts have held that the state has a legitimate interest in ensuring that its youth receive a competent education, and that this interest justifies "reasonable" governmental regulation of private schools.[49] One court has observed that "[n]umerous decisions of the Supreme Court of the United States over the years have clearly sounded the death knell" for the assertion that "the state is devoid of all power to promulgate and enforce reasonable regulations affecting the operation of nonpublic schools."[50] To illustrate, the Supreme Court has held that "[t]here is no doubt as to the power of a State, having a high responsibility for education of its citizens, to impose reasonable regulations for the control and duration of basic education."[51] The Court has also observed:

> [A] substantial body of case law has confirmed the power of the States to insist that attendance at private schools, if it is to satisfy state compulsory-attendance laws, be at institutions which provide minimum hours of instruction, employ teachers of specified training, and cover prescribed subjects of instruction . . . [and that] if the State must satisfy its interest in secular education through the instrument of private schools, it has a proper interest in the manner in which those schools perform their secular educational function.[52]

Many states in the exercise of their authority to provide for the competent education of their citizens have enacted laws applying directly to private schools. Many of these laws are part of a general compulsory attendance statute requiring that all children of prescribed ages attend a public or state-approved private school. State approval of private schools generally is based upon such criteria as teacher certification, length of school day and year, curriculum content, and compliance with safety laws. Such laws have generally been upheld by the courts. To illustrate, the State of North Dakota has a compulsory attendance law requiring all children between seven and sixteen years of age to attend a public school or a state-approved private school. To receive state approval, a private school must use only state-certified teachers, teach a minimum of prescribed courses, and comply with all municipal and state health, fire, and safety laws. The state prosecuted two families who sent their children to a nonap-

---

[48]Albemarle Educational Foundation, Inc. v. Basnight, 167 S.E.2d 486 (N.C. 1969).
[49]*See generally* chapter 16, § G, *infra*, and chapter 11, *supra*.
[50]State of Ohio v. Whisner, 351 N.E.2d 750, 760 (Ohio 1976).
[51]Wisconsin v. Yoder, 406 U.S. 205, 213 (1972).
[52]Board of Education v. Allen, 392 U.S. 236, 245-46 (1968).

proved church school for violation of the compulsory attendance law. The parents challenged the constitutionality of the state's compulsory attendance law as applied to church schools.[53] In particular, the parents argued that the Bible commands parents to educate their children according to the scriptures and to raise them in the nurture and admonition of the Lord, and thus parents have an obligation to send their children to a school where Christian values and beliefs can be taught without state interference.

The state countered by demonstrating that the school used a self-study curriculum that did not require the use of state-certified teachers, that the school had never sought approval for its program, and that the state had a significant interest in ensuring that all children receive a competent education and that this responsibility justified the state's approval of private schools.

In resolving the issue the court applied a three-pronged test formulated by the United States Supreme Court:[54]

1. Was the activity with which the state interfered motivated by and rooted in a legitimate and sincerely held religious belief?
2. Was the right to the free exercise of religion unduly burdened by the state regulation, and if so, what was the extent of its impact on religious practices?
3. Did the state have a sufficiently "compelling" interest in the regulation to justify the burden on the free exercise of religion?

The court concluded that the activity interfered with by the state was motivated by and rooted in a legitimate and sincerely held religious belief, and assumed for the sake of argument that the parents' right to freely exercise their religion had been unduly burdened by the state's compulsory attendance law. However, the court concluded that the state did have a "compelling" interest in reasonably regulating private education that justified the burden on the parents' free exercise of religion:

> Absent the approval requirement, the state would have virtually no assurance that children, who are not in attendance at a public school, are in fact attending either a private or parochial school, and, if so, are receiving and will continue to receive a good education in a safe, healthy environment.[55]

The court rejected the parents' contention that the state could fulfill its

---

[53]State v. Shaver, 294 N.W.2d 883 (N.D. 1980). *Accord* Lanner v. Wimmer, 662 F.2d 1349 (10th Cir. 1981); Windsor Park Baptist Church, Inc., v. Arkansas Activities Association, 658 F.2d 618 (8th Cir. 1981).

[54]Wisconsin v. Yoder, 406 U.S. 205 (1972).

[55]294 N.W.2d at 897.

responsibility of providing a competent education for its youth through the less restrictive means of a standardized achievement testing program.

In a similar case, the Supreme Court of Nebraska upheld the constitutionality of a state compulsory attendance law requiring children between seven and sixteen years of age to attend either public schools or state-approved private schools.[56] To receive state approval, a private school had to meet various requirements relating to curriculum, length of school day and year, and health and safety. In addition, private schools were required to file reports with the state and could employ only state-certified teachers. The State of Nebraska filed suit to halt further operation of a particular church school on the ground that it was not in compliance with the state compulsory attendance law. In particular, the state alleged that the school used a self-study curriculum "not unlike a correspondence course" that utilized noncertified teachers, and that state reporting requirements were not being followed. The church countered by arguing that its school was an extension of the church and thus the state had no authority to approve it. The church also maintained that the First Amendment's guaranty of the free exercise of religion insulated its school from state regulation, and that the state was incapable of judging the quality of a religious school.

The court concluded that the state had a "compelling" and critical interest in the quality of the education provided its youth that justified reasonable regulation of nonpublic religious schools. Accordingly, the court upheld the validity of the compulsory attendance law, including the requirement that private school teachers be state-certified. The court observed:

> We are not suggesting as an absolute that every person who has earned a baccalaureate degree in teaching is going to become a good teacher, any more than one who has obtained the appropriate training and education will become a good engineer, lawyer, beauty operator, welder, or pipefitter. However, we think it cannot fairly be disputed that such a requirement is neither arbitrary nor unreasonable; additionally, we believe it is also a reliable indicator of the probability of success in that particular field. We believe that it goes without saying that the State has a compelling interest in the quality and ability of those who are to teach its young people.[57]

The court, in rejecting the church's contention that the state's legitimate interest in providing quality education could better be served by annual comparative testing, observed that the "problem with testing is that it comes too

---

[56]State ex rel. Douglas v. Faith Baptist Church, 301 N.W.2d 571 (Nebr. 1981), *appeal dismissed*, 102 S. Ct. 75 (1981).

[57]*Id.* at 579.

late. If the deficiency of the education being afforded is not discovered until the end of the year, the child has wasted that year."[58]

The Supreme Court of New Mexico has held that

> the state may impose minimum scholastic and training standards, including qualifications for teachers, for both public and private nurseries, kindergartens and elementary schools. Above and beyond such minimum standards the private institution may furnish a better curriculum if it desires to do so. But the state has a preeminent interest in basic or minimum standards.[59]

The Supreme Court of Massachusetts has held that a church-operated school may not avoid state regulation by characterizing itself as a part of the church, and that a state law requiring private schools to report the name, age, and residence of every student did not violate the church school's First Amendment right to freely exercise its religion and did not interfere with any privacy rights.[60] In determining whether the state law violated the First Amendment's free exercise clause, the court applied the three-pronged test formulated by the United States Supreme Court[61] (see p. 313). The court reasoned that the school satisfied the first element of this test, but concluded that the second and third elements were not satisfied since an application of the state reporting law to private religious schools had only an incidental burden on the right of such schools to practice their religion and was justified by the state's compelling interest in providing a quality education for all its youth. The court emphasized that the law in no way interfered with a church school's right to teach religious doctrine. Finally, the court rejected the school's claims that the state law constituted an impermissible "establishment of religion" since it inhibited religion and created an excessive entanglement between church and state, and that the law unconstitutionally burdened the First Amendment right of association. With regard to the latter contention, the court observed that "the State's interest in compulsory education is so compelling and the information sought so relevant that it justifies the burden on the [school's], the parents', and the children's right to freedom of association."[62]

It has also been held that a parent who removes his child from the public schools and attempts to teach him at home does not satisfy state compulsory attendance requirements and thus such education can be halted since "the

---

[58]*Id.*

[59]Santa Fe Community School v. New Mexico State Board of Education, 518 P.2d 272, 274 (N.M. 1974).

[60]Attorney General v. Bailey, 436 N.E.2d 139 (Mass. 1982).

[61]Wisconsin v. Yoder, 406 U.S. 205 (1972).

[62]436 N.E.2d at 148.

natural rights of a parent to the custody and control of his child are subordinate to the police power of the state and may be restricted and regulated by municipal law providing minimum educational standards."[63]

A substantial body of case law has confirmed the power of the states "to insist that attendance at private schools, if it is to satisfy state compulsory attendance laws, be at institutions which provide minimum hours of instruction, employ teachers of specified training, and cover prescribed subjects of instruction."[64] However, case law also demonstrates that unreasonable state regulation of private education will not be tolerated. To illustrate, the Supreme Court of Ohio struck down the application to private religious schools of a series of "minimum standards" promulgated by the Ohio State Board of Education.[65] The minimum standards regulated the content of the curriculum, the manner in which it was taught, the physical layout of the educational buildings, the hours of instruction, the educational policies to be achieved, and the amount of instructional time to be allocated to the subjects offered. The minimum standards left no time for Biblical or spiritual training, required a minimum number of students, required that all activities "shall conform to policies adopted by the board of education," prohibited the release of child study information to parents, and required that "organized group life of all types must act in accordance with established rules of social relationships and a system of social controls." The court concluded that these standards unduly burdened the First Amendment right of parents to send their children to private religious schools since "these 'minimum standards' overstep the boundary of *reasonable* regulation as applied to a nonpublic religious school."[66] The court also found that the right of parents to direct the upbringing and education of their children in a manner they deem advisable was also denied by the application of the "minimum standards" to private religious schools:

> These standards are so pervasive and all-encompassing that total compliance with each and every standard by a nonpublic school would effectively eradicate the distinction between public and nonpublic education, and thereby deprive [parents] . . . of their traditional interest . . . to direct the upbringing and education of their children.[67]

The Supreme Court of Kentucky has held that the state cannot require nonpublic schools to comply with curriculum, teacher certification, and text-

---

[63]State v. Garber, 419 P.2d 896, 900 (Kan. 1966).

[64]Board of Education v. Allen, 392 U.S. 236, 245-46 (1968).

[65]State of Ohio v. Whisner, 351 N.E. 2d 750 (Ohio 1976).

[66]*Id.* at 764.

[67]*Id.* at 768.

book standards because such requirements would violate Section 5 of the Kentucky Constitution which states: "[N]or shall any man be compelled to send his child to any school to which he may be conscientiously opposed." The court added that if the state legislature wished to monitor the work of private schools in accomplishing the state's obligation to provide its youth with a competent education, "it may do so by an appropriate standardized achievement testing program."[68]

The previous two decisions have been distinguished by some courts on the following grounds: (1) the regulations in the first case (*i.e.*, *Whisner*) were so pervasive as to be unreasonable, (2) the second case (*i.e.*, *Rudasill*) involved a unique state constitutional provision, and (3) both cases involved actual or threatened criminal sanctions that greatly increased the burden on religious practices.[69]

Finally, in *Yoder v. Wisconsin* the United States Supreme Court ruled that the First Amendment's free exercise clause prevents a state from compelling Old Order Amish parents to send their children to school after graduation from the eighth grade.[70] The Amish demonstrated that their religion was characterized by a fundamental belief that salvation requires life in a church community separate and apart from the world and worldly influence, and that formal education of Amish children beyond the eighth grade would expose them to unacceptable worldly influences and values such as intellectual and scientific achievement, self-distinction, competitiveness, material success, and social conformity. The Amish did not object to formal education through eighth grade because they believed that their children should have sufficient skills to read the Bible and to be able to deal with non-Amish people when necessary in the course of daily affairs.

The Court acknowledged the power of a state to impose reasonable regulations "for the control and duration of basic education."[71] It added, however, that "a State's interest in universal education, however highly we rank it, is not totally free from a balancing process when it impinges on fundamental rights and interests such as those specifically protected by the Free Exercise Clause of the First Amendment, and the traditional interest of parents with respect to the religious upbringing of their children . . . ."[72]

The Court formulated a three-pronged test for determining whether Wis-

[68]Kentucky State Board for Elementary and Secondary Education v. Rudasill, 589 S.W.2d 877, 884 (Ky. 1979), *cert. denied*, 446 U.S. 938 (1980).

[69]Windsor Park Baptist Church, Inc. v. Arkansas Activities Association, 658 F.2d 618 (8th Cir. 1981).

[70]406 U.S. 205 (1972).

[71]*Id.* at 213.

[72]*Id.* at 214.

consin's compulsory attendance law was unconstitutional as applied to Amish parents. The test involved a determination of (1) whether the activity interfered with by the state was motivated by and rooted in a legitimate and sincerely held religious belief; (2) whether the Amish parents' free exercise of religion had been unduly and substantially burdened by the regulation to the extent of affecting religious practices; and (3) whether or not the state had a compelling interest in the regulation that justified the burden on the free exercise of religion and overrode the interest of the Amish parents in exercising their religious practices. This three-pronged test has been employed by a number of other courts in subsequent cases, and may be considered a general test for determining whether a particular state law or regulation may apply to private religious schools.

With respect to the first prong of the test, the Court concluded that the opposition of the Amish parents to formal secondary education was motivated by and rooted in legitimate and sincerely held religious beliefs. As to the second prong, the Court observed:

> [T]he unchallenged testimony of acknowledged experts in education and religious history, almost 300 years of consistent practice, and strong evidence of a substantial faith pervading and regulating [the Amish members'] entire mode of life support the claim that enforcement of compulsory formal education after the eighth grade would gravely endanger if not destroy the free exercise of [their] religious beliefs.[73]

Finally, the Court concluded that the State of Wisconsin lacked a compelling interest in requiring Amish children to attend school after graduation from the eighth grade:

> It is one thing to say that compulsory education for a year or two beyond the eighth grade may be necessary when its goal is the preparation of the child for life in modern society as the majority live, but it is quite another if the goal of education be viewed as the preparation of the child for life in the separated agrarian community that is the keystone of the Amish faith.[74]

The Court emphasized that the Old Order Amish were one of a very few religious groups that could successfully argue that the application of a state compulsory attendance law violated their First Amendment right to the free exercise of religion.

In summary, it is the prevailing view that a state is responsible for providing a competent education for its citizens and that this responsibility justifies reasonable state regulation of private religious schools unless such regulation fails

[73]*Id.* at 219.
[74]*Id.* at 222.

the Supreme Court's three-pronged test. Presumably, most state laws regulating private education will satisfy this test unless (1) they are so patently unreasonable and pervasive as to in effect obliterate any distinction between public and private education, as was the case in *Whisner*;[75] (2) they adversely affect in a substantial way the religious tenets of a church-operated school; or (3) a less restrictive means of accomplishing the purpose of the regulation is available to the state.

## §I. Zoning Laws

Most courts hold that churches may establish private schools on church-owned property that is zoned for either residential or church use.[76] This view has been based on a number of grounds, including the following: (1) a private school is a permissible "accessory use" of church property; (2) a church school is an integral and inseparable part of a church and therefore is a permissible use wherever churches are permitted; (3) a zoning law that excludes private schools from church-owned property bears no reasonable relation to the promotion of public health, safety, morals, or general welfare and is therefore invalid; and (4) schools are permitted in residential districts where churches generally are located.[77]

Obviously, a zoning ordinance that excludes private schools from an entire municipality is invalid.[78] It has also been held that a zoning ordinance that imposed conditions on private schools that were so burdensome that no school could reasonably be expected to comply amounted to an impermissible exclusion of such schools from a municipality.[79] Zoning ordinances that exclude private schools from certain districts within a municipality likewise have been invalidated if public schools were permitted in the same districts,[80] or if such an exclusion bore no reasonable relation to the promotion of the public health, safety, morals, or general welfare.[81]

---

[75]*See* note 65, *supra*, and accompanying text.

[76]*See generally* A. RATHKOPF, THE LAW OF ZONING AND PLANNING § 20.02 (1982).

[77]*See generally* RATHKOPF, *supra* note 76, at § 20.02; Annot., 74 A.L.R.3d 14 (1976).

[78]Mooney v. Village of Orchard Lake, 53 N.W.2d 308 (Mich. 1952).

[79]Incorporated Village of Brookville v. Paulgene Realty Corp., 200 N.Y.S.2d 126 (1960), *aff'd*, 225 N.Y.S.2d 750 (1962).

[80]Roman Catholic Welfare Corporation v. Piedmont, 289 P.2d 438 (Cal. 1955), *aff'd*, 278 P.2d 943 (Cal. 1955); Chicago v. Sachs, 115 N.E.2d 762 (Ill. 1953); Diocese of Rochester v. Planning Board, 154 N.Y.S.2d 849 (1956).

[81]Urnstein v. Village of Town and Country, 368 S.W.2d 390 (Mo. 1963). As has been noted elsewhere, states possess inherent authority to enact laws in furtherance of the public health, safety, morals, and general welfare. This authority is referred to as the police power. Most municipalities possess a limited police power by virtue of delegation of authority by the state legislature. *See generally* chapter 11, § E, *supra*.

Zoning ordinances permitting church schools in certain districts only by special permit generally have been upheld. In a leading case, one court observed that the use of private property, including church-owned property, may be regulated by a municipality in the interest of the public health, safety, morals, or general welfare. Therefore, reasoned the court, it is appropriate to prevent churches from constructing or operating a private school on church-owned property unless they have applied for and received a special permit from municipal authorities, following a comprehensive review by the city of the impact of such a school on the public health, safety, morals, and general welfare.[82] Most courts have found the following grounds to be insufficient justification for denying a special permit authorizing the creation of a private school on church property or otherwise excluding private schools from certain districts: adverse effect on the value of neighboring properties, loss of tax revenues, decreased enjoyment of neighboring property because of the increase in noise and other inconveniences, traffic hazards, and neighborhood opposition.[83]

## §J. Safety and Health Regulations

It is well-established that states and municipalities may require private schools to comply with reasonable health, fire, and safety regulations. The Supreme Court of Kentucky, in the same decision in which it invalidated a state law requiring private schools to use only state-certified teachers and state-approved textbooks, upheld the right of the state to require private schools to comply with health, fire, and safety regulations.[84] In the Yoder[85] case, the United States Supreme Court observed: "It is true that activities of individuals, even when religiously based, are often subject to regulation by the States in the exercise of their undoubted power to promote the health, safety, and general welfare . . . ."[86]

In one case, a municipality sued to prevent the continued operation of a church school in a church basement that failed to meet building code safety

[82]St. John's Roman Catholic Church v. Town of Darien, 184 A.2d 42 (Conn. 1962).

[83]Board of Cooperative Educational Services v. Gaynor, 303 N.Y.S.2d 183 (1969), aff'd, 306 N.Y.S.2d 216 (1969), appeal denied, 310 N.Y.S.2d 1025 (1970); Meadows v. Binkowski, 269 N.Y.S.2d 331 (1966), aff'd, 279 N.Y.S.2d 1019 (1967); Diocese of Rochester v. Planning Board, 154 N.Y.S.2d 849 (1956); Dietrich v. District of Columbia Board of Zoning Adjustments, 320 A.2d 282 (D.C. 1974).

[84]Kentucky State Board for Elementary and Secondary Education v. Rudasill, 589 S.W.2d 877 (Ky. 1979), cert. denied, 446 U.S. 938 (1980).

[85]Wisconsin v. Yoder, 406 U.S. 205 (1972). See note 70, supra, and accompanying text.

[86]Id. at 220.

standards applicable to buildings used for educational purposes.[87] The church contended that its school was substantially in compliance with the building code, that the alleged violations were highly technical and did not endanger the lives or safety of students, that prohibitively costly structural and mechanical modifications would be required to bring the school into full compliance with the code, and that the right of parents to freely exercise their religion by providing a Christian education for their children would be abridged by requiring strict compliance with the code. The Supreme Court of Washington State agreed that an "uncompromising enforcement" of the municipal building code would result in the closing of the school and that this would deny church members the right to guide the education of their children and to freely exercise their religion. However, the court also acknowledged that the municipality was responsible for the safety and health of school children. The court observed that when two legitimate and substantial interests collide, one may have to give way, and it is the courts' function "to balance the interests of the parties and if an accommodation can be effected, determin[e] which interest must yield."[88] The court concluded that reasonable health, fire, and safety standards

> will be enforced against religious schools when the state proves that the specific concerns addressed by the regulations are of sufficient magnitude to outweigh the free exercise claim, that the nonapplication of the regulations will threaten the public health or other vital interests, and that the state's interest could not otherwise be satisfied in a way which would not infringe on religious liberty.[89]

The court suggested that when a municipality, in the exercise of its power to promote the public health, safety, morals, or general welfare is confronted with rights protected by the First Amendment, "it should not be uncompromising and rigid" but rather should approach the problem with flexibility since there should be "some play in the joints of both the zoning ordinance and the building code."[90] The court sent the case back to the trial court for reconsideration.

## §K. Taxation

As has been noted earlier in the present chapter, most church-operated schools share the federal income tax exemption of their parent church. Such schools are also exempt from payment of social security taxes until 1984 unless

[87]City of Sumner v. First Baptist Church, 639 P.2d 1358 (Wash. 1982).
[88]Id. at 1362.
[89]Id. at 1363.
[90]Id.

they waive the exemption.[91] Church schools automatically are covered by social security taxes after 1983. There are no exceptions or exemption provisions. Church schools are subject to the same withholding and wage reporting requirements as churches,[92] and, like churches, are exempt from the requirement of filing an annual information return (Form 990) with the IRS.[93]

The United States Supreme Court has struck down state laws allowing income tax benefits to parents of children attending private schools on the ground that such laws constitute an establishment of religion.[94] In one case, after noting that the vast majority of students attending nonpublic schools attend church-related schools, the Court held:

> Special tax benefits, however, cannot be squared with the principle of neutrality established by the decisions of this Court. To the contrary, insofar as such benefits render assistance to parents who send their children to sectarian schools, their purpose and inevitable effect are to aid and advance those religious institutions.[95]

It is clear that tuition payments made to a church school are not deductible as charitable contributions by a parent.[96] Neither are tuition payments made deductible because they are made directly to the church rather than to its school,[97] or because they are designated a "donation" that is paid instead of tuition. The IRS denied a charitable contribution deduction to a parent who was required to pay a fixed amount designated as a "donation" in addition to a tuition fee as a condition of enrolling his children in a church-operated school.[98] The IRS observed:

> A gift is generally defined as a voluntary transfer of property by its owner to another with donative intent and without consideration. If a payment proceeds primarily from the incentive of anticipated benefit to the payor beyond the sat-

[91] See chapter 10, § B, supra.

[92] See chapter 10, § A, supra.

[93] Treas. Reg. § 1.6033-2(g)(1)(a)(vii).

[94] Sloan v. Lemon, 413 U.S. 825 (1973); Committee for Public Education and Religious Liberty v. Nyquist, 413 U.S. 756 (1973). But see Mueller v. Allen, 676 F.2d 1195 (8th Cir. 1982).

[95] Committee for Public Education and Religious Liberty v. Nyquist, 413 U.S. 756, 793 (1973).

[96] Ryan v. Commissioner, 28 T.C.M. 1120 (1969); Casey v. Commissioner, 24 T.C.M. 1558 (1965).

[97] Haak v. United States, 451 F. Supp. 1087 (W.D. Mich. 1978) (rejecting claim that taxpayers' First Amendment right to the free exercise of religion was violated); Rev. Rul. 54-580, 1954-2 C.B. 97.

[98] Rev. Rul. 71-112, 1971-1 C.B. 93.

isfaction which flows from the performance of a generous act, is not a gift. In this case payments of both the tuition fee and the so-called "donation" represent consideration between the parties. Therefore, each lacks a donative intent and is not a gift . . . . Accordingly . . . no deduction for a charitable contribution is allowable . . . .[99]

Similarly, the IRS has ruled that a parent who sent his child to a church school that charged no tuition but that solicited funds from parents and others was entitled to a charitable contribution deduction only to the extent that "contributions" made to the school exceeded the fair market value of the child's education.[100] The IRS has also disallowed a deduction for amounts contributed to an education fund maintained by a church and used to help finance the education of children of church members who attended nonpublic schools.[101]

In addition, the IRS maintains that contributions to racially restricted private schools are not deductible by the donor in computing federal income taxes.[102]

Finally, it is a well-settled rule of law that a parent whose child attends a church school may not deduct as a charitable contribution a "scholarship gift" made to the school and earmarked for the use and benefit of his child. The IRS has noted:

Section 170 of the Code provides for the deduction, in computing taxable income, of charitable contributions, the payment of which is made within the taxable year to certain organizations described therein. Section 262 of the Code provides, generally, that no deduction shall be allowed for personal, living, or family expenses. If contributions to the fund are earmarked by the donor for a particular individual, they are treated, in effect, as being gifts to the designated individual and are not deductible. However, a deduction will be allowable where it is established that a gift is intended by a donor for the use of the organization and not as a gift to an individual. The test in each case is whether the organization has full control of the donated funds, and discretion as to their use, so as to insure that they will be used to carry out its functions and purposes.[103]

[99]*Id.*
[100]Rev. Rul. 79-99, 1979-1 C.B. 108. *See also* Rev. Rul. 78-189, 1978-1 C.B. 68.
[101]Winters v. Commissioner of Internal Revenue, 468 F.2d 778 (2nd Cir. 1972).
[102]Rev. Rul. 75-231, 1975-1 C.B. 158.
[103]Rev. Rul. 62-113, 1962-2 C.B. 10.

Form **5578**

(Rev. Nov. 1981)

Department of the Treasury
Internal Revenue Service

## Annual Certification of Racial Nondiscrimination
## for a Private School Exempt from Federal Income Tax
(For Use by Organizations That Do Not File Form 990)

OMB No. 1545-0213

Expires 10-31-84

For IRS
use ONLY ▶

For the period beginning _____ , 19____ , and ending _____ , 19____

| 1(a) Name of organization which operates, supervises, and/or controls school(s) | (b) Employer identification number (see instructions under **Definitions**) |
|---|---|
| Address (number and street) | |
| City or town, State, and ZIP code | |

| 2(a) Name of central organization holding group exemption letter covering the school(s). (If the same as the organization in 1(a) above, write "Same" and complete 2(c).) If the organization in 1(a) above holds an individual exemption letter, write "Not Applicable." | (b) Employer identification number |
|---|---|
| Address (number and street) | (c) Group exemption number (see instructions under **Definitions**) |
| City or town, State, and ZIP code | |

| 3(a) Name of school (if more than one school, write "See Attached," and attach list of the names, addresses, ZIP codes, and employer identification numbers of the schools). If same as the organization in 1(a) above, write "Same." | (b) Employer identification number, if any |
|---|---|
| Address (number and street) | |
| City or town, State, and ZIP code | |

Under penalties of perjury, I hereby certify that I am authorized to take official action on behalf of the above school(s) and that to the best of my knowledge and belief the school(s) has (have) satisfied the applicable requirements of sections 4.01 through 4.05 of Revenue Procedure 75–50 for the period covered by this certification.

_____ (Signature)     _____ (Title or authority of signer)     _____ (Date)

## Instructions

*This Form is Open to Public Inspection*

**Paperwork Reduction Act Notice.**—The Paperwork Reduction Act of 1980 says we must tell you why we are collecting this information, how we will use it, and whether you have to give it to us. We ask for the information to carry out the Internal Revenue laws of the United States. We need it to ensure that you are complying with these laws. You are required to give us this information.

**Who Must File**

Every organization that claims exemption from Federal income tax under section 501(c)(3) of the Code and that operates, supervises, or controls a private school or schools must file a certification of racial nondiscrimination. If an organization is required to file Form 990, Return of Organization Exempt from Income Tax, either as a separate return or as part of a group return, the certification should be made on Schedule A (Form 990) rather than on this form.

An authorized official of a central organization may file one form to certify for the school activities of subordinates, that would otherwise be required to file on an individual basis, but only if the central organization has enough control over the schools listed on the form to ensure that the schools maintain a racially nondiscriminatory policy as to students.

**Definitions**

A "racially nondiscriminatory policy as to students" means that the school admits the students of any race to all the rights, privileges, programs, and activities generally accorded or made available to students at that school and that the school does not discriminate on the basis of race

in the administration of its educational policies, admissions policies, scholarship and loan programs, and other school-administered programs.

The Service considers discrimination on the basis of race to include discrimination on the basis of color and national or ethnic origin.

A **school** is an educational organization which normally maintains a regular faculty and curriculum and normally has a regularly enrolled body of pupils or students in attendance at the place where its educational activities are regularly carried on. The term includes primary, secondary, preparatory, or high schools, and colleges and universities, whether operated as a separate legal entity or as an activity of a church or other organization described in section 501(c)(3) of the Code. The term also includes pre-schools and any other organization that is a school as defined in section 170(b)(1)(A)(ii) of the Code.

A **central organization** is an organization which has one or more subordinates under its general supervision or control. A subordinate is a chapter, local, post, or other unit of a central organization. A central organization may also be a subordinate, as in the case of a State organization which has subordinate units and is itself affiliated with a national organization.

The **employer identification number (EIN)** is a nine-digit number issued by the Service to identify organizations subject to various provisions of the tax law.

The **group exemption number (GEN)** is a four-digit number issued to a central organization by the Service. It identifies a central organization that has received a ruling from the Service recognizing on a group basis the exemption from Federal income tax of the central organization and its covered subordinates.

**When to File**

Under Rev. Proc. 75–50, 1975–2 C.B. 587, a certification of racial nondiscrimination must be filed annually. File Form 5578 by the 15th day of the 5th month following the end of the organization's calendar year or fiscal period.

**Where to File**

| If your principal office is located in— | Send your return to the Internal Revenue Service Center below— |
|---|---|
| Connecticut, New Hampshire, Maine, Massachusetts, Rhode Island, or Vermont | Andover, MA 05501 |
| Alabama, Florida, Georgia, Mississippi, North Carolina, South Carolina, or Tennessee | Atlanta, GA 31101 |
| Arkansas, Colorado, Kansas, Louisiana, New Mexico, Oklahoma, Texas, or Wyoming | Austin, TX 73301 |
| Indiana, Kentucky, Michigan, Ohio, or West Virginia | Cincinnati, OH 45999 |
| Arizona, California, Hawaii, Nevada, or Utah | Fresno, CA 93888 |
| New Jersey or New York | Holtsville, NY 00501 |
| Illinois, Iowa, Missouri, or Nebraska | Kansas City, MO 64999 |
| Alaska, Idaho, Minnesota, Montana, North Dakota, Oregon, South Dakota, Washington, or Wisconsin | Ogden, UT 84201 |

Delaware, Maryland,
Pennsylvania, Virginia,
District of Columbia,        Philadelphia, PA  19255
any U.S. possession, or
foreign country

## Certification Requirement

Section 4.06 of Rev. Proc. 75–50 requires an individual authorized to take official action on behalf of a school that claims to be racially nondiscriminatory as to students to certify annually, under penalties of perjury, that to the best of his or her knowledge and belief the school has satisfied the applicable requirements of sections 4.01 through 4.05 of the Procedure, reproduced below:

### Rev. Proc. 75–50

4.01 *Organizational requirements.* A school must include a statement in its charter, bylaws, or other governing instrument, or in a resolution of its governing body, that it has a racially nondiscriminatory policy as to students and therefore does not discriminate against applicants and students on the basis of race, color, and national or ethnic origin.

4.02 *Statement of Policy.* Every school must include a statement of its racially nondiscriminatory policy as to students in all its brochures and catalogues dealing with student admissions, programs, and scholarships. A statement substantially similar to that of section 4.03, *infra*, will be acceptable for this purpose. Further, every school must include a reference to its racially nondiscriminatory policy in other written advertising that it uses as a means of informing prospective students of its programs. The following references will be acceptable:

The M school admits students of any race, color, and national or ethnic origin.

4.03 *Publicity.* The school must make its racially nondiscriminatory policy known to all segments of the general community served by the school.

1. The school must use one of the following two methods to satisfy this requirement:

(a) The school may publish a notice of its racially nondiscriminatory policy in a newspaper of general circulation that serves all racial segments of the community. This publication must be repeated at least once annually during the period of the school's solicitation for students or, in the absence of a solicitation program, during the school's registration period. Where more than one community is served by a school, the school may publish its notice in those newspapers that are reasonably likely to be read by all racial segments of the communities that it serves. The notice must appear in a section of the newspaper likely to be read by prospective students and their families and it must occupy at least three column inches. It must be captioned in at least 12 point bold face type as a notice of nondiscriminatory policy as to students, and its text must be printed in at least 8 point type. The following notice will be acceptable:

## NOTICE OF
## NONDISCRIMINATORY POLICY
## AS TO STUDENTS

The M school admits students of any race, color, national and ethnic origin to all the rights, privileges, programs, and activities generally accorded or made available to students at the school. It does not discriminate on the basis of race, color, national and ethnic origin in administration of its educational policies, admissions policies, scholarship and loan programs, and athletic and other school-administered programs.

(b) The school may use the broadcast media to publicize its racially nondiscriminatory policy if this use makes such nondiscriminatory policy known to all segments of the general community the school serves. If this method is chosen, the school must provide documentation that the means by which this policy was communicated to all segments of the general community was reasonably expected to be effective. In this case, appropriate documentation would include copies of the tapes or script used and records showing that there was an adequate number of announcements, that they were made during hours when the announcements were likely to be communicated to all segments of the general community, that they were of sufficient duration to convey the message clearly, and that they were broadcast on radio or television stations likely to be listened to by substantial numbers of members of all racial segments of the general community. Announcements must be made during the period of the school's solicitation for students or, in the absence of a solicitation program, during the school's registration period.

Communication of a racially nondiscriminatory policy as to students by a school to leaders of racial groups as the sole means of publicity generally will not be considered effective to make the policy known to all segments of the community.

2. The requirements of subsection 1 of this section will not apply when one of the following paragraphs applies:

(a) If for the preceding three years the enrollment of a parochial or other church-related school consists of students at least 75 percent of whom are members of the sponsoring religious denomination or unit, the school may make known its racially nondiscriminatory policy in whatever newspapers or circulars the religious denomination or unit utilizes in the communities from which the students are drawn. These newspapers and circulars may be those distributed by a particular religious denomination or unit or by an association that represents a number of religious organizations of the same denomination. If, however, the school advertises in newspapers of general circulation in the community or communities from which its students are drawn and paragraphs (b) and (c) of this subsection are not applicable to it, then it must comply with paragraph (a) of subsection 1 of this section.

(b) If a school customarily draws a substantial percentage of its students nationwide or worldwide or from a large geographic section or sections of the United States and follows a racially nondiscriminatory policy as to students, the publicity requirement may be satisfied by complying with section 4.02, *supra.* Such a school may demonstrate that it follows a racially nondiscriminatory policy within the meaning of the preceding sentence either by showing that it currently enrolls students of racial minority groups in meaningful numbers or, when minority students are not enrolled in meaningful numbers, that its promotional activities and recruiting efforts in each geographic area were reasonably designed to inform students of all racial segments in the general communities within the area of the availability of the school. The question whether a school satisfies the preceding sentence will be determined on the basis of the facts and circumstances of each case.

(c) If a school customarily draws its students

U.S. GOVERNMENT PRINTING OFFICE : 1981  O-343-367

from local communities and follows a racially nondiscriminatory policy as to students, the publicity requirement may be satisfied by complying with section 4.02, *supra.* Such a school may demonstrate that it follows a racially nondiscriminatory policy within the meaning of the preceding sentence by showing that it currently enrolls students of racial minority groups in meaningful numbers. The question whether a school satisfies the preceding sentence will be determined on the basis of the facts and circumstances of each case. One of the facts and circumstances that the Service will consider is whether the school's promotional activities and recruiting efforts in each area were reasonably designed to attract students of all racial segments in the general communities within the area of the availability of the school. The Service recognizes that the failure by a school drawing its students from local communities to enroll racial minority group students may not necessarily indicate the absence of a racially nondiscriminatory policy as to students when there are relatively few or no such students in these communities. Actual enrollment is, however, a meaningful indication of a racially nondiscriminatory policy in a community in which a public school or schools became subject to a desegregation order of a federal court or otherwise expressly became obligated to implement a desegregation plan under the terms of any written contract or other commitment to which any Federal agency was a party.

The Service encourages schools to satisfy the publicity requirement by the methods described in subsection 1 of this section, regardless of whether a school considers itself within subsection 2, because it believes these methods to be the most effective to make known a school's racially nondiscriminatory policy. In this regard it is each school's responsibility to determine whether paragraph (a), (b), or (c) of subsection 2 applies to it. On audit, a school must be prepared to demonstrate that the failure to publish its racially nondiscriminatory policy in accordance with subsection 1 of this section was justified by the application to it of paragraph (a), (b), or (c) of subsection 2. Further, a school must be prepared to demonstrate that it has publicly disavowed or repudiated any statements purported to have been made on its behalf (after November 6, 1975) that are contrary to its publicity of a racially nondiscriminatory policy as to students, to the extent that the school or its principal official were aware of such statements.

4.04 *Facilities and Programs.* A school must be able to show that all of its programs and facilities are operated in a racially nondiscriminatory manner.

4.05 *Scholarship and loan programs.* As a general rule, all scholarship or other comparable benefits procurable for use at any given school must be offered on a racially nondiscriminatory basis. Their availability on this basis must be known throughout the general community being served by the school and should be referred to in the publicity required by this section in order for that school to be considered racially nondiscriminatory as to students. . . . . [S]cholarships and loans that are made pursuant to financial assistance programs favoring members of one or more racial minority groups that are designed to promote a school's racially nondiscriminatory policy will not adversely affect the school's exempt status. Financial assistance programs favoring members of one or more racial groups that do not significantly derogate from the school's racially nondiscriminatory policy similarly will not adversely affect the school's exempt status.

# 14

# TAXATION OF CHURCHES

## §A. Introduction

Federal, state, and local governments have enacted a variety of tax laws to finance the enormous costs of government. The primary sources of federal revenue are individual and corporate income taxes and social security taxes. Other federal taxes include unemployment, estate, and excise taxes. State and local governments often impose income, sales, and property taxes, and in addition provide employment security through unemployment taxes. The applicability of any of these various taxes to churches depends upon the following factors:

1. whether the statute that imposes the tax specifically exempts churches
2. if churches are exempt, whether all statutory preconditions to exempt status have been satisfied
3. whether a tax that purports to apply to churches is permissible under state and federal constitutions

These factors will be considered in detail in the materials that follow.

## §B. Federal Income Taxation

### 1. EXEMPTION OF CHURCHES

#### a. *In General*

Section 501(a) of the Internal Revenue Code exempts organizations described in section 501(c) from federal income taxation. Section 501(c) lists several exempt organizations, including

[c]orporations . . . organized and operated exclusively for religious, charitable . . . or educational purposes . . . no part of the net earnings of which inures to

327

the benefit of any private shareholder or individual, no substantial part of the activities of which is carrying on propaganda, or otherwise attempting, to influence legislation . . . and which does not participate in, or intervene in (including the publishing or distributing of statements), any political campaign on behalf of any candidate for public office.[1]

The quoted section exempts churches from federal income taxation. Note that the exemption is conditioned upon the following six factors: (1) the church is a corporation, (2) the church is organized exclusively for exempt purposes, (3) the church is operated exclusively for exempt purposes, (4) none of the church's net earnings inures to the benefit of any private individuals, (5) the church does not engage in substantial efforts to influence legislation, and (6) the church does not intervene or participate in political campaigns. These factors will be considered individually.

### (1) *The Church Is a Corporation*

While the Internal Revenue Code would appear to exempt only those churches that are incorporated, the IRS maintains that unincorporated churches are eligible for exemption. In its *Exempt Organizations Handbook,* the IRS states that "the typical nonprofit association formed under a constitution or bylaws, with elective officers empowered to act for it, would be treated as a corporation . . . ."[2]

### (2) *The Church Is Organized Exclusively for Exempt Purposes*

To be exempt from federal income tax, a church must be "organized exclusively" for exempt purposes. This requirement is referred to by the IRS as the "organizational test" of tax-exempt status. The income tax regulations state that an organization will be deemed to be "organized exclusively" for exempt purposes only if its articles of incorporation[3] limit the purposes of the organization to one or more of the exempt purposes listed in section 501(c)(3) of the Code and do not expressly empower the organization to engage, otherwise than as an insubstantial part of its activities, in activities that in themselves are not in

---

[1]I.R.C. § 501(c)(3).

[2]IRS EXEMPT ORGANIZATIONS HANDBOOK § 321.4 (1982). Besides corporations, § 501(c)(3) of the Code also exempts community chests, funds, and foundations that meet the prerequisites to tax-exempt status. Since none of these other forms of organization ordinarily applies to churches, they are not considered in this chapter.

[3]Treas. Reg. § 1.501(c)(3)-1(b)(2) defines "articles of incorporation" to include "the trust instrument, the corporate charter, the articles of association, or any other written instrument by which an organization is created."

furtherance of one or more exempt purposes.[4] Section 501(c)(3) of the Code lists the following exempt purposes: religious, charitable, scientific, testing for public safety, literary, educational, and prevention of cruelty to children or animals. A church's purposes may be as broad as, or more specific than, the purposes stated in section 501(c)(3). But in no event will a church be considered organized exclusively for one or more exempt purposes if by the terms of its articles of incorporation its purposes are broader than the purposes stated in section 501(c)(3).[5] The fact that the actual operation of a church whose purposes are broader than those stated in section 501(c)(3) is exclusively in furtherance of one or more exempt purposes will not be sufficient to permit the church to satisfy the organizational test. Similarly, a church whose purposes are broader than those stated in section 501(c)(3) will not meet the organizational test as a result of statements or other evidence that its members intend to operate it solely in furtherance of one or more exempt purposes. In summary, a church can be organized for purposes other than religious if such purposes are among those listed in section 501(c)(3). At a minimum, however, a church's purposes must be either religious or charitable. The IRS maintains that a church may be organized exclusively for charitable purposes since the term *charitable* encompasses the advancement of religion.

Section 502 of the Internal Revenue Code states that "[a]n organization operated for the primary purpose of carrying on a trade or business for profit shall not be exempt from taxation under section 501 on the ground that all of its profits are payable to one or more organizations exempt from taxation under section 501." Such organizations are referred to as feeder organizations. To illustrate, in Revenue Ruling 73-164 the IRS ruled that a church-controlled commercial printing corporation whose business earnings were paid to the church but that had no other significant charitable activity was a feeder organization that did not qualify for exemption under section 501(c)(3). Section 502 specifies that an organization will not be considered to be a feeder organization if (1) its earnings consist of rents that would be excluded from the definition of unrelated business income under section 512 of the Code, (2) substantially all of its work is performed without compensation, or (3) its earnings derive from the selling of merchandise substantially all of which was received as gifts or contributions.

The regulations also specify that an organization is not organized exclusively for exempt purposes unless its assets are dedicated to an exempt purpose, and that an organization's assets will be presumed to be dedicated to an exempt purpose if, upon dissolution, the assets would by reason of a provision in the organization's articles of incorporation be distributed to another exempt or-

[4]Treas. Reg. § 1.501(c)(3)-1(b)(1)(i).
[5]Treas. Reg. § 1.501(c)(3)-1(b)(1)(iv).

ganization. Finally, the regulations state that an organization will not be considered organized exclusively for exempt purposes if its articles of incorporation empower it to devote more than an insubstantial part of its activities to attempting to influence legislation, or directly or indirectly to participate in or intervene in any political campaign on behalf of or in opposition to any candidate for public office.[6]

The IRS has drafted the following paragraphs which, if inserted in a church's articles of incorporation, will indicate compliance with the organizational test:

> Said corporation is organized exclusively for charitable, religious, [and] educational . . . purposes, including, for such purposes, the making of distributions to organizations that qualify as exempt organizations under section 501(c)(3) of the Internal Revenue Code of 1954 (or the corresponding provision of any future United States Internal Revenue Law).
>
> No part of the net earnings of the corporation shall inure to the benefit of, or be distributable to its members, trustees, officers, or other private persons, except that the corporation shall be authorized and empowered to pay reasonable compensation for services rendered and to make payments and distributions in furtherance of the purposes set forth [herein]. No substantial part of the activities of the corporation shall be the carrying on of propaganda, or otherwise attempting to influence legislation, and the corporation shall not participate in, or intervene in (including the publishing or distribution of statements) any political campaign on behalf of any candidate for public office.
>
> Notwithstanding any other provision of these articles, the corporation shall not carry on any other activities not permitted to be carried on (a) by a corporation exempt from Federal income tax under section 501(c)(3) of the Internal Revenue Code of 1954 (or the corresponding provision of any future United States Internal Revenue Law) or (b) by a corporation, contributions to which are deductible under section 170(c)(2) of the Internal Revenue Code of 1954 (or the corresponding provision of any future United States Internal Revenue Law).
>
> Upon dissolution of the corporation, the Board of Trustees shall, after paying or making provision for the payment of all of the liabilities of the corporation, dispose of all of the assets of the corporation exclusively for the purposes of the corporation in such manner, or to such organization or organizations organized and operated exclusively for charitable, educational, religious, or scientific purposes as shall at the time qualify as an exempt organization or organizations under section 501(c)(3) of the Internal Revenue Code of 1954 (or the corresponding provision of any future United States Internal Revenue Law), as the Board of Trustees shall determine. Any such assets not so disposed of shall be disposed of by the Court of Common Pleas of the county in which the principal office of the corporation is then located, exclusively for such purposes or to such organizations,

[6]Treas. Reg. § 1.501(c)(3)-1(b)(3).

as said Court shall determine, which are organized and operated exclusively for such purposes.[7]

It is difficult to define what is meant by a religious purpose. The IRS, in its *Exempt Organizations Handbook,* acknowledges that the term *religion* cannot be defined with precision. The IRS does acquiesce in federal court rulings defining religion to include beliefs not encompassing a Supreme Being in the conventional sense, such as Taoism, Buddhism, and secular humanism.[8] The IRS also maintains that religion is not confined to a sect or a ritual.[9] Activities carried on in furtherance of the belief must be exclusively religious. If the activities promote some nonreligious purpose, exemption may be denied. In one case, it was held that an organization dominated by one individual was not exempt as a religious organization since its purpose was to carry on the founder's feud with a local newspaper.[10] Religious organizations that engage in substantial legislative activity are disqualified from tax exemption regardless of the motivation or purpose of that activity.[11] Religious publishing has been held to be a commercial, nonexempt activity regardless of religious motivation if literature is sold to the general public at a profit.[12] But where a religious organization publishes literature to promote its own beliefs, and revenues are used to defray expenses and to further the religious purposes of the organization, the activity is considered to be religious.[13] These same principles apply to religious broadcasting activities. Thus, in one case a nonprofit religious broadcasting station whose broadcasting time was devoted to worship services and other religious

[7]IRS Publication 557.

[8]IRS EXEMPT ORGANIZATIONS HANDBOOK § 344.2 (1982).

[9]*Id.*

[10]Puritan Church of America v. Commissioner, 10 T.C.M. 485 (1951), *aff'd per curiam,* 209 F.2d 306 (D.C. Cir. 1953), *cert. denied,* 350 U.S. 810 (1955).

[11]Christian Echoes National Ministry, Inc. v. United States, 470 F.2d 849 (10th Cir. 1972), *cert. denied,* 414 U.S. 864 (1973).

[12]Parker v. Commissioner, 365 F.2d 792 (8th Cir. 1966), *cert. denied,* 385 U.S. 1026 (1967); Incorporated Trustees of the Gospel Worker Society v. United States, 510 F. Supp. 374 (D.D.C. 1981), *aff'd,* 672 F.2d 894 (D.C. Cir. 1981); Fides Publishers Assoc. v. United States, 263 F. Supp. 924 (N.D. Ind. 1967); Scripture Press Foundation v. United States, 285 F.2d 800 (Ct. Cl. 1961); Presbyterian and Reformed Publishing Co. v. Commissioner, 79 T.C. 69 (1982); Christian Manner International v. Commissioner, 71 T.C. 661 (1979); Rev. Rul. 73-164, 1973-1 C.B. 223; Rev. Rul. 68-26, 1968-1 C.B. 272.

[13]Elisian Guild, Inc. v. United States, 412 F.2d 121 (1st Cir. 1969); Pulpit Resource v. Commissioner, 70 T.C. 594 (1978); Saint Germain Foundation v. Commissioner, 26 T.C. 648 (1956); Unity School of Christianity v. Commissioner, 4 B.T.A. 61 (1962); Rev. Rul. 68-26, 1968-1 C.B. 272. *See generally* IRS EXEMPT ORGANIZATIONS HANDBOOK § 344.4 (1982).

programs and which did not sell commercial or advertising time was found to be exempt.[14]

The following activities have also been held to be sufficiently religious in nature to entitle the organization to exempt status: a nonprofit organization formed by local churches to operate a supervised facility known as a coffeehouse in which persons of college age were brought together with church leaders, educators, and businessmen for discussion of religion and current events;[15] a nonprofit organization formed to complete genealogical research data on its family members in order to perform religious ordinances in accordance with the precepts of the religious denomination to which family members belonged;[16] a nonprofit organization that supervised the preparation and inspection of food products prepared commercially in order to ensure that they satisfied the dietary rules of a particular religion, thereby assisting members of the religion to comply with its tenets;[17] an organization formed and controlled by an exempt conference of churches that borrowed funds from individuals and made mortgage loans at less than commercial rates of interest to affiliated churches to finance the construction of church buildings;[18] and an organization established to provide temporary low-cost housing and related services for missionary families on furlough in the United States from their assignments abroad.[19]

Not every organization claiming to be religious is entitled to exemption from federal income taxes. The IRS has denied tax-exempt status to several organizations on the ground that they were not organized exclusively for religious purposes. Illustratively, the following activities have been denied exempt status: a religious organization whose primary activity was the operation of a commercial restaurant;[20] a church that engaged in substantial social and political activities;[21] an organization incorporated for religious purposes but which conducted no religious services and whose primary activity was making investments to accumulate monies for its "building fund";[22] and a "church" consisting of

[14]Rev. Rul. 68-563, 1968-2 C.B. 212.

[15]Rev. Rul. 68-72, 1968-1 C.B. 250.

[16]Rev. Rul. 71-580, 1971-2 C.B. 235.

[17]Rev. Rul. 74-575, 1974-2 C.B. 161.

[18]Rev. Rul. 75-282, 1975-2 C.B. 201.

[19]Rev. Rul. 75-434, 1975-2 C.B. 205.

[20]Riker v. Commissioner, 244 F.2d 220 (9th Cir. 1957), cert. denied, 355 U.S. 839 (1957).

[21]First Libertarian Church v. Commissioner, 74 T.C. 396 (1980).

[22]Western Catholic Church v. Commissioner, 73 T.C. 196 (1979), aff'd, 631 F.2d 736 (7th Cir. 1980), cert. denied, 101 S. Ct. 1515 (1981).

three family members that held Christmas and Easter services but otherwise engaged in no regular or substantial religious activities.[23]

Charitable purposes, like religious purposes, constitute a basis for exemption under the Internal Revenue Code. Many churches define their purposes to include both religious and charitable purposes. The income tax regulations define *charitable* as follows:

> Relief of the poor and distressed or of the underprivileged; advancement of religion; advancement of education or science; erection or maintenance of public buildings, monuments, or works; lessening of the burdens of Government; and promotion of social welfare by organizations designed to accomplish any of the above purposes, or (i) to lessen neighborhood tensions; (ii) to eliminate prejudice and discrimination; (iii) to defend human and civil rights secured by law; or (iv) to combat community deterioration and juvenile delinquency.[24]

Churches occasionally engage in activities of a charitable nature. Examples include day-care centers, homes for the aged, orphanages, and halfway houses. Although a church may contend that these activities are religious, it is clear that the IRS views them as charitable.[25] Therefore, it is important for a church contemplating any such activities to be sure that its articles of incorporation or other organizing document lists charitable purposes among the purposes of the church.

Similarly, educational purposes, like religious and charitable purposes, constitute a basis for exemption under the Code. The income tax regulations define *educational* as follows: "The instruction or training of the individual for the purpose of improving or developing his capabilities; or the instruction of the public on subjects useful to the individual and beneficial to the community."[26]

The IRS maintains that even if a school is operated by a church, it is an educational organization if it has a regularly scheduled curriculum, a regular faculty, and a regularly enrolled body of students in attendance at a place where the educational activities are regularly carried on.[27] Thus, the IRS considers many church-operated primary and secondary schools to be educational and not religious institutions. Some courts have held that church-operated schools can be considered a religious function.[28] The distinction is important, for the

---

[23]Bubbling Well Church of Universal Love, Inc. v. Commissioner, 74 T.C. 531 (1980), *aff'd,* 670 F.2d 104 (9th Cir. 1981).

[24]Treas. Reg. § 1.501(c)(3)-1(d)(2).

[25]IRS EXEMPT ORGANIZATIONS HANDBOOK § 343.9 (1982).

[26]Treas. Reg. § 1.501(c)(3)-1(d)(3).

[27]Treas. Reg. § 1.501(c)(3)-1(d)(3)(ii).

[28]*See, e.g.,* Concord v. New Testament Baptist Church, 382 A.2d 377 (N.H. 1978); Employment Division v. Archdiocese of Portland, 600 P.2d 926 (Ore. 1979).

IRS maintains that *schools*—including those operated by churches—must affirmatively demonstrate to the IRS that they have adopted and are operating under a racially nondiscriminatory policy toward students, and that they have made such a policy known to all segments of the general community they serve.[29]

### (3) *The Church Is Operated Exclusively for Exempt Purposes*

To be exempt from federal income taxes, section 501(c)(3) of the Code requires that a church be "operated exclusively" for exempt purposes. This requirement is referred to as the operational test. The regulations specify that an organization will be regarded as "operated exclusively" for one or more exempt purposes only if it engages primarily in activities that accomplish one or more of the exempt purposes specified in section 501(c)(3), and if no more than an insubstantial part of its activities are not in furtherance of an exempt purpose.

To illustrate, the tax-exempt status of the following religious organizations was revoked on the ground that they were not operated exclusively for exempt purposes: a church that operated a medical assistance plan that helped members pay medical expenses,[30] a religious retreat that offered recreational and social activities for a fee similar to those of most other commercial vacation resorts,[31] a religious organization that operated a commercial restaurant,[32] a church that conducted no religious services and whose primary activity was the accumulation of contributions for its building fund,[33] a church that conducted purely social and political meetings,[34] and an independent publisher that sold religious literature to the general public at a profit.[35]

---

[29]Rev. Proc. 75-50, 1975-2 C.B. 587; Rev. Rul. 75-231, 1975-1 C.B. 158. *See* chapter 13, § B, *supra*.

[30]Bethel Conservative Mennonite Church v. Commissioner, 80 T.C. 352 (1983).

[31]Schoger Foundation v. Commissioner, 76 T.C. 380 (1981). *But see* Rev. Rul. 77-340, 1977-2 C.B. 341 (exempt status of religious retreat upheld since no fees were charged).

[32]Christ's Church of Golden Rule v. Commissioner, 244 F.2d 220 (9th Cir. 1957), *cert. denied*, 355 U.S. 839 (1957).

[33]Western Catholic Church v. Commissioner, 73 T.C. 196 (1979), *aff'd mem.*, 631 F.2d 736 (7th Cir. 1980), *cert. denied*, 101 S. Ct. 1515 (1980).

[34]First Libertarian Church v. Commissioner, 74 T.C. 396 (1980).

[35]Parker v. Commissioner, 365 F.2d 792 (8th Cir. 1966), *cert. denied*, 385 U.S. 1026 (1967); Scripture Press Foundation v. United States, 285 F.2d 800 (Ct. Cl. 1961); Presbyterian and Reformed Publishing Co. v. Commissioner, 79 T.C. 69 (1982).

## (4) No Inurement of Net Earnings to Private Individuals

A church is not entitled to exemption from federal income taxes if any part of its net earnings inures, or accrues, to the benefit of a private individual. The IRS construes this requirement as follows:

> An organization's trustees, officers, members, founders, or contributors may not, by reason of their position, acquire any of its funds. They may, of course, receive reasonable compensation for goods or services or other expenditures in further-ance of exempt purposes. If funds are diverted from exempt purposes, however, exemption is in jeopardy. . . . The prohibition of inurement, in its simplest terms, means that a private . . . individual cannot pocket the organization's funds except as reasonable payment for goods or services.[36]

The IRS has denied tax-exempt status to many churches on the basis of inurement of net earnings to the benefit of private individuals. To illustrate, the IRS has found private inurement in each of the following situations: a church consisting mostly of family members and conducting few if any religious services paid rent on a residence for the church's ministers, paid for a "church car" that was used by church members, and purchased a "church camp" for church members;[37] a religious denomination whose assets could be distributed to members upon dissolution;[38] a church that made cash grants of twenty percent of its income to officers and other individuals based on no fixed criteria and with no provision for repayment;[39] a church that received almost all of its income from its minister and in turn paid back ninety percent of such income to the minister in the form of living expenses;[40] a church comprised of three minister-members that paid each minister a salary based on a fixed percentage of the church's gross receipts;[41] a religious community comprised in part of members who committed all of their possessions to the community and that returned bene-fits to members in the form of food, shelter, clothing, medical care, educational services, and recreational facilities;[42] and the founder of a church who was paid ten percent of the church's gross income, received a residence and car at the

---

[36]IRS EXEMPT ORGANIZATIONS HANDBOOK § 381.1 (1982).

[37]Riemers v. Commissioner, 42 T.C.M. 838 (1981).

[38]General Conference of the Free Church of America v. Commissioner, 71 T.C. 920 (1979).

[39]Church in Boston v. Commissioner, 71 T.C. 102 (1978).

[40]Baker v. Commissioner, 40 T.C.M. 1174 (1980). See also The Basic Unit Ministry of Schurig v. United States, 511 F. Supp. 166 (D.C. Cir. 1981) (70 percent of members' offerings expended for the support of members).

[41]People of God Community v. Commissioner, 75 T.C. 127 (1980).

[42]New Life Tabernacle v. Commissioner, 44 T.C.M. 309 (1982).

church's expense, and received loans and unexplained reimbursements from the church.[43] In the last-cited case, the court held that an organization's net earnings may inure to the benefit of a private individual in ways other than excessive salaries, such as loans. The court also emphasized that the Internal Revenue Code specifies that "no part" of the net earnings of a religious organization may inure to the benefit of a private individual, and therefore the amount or extent of benefit is immaterial.

### (5) No Substantial Efforts to Influence Legislation

A religious corporation is not entitled to an exemption from federal income tax if a substantial part of its activities consists of the carrying on of propaganda or otherwise attempting to influence legislation.[44] The income tax regulations state that an organization will be regarded as attempting to influence legislation if it contacts or urges the public to contact members of a legislative body for the purpose of proposing, supporting, or opposing legislation, or if it advocates the adoption or rejection of specific legislation.[45] The regulations define *legislation* to include action by the Congress, by any state legislature, by any local governing body, or by the public in a referendum, initiative, constitutional amendment, or similar procedure.[46] The regulations use the term *action organization* in referring to an organization engaged in substantial attempts to influence legislation.[47]

The IRS maintains that appearances before legislative committees in response to official requests for testimony do not constitute attempts to influence legislation.[48] The IRS also has acknowledged that study, research, and discussion of matters pertaining to government and even to specific legislation under some circumstances may constitute educational activities rather than attempts to influence legislation. To illustrate, a nonprofit organization was held to be

---

[43]The Founding Church of Scientology v. United States, 412 F.2d 1197 (Ct. Cl. 1969), *cert. denied,* 397 U.S. 1009 (1970).

[44]*See generally* B. HOPKINS, THE LAW OF TAX-EXEMPT ORGANIZATIONS (3rd ed. 1979); Weinberg, *Political Activities by Charities—Sorting Out the IRS Position,* 9 TAX ADVISER 466 (1978); Whaley, *Political Activities of Section 501(c)(3) Organizations,* 29 SO. CALIF. TAX INST. 195 (1977); Woodworth, *Legislative Activities of 501(c)(3) Organizations,* 23 CATH. LAW. 175 (1978); Note, *Church Lobbying: The Legitimacy of the Controls,* 16 HOUSTON L. REV. 480 (1979); Note, *Tax Code's Differential Treatment of Lobbying Under Section 501(c)(3): A Proposed First Amendment Analysis,* 66 VA. L. REV. 1513 (1980).

[45]Treas. Reg. § 1.501(c)(3)-1(c)(3)(ii).

[46]*Id.*

[47]*Id.*

[48]IRS EXEMPT ORGANIZATIONS HANDBOOK § 392 (1982).

exempt under section 501(c)(3) although it was engaged in nonpartisan study, research, and compilation of materials on court reform legislation and disseminated the materials to the public.[49] Another nonprofit organization that conducted research to develop solutions to a variety of urban problems but that did not advocate any legislative action to implement its findings was held to qualify for tax-exempt status.[50] However, an organization whose primary activity was the promotion of a theory that could become effective only through the enactment of legislation was found to be ineligible for an exemption.[51]

The IRS has ruled that the term *legislation* contemplates foreign as well as domestic laws, and thus a nonprofit organization that attempted to change the laws of a foreign country was denied exempt status.[52] The legislative activity must be carried on by the nonprofit organization itself, and therefore a university is not barred from tax-exempt status because a campus newspaper prints editorials on legislative matters.[53]

No distinction is made between "good" and "bad" legislation. Thus, a nonprofit organization is ineligible for tax-exempt status even if it is engaged in substantial activities to promote socially desirable legislation. The Supreme Court has observed that "political agitation is outside the statute, however innocent the aim."[54] Another court has stated that a religious organization that engages in substantial activity aimed at influencing legislation "is disqualified from tax exemption, whatever its motivation."[55]

Attempts to influence legislation that amount to less than a substantial part of an organization's activities will not deprive it of exempt status. The IRS maintains that whether a specific activity constitutes a "substantial" portion of an exempt organization's total activities is a factual question, and that there is no simple rule for what amount of activities is "substantial."[56] One court has suggested that attempts to influence legislation are not substantial if they constitute less than five percent of a nonprofit organization's total activities,[57] but the IRS maintains that this test provides only limited guidance because the court's view of what sort of activities were to be measured "is no longer sup-

[49]Rev. Rul. 64-195, 1964-2 C.B. 138.

[50]Rev. Rul. 70-79, 1970-1 C.B. 127.

[51]Rev. Rul. 62-71, 1962-1 C.B. 85.

[52]Rev. Rul. 73-440, 1973-2 C.B. 177.

[53]Rev. Rul. 72-513, 1972-2 C.B. 246.

[54]Cammarano v. United States, 358 U.S. 498, 512 (1959).

[55]Christian Echoes National Ministry, Inc. v. United States, 470 F.2d 849, 854 (10th Cir. 1972), *cert. denied,* 414 U.S. 864 (1973).

[56]IRS EXEMPT ORGANIZATIONS HANDBOOK § 394 (1982).

[57]Murray Seasongood v. Commissioner, 227 F.2d 907 (6th Cir. 1955).

ported by the weight of precedent."[58] The IRS has noted that "[m]ost cases have attempted to avoid . . . a percentage measurement of activities."[59] Some courts have held that a percentage test is inappropriate.[60] Other courts consider a percentage measurement of activities relevant but not controlling. In one case, the Tax Court held that a church expending approximately twenty-two percent of its revenues on members' medical bills was engaged in a "substantial nonexempt activity" and therefore was not operated exclusively for exempt purposes.[61] Section 501(h) of the Code, which was part of the Tax Reform Act of 1976, permits certain charitable organizations to make expenditures in an attempt to influence legislation if the expenditures do not exceed prescribed levels. This section does not apply to churches.

In a leading case involving the application of these rules to a religious organization, a federal appeals court found that a nonprofit religious organization had engaged in substantial and continuous activities to influence legislation. It accordingly revoked the organization's tax-exempt status.[62] The organization had been organized in 1951 to "proclaim the essential truths of Christianity" through weekly radio and television broadcasts, the creation of a national religious magazine, and the development of religious educational institutions. In its efforts to promote Christian truth, the organization attacked communism, socialism, and political liberalism, all of which it considered to be enemies of the Christian faith. It appealed to the readers of its publications to write their Congressmen to influence decisions in Washington; work at the precinct level; support various bills and amendments; purge the media of bias; demand the retention of the House Committee on Un-American Activities; demand that Congress limit foreign aid spending; urge support of restoration of prayer in the public schools; discourage support of the World Court; cut off diplomatic relations with all communist nations; stop federal aid to education, socialized medicine, and public housing; abolish the federal income tax; withdraw from the United Nations; outlaw the Communist Party in the United States; and adopt strict immigration laws. In addition, the organization intervened in political campaigns. While it did not formally endorse specific candidates, it did use its publications and broadcasts to attack candidates and incumbents who were considered too liberal.

[58]IRS Exempt Organizations Handbook § 394 (1982).

[59]Id.

[60]Haswell v. United States, 500 F.2d 1133 (Ct. Cl. 1974), cert. denied, 419 U.S. 1107 (1975).

[61]Bethel Conservative Mennonite Church v. Commissioner, 80 T.C. 352 (1983).

[62]Christian Echoes National Ministry, Inc. v. United States, 470 F.2d 849 (10th Cir. 1972), cert. denied, 414 U.S. 864 (1973). See also Abortion Rights Mobilization, Inc. v. Regan, No. 53431 (S.D.N.Y. July 19, 1982).

The IRS retroactively revoked the organization's tax-exempt status on the grounds that (1) it was not operated exclusively for charitable, educational, or religious purposes; (2) it had engaged in substantial activities aimed at influencing legislation; and (3) it had directly and indirectly intervened in political campaigns on behalf of candidates for public office.

The organization defended its exemption on the grounds that all of its activities were motivated by sincere religious convictions and that the First Amendment prohibits the government from determining whether activities are religious or political. A federal district court upheld the organization's exempt status, and the government appealed. The appeals court agreed with the government's contentions that a substantial part of the organization's activities did consist of attempts to influence legislation and that the organization had participated or intervened in political campaigns on behalf of candidates for public office. The court began its opinion by noting that the limitations in section 501(c)(3) relating to legislative and political activity stem from a congressional policy that the government should be neutral in political affairs and that substantial efforts to influence legislation or affect political campaigns should not be subsidized through tax exemptions. The court acknowledged that the organization was a religious organization and that its activities had been religiously motivated. However, the court emphasized that religious organizations engaging in substantial activities aimed at influencing legislation are disqualified from tax exemption whatever the motivation.

The court rejected a "percentage test" in determining whether the organization's activities were substantial, since such a test would obscure "the complexity of balancing the organization's activities in relation to its objectives and circumstances."[63] The court concluded that the organization's many efforts to influence legislation "were not incidental, but were substantial and continuous."[64]

Finally, the court rejected the argument that a denial of the organization's tax-exempt status violated its First Amendment rights of free speech and free exercise of religion. Noting that First Amendment rights are not absolute, and that tax-exempt status is a matter of legislative grace rather than right, the court concluded that the First Amendment was not violated by restrictions imposed by Congress against legislative and political activity by tax-exempt organizations.

Some organizations have challenged the prohibition of substantial efforts to

[63]*Id.* at 855.
[64]*Id.* at 856.

influence legislation on the ground that their First Amendment right of free speech was being abridged.[65] Thus far none of these challenges has been successful.

### (6) *No Intervention or Participation in Political Campaigns*

A religious organization is not entitled to an exemption from federal income taxes if it participates or intervenes in any political campaign on behalf of any candidate for public office. The income tax regulations state that the term *candidate for public office* means an individual

> who offers himself, or is proposed by others, as a contestant for an elective public office, whether such office be national, state or local. Activities which constitute participation or intervention in a political campaign on behalf of or in opposition to a candidate include, but are not limited to, the publication or distribution of written or printed statements or the making of oral statements on behalf of or in opposition to such a candidate.[66]

The regulations use the term *action organization* in referring to an organization that intervenes or participates in political campaigns.[67]

The prohibition of intervention or participation in political campaigns is absolute. There is no requirement that such activities amount to a "substantial" part of an organization's activities as in the case of efforts to influence legislation.

The intervention or participation in a political campaign must be "on behalf of or in opposition to a candidate." Thus it has been held that an organization that operated a broadcasting station presenting religious, educational, and public interest programs was not participating in a political campaign on behalf of public candidates by providing reasonable air time equally to all candidates for a particular political office.[68]

Another religious organization that used its publications and broadcasts to attack specific candidates and incumbents who were considered "too liberal" and that urged its followers to elect "conservatives" was found to have intervened in political campaigns even though it generally did not formally endorse specific candidates.[69]

The IRS has ruled that exempt organizations can engage in limited "voter education" activities without actually intervening or participating in political

---

[65]*See, e.g.,* Taxation With Representation v. United States, 585 F.2d 1219 (4th Cir. 1978), *cert. denied,* 441 U.S. 905 (1979).

[66]Treas. Reg. § 1.501(c)(3)-1(c)(3)(iii).

[67]*Id.*

[68]Rev. Rul. 74-574, 1974-2 C.B. 160.

[69]Christian Echoes National Ministry, Inc. v. United States, 470 F.2d 849 (10th Cir. 1972), *cert. denied,* 414 U.S. 864 (1973).

campaigns. In Revenue Ruling 78-248 the IRS stated that the following two "voter education" activities do not constitute prohibited political activity if conducted in a nonpartisan manner: (1) preparation and public distribution of the voting records of all members of Congress on major legislative issues involving a wide range of subjects if no editorial opinions are presented and the contents and structure of the publication do not imply approval or disapproval of any members based on their voting records, and (2) submission of a questionnaire to all candidates for governor in a particular state requesting a brief statement of each candidate's position on a wide variety of issues if the results are generally made available to the public and neither the questionnaire nor the voters' guide in content or structure manifests a bias or preference with respect to the views of any candidate or group of candidates. Revenue Ruling 78-248 specifically holds that an organization participates in a political campaign and thus is disqualified as an exempt organization if it engages in voter education activities that are biased. As an example, Revenue Ruling 78-248 states that an organization that sends a questionnaire to political candidates containing questions that indicate a bias on certain issues is participating in a political campaign. Thus, an organization would be disqualified if it sent a questionnaire to congressional candidates requesting their positions on abortion and if the results were disseminated in a pamphlet advocating the election of only those candidates who opposed abortion.

### b. *Basis for the Exemption*

Is the exemption of churches and other religious organizations from federal income taxation mandated by the First Amendment or is it merely a matter of legislative grace? This is a question that has eluded a definitive answer.[70] Several courts have held that religious organizations have no constitutional right to be exempted from federal income taxes. For example, one federal court has held that "tax exemption is a privilege, a matter of grace rather than right,"[71] and another federal court has observed:

> We believe it is constitutionally permissible to tax the income of religious organizations. In fact there are those who contend that the failure to tax such organizations violates the "no establishment clause" of the First Amendment. Since

---

[70] *See generally* B. HOPKINS, THE LAW OF TAX-EXEMPT ORGANIZATIONS (3rd ed. 1979); P. Kauper, *The Constitutionality of Tax Exemptions for Religious Activities,* THE WALL BETWEEN CHURCH AND STATE 95 (D. Oaks ed. 1963); D. KELLEY, WHY CHURCHES SHOULD NOT PAY TAXES (1977); Bittker & Rahdert, *The Exemption of Nonprofit Organizations From Federal Income Taxation,* 85 YALE L.J. 301 (1976); Note, *Constitutionality of Tax Benefits Accorded Religion,* 49 COLUM. L. REV. 968 (1949).

[71] Christian Echoes National Ministry, Inc. v. United States, 470 F.2d 849, 857 (10th Cir. 1972), *cert. denied,* 414 U.S. 864 (1973).

the government may constitutionally tax the income of religious organizations, it follows that the government may decide not to exercise this power and grant reasonable exemptions to qualifying organizations, while continuing to tax those who fail to meet these qualifications. The receiving of an exemption is thus a matter of legislative grace and not a constitutional right.[72]

It is nevertheless true that for as long as federal income taxes have had any potential impact on churches, religious organizations have been expressly exempted from such taxes.[73] Significantly, the exemption of churches, conventions and associations of churches, and integrated auxiliaries of churches is automatic. Unlike other charities, such organizations are not required to apply for and receive IRS recognition of tax-exempt status.[74] This of course assumes that a church, convention or association of churches, or integrated auxiliary of a church satisfies the conditions enumerated in section 501(c)(3). Whether this legislative history indicates a congressional determination that tax exemption of religious organizations is constitutionally mandated is unclear. Congress does require religious organizations other than churches, conventions or associations of churches, and integrated auxiliaries of churches to apply for and receive IRS recognition of tax-exempt status. And, in 1969 Congress elected to tax the "unrelated business income" of all religious organizations including churches, conventions or associations of churches, and integrated auxiliaries of churches.[75] Finally, as has been noted elsewhere,[76] religious organizations that engage in substantial efforts to influence legislation, that intervene in political campaigns, that are not operated exclusively for religious purposes, that are not organized exclusively for religious purposes, or the net earnings of which inures to the benefit of a private individual are not entitled to exemption. Certainly such factors militate against the conclusion that religious organizations are constitutionally immune from taxation.

The United States Supreme Court, in upholding the constitutionality of state

---

[72]Parker v. Commissioner, 365 F.2d 792, 795 (8th Cir. 1966) (citations omitted), *cert. denied*, 385 U.S. 1026 (1967). *See also* Bethel Conservative Mennonite Church v. Commissioner, 80 T.C. 352 (1983) ("a bona fide church is not per se exempt from taxation as a religious organization . . . [e]xemption from Federal income taxation is a privilege provided as a matter of legislative grace, not a right"); Parshall Christian Order v. Commissioner, 45 T.C.M. 488 (1983) ("Exemption from tax is a matter of grace rather than right."); People v. Life Science Church, 450 N.Y.S.2d 664, 669 (1982) ("Taxation of religious organizations is constitutionally permissible under the free exercise of religion clause of the First Amendment to the Constitution.").

[73]Walz v. Tax Commission, 397 U.S. 664, 676 n.4 (1970).

[74]I.R.C. § 508(c)(1)(A).

[75]I.R.C. § 511(a)(2)(A).

[76]*See* chapter 14, § B.1, *supra*.

property tax exemptions for properties used solely for religious worship, suggested that a constitutional basis may exist for property tax exemptions. The Court emphasized that the First Amendment forbids the government from following a course of action, be it taxation of churches or exemption, that results in an excessive governmental entanglement with religion. The Court reasoned that eliminating the tax exemption of properties used exclusively for religious worship would be unconstitutional since it would expand governmental entanglement with religion: "Elimination of exemption would tend to expand the involvement of government by giving rise to tax valuation of church property, tax liens, tax foreclosures, and the direct confrontations and conflicts that follow in the train of those legal processes."[77]

The Court observed that "exemption creates only a minimal and remote involvement between church and state and far less than taxation of churches"[78] and that "[t]he hazards of churches supporting government are hardly less in their potential than the hazards of government supporting churches."[79] The Court concluded that the grant of a tax exemption is not an impermissible "sponsorship" of religion since "the government does not transfer part of its revenue to churches but simply abstains from demanding that the church support the state."[80] Such reasoning suggests that the exemption of religious organizations from federal income taxation may be rooted in part in the United States Constitution, at least to the extent that it can be demonstrated that the taxation of religious organizations would lead to substantial governmental entanglement with religion far greater than the entanglement occasioned by exemption.[81]

Finally, it is a well-settled principle of law that the exemption of religious organizations from federal income taxation does not constitute an impermissible "establishment of religion" in violation of the First Amendment.[82]

c. *Recognition of Exemption*

Before 1969 the statutory requirement that an organization file a notice or application with the IRS in order to be exempt was nonexistent. An organization was automatically exempt if it met the requirements of section 501(c)(3) of the

---

[77]Walz v. Tax Commission, 397 U.S. 664, 674 (1970).

[78]*Id.* at 676.

[79]*Id.* at 675.

[80]*Id.*

[81]*See also* Committee for Public Education and Religious Liberty v. Nyquist, 413 U.S. 756, 792-93 (1973).

[82]Swallow v. United States, 325 F.2d 97 (10th Cir. 1963), *cert. denied,* 377 U.S. 951 (1964).

Internal Revenue Code. Although many organizations applied for recognition of exemption by filing a Form 1023 (Application for Recognition of Exemption Under Section 501(c)(3) of the Internal Revenue Code),[83] some did not.

The Tax Reform Act of 1969 added section 508 to the Internal Revenue Code. This section stipulated that after October 9, 1969, no organization, with a few exceptions, would be treated as exempt unless it gave notice to the IRS, in the manner prescribed by regulation, that it was applying for recognition of exempt status under section 501(c)(3). This is commonly referred to as the "508(a) notice." The income tax regulations state that notice is given by submitting a properly completed Form 1023 to the appropriate IRS district director.[84] The regulations further state that the notice must be filed within fifteen months of the end of the month in which the organization was organized. Organizations that were in existence on October 9, 1969, were required to file the notice with the appropriate IRS district director by March 22, 1973. The regulations allow for extensions of time for filing the notice when a reasonable basis exists.[85]

If an organization files its Form 1023 after the fifteen-month period it may be recognized as exempt only from the date its application was filed.[86] It follows that the organization would be a taxable organization under such circumstances and thus would be unable to receive deductible contributions for the period preceding the date the application was filed.

Since an "incomplete" application does not constitute notice under section 508(a), the distinction between such an application and a completed application should be recognized. The IRS recognizes that cases will arise when the criteria of a completed application is met but additional information is needed for a determination of exempt status. In such cases the notice requirement of section 508(a) is considered to be satisfied whether or not the additional information is timely received. The IRS has stated that the absence of any of the following materials will cause an application to be regarded as incomplete: an authorized signature, an employer identification number or a completed application for an employer identification number, a statement of receipts and expenditures

[83]Form 1023 is the application form used by § 501(c)(3) organizations. It is also used by cooperative hospital associations and cooperative service organizations under section 501(e) and 501(f) of the Code. Most other organizations use Form 1024 in applying for exemption.

[84]Treas. Reg. § 1.508-1(a)(2). Among other things, Form 1023 calls for the name and address of the applicant organization, the applicant's employer identification number, date of incorporation or formation, a detailed statement of the activities carried on by the organization, names and addresses of officers and directors, sources of financial support, description of fundraising activities, detailed financial information, and the basis for nonprivate foundation status.

[85]Treas. Reg. § 1.508-1(a)(2)(ii).

[86]Treas. Reg. § 1.508-1(a)(1)(ii).

and a balance sheet for the current year and the three preceding years or the years the organization has been in existence if less than four years, a statement of proposed activities and a description of anticipated receipts and contemplated expenditures, a copy of the organization's "organizing document" signed by a principal officer, and a copy of the organization's bylaws.[87] If information submitted in the application is incomplete and the organization supplies the necessary additional information requested by the IRS within the additional time stipulated in the request, the application will be considered timely filed.[88]

An application for recognition of exemption is considered by the "key district director"[89] who either refers the case to the IRS National Office for advice or a ruling, issues a favorable determination letter recognizing an organization's exempt status, or issues a proposed adverse determination letter denying exempt status. Exempt status can be recognized in advance of actual operations if proposed operations can be described in sufficient detail to permit a conclusion that the organization will clearly meet the requirements of section 501(c)(3). A mere restatement of purposes or a statement that the proposed activities will be in furtherance of such purposes will not satisfy this requirement.

Section 508(c) and the income tax regulations state that the following organizations are immune from section 508(a) notice requirements and therefore are not required to file a Form 1023 to be exempt from federal income tax or to receive tax deductible contributions:

1. churches, interchurch organizations of local units of a church, conventions or associations of churches, or integrated auxiliaries of a church, such as a men's or women's organization, religious seminary, mission society, or youth group

2. any organization that is not a private foundation and the gross receipts of which in each taxable year are normally not more than $5,000

3. subordinate organizations covered by a group exemption letter

The recognition of the exempt status of such organizations without the need for complying with the section 508(a) notice requirements of course assumes that all of the prerequisites contained in section 501(c)(3) of the Code have been satisfied.[90]

The IRS maintains that although such organizations are not required to file a Form 1023 to be exempt from federal income tax or to receive tax deductible contributions, they may "find it advantageous to obtain recognition of exemp-

[87]Rev. Proc. 80-25, 1980-1 C.B. 667.

[88]Treas. Reg. § 1.508-1(a)(2)(ii).

[89]The term *key district director* means the district director of each of the 17 IRS key district offices for exempt organization matters.

[90]*See* § B, *supra*.

tion."[91] Presumably, such organizations might voluntarily wish to obtain IRS recognition of tax-exempt status in order to assure contributors that donations will be tax deductible. The IRS publishes a cumulative listing (Publication 78) of organizations that have been determined to be exempt from federal income tax, contributions to which are tax deductible.[92] Contributions made to an organization whose name does not appear in Publication 78 may be questioned by the IRS, in which case the contributor would have to substantiate the deductibility of his contribution by demonstrating that the donee met the requirements of section 501(c)(3) and was exempt from the notice requirements. Similarly, some potential contributors may be reluctant to contribute to a religious organization not listed in Publication 78.

Although the vast majority of applications for recognition of tax-exempt status are approved by the IRS,[93] some result in adverse determinations. If the IRS issues an adverse determination letter, it must advise the organization of its right to protest the determination by requesting consideration by an IRS Appeals Office. To do this, the organization must submit to the appropriate district director within thirty days from the date of the adverse letter a statement of the facts, law, and arguments in support of its position.[94] If the Appeals Office upholds the adverse determination, the organization may file a suit for a declaratory judgment in federal court.[95] The declaratory judgment remedy cannot be used unless either all remedies within the IRS have been exhausted or 270 days have elapsed since the organization requested a determination and the organization has taken in a timely manner all reasonable steps to secure such a determination.

Finally, it should be noted that recognition of exemption from federal income tax under section 501(c)(3) of the Internal Revenue Code may be obtained on a group basis for "subordinate organizations" affiliated with and under the supervision or control of a "central organization."[96] This procedure relieves each of the subordinates covered by a group exemption letter of the necessity of filing its own application for recognition of exemption. To be eligible for a group exemption ruling, a central organization must obtain recognition of its own exempt status. It must also submit the following information on behalf of those subordinates to be included in the group exemption letter:

[91]IRS Publication 557.

[92]See also Rev. Proc. 82-39, 1982-27 I.R.B. 18.

[93]For example, the IRS annual report for 1981 reveals that only 913 out of a total of 27,676 applications for recognition of tax-exempt status by religious organizations were denied in 1981.

[94]Rev. Proc. 80-25, 1980-1 C.B. 667.

[95]Rev. Proc. 80-28, 1980-1 C.B. 680.

[96]Rev. Proc. 80-27, 1980-1 C.B. 677.

1. A letter signed by a principal officer of the central organization setting forth or including as attachments the following:

   a. information verifying that the subordinates to be included in the group exemption letter are affiliated with the central organization; are subject to its general supervision or control; are all eligible to qualify for exemption under the same paragraph of section 501(c) of the Code, though not necessarily the paragraph under which the central organization is exempt; are not private foundations; and are organizations that have been formed within the fifteen-month period prior to the date of submission of the group exemption application if they are claiming section 501(c)(3) status and are subject to the notice requirements of section 508(a)[97]

   b. a detailed description of the purposes and activities of the subordinates including the source of receipts and the nature of expenditures

   c. a sample copy of a uniform governing instrument (such as a charter or articles of association) adopted by the subordinates, or in its absence, copies of representative instruments

   d. an affirmation to the effect that, to the best of the officer's knowledge, the purposes and activities of the subordinates are as stated

   e. a statement that each subordinate to be included in the group exemption letter has furnished written authorization to that effect, signed by a duly authorized officer of the subordinate, to the central organization

   f. a list of subordinates to be included in the group exemption letter to which the IRS has already issued an outstanding ruling or determination letter relating to exemption

   g. if the application for a group exemption letter involves section 501(c)(3) of the Code and is subject to the provisions of the Code requiring that the central organization give timely notice that it is not a private foundation, an affirmation to the effect that, to the best of the officer's knowledge and belief, no subordinate to be included in the group exemption letter is a private foundation

   h. for each subordinate that is a school, the information required by Revenue Ruling 71-447 and Revenue Procedure 75-50 relating to proof of nondiscrimination

2. A list of the names, mailing addresses, actual addresses, and employer identification numbers of subordinates to be included in the group exemption letter. A current directory of subordinates may be furnished in lieu of the list if it includes the required information and if the subordinates not to be included in the group exemption letter are identified.

---

[97]As mentioned earlier in the present chapter, churches, conventions and associations of churches, and integrated auxiliaries of churches are exempt from the section 508(a) notice requirements.

If the central organization does not have an employer identification number, it must submit a completed application (Form SS-4) for such a number with its group exemption application.

An incorporated subordinate unit of a central organization may be included in a group exemption letter if the central organization submits evidence to show that it maintains adequate control over the incorporated subordinate unit, and that the subordinate is otherwise qualified. However, a subordinate that is organized and operated in a foreign country may not be included in a group exemption letter.

A new organization that wishes to be included in a group exemption letter must submit its authorization to the central organization before the end of the fifteenth month after it was formed in order to satisfy the section 508(a) notice requirements.[98] The central organization must also include all new subordinates in its next annual submission of information.

To maintain a group exemption letter, the central organization must submit the following information to the appropriate IRS center each year within ninety days before the close of its annual accounting period: (1) information regarding all changes in the purposes, character, or method of operation of the subordinates included in the group exemption letter; (2) a separate list including names, addresses, and employer identification numbers of subordinates that have changed their names or addresses during the year, that no longer are to be included in the group exemption letter because they have ceased to exist, disaffiliated, or withdrawn their authorization to the central organization, or that are to be added to the group exemption letter because they are newly organized or affiliated or because they have recently authorized the central organization to include them; and (3) the information required of a central organization on behalf of subordinates to be added to the group exemption letter.

The continued effectiveness of a group exemption letter is based on the following conditions: (1) the continued existence of the central organization, (2) the continued qualification of the central organization for exemption under section 501(c)(3) of the Code, (3) the submission by the central organization of the information required annually, and (4) the annual filing of an information return (Form 990) by the central organization if such a return is required.

### d. Annual Information Return Requirements

Most organizations exempt from federal income tax must file an annual information return with the IRS on Form 990. The following organizations, among

---

[98]Churches, conventions and associations of churches, and integrated auxiliaries of churches are not subject to the section 508(a) notice requirements.

others, are specifically exempted from this requirement: (1) a church, inter-church organization of local units of a church, a convention or association of churches, or an integrated auxiliary of a church such as a men's or women's organization, religious seminary, mission society, or youth group; (2) an exclusively religious activity of a religious order; (3) religious, educational, or other exempt organizations whose annual gross receipts normally do not exceed $25,000; (4) a mission society sponsored by or affiliated with one or more churches or church denominations, more than half of the activities of which are conducted in or directed at persons in foreign countries; and (5) a school below college level affiliated with a church or operated by a religious order, even though it is not an integrated auxiliary of a church.[99]

In general, Form 990 requests information regarding an exempt organization's income, disbursements, assets, and liabilities.[100]

The regulations state that an organization that has been determined by the IRS to be exempt may rely upon such determination "so long as there are no substantial changes in the organization's character, purposes, or methods of operation."[101] Thus, the IRS maintains that all exempt organizations are under a duty to notify the IRS of any substantial changes in character, purposes, or methods of operation.

### e. *Loss of Exemption*

An exemption ruling or determination letter may be revoked or modified by a ruling or determination letter addressed to the organization or by a revenue ruling or other statement published in the Internal Revenue Bulletin. The revocation or modification may be retroactive if the organization omitted or misstated a material fact or operated in a manner materially different from that originally represented.[102] In any event, revocation or modification ordinarily will take effect no earlier than the time at which the organization received written notice that its exemption ruling or determination letter might be revoked or modified.

### f. *Consequences of Exemption*

The IRS lists the following "collateral benefits" of exemption from federal income taxes:[103]

---

[99]I.R.C. § 6033; Treas. Reg. § 1.6033-2(g)(1).

[100]Treas. Reg. § 1.6033-2(a)(2)(ii).

[101]Treas. Reg. § 1.501(a)-1(a)(2).

[102]Treas. Reg. § 601.201(n)(6)(i).

[103]IRS EXEMPT ORGANIZATIONS HANDBOOK § 314 (1982).

1. In addition to the exemption from the payment of federal income tax, organizations recognized as exempt under section 501(c)(3) may enjoy collateral tax exemption under some state and local income, property, sales, use or other forms of taxation.

2. Contributions to organizations recognized as exempt under section 501(c)(3) are deductible as charitable contributions on the individual or corporate donor's federal income tax return.

3. Services performed for an organization described in section 501(c)(3) may be exempt from social security taxes, unemployment taxes, and certain excise taxes.

4. Religious organizations are among those listed under United States Postal Service regulations as being eligible to mail at preferred postal rates. The regulations state that exemption from federal income taxes will be considered as evidence of qualification for preferred postal rates but will not be controlling.

5. Organizations recognized as exempt under section 501(c)(3) are able to offer employees the benefit of special taxation of annuity provisions under section 403(b) of the Code.

### g. Mail Order Churches

In recent years, many taxpayers have attempted to exclude all or part of their income from federal taxation through the creation of a mail order church. Mail order churches ordinarily involve some or all of the following characteristics: An individual forms his own church, assigns all or a substantial part of his income to the church, takes a "vow of poverty," declares himself to be the minister, retains control over all church funds and property, designates a substantial housing allowance for himself, and reports the income that he has assigned to his church as a charitable contribution deduction on his federal tax return. In most cases the church has no building other than the personal residence of the minister, and it conducts few if any religious activities. Since the minister often purchases his credentials and church charter by mail, such schemes commonly are referred to as mail order churches.

The IRS has challenged the tax-exempt status of several mail order churches on the ground that they fail to meet one or more of the six prerequisites of exempt status discussed previously. Ordinarily, the IRS asserts that the church is ineligible for exempt status since its net earnings inure to the benefit of private individuals. The IRS acknowledges that payment of reasonable compensation for services rendered does not constitute inurement of an exempt organization's net earnings to a private individual.[104]

However, it maintains that inurement does occur if (1) compensation paid

---

[104]IRS Exempt Organizations Handbook § 381.1 (1982).

by an exempt organization is excessive in light of services rendered, (2) the value of services performed and of the corresponding compensation paid cannot be established objectively, (3) payments are not compensation for services rendered, (4) material benefits are provided in addition to regular wages, (5) compensation is based on a percentage of a church's gross receipts, (6) substantially all of a church's gross receipts come from its minister and are returned to him in the form of compensation or reimbursement of personal expenses, or (7) a church exists primarily to facilitate the personal financial transactions of its founder. To illustrate, inurement has been found in the following contexts: church ministers received fees, commissions, royalties, loans, a personal residence, and a car, in addition to ordinary wages;[105] a church devised a formula for determining the percentage of its gross receipts that would be payable to its minister, under which formula the minister received sixty-three percent of the church's gross receipts in one year and fifty-three percent in the next;[106] a boilermaker was ordained and chartered as a "church personally" by a mail order organization, took a vow of poverty, continued to work full time in secular employment, assigned his salary to his church account over which he maintained complete control, paid all of his personal expenses out of the church account, and claimed the maximum charitable contribution deduction for the amounts he transferred to the church account;[107] a married couple was ordained by and received a church charter from a mail order organization, established a church in their home, conducted religious services for between three and ten persons, paid all of their secular income to the church, and received such income back in the form of compensation and a housing allowance;[108] a married couple took

[105]Founding Church of Scientology v. Commissioner, 412 F.2d 1197 (Ct. Cl. 1969), cert. denied, 397 U.S. 1009 (1970).

[106]People of God Community v. Commissioner, 75 T.C. 127 (1981). The court concluded that "paying over a portion of gross earnings to those vested with the control of a church organization constitutes private inurement . . . ."

[107]Hall v. Commissioner, 41 T.C.M. 1169 (1981). See also McGahen v. Commissioner, 76 T.C. 468 (1981).

[108]Church of the Transfiguring Spirit v. Commissioner, 76 T.C. 1 (1981). In all of the following cases, individuals were ordained by and received a church charter from a mail order organization, established a church in their homes, conducted few if any religious services, assigned their secular income to the church checking account out of which they paid most of their personal expenses, and attempted to claim the maximum charitable contribution deduction allowable for the income assigned. An IRS finding of inurement was upheld in each case. Basic Unit Ministry of Schurig v. Commissioner, 670 F.2d 1210 (D.C. Cir. 1982); Solander v. Commissioner, 43 T.C.M. 934 (1982); Riemers v. Commissioner, 42 T.C.M. 838 (1981); Southern Church of Universal Brotherhood Assembled v. Commissioner, 74 T.C. 1223 (1980); Bubbling Well Church of Universal Love v. Commissioner, 74 T.C. 531 (1980); Rev. Rul. 81-94, 1981-12 I.R.B. 15.

a vow of poverty and established a religious order in which they and their children were the only members, assigned all of their secular income to the order, and claimed a charitable contribution deduction for the income assigned;[109] a taxpayer was ordained by and received a church charter from a mail order organization, established a church in his home, declared himself and two others to be its ministers, assigned all of his secular income to the church, and received substantially all of it back in the form of wages, a housing allowance, loans, and travel allowances;[110] a church made substantial cash grants to its officers without provision for repayment;[111] and a mail order church could not support substantial payments made to its founder.[112]

The IRS often asserts that mail order churches are ineligible for tax-exempt status since they are not organized or operated exclusively for exempt purposes. This assertion often is based upon section 1.501(c)(3)-1(d)(1)(ii) of the income tax regulations, which specifies that

> [a]n organization is not organized or operated exclusively for one or more [exempt purposes] unless it serves a public rather than a private interest. Thus, to meet [this] requirement . . . it is necessary for an organization to establish that it is not organized or operated for the benefit of private interests such as designated individuals, the creator or his family, shareholders of the organization, or persons controlled, directly or indirectly, by such private interests.

Thus, if a church exists primarily to serve the private interests of its creator or some identifiable group, it is not serving a public interest and therefore is not organized or operated for exempt purposes. Such a finding will be made whenever a church exists primarily as a vehicle for handling the personal financial transactions of its founder.

To illustrate, in Revenue Ruling 81-94[113] the IRS denied exempt status to a mail order church founded by a nurse. Following a vow of poverty, the nurse had transferred all of her assets, including her home and automobile, to her church and assigned her secular income to the church's checking account. In return, all of her expenses, such as her home mortgage and all outstanding

---

[109]Greeno v. Commissioner, 42 T.C.M. 1112 (1981).

[110]Unitary Mission Church v. Commissioner, 74 T.C. 507 (1980). Besides finding the amount of ministerial wages paid by the church to be excessive, the court observed that housing allowances also may be so excessive as to constitute unreasonable compensation. In either case, inurement occurs. The court rejected the church's argument that the First Amendment prohibits the courts from inquiring into the reasonableness of church salaries, at least where such inquiries involve no analysis of religious doctrine.

[111]Church in Boston v. Commissioner, 71 T.C. 102 (1978).

[112]Bubbling Well Church of Universal Love v. Commissioner, 74 T.C. 531 (1980). See also Truth Tabernacle v. Commissioner, 41 T.C.M. 1405 (1981).

[113]Rev. Rul. 81-94, 1981-12 I.R.B. 15.

credit card balances, were assumed by the corporation. The nurse was also provided with a full living allowance sufficient to maintain her previous standard of living. The church permitted her to use the home and automobile for personal uses. While the church's charter stated that it was organized exclusively for religious and charitable purposes, including a religious mission of healing the spirit, mind, emotions, and body, the church conducted few if any religious services and performed virtually no religious functions. The IRS concluded that the church existed primarily as a vehicle for handling the nurse's personal financial transactions and thus it was operated for the private interests of a designated individual rather than for a public interest.[114]

Predictably, standards that are comprehensive enough to deal effectively with the abuses of mail order churches may be sufficiently broad to negatively affect some legitimate churches. For example, the Tax Court denied exempt status to a church having fifty-six members that conducted regular evangelistic worship services; performed baptisms, communion services, weddings, and burials; whose beliefs included the infallibility of the Bible; and whose pastor testified that "we do not have a creed but Christ; no law but love; no book but the Bible."[115] The IRS contended that the church was not entitled to exempt status since it had not established that (1) its charter or bylaws provided for the distribution of church property to another exempt organization upon dissolution, (2) it was operated exclusively for religious purposes, (3) it was operated for public rather than private interests, and (4) its net earnings did not inure to the benefit of private individuals.

Churches, like any other exempt organization, have the burden of proving that they meet each of the prerequisites to exempt status. The burden of proof is not on the IRS to disprove eligibility for exempt status. Many mail order churches have been denied exempt status because they could not prove that they in fact were organized or operated exclusively for exempt purposes or that none of their net earnings inured to the benefit of private individuals.

Many mail order church schemes involve the assignment of a founder's secular income to his church's checking account, and the founder's claiming the largest allowable charitable contribution deduction on his federal income tax return. Since a charitable contribution deduction is available only to donors who make contributions to an exempt organization, the deductibility of charitable contributions to mail order churches often is challenged by the IRS. Unless a taxpayer can prove that his contribution was made to a church that

---

[114]See also New Life Tabernacle v. Commissioner, 44 T.C.M. 309 (1982); Solander v. Commissioner, 43 T.C.M. 934 (1982); Self v. Commissioner, 41 T.C.M. 1465 (1981); Basic Bible Church v. Commissioner, 74 T.C. 846 (1980); Southern Church of Universal Brotherhood Assembled, Inc. v. Commissioner, 74 T.C. 1223 (1980).

[115]Truth Tabernacle v. Commissioner, 41 T.C.M. 1405 (1981).

satisfies the prerequisites to exempt status listed in section 501(c)(3) of the Internal Revenue Code, his deduction will be disallowed. Occasionally, the IRS challenges a charitable contribution to a mail order church on the ground that such a transfer does not constitute a contribution. To illustrate, in Revenue Ruling 78-232[116] the IRS disallowed a charitable contribution deduction for any part of a taxpayer's secular income that he assigned to his mail order church's checking account, since

> [s]ection 170 of the Code provides . . . a deduction for charitable contributions to or for the use of [exempt] organizations . . . . Section 170(c)(2) of the Code provides, in part, that the term "charitable contribution" means a contribution or gift to or for the use of a corporation organized and operated exclusively for religious or other charitable purposes, no part of the net earnings of which inures to the benefit of any private shareholder or individual.
>
> The term "charitable contribution," as used in section 170 of the Code, has been held to be synonymous with the word "gift." A gift for purposes of section 170 is a voluntary transfer of money or property that is made with no expectation of procuring a commensurate financial benefit in return for the transfer. It follows that if the benefits the donor can reasonably expect to obtain by making the transfer are sufficiently substantial to provide a *quid pro quo* for it, then no deduction under section 170 is allowable.
>
> In the instant case the money deposited by the taxpayer in the . . . church account was used or available for use for the taxpayer's benefit. . . . Accordingly, the amount of the salary checks deposited by the taxpayer in the bank account maintained in the name of the . . . church is not deductible as a "charitable contribution" under section 170 of the Code.

Finally, as part of its Illegal Tax Protester Program the IRS has developed guidelines to assist its agents in recognizing mail order churches.[117] In addition, the IRS is strictly construing the requirements of section 501(c)(3) when assessing the eligibility of a mail order church for exempt status, and it is threatening criminal prosecution of taxpayers who persist in using these tax evasion schemes.

## 2. CHARITABLE CONTRIBUTIONS

Certainly one of the most valuable benefits of tax-exempt status is the ability to attract tax-deductible contributions. Section 170 of the Internal Revenue Code states in part: "There shall be allowed as a deduction any charitable contribution . . . payment of which is made within the taxable year." To be deductible, a contribution must meet the following conditions: (1) a gift of cash

---

[116]Rev. Rul. 78-232, 1978-1 C.B. 69 (citations omitted).
[117]INTERNAL REVENUE MANUAL § 426 (26).5.

or other property, (2) made before the close of the tax year for which the contributor is claiming a deduction, (3) unconditional and without material personal benefit to the contributor, (4) made to or for the use of a qualified organization, (5) not in excess of the amount allowed by law, and (6) subject to substantiation. These conditions will be considered individually.

### a. *Gift of Cash or Other Property*

Generally only contributions of cash or other property are deductible. No deduction is allowable for a contribution of services. Thus, a church member who donates his labor in helping to construct a church is not entitled to deduct the value of his labor.

However, the IRS maintains that unreimbursed expenditures incurred because of the performance of services for an exempt organization may constitute a deductible contribution.[118] For example, the cost of a uniform required in performing donated services and unsuited for everyday use is deductible.[119] Similarly, out-of-pocket transportation expenses incurred in performing donated services are deductible. To illustrate, it has been held that a minister who served without pay could deduct his automobile expenses incurred in the course of church work as a charitable contribution.[120] And a taxpayer was allowed to deduct out-of-pocket expenses incurred in carrying out evangelistic work for his church.[121] A standard rate per mile is available for those not wishing to deduct actual expenses. General repair and maintenance expenses, insurance, and depreciation are not deductible.[122] Reasonable expenditures for meals and lodging incurred while away from home in the course of performing donated services are also deductible.[123]

Expenses incurred in attending a church convention may not be deducted unless one goes as a chosen representative.[124] Chosen representatives may deduct unreimbursed expenses for travel and transportation, and also may deduct a reasonable amount for meals and lodging while away from home overnight in connection with the convention.[125] Travel, meals, and lodging expenses of a spouse and children may not be deducted since these are personal

---

[118]Treas. Reg. § 1.170A-1(g); IRS Publication 526.
[119]Rev. Rul. 56-508, 1956 C.B. 126.
[120]Rev. Rul. 69-645, 1969-2 C.B. 37.
[121]Smith v. Commissioner, 60 T.C. 988 (1974).
[122]Orr v. United States, 343 F.2d 553 (5th Cir. 1965).
[123]Treas. Reg. § 1.170A-1(g); IRS Publication 526.
[124]Rev. Rul. 61-46, 1961-1 C.B. 51.
[125]Rev. Rul. 58-240, 1958-1 C.B. 141.

expenses.[126] If an individual donates his time and services to a charitable organization and receives a daily allowance to cover reasonable travel expenses, including meals and lodging, he must include as income the amount that exceeds his actual travel expenses. He may, however, deduct necessary travel expenses that exceed the allowance.

Virtually any kind of property, whether tangible or intangible, can constitute a charitable contribution, including cash, charges to a bank credit card,[127] real estate, promissory notes, pew rents,[128] stocks, church bonds, automobiles, boats, aircraft, art objects, books, documents, music manuscripts, building materials, collections, jewelry, easements, insurance policies,[129] inventory, and sound equipment. A deduction is allowed if a contributor borrows funds from a third party and uses the funds to make a contribution. When property other than cash is given, its value is often difficult to determine. Valuation of contributions is considered later in the present chapter.

Contributions of less than a donor's entire interest in property are not deductible unless they fit within one of the following exceptions:

1. A contribution not in trust of an irrevocable remainder interest in a personal residence or farm. For example, a donor can contribute a remainder interest in his residence to an exempt organization and retain a life estate in the property. In such a case, the donor has contributed only a partial interest in property, but a charitable contribution deduction is permitted.[130]

2. A contribution not in trust of an undivided portion of a donor's entire interest in property. For example, if a donor owns one hundred acres of land and makes a contribution of fifty acres to an exempt organization, a deduction is permitted even though the donor has contributed less than his entire interest.[131]

---

[126]Lemmon v. Commissioner, 27 T.C.M. 503 (1968).

[127]Rev. Rul. 78-38, 1978-1 C.B. 67.

[128]Rev. Rul. 70-47, 1970-1 C.B. 49.

[129]Premiums paid on a life insurance policy irrevocably assigned to the benefit of an exempt organization are deductible as a charitable contribution. A deduction is also allowable for an irrevocable assignment of the cash surrender value of a life insurance policy to an exempt organization. However, if a donor reserves significant rights in a policy, he will not be entitled to a deduction. Thus, the IRS has disallowed a deduction for a contribution of the cash surrender value of a life insurance policy to an exempt organization since the donor had reserved the right to designate the beneficiary and to assign the balance of the policy. Rev. Rul. 76-143, 1976-1 C.B. 57.

[130]I.R.C. § 170(f)(3)(B)(i). The value of the donated remainder interest is determined under § 20.2031-10 of the estate tax regulations and § 1.170A-12 of the income tax regulations.

[131]I.R.C. § 170(f)(3)(B)(ii).

3. A contribution of certain partial interests in property exclusively for conservation purposes.[132]

4. A contribution of an irrevocable remainder interest in property to a charitable remainder trust or a pooled income fund. Generally, a charitable remainder trust is a trust that provides for a specified distribution, at least annually, to one or more beneficiaries, at least one of which is not an exempt organization, for life or for a term of years, with an irrevocable remainder interest to be held for the benefit of, or paid to, an exempt organization. A trust is a charitable remainder trust only if it is either a charitable remainder annuity trust or a charitable remainder unitrust.

A deduction of the fair market value of a partial interest in property donated to an exempt organization will not be allowed unless it fits within one of these four exceptions. Thus, for example, an individual owning an office building who donates the rent-free use of a portion of the building to a charitable organization is not entitled to a charitable contribution deduction since his contribution consists of a partial interest in property that does not fit within one of the four exemptions previously discussed.[133] A deduction is allowed, however, of a partial interest in property if such interest is the donor's entire interest in the property and the property was not divided solely to facilitate the charitable contribution deduction.

Pledges or subscriptions are commitments to contribute a fixed sum of money or designated property to a charitable organization. They can be oral or in writing. Traditionally, the courts refused to enforce pledges on the basis of contract law. A contract essentially is an agreement between two parties to do a particular thing, with each party receiving some benefit or "consideration" from the other. If only one party benefits, the agreement is deemed illusory and is unenforceable. Since a donor typically receives nothing in exchange for his promise to make a future contribution, the agreement formerly was considered illusory and unenforceable.

In recent years, however, several courts have found pledges to be enforceable on either of two grounds. First, some courts have held that an enforceable contract occurs when a donee charity incurs debts or other obligations in reliance on the pledge. To illustrate, one court has held that

the consideration for a pledge to an eleemosynary [*i.e.*, charitable] institution or organization is the accomplishment of the purposes for which such institution or organization was organized and created and in whose aid the pledge is made, and such consideration is sufficient. We therefore conclude that pledges made in

[132]I.R.C. §§ 170(f)(3)(B)(iii), 170(h).
[133]I.R.C. § 170(f)(3)(A).

writing to eleemosynary institutions and organizations are enforceable debts supported by consideration, unless the writing itself otherwise indicates or it is otherwise proved.[134]

In another case, a court enforced the promise of a trustee of a religious organization to pay the balance due on a building that had been purchased at his suggestion.[135]

Second, some courts have held that the promises of other donors is sufficient consideration for the promise of each. To illustrate, one court has held that "[i]t is elemental that one donor is not likely to give unless other donors give, and bound together as they are, inextricably linked in a project for the benefit of all of them, they must support one another rather than be afforded a unilateral opportunity to withdraw."[136]

A few states have enacted statutes authorizing the executor of an estate to honor pledges made by the decedent during his lifetime.[137]

But even in those states that consider pledges to be legally enforceable obligations, a cash-basis donor may claim a charitable contribution deduction only for the amount of a pledge actually paid during the current year.[138] The IRS has ruled that a donor who makes a legally enforceable pledge to a charitable organization that loses its exempt status before the date the pledge is fully met may deduct the balance of his pledge with IRS approval unless he (1) had knowledge of the revocation of exemption, (2) was aware that such revocation was imminent, or (3) was in part responsible for, or was aware of, the activities on the part of the organization that gave rise to the loss of exemption.[139]

### b. *Time of Contribution*

Ordinarily, a contribution is made at the time of delivery. The unconditional delivery or mailing of a check that clears in due course will constitute an effective contribution on the date of delivery or mailing. Contributions of real estate ordinarily are deductible in the year that a deed to the property is delivered to the donee organization. If a taxpayer unconditionally delivers or mails a properly endorsed stock certificate to an exempt organization, the gift is completed on the date of delivery or if such certificate is received in the ordinary

---

[134]Hirsch v. Hirsch, 289 N.E.2d 386 (Ohio 1972).

[135]Estate of Timko v. Oral Roberts Evangelistic Assoc., 215 N.W.2d 750 (Mich. 1974).

[136]Congregation B'Nai Sholom v. Martin, 160 N.W.2d 784 (Mich. 1968), *rev'd on other grounds,* 173 N.W.2d 504 (Mich. 1969).

[137]*See, e.g.,* ARIZ. REV. STAT. § 14-3715; NEB. REV. STAT. § 30-2476(4).

[138]Mann v. Commissioner, 35 F.2d 873 (D.C. Cir. 1929).

[139]Rev. Proc. 82-39, 1982-27 I.R.B. 18.

course of the mails, on the date of mailing. If a stock certificate is given to the contributor's agent or to the issuing corporation for transfer to the name of an exempt organization, the gift is not completed until the date the stock is transferred on the books of the issuing corporation.

If a contributor issues a promissory note to an exempt organization, a gift ordinarily is not made until the contributor makes the note payments.[140]

A taxpayer who telephoned a religious organization on the evening of December 31, 1967, and informed it that he was making a gift of an interest in land to the organization and who sent a notarized letter acknowledging the gift before midnight the same evening was found not to have made a valid gift for tax purposes in 1967 because he added several conditions to the gift in the letter.[141]

The amount of a pledge by a cash-basis taxpayer to a church or other charitable organization is deductible in the year of the pledge only to the extent that it is paid.[142]

c. *Unconditional and Without Personal Benefit*

It is well-settled that the term *contribution* is synonymous with the term *gift,* and therefore a contribution is not deductible unless it constitutes a valid gift.[143] Since no gift exists in a legal sense unless a donor absolutely and irrevocably divests himself of title, dominion, and control over the gift, it is the prevailing view that no charitable contribution deduction is available unless the contribution is unconditional. The income tax regulations stipulate that if as of the date of a gift a transfer of property to an exempt organization is dependent upon the performance of some act or the happening of some event in order to become effective, no deduction is allowable unless the possibility that the gift will not become effective is so remote as to be negligible.[144] The regulations further state that if a transfer of property vests in an exempt organization on the date of the gift and the gift would be voided by the subsequent performance of some act or the happening of some event the possibility of which appears on the date of the gift to be so remote as to be negligible, the deduction is allowable.[145] For example, if a contributor transfers land to a church on the condition that the land will be used for church purposes, he is entitled

---

[140]Rev. Rul. 68-174, 1968-1 C.B. 81.

[141]Dalton v. Commissioner, 32 T.C.M. 782 (1973).

[142]Mann v. Commissioner, 35 F.2d 873 (D.C. Cir. 1929).

[143]DeJong v. Commissioner, 36 T.C. 896 (1961), *aff'd,* 309 F.2d 373 (9th Cir. 1962). *See also* Rev. Rul. 78-232, 1978-1 C.B. 69.

[144]Treas. Reg. § 1.170A-1(e).

[145]*Id.*

to a charitable contribution deduction if on the date of the transfer the church does plan to use the land for church purposes and the possibility that the church will not use the land for such purposes is so remote as to be negligible.

Similarly, a charitable contribution deduction is not allowed if the contributor receives a direct and material benefit for his contribution, since a gift by definition is a gratuitous transfer of property without consideration or advantage to the donor other than the feeling of satisfaction that it inspires. Thus, one court has held that membership dues paid to a charitable organization are deductible as charitable contributions only to the extent that members do not receive any benefits or privileges in return for their payment.[146] If members do receive benefits from membership in a charitable organization, they may deduct dues paid to such an organization only to the extent that they exceed the monetary value of the benefits available by reason of such payment.[147] It has been held that a fee paid to a church for the use of a church social hall for a wedding is not deductible as a charitable contribution since the donor receives material benefit for his contribution.[148] And it has been held that travel expenses incurred in commuting to and from church choir practice are not deductible since participation in a church choir is a form of religious worship that primarily benefits the member and only indirectly benefits the church.[149] Charitable contribution deductions have also been denied for the value of memorial plaques presented to charitable organizations in the name of a deceased relative[150] and for tuition payments made by a parent to a church-operated school[151] on the ground that such contributions result in direct benefit to the donor and therefore are not valid gifts. Furthermore, amounts paid to buy raffle tickets or to play bingo or other games of chance are not deductible as charitable contributions. These are gambling losses that may be deducted only to the extent of gambling gains.

Obviously, loans to exempt organizations and the purchase of church bonds do not constitute charitable contributions since in neither case does a donor irrevocably divest himself of control over any property. A charitable contribution deduction is permitted for the value of a loan that is forgiven or for the value of church bonds donated to a church.

It is a common practice for charitable organizations to offer books, tickets, and other promotional materials to donors as a means of soliciting contributions. A donor may deduct as a charitable contribution only the amount by which his

[146]Rev. Rul. 54-565, 1954-2 C.B. 95.
[147]Rev. Rul. 68-432, 1968-2 C.B. 104.
[148]Summers v. Commissioner, 33 T.C.M. 696 (1974).
[149]Churukian v. Commissioner, 40 T.C.M. 475 (1980).
[150]Reese v. Commissioner, 8 T.C.M. 99 (1949).
[151]Rev. Rul. 54-580, 1954-2 C.B. 97.

contribution exceeds the fair market value of the books or other promotional merchandise that he receives in return for his gift. For example, if an organization offers a book having a fair market value of $5 to persons who contribute $20 or more, a person who contributes $20 is entitled to deduct only $15 as a charitable contribution. Organizations offering promotional gifts to contributors should be careful not to represent that contributions are "fully deductible."[152] It is a more appropriate practice to state that contributions are fully deductible as allowed by law. Furthermore, the fair market value of promotional gifts should be stated in the tax receipts that are provided to contributors, with some indication that a contributor may deduct only the excess of his contribution over the value of the promotional gift.

### d. *Made to or for the Use of a Qualified Organization*

Only those contributions made to qualified organizations are deductible. Section 170(c) of the Code defines *qualified organizations* to include, among others, a corporation, trust, or fund

1. created or organized in the United States or in any United States possession
2. organized and operated exclusively for religious, educational, or other charitable purposes
3. no part of the net earnings of which inures to the benefit of any private individual
4. not disqualified for tax exemption under section 501(c)(3) by reason of attempting to influence legislation, and which does not participate or intervene in any political campaign on behalf of any candidate for public office

IRS Publication 78 lists those organizations that are presumptively qualified.[153] This listing of course is not exhaustive since many organizations, including churches, are automatically exempt from federal income taxes without filing an exemption application and therefore their names ordinarily do not appear in the IRS cumulative listing.

To be deductible, a contribution must be made "to or for the use of" a qualified organization. Contributions and gifts made directly to individuals are not deductible. Thus, it has been held that payments made directly to a religious

---

[152]It is imprudent for any charitable organization to state that contributions are "fully deductible," for in many cases this will not be true. For example, a contributor who has already exceeded his percentage limitations may not be able to deduct any part of a gift to such an organization.

[153]Rev. Proc. 82-39, 1982-27 I.R.B. 18.

science practitioner,[154] to individual ministers of the gospel,[155] or to needy individuals are not deductible. However, even if a contribution is made directly to an individual, the contribution may be deductible if it was made "for the use of" an exempt organization. To illustrate, a taxpayer who sent a check to a Presbyterian missionary in Brazil with the stipulation that the funds be used for missions work was found to be entitled to a charitable contribution deduction for the amount of the check.[156] The court concluded that the funds were contributed "for the use of" the Presbyterian mission in Brazil and were not a nondeductible gift to an individual. Another court upheld the deductibility of a contribution to a fund established by three Presbyterian churches for the support of a particular missionary, even though the contribution mentioned the missionary's name, since the contribution was "for the use of" an exempt missions organization.[157] A contribution given directly to a Jesuit priest was held to be deductible on the theory that members of the Jesuit Order are under a vow of poverty obligating them to give to the Order all property received by them, and thus a gift to a priest in reality is a gift "to or for the use of" the Order.[158] The IRS, in upholding the deductibility of a taxpayer's contribution to a church fund out of which missionaries, including his son, were compensated, stated the test for determining the deductibility of "designated" contributions as follows:

> If contributions to the fund are earmarked by the donor for a particular individual, they are treated, in effect, as being gifts to the designated individual and are not deductible. However, a deduction will be allowable where it is established that a gift is intended by a donor for the use of the organization and not as a gift to an individual. The test in each case is whether the organization has full control of the donated funds, and discretion as to their use, so as to insure that they will be used to carry out its functions and purposes. In the instant case, the son's receipt of reimbursements from the fund is alone insufficient to require a holding that this test is not met. Accordingly, unless the taxpayer's contributions to the fund are distinctly marked by him so that they may be used only for his son or are received by the fund pursuant to a commitment or understanding that they

[154]Miller v. Commissioner, 40 T.C.M. 243 (1980).

[155]Cook v. Commissioner, 37 T.C.M. 771 (1978).

[156]Lesslie v. Commissioner, 36 T.C.M. 495 (1977). The court added: "It seems to us that the [IRS] has chosen the wrong case to be puristic in [its] effort to collect the sovereign's revenue."

[157]Winn v. Commissioner, 595 F.2d 1060 (5th Cir. 1979).

[158]Ratterman v. Commissioner, 11 T.C. 1140 (1948), aff'd, 177 F.2d 204 (6th Cir. 1949).

will be so used, they may be deducted by the taxpayer in computing his taxable income . . . .[159]

Contributions to foreign organizations are not deductible. Thus, no deduction was allowed for contributions to churches in France,[160] to a Swiss church,[161] or to the State of Israel.[162] The IRS maintains that contributions to a United States organization that transfers the funds to a charitable foreign organization are deductible if the United States organization controls the use of the funds or if the foreign organization is only an administrative arm of the United States organization.

### e. *Amount Deductible*

A taxpayer can deduct contributions to most charitable organizations up to fifty percent of his adjusted gross income. The fifty-percent limit applies to contributions to all public charities including churches, conventions or associations of churches, and religious organizations that receive a substantial part of their support (other than income from religious activities) from public contributions.[163] Contributions to nonpublic charities, including certain private nonoperating foundations, veterans' organizations, and fraternal societies are deductible only up to twenty percent of adjusted gross income.[164] The IRS maintains that any contribution "for the use of" rather than "to" a charitable organization, including religious organizations, is deductible only up to twenty percent of adjusted gross income.[165] For example, the IRS has held that out-of-pocket expenses incurred for a charitable organization are subject to the

---

[159]Rev. Rul. 62-113, 1962-2 C.B. 10.

[160]Herter v. Commissioner, 20 T.C.M. 78 (1961).

[161]Welti v. Commissioner, 1 T.C. 905 (1943).

[162]Hess v. Commissioner, 30 T.C.M. 1043 (1971).

[163]I.R.C. § 170(b)(1)(A). The 50-percent limit also applies to contributions to (1) educational organizations, (2) hospitals and medical research organizations, (3) organizations operated for the benefit of certain state and municipal colleges and universities, (4) governmental units, (5) "publicly supported" organizations that normally receive a substantial part of their support from a governmental unit or from the general public, (6) certain private foundations, and (7) organizations that normally receive more than one-third of their support from gifts, grants, contributions, membership fees, and receipts from admissions, sales, or performance of services.

[164]I.R.C. § 170(b)(1)(B).

[165]IRS Publication 526.

twenty-percent limitation.[166] There is also a thirty-percent limit that applies to contributions of certain capital gain property to public charities.[167]

To compute one's aggregate annual charitable contribution deduction, the following steps are taken: (1) consider gifts to charitable organizations to which the fifty-percent limit applies; (2) next consider gifts to which the twenty-percent limit applies, and only to the extent of the lesser of twenty percent of adjusted gross income or fifty percent of adjusted gross income minus the contributions to which the fifty-percent limit applies, without regard to the special thirty-percent limit; (3) consider gifts of capital gain property to which the special thirty-percent limit applies after all other gifts. If contributions to organizations to which the fifty-percent limit applies are more than fifty percent of adjusted gross income, or thirty percent for certain capital gain property, the excess may be carried over and deducted in each of the five succeeding years until it is used up. Gifts to which the twenty-percent limit applies may not be carried over. An amount carried over to the following year may be deducted to the extent that it is not more than fifty percent of adjusted gross income for that year (or thirty percent for certain capital gain property) less the amount donated to qualified organizations during the year. For example, if a taxpayer had adjusted gross income of $20,000 in 1982 and contributed $11,000 to his church in the same year, he may deduct $10,000 in 1982 (50% of $20,000) and carry over the $1,000. In 1983, if the taxpayer again had adjusted gross income of $20,000 and contributed $9,000 or less during the year, he may deduct the entire carryover from 1982. However, if he contributed $9,500 during 1983, he may deduct only $500 of the carryover. The balance of $500 is carried over to 1984.

Corporations may deduct charitable contributions of up to ten percent of taxable income computed without regard to certain items.[168]

In order to apply the percentage limitations, the value of charitable contributions must be determined. Cash gifts obviously present no valuation problem, and gifts of other property generally are deductible at their fair market value at the time of the gift. Fair market value refers to the price at which property would change hands between a willing buyer and a willing seller, neither being under any compulsion to buy or sell and both having reasonable knowledge of the relevant facts. The value of used personal property is generally less than its original cost.[169] If a taxpayer contributes property subject to a debt obligation, he must reduce the fair market value of the property by the amount of the

[166]*Id. See also* Rev. Rul. 58-279, 1958-1 C.B. 145. *Contra* Rockefeller v. Commissioner, 676 F.2d 35 (2d Cir. 1982).

[167]I.R.C. § 170(b)(1)(C).

[168]I.R.C. § 170(b)(2).

[169]*See generally* IRS Publication 561.

outstanding debt. Further, any prepaid interest must be deducted from the amount of a contribution of property in order to avoid a double deduction.

A taxpayer can deduct the fair market value of donated bonds, notes, certificates, or other evidences of debt. A taxpayer must subtract from the fair market value any interest paid or to be paid on money borrowed for buying or carrying the instrument if the interest is for any period before the contribution. However, this reduction is limited to not more than the interest (including bond discounts and other items that are the same as interest) on the instrument for the period before the contribution that is not included in income because of one's accounting method.[170]

If a taxpayer donates appreciated property having a fair market value that exceeds his basis (generally his cost) in the property, he may have to reduce the fair market value by all or a part of the appreciation (increase in value) when computing his deduction. The amount of the reduction depends on whether the property is ordinary income property or capital gain property.

A "bargain sale" is a sale of property to a charity at less than its fair market value. The bargain sale is in part a sale of property and in part a charitable contribution.

f. *Substantiation*

Section 170 of the Internal Revenue Code, which authorizes deductions for charitable contributions, states that a charitable contribution shall be allowable as a deduction only if verified. Taxpayers should keep records, receipts, canceled checks, or other written evidence of charitable contributions. Prior to 1983, a taxpayer who claimed a contribution of money but lacked written evidence of his contribution occasionally was allowed a deduction for all or part of the contribution if supported by convincing oral testimony. To illustrate, one court held that a taxpayer was entitled to deduct all of his claimed cash contributions to his church even though no written records supported them since oral testimony established (1) that the taxpayer regularly attended church and (2) the amount of money that he habitually contributed.[171] In another case, an IRS attempt to limit a taxpayer's unsubstantiated church contributions to the amount he had contributed in the previous year was overruled by the Tax Court since the taxpayer's testimony established that he had given additional contributions toward a newly created building fund.[172] The Tax Court also overruled an IRS attempt to disallow entirely for lack of substantiation a $100 charitable contribution deduction allegedly made by a taxpayer to her church.

---

[170]*See generally* Treas. Reg. § 1.170A-3(c).

[171]Novaky v. Commissioner, 36 T.C.M. 1601 (1977).

[172]Russos v. Commissioner, 36 T.C.M. 1222 (1977).

The court concluded that the claimed contribution "was reasonable in amount for someone who attended church on a weekly basis" and who testified that she generally made weekly cash contributions of between one and five dollars.[173]

The Tax Court in another case observed:

> Petitioner regularly attended St. Theresa's each week during 1975 and made cash contributions which he claims totaled $520. However, he failed to substantiate his alleged contributions as he should have. Nevertheless, petitioner's testimony was candid, forthright, and credible, and we are convinced that he regularly attended and made cash contributions to St. Theresa's throughout 1975. Using our best judgment and bearing heavily against petitioner whose inexactitude is of his own making, we hold that petitioner is entitled to a $260 charitable contribution deduction.[174]

Taxpayers who before 1983 made contributions of property other than money and claimed a deduction in excess of $200 were required to attach the following information to their income tax returns:

1. The name and address of the organization to which the contribution was made.

2. The date of the actual contribution.

3. A description of the property in sufficient detail to identify the particular property contributed, including in the case of tangible personal property the physical condition of the property.

4. The approximate date the taxpayer acquired the property, and the manner in which it was acquired.

5. The fair market value of the property at the time the contribution was made, and the method used to determine fair market value. If it was determined by appraisal, a signed copy of the appraiser's report was to be attached.

6. The cost or other basis, as adjusted, of appreciated property other than securities if it was held for less than five years.

7. The cost or other basis of ordinary income property or short-term capital gain property, and the amount of ordinary income or short-term capital gain that would have been realized had the property been sold at its fair market value.

8. The terms of any agreement or understanding entered into with the charitable organization that related to the use, sale, or disposition of the property contributed, as, for example, the terms of any agreement or understanding that restricted the donee organization's right to dispose of donated property;

[173]Reinert v. Commissioner, 39 T.C.M. 770 (1979).
[174]Johnson v. Commissioner, 39 T.C.M. 868 (1980).

that reserved to or conferred upon anyone other than the donee organization any right to the income from donated property, to the possession of such property, or to acquire such property; or that earmarked donated property for a particular charitable use.

9. The amount claimed as a deduction for the tax year as a result of the contribution.[175]

The regulations also state that any deduction for a charitable contribution must be substantiated, as may be required by the IRS district director, by a statement from the organization to which the contribution was made indicating whether the organization is a domestic organization, the name and address of the contributor, the amount of the contribution, the date of the actual receipt of the contribution, and such other information as the district director may deem necessary.[176] Section 1.170A-13 of the income tax regulations, proposed by the IRS on April 6, 1983, would require a taxpayer making a charitable contribution of *money* to maintain one of the following for each contribution:

1. A cancelled check;
2. A receipt from the donee charitable organization showing the date of the contribution, the amount, and the name of the donee (including a letter, or other communication from the donee, acknowledging receipt of the contribution and showing the date and amount of the contribution);
3. In the absence of a cancelled check or a receipt from the donee charitable organization, other reliable written evidence showing the name of the charitable donee and the date and amount of the contribution. The reliability of such other written evidence is to be determined on the basis of all of the facts and circumstances of a particular case. In all events, however, the burden shall be on the taxpayer to establish reliability. Factors indicating that such other written evidence is reliable include, but are not limited to:
(i) The contemporaneous nature of the writing evidencing the contribution and the regularity of the taxpayer's recordkeeping procedures. For example, a contemporaneous diary entry stating the amount and date of the donation and the name of the donee charitable organization made by a taxpayer who regularly makes such diary entries would generally be considered reliable.
(ii) In the case of a contribution of a small amount, any written or other evidence from the donee charitable organization evidencing receipt of a donation that would not otherwise constitute a receipt under paragraph . . . (2) of this section . . . .

The proposed regulation would generally require a taxpayer making a charitable contribution of *property other than money* to have (1) a receipt from the

---

[175]Treas. Reg. § 1.170A-1(a)(2)(ii).
[176]Treas. Reg. § 1.170A-1(a)(2)(iii).

donee charitable organization that includes the name of the organization to which the contribution was made, the date and location of the actual contribution, and a description of the property adequate to identify it, and (2) a "reliable written record" for each item of donated property that contains essentially the same nine categories of information (discussed previously) formerly required of taxpayers who made noncash contributions of property and claimed a charitable contribution deduction in excess of $200, except for the date the taxpayer acquired the property and the manner in which it was acquired. For noncash charitable contributions of property for which the taxpayer claims a deduction in excess of $500, the taxpayer would be required to maintain additional records regarding the manner of acquisition of the property and the property's cost or other basis if it was held for less than one year prior to the date of contribution. The information required by the proposed amendments would have to be stated in the taxpayer's income tax return only if required by the return form or its instructions.

The proposed regulation, if adopted, would make oral substantiation of charitable contributions much more difficult, if not impossible.

### 3. TAX ON UNRELATED BUSINESS INCOME

#### a. *In General*

Prior to 1950, a growing number of exempt organizations were engaged in profitable business activities in competition with taxable organizations. In some cases, these business activities had little or no relation to the exempt organization's purposes other than the production of revenue to carry out those purposes. This led Congress, in the Revenue Act of 1950, to impose a tax on the "unrelated business taxable income" of certain otherwise exempt organizations. The Report of the Senate Finance Committee stated the purpose of the new tax as follows:

> The problem at which the tax on unrelated business income is directed is primarily that of unfair competition. The tax-free status of section [501] organizations enables them to use their profits tax-free to expand operations, while their competitors can expand only with the profits remaining after taxes. In neither the House bill nor your committee's bill does this provision deny the exemption where the organizations are carrying on unrelated active business enterprises, nor require that they dispose of such businesses. Both provisions merely impose the same tax on income derived from an unrelated trade or business as is borne by their competitors. In fact it is not intended that the tax imposed on unrelated business income will have any effect on the tax-exempt status of any organization.[177]

---

[177]S. Rep. No. 2375, 81st Cong., 2d Sess. 27 (1950).

The Revenue Act of 1950 exempted certain organizations from the unrelated business income tax provisions, including churches and conventions or associations of churches. However, it soon became apparent that many of the exempted organizations were engaging, or were apt to engage, in unrelated business. For example, churches were involved in various types of commercial activities, including publishing houses, hotels, factories, radio and television stations, parking lots, newspapers, bakeries, and restaurants. Congress responded in the Tax Reform Act of 1969 by subjecting almost all exempt organizations, including churches and conventions or associations of churches, to the tax on unrelated business income.[178] Thus, for taxable years beginning after December 31, 1969, churches and conventions or associations of churches became subject to the tax on unrelated business income unless the unrelated business was being carried on before May 27, 1969, in which case the tax applies only to years beginning after December 31, 1975.[179]

### b. *Unrelated Business Income*

Section 511 of the Code imposes a tax on "unrelated business taxable income." Section 512 defines *unrelated business taxable income* as "the gross income derived by any organization from any unrelated trade or business regularly carried on by it" less certain deductions. Section 513 defines the term *unrelated trade or business* as

> any trade or business the conduct of which is not substantially related (aside from the need of such organization for income or funds or the use it makes of the profits derived) to the exercise or performance by such organization of its charitable, educational, or other purpose or function constituting the basis for its exemption under section 501 . . . .

Thus, the following three conditions must be met before an activity of an exempt organization may be classified as an unrelated trade or business and the gross income of such activity subjected to the tax on unrelated business taxable income:

1. the activity must be a trade or business
2. the trade or business must be regularly carried on
3. the trade or business must not be substantially related to exempt purposes

The term *trade or business* generally includes any activity carried on for the production of income from the sale of goods or performances of services. The IRS maintains that the term includes activities such as selling goods at a church

---

[178] I.R.C. § 511(a)(2)(A).
[179] I.R.C. § 512(b)(14).

bazaar, selling commercial advertising in an exempt organization's magazine, and the operation of factories, bingo games, publishing houses, hotels, radio and television stations, grocery stores, restaurants, newspapers, parking lots, record companies, and cleaners.[180] The regulations state that an activity does not lose its identity as a trade or business merely because it is carried on within a larger aggregate of similar activities or within a larger complex of other endeavors which may or may not be related to the exempt purposes of the organization.[181] Thus, for example, when a church's parking lot is used by the church as a commercial lot during the week, the fees received are income from an unrelated trade or business even though the lot is necessary for the church's exempt purposes. Similarly, commercial advertising does not lose its identity as a trade or business simply because it is contained in a magazine published by an exempt organization.[182]

To be subject to the tax on unrelated business income, an activity constituting a trade or business must be "regularly carried on." The regulations specify that in determining whether a trade or business is regularly carried on, regard must be had to the "frequency and continuity with which the activities . . . are conducted and the manner in which they are pursued."[183] The regulations further stipulate that this requirement must be applied in light of the purpose of the unrelated business income tax to place the business activities of exempt organizations on the same tax basis as the taxable business endeavors with which they compete.[184] Thus, if a particular income-producing activity is of a kind normally conducted by taxable commercial organizations on a year-round basis, the conduct of such activities by an exempt organization over a period of only a few weeks does not constitute the regular carrying on of a trade or business. For example, the operation of a sandwich stand by a church for only two weeks at a county fair is not "regularly carried on" since such a stand would not compete with a similar facility of a commercial organization that ordinarily would operate on a year-round basis.[185] On the other hand, if a particular income-producing activity is of a type that is ordinarily conducted on a seasonable basis by commercial organizations, then a similar activity conducted by a church for a substantial part of the season would be regularly carried on. The IRS maintains that an activity carried on one day a week on a year-round basis, such as the use of a church parking lot for commercial parking every

---

[180]IRS Publication 1018.
[181]Treas. Reg. § 1.513-1(b).
[182]*Id.*
[183]Treas. Reg. § 1.513-1(c)(1).
[184]*Id.*
[185]IRS Publication 1018.

Saturday, is regularly carried on.[186] However, the regulations state that certain intermittent income-producing activities occur so infrequently that they will not be regarded as a trade or business regularly carried on.[187] For example, an income-producing activity lasting for a short period of time and conducted on an annual basis will not be considered regularly carried on.[188]

Finally, to be exempt from the tax on unrelated business income, an activity constituting a trade or business must be substantially related to exempt purposes. The regulations stipulate that for the conduct of a trade or business to be substantially related, the activity must "contribute importantly to the accomplishment of those purposes."[189] If a particular activity does not "contribute importantly" to the accomplishment of an organization's exempt purposes, the income realized from the activity does not derive from the conduct of a "related" trade or business. Whether a particular activity "contributes importantly" to the accomplishment of an organization's exempt purposes depends in each case upon the facts and circumstances involved. The regulations do specify that in determining whether a particular activity contributes importantly to the accomplishment of an exempt purpose, the size and extent of the activity involved must be considered "in relation to the nature and extent of the exempt function which they purport to serve."[190] Thus, where income is realized by an exempt organization from activities that are in part related to the performance of its exempt functions but that are conducted on a larger scale than is reasonably necessary for the performance of such functions, the gross income attributable to that portion of the activities in excess of the needs of exempt functions constitutes gross income from the conduct of an unrelated trade or business.

The IRS maintains that the sale of religious articles and publications with substantial religious content is related to the exempt purposes of a church, as is a church's operation of a religious school since religious training contributes importantly to the exempt purposes of the church.[191] However, it is important to recognize that the accomplishment of a church's exempt purposes does not include a church's need for income or its ultimate use of income. If a church receives income from an unrelated trade or business, the income is taxable even though it is used exclusively for religious purposes such as maintaining the church building, purchasing hymnals, or supporting missions.

---

[186]*Id.*
[187]Treas. Reg. § 1.513-1(c)(2)(iii).
[188]*Id.*
[189]Treas. Reg. § 1.513-1(d)(2).
[190]Treas. Reg. § 1.513-1(d)(3).
[191]IRS Publication 1018.

c. *Exceptions*

Section 513(a) of the Code specifically states that the term *unrelated trade or business* does not include

1. activities in which substantially all the work is performed by unpaid volunteers
2. activities carried on by a church or other charitable organization primarily for the convenience of its members, students, or employees
3. selling merchandise substantially all of which has been received by the exempt organization as gifts or contributions

Several income-producing activities of churches are exempt from the tax on unrelated business income for more than one reason. For example, church bake sales ordinarily are exempt because all of the work is performed by unpaid volunteers, the bakery goods are donated to the church, and the activity is not regularly carried on. Similarly, income from a "thrift shop" operated by a church or other exempt organization ordinarily is exempt from the tax on unrelated business income because all or most of the work is performed by unpaid volunteers and because most of the merchandise sold by the thrift shop is donated. Car washes, fundraising dinners, bazaars, bingo games (if they do not compete with lawful bingo games of for-profit organizations), and many similar income-producing activities of churches are exempt from the tax on unrelated business income because of one or more of the exceptions discussed above or because the activity is not regularly carried on.

In addition, section 512(b) exempts dividends, interest, annuities, royalties, capital gains and losses, and rents from real property from the tax on unrelated business income. These exemptions are limited, however, in two ways. Section 514 of the Code states that the exclusion of dividends, interest, annuities, royalties, rents, and capital gains and losses from the definition of unrelated business income does not apply in the case of unrelated "debt-financed property." *Debt-financed property* is defined as any property held to produce income and that is subject to an "acquisition indebtedness," such as a mortgage, at any time during the tax year.[192] Income derived from debt-financed property generally is included in unrelated business taxable income unless the property falls within one of the following exceptions:

1. Substantially all (eighty-five percent or more) of the property is used for exempt purposes. Property is not used for exempt purposes merely because income derived from the property is expended for exempt purposes. If less than eighty-five percent of the use of property is devoted to exempt purposes,

[192]I.R.C. § 514(b).

only that part of the property that is not used to further exempt purposes is treated as unrelated debt-financed property.[193]

2. Income from debt-financed property is otherwise taken into account in computing the gross income of any unrelated trade or business.

3. The property is used in a trade or business that is substantially supported by volunteer workers; that is carried on primarily for the convenience of its members, students, or employees; or that involves the selling of merchandise substantially all of which has been received by the organization as gifts or contributions.[194]

In addition, the Code specifies that if a church acquires real property for the principal purpose of using it substantially for exempt purposes within fifteen years of the time of acquisition, the property is not treated as unrelated debt-financed property even though it may otherwise meet the definition. Furthermore, contrary to the rule applicable to other exempt organizations, the property need not be located in the vicinity of the church.[195]

The second limitation relates to the interest, annuities, royalties, and rents of organizations that are controlled by a tax-exempt organization. Under section 512(b)(13) of the Code, the exclusion of interest, annuities, royalties, and rents from the definition of unrelated business income may not apply if such amounts are derived from organizations that are controlled by a church or other tax-exempt organization. The regulation states that in the case of a nonstock organization the term *control* means that at least eighty percent of the directors or trustees of such organization are either representatives of or directly or indirectly controlled by an exempt organization. A trustee or director is controlled by an exempt organization if the organization has the power to remove the trustee or director and designate a new trustee or director. In general, if a tax-exempt organization has control of another organization, the interest, annuities, royalties, and rents received by the controlling organization from the controlled organization are taxable at a specific ratio depending on whether the controlled organization is exempt or nonexempt.[196]

---

[193]*See generally* IRS Publication 598; Treas. Reg. § 1.514(b)-1(b)(1).

[194]I.R.C. § 514(b)(1).

[195]I.R.C. § 514(b)(3)(E).

[196]Regulation 1.512(b)-1(*l*) stipulates that if the controlled organization is exempt from taxation under section 501 of the Code and if its taxable income (computed as if the organization were not exempt from tax) exceeds its unrelated business taxable income, then the controlling organization must report as unrelated business taxable income the portion of the interest, annuities, royalties, and rents that it receives from the controlled organization that bears the same ratio as the controlled organization's unrelated business taxable income bears to its taxable income. If the controlled organization's unrelated business taxable income equals or exceeds its taxable income, then the controlling

### d. *Computation of the Tax*

Section 511 imposes a tax on "unrelated business taxable income." Section 512 defines *unrelated business taxable income* as the gross income derived from any unrelated trade or business regularly carried on less the deductions directly connected with such trade or business, both computed with the modifications set forth in section 512(b). To qualify as an allowable deduction, an expense must qualify as an income tax deduction and be directly connected with the carrying on of the unrelated trade or business. Expenses that are incurred to carry out both an unrelated trade or business and an organization's exempt functions must be allocated between the two uses on a reasonable basis. For example, if an exempt organization pays its president an annual salary of $20,000, and the president devotes approximately ten percent of his time to an unrelated trade or business conducted by the organization, a deduction of $2,000 (10% of $20,000) would be allowable as a salary expense in computing unrelated business taxable income.

Expenses attributable to an unrelated trade or business that exploits exempt activities for commercial gain, such as the sale of commercial advertising in the periodical of an exempt organization, are deductible if (1) the unrelated trade or business is the kind carried on for profit by taxable organizations, (2) the activity being exploited is of a type normally carried on by taxable corporations, (3) the expenses exceed the income from or attributable to the exempt activity, and (4) the allocation of the excess expenses to the unrelated business does not result in a loss from the unrelated trade or business. Thus, the expenses are allocated first to the exempt activity to the extent of any income derived from or attributable to that activity. Any excess expense is allocated to the unrelated business, but only to the extent that the allocation does not result in a loss carryover or carryback to the unrelated business.

In addition to allowable deductions, an exempt organization is entitled to various "modifications" in computing unrelated business taxable income. These include (1) dividends, interest, annuities, and royalties, except with respect to the limitations that apply in connection with debt-financed property and controlled organizations;[197] (2) rents from real property; (3) capital gains and losses; (4) charitable contributions of up to five percent of unrelated business taxable income; and (5) a specific deduction of $1,000.

Once all available deductions and modifications have been considered and

---

organization must report all of the interest, annuities, royalties, and rents it receives from the controlled organization as unrelated business taxable income. The computation of the controlled organization's taxable income and its unrelated business taxable income are made without regard to any amounts paid directly or indirectly to the controlling organization.

[197]These limitations were discussed earlier in the present chapter.

unrelated business taxable income is determined, the tax is computed by multiplying unrelated business taxable income times the corporate income tax rates. Presently the corporate tax rate is 15% of so much of an organization's taxable income as does not exceed $25,000; 18% of taxable income exceeding $25,000 but less than $50,000; 30% of taxable income exceeding $50,000 but less than $75,000; 40% of taxable income exceeding $75,000 but less than $100,000; and 46% of taxable income exceeding $100,000. [198]

### e. Returns

To report income received from an unrelated trade or business, all churches receiving $1,000 or more in net income from unrelated business must file IRS Form 990-T on or before the fifteenth day of the fifth month following the close of the organization's tax year. Thus, a church that ends its accounting year on December 31 is required to file a Form 990-T by May 15 of the following year. Extensions of time for filing the return are available upon filing a Form 7004. Penalties and interest may be assessed for failure to file a timely return.

### f. Effect on Tax-Exempt Status

A tax-exempt organization will not lose its exempt status by engaging in an unrelated trade or business so long as the trade or business does not constitute more than an insubstantial part of its activities.

### g. IRS Audits

As was noted in a previous chapter, [199] the IRS possesses authority under section 7605(c) of the Internal Revenue Code to audit the books of account of a church or convention or association of churches "to determine whether such organization may be engaged in the carrying on of an unrelated trade or business . . . ." Section 301.7605-1(c)(2) of the income tax regulations specifies that the IRS may conduct such an audit only if it (1) has some reasonable basis for believing that a church or convention or association of churches is engaged in an unrelated trade or business, and (2) notifies the church or convention or association of churches in writing at least thirty days prior to the audit.

### §C. Social Security

The subject of social security taxes has been discussed fully in another chapter. [200] It will suffice for purposes of the present chapter to repeat that services

[198] I.R.C. § 11(b).
[199] See chapter 8, § C, supra.
[200] See chapter 8, § C, and chapter 10, § B, supra.

performed in the employ of a religious, charitable, or educational organization are exempt from social security taxes through December 31, 1983, unless the exemption is waived. The exemption can be waived through the filing of IRS Forms SS-15 and SS-15a, or through the intentional or inadvertent payment of social security taxes on any employee.

However, the Social Security Act amendments of 1983 removed the exemption of services performed in the employ of a religious, charitable, or educational organization from social security taxes. Thus, beginning on January 1, 1984, all churches and religious organizations must pay social security taxes on the wages of nonministerial employees. A minister is deemed self-employed for social security purposes, and therefore his church does not pay social security taxes on his wages even if he otherwise is treated as an employee and has not waived his personal exemption from social security on the basis of religious conviction.

## §D. Unemployment Taxes

As has been noted elsewhere,[201] service performed in the employ of a church or other religious organization is not subject to the federal unemployment tax provisions. In addition, nearly every state unemployment tax law specifically exempts churches from the tax by excluding "services performed in the employ of a church" from the definition of employment.

## §E. State Taxes

### 1. STATE INCOME TAXES

Most states impose a tax on the gross income of corporations. Although nearly all the income of most religious organizations is in the form of gifts that generally are excludable from the donee organization's income, most states expressly exempt religious organizations from the tax on corporate income. Some state corporate income tax laws exempt any corporation that is exempt from federal income tax.[202] Others specifically exempt various charitable organizations, including religious and educational organizations.[203] A number of states impose a tax on the "unrelated business income" of exempt organizations.[204]

---

[201]See chapter 10, § C, supra.

[202]COLO. REV. STAT. § 39-22-117; GA. CODE § 92-3105; IND. CODE § 6-3-2-3; KAN. STAT. ANN. § 79-32,113; MD. ANN. CODE art. 81, § 288; MICH. STAT. ANN. § 208.35.

[203]ARIZ. REV. STAT. ANN. §§ 20-1566, 43-1201; IOWA CODE § 422.34; N.C. GEN. STAT. §§ 57-14, 105-130.11; S.C. CODE ANN. § 12-7-330.

[204]COLO. REV. STAT. § 39-22-117; KAN. STAT. ANN. § 79-32,113; MD. ANN. CODE art. 81, § 288(d)(5); ORE. REV. STAT. § 317.920.

## 2. State Sales Taxes

Most states impose a tax on the sale of tangible personal property or the rendering of various services for compensation. Sales made *to* religious organizations are exempted from sales taxes in many states.[205] A few states exempt sales made *by* religious organizations,[206] and a few others exempt sales *to or by* religious organizations.[207] Many states that exempt sales of property made to religious organizations stipulate that the exemption is available only if the organization uses the purchased property for exempt purposes.[208] Some states are even more restrictive. For example, one state limits the exemption to sales made by a religious organization to its members in furtherance of the organization's exempt purposes or involving products that are not sold by taxable organizations.[209] Another state limits the exemption to fundraising sales of religious organizations.[210] Other states limit the exemption to sales made to domestic religious corporations;[211] to sales of Bibles, hymnals, prayerbooks, or textbooks to religious organizations;[212] and to the sales of items used in religious worship or education.[213]

The exemption of religious organizations from state sales taxes is available only to bona fide religious organizations, and ordinarily is available only to those organizations that make application. It has been held that a religious organization was properly denied an exemption from a state's sales tax when it refused to submit sufficient information with its exemption application to establish that it was in fact a religious organization.[214]

## 3. Property Taxes

The exemption of religious organizations from property taxes is a practice that dates back to ancient times. The Bible records that "Joseph made it a law

[205]Colo. Rev. Stat. § 39-26-102; Conn. Gen. Stat. § 12-408; Tenn. Code Ann. § 67-3014; Tex. Tax Code Ann. title 2, § 151.310.

[206]Ark. Stat. Ann. § 84-1904; N.M. Stat. Ann. §§ 7-9-12 to 7-9-42. Ohio Rev. Code Ann. § 5739.02 (if the number of sale days does not exceed six in any calendar year or one in any calendar quarter).

[207]Mo. Rev. Stat. § 144.030; Okla. Stat. Ann. title 68, § 1356. *See generally* Annot., 54 A.L.R.3d 1204 (1974).

[208]Minn. Stat. § 297A; Pa. Stat. Ann. title 72, § 7204; Utah Code Ann. § 59-15-6.

[209]Ill. Rev. Stat. ch. 120, para. 440.

[210]Ga. Code § 92-2150.3.

[211]Md. Tax. & Rev. Code Ann. §§ 81-324 to 81-326.

[212]N.D. Cent. Code § 57-39.2-04.

[213]Va. Code § 58.441.6.

[214]First Lutheran Mission v. Department of Revenue, 613 P.2d 351 (Colo. 1980).

over the land of Egypt . . . that Pharaoh should have the fifth part; except the land of the priests only, which became not Pharaoh's."[215] The emperor Constantine exempted churches from property taxes in the fourth century.[216] Medieval Europe generally exempted church property from property taxes.[217] This tradition of exemption was adopted by the American colonies.[218] All fifty states presently recognize some form of exemption of religious organizations from property taxes.[219] Most states have adopted constitutional or statutory provisions that exempt real and personal property used exclusively for religious purposes from property taxes.[220] Some states have adopted narrower exemptions. For example, a number of states exempt only houses of religious worship.[221] One state limits the exemption to buildings used for religious worship and the surrounding property up to a maximum of one acre.[222] Several states specifically exempt parsonages from the property tax, but in most cases this exemption is limited to parsonages owned by churches and thus is not available to privately owned ministers' residences.[223] A minister who purchased his church's parsonage and had the title conveyed to himself and his wife as trustees of the church, with the understanding that if he ever left the church then the church would buy the property back by paying him the purchase price he had paid plus the appreciation value, was held not to be entitled to a property tax exemption since in reality the "parsonage" was owned by a private individual and not by the church.[224] A minister of course is entitled to exclude a housing allowance for federal income tax purposes even though he owns his home.

---

[215]*Genesis* 47:26 (KJV).

[216]A. STOKES & L. PFEFFER, CHURCH AND STATE IN THE UNITED STATES 546 (1964).

[217]*See generally* Stimson, *The Exemption of Property From Taxation in the United States,* 18 MINN. L. REV. 411 (1934).

[218]*See generally* C. ANTIEAU, A. DOWNEY, & E. ROBERTS, FREEDOM FROM FEDERAL ESTABLISHMENT 20-21, 73-74, 175 (1964).

[219]*See* Walz v. Tax Commission, 397 U.S. 664, 676 (1970).

[220]*See, e.g.,* ALA. CODE § 40-9-1; ALASKA STAT. § 29.53.020; CONN. GEN. STAT. § 12-81; ILL. REV. STAT. ch. 120, para. 500.2; KAN. STAT. ANN. § 79-201; MISS. CODE ANN. § 27-31-1; MO. REV. STAT. § 137.100; NEB. REV. STAT. § 77-202; OKLA. STAT. ANN. title 68, § 2405.

[221]ARK. STAT. ANN. § 84-206; FLA. STAT. ANN. § 196; GA. CODE § 92-201; MASS. GEN. LAWS ANN. ch. 59, § 5; MICH. STAT. ANN. § 211.7; MONT. REV. CODES ANN. §§ 15-6-201 to 15-6-209; N.C. GEN. STAT. § 105-278; PA. STAT. ANN. title 72, § 5020-204; R.I. GEN. LAWS § 44-3-3.

[222]R.I. GEN. LAWS § 44-3-3.

[223]ARK. STAT. ANN. § 84-206; GA. CODE § 92-201; MD. ANN. CODE art. 81 § 9; N.J. REV. STAT. § 54:4-3.6; N.Y. REAL PROP. TAX LAW §§ 421a, 438; TENN. CODE ANN. § 67-513; TEX. TAX CODE ANN. title 1, § 11.20; WIS. STAT. § 70.11; WYO. STAT. § 39-1-201.

[224]Watts v. Board of Assessors, 414 N.E.2d 1003 (Mass. 1981).

Generally, the term *parsonage* refers to church-owned dwellings provided to clergymen and thus a property tax exemption that refers to "parsonages" may reasonably be construed to apply only to church-owned dwellings.[225] Some states stipulate that the exemption of parsonages is available only up to a prescribed dollar value.[226] Church-owned parsonages may be considered exempt from property taxation even though they enjoy no specific statutory exemption. For example, one court has held that a church-owned parsonage that served various religious purposes, such as a meeting place for church groups and as a place for providing religious services including pastoral counseling, was exempted from taxation by the general exemption of property used exclusively for religious purposes.[227] But several other courts have held that parsonages are taxable unless they are specifically exempted.[228]

In general, to be exempt from property taxation a parsonage must be actually and exclusively used as an integral part of the operations of the church rather than as a mere convenience to a clergyman.[229] To illustrate, one court held that a dwelling used for several hours a week by a clergyman for commercial purposes did not qualify for a property tax exemption.[230] However, one court upheld the exemption of a parsonage even though the clergyman's wife engaged in a part-time interior designing business and occasionally used a bedroom for business purposes.[231]

Some courts have held that the term *parsonage* applies only to a dwelling provided by a local church to its full-time minister and thus does not apply to the dwelling place of a full-time evangelist,[232] an executive of a religious de-

---

[225]East Coast Conference of the Evangelical Covenant Church of America, Inc. v. Supervisor of Assessments, 388 A.2d 177 (Md. 1978); In re Marlow, 237 S.E.2d 57 (S.C. 1977); St. Matthew Lutheran Church v. Delhi Township, 257 N.W.2d 183 (Mich. 1977).

[226]COLO. REV. STAT. §§ 39-3-101 to 39-3-102 (up to $16,000); R.I. GEN. LAWS § 44-3-3 (up to $50,000).

[227]Immanuel Baptist Church v. Glass, 497 P.2d 757 (Okla. 1972).

[228]*See, e.g.,* Congregation B'Nai Jeshurun v. Board of Review, 301 N.W.2d 755 (Iowa 1981); Borough of Harvey Cedars v. Sisters of Charity, 395 A.2d 518 (N.J. 1978) (summer residences); Salt Lake County v. Tax Commission ex rel. Good Shepherd Lutheran Church, 548 P.2d 630 (Utah 1976).

[229]Clinton Township v. Camp Brett-Endeavor, Inc., 1 N.J. Tax 54 (1980); German Apostolic Christian Church v. Department of Revenue, 569 P.2d 596 (Ore. 1977).

[230]Ballard v. Supervisor of Assessments, 306 A.2d 506 (Md. 1973).

[231]Congregation Beth Mayer, Inc. v. Board of Assessors, 417 N.Y.S.2d 754 (1979).

[232]Blackwood Brothers Evangelistic Association v. State Board of Equalization, 614 S.W.2d 364 (Tenn. 1980).

nomination,[233] or a minister employed by a religious denomination to establish new churches in a particular region.[234] Other courts have construed the term *parsonage* more broadly, including within the term dwellings owned by a religious denomination and used by denominational executives.[235]

Church-owned parsonages used by ordained ministers of music have been held to qualify for exemption under a statute exempting parsonages from property taxation.[236] However, parsonages used by unordained ministers of music have been held not to qualify for exemption.[237] Similarly, church-owned dwellings used by a superintendent of a church-operated school,[238] an instructor at a church-operated school,[239] an unordained youth minister,[240] the widow of a deceased minister,[241] and a church sexton[242] have been held not to qualify for exempt status.

Generally the courts have held that a church is not limited to one parsonage. Thus, a church having two or more full-time ministers ordinarily may provide a tax-free parsonage to each.[243]

Other forms of church-owned property have presented more difficult questions. For example, is a large tract of vacant land owned by a church exempt from property taxation under a statute that exempts property "used exclusively for religious purposes"? A number of courts have held that vacant land ordinarily is not used exclusively for religious purposes and thus does not qualify for

[233]Pentecostal Church of God of America v. Hughlett, 601 S.W.2d 666 (Mo. 1980); Pacific Northwest Annual Conference of the United Methodist Church v. Walla Walla County, 508 P.2d 1361 (Wash. 1973).

[234]East Coast Conference of Evangelical Covenant Church of America, Inc. v. Supervisor of Assessments, 388 A.2d 177 (Md. 1978).

[235]McCreless v. City of San Antonio, 454 S.W.2d 393 (Tex. 1970); Cudlipp v. City of Richmond, 180 S.E.2d 525 (Va. 1971).

[236]City of Amarillo v. Paramount Terrace Christian Church, 530 S.W.2d 323 (Tex. 1975).

[237]In re Marlow, 237 S.E.2d 57 (S.C. 1977).

[238]St. Matthew Lutheran Church v. Delhi Township, 257 N.W.2d 183 (Mich. 1977).
[239]Id.

[240]Id. See also Borough of Cresskill v. Northern Valley Evangelical Free Church, 312 A.2d 641 (N.J. 1973).
[241]Id.

[242]Episcopal Parish of Christ Church v. Kinney, 389 N.E.2d 847 (Ohio 1979).

[243]Congregation B'Nai Jacob v. City of Oak Park, 302 N.W.2d 296 (Mich. 1981); In re Marlow, 237 S.E.2d 57 (S.C. 1977); Cudlipp v. City of Richmond, 180 S.E. 525 (Va. 1971).

exemption.[244] Similarly, a religious organization that owned farm land from which it derived income was required to pay property taxes on such land.[245]

Church-owned camp grounds have presented considerable difficulty. It is the prevailing view that a camp ground or retreat center owned and operated by a religious organization is exempt from property taxation in jurisdictions that allow an exemption for property used exclusively for religious purposes[246] if all the activities conducted on the property are directly related to the religious purposes for which the organization was established.

A few courts have denied exempt status to camp grounds. In one case, exemption was denied to a 155-acre church camp used for recreational, craft, and religious activities since the property tax law exempted only actual places of religious worship from the tax.[247] Another court denied exemption to a church camp that derived twenty-five percent of its income from nonexempt uses since the nonexempt uses cumulatively were substantial enough to preclude a finding that the property was used exclusively for religious purposes.[248] Any portion of a church camp that is owned by private individuals will not be exempt from property taxation, even if the individuals are members or adherents of the church that owns the camp.[249] And if a religious organization is not actually using a portion of its camp grounds, there is legal basis for the position that only the portion that actually is being used is entitled to an exemption.[250]

The taxability of property owned by a religious organization and used for publishing activities has also been a source of some confusion. Again, most courts have held that property owned by a religious organization and used for

[244]Seventh-Day Adventists Kansas Conference Association v. Board of County Commissioners, 508 P.2d 911 (Kan. 1973); St. Matthew Lutheran Church v. Delhi Township, 257 N.W.2d 183 (Mich. 1977).

[245]Kunes v. Mesa Stake of Church of Jesus Christ of Latter-Day Saints, 498 P.2d 525 (Ariz. 1972); Corporation of Presiding Bishop of Church of Jesus Christ of Latter-Day Saints v. Department of Revenue, 556 P.2d 685 (Ore. 1976).

[246]North Idaho Jurisdiction of Episcopal Churches, Inc. v. Kootenai County, 496 P.2d 105 (Idaho 1972); Jewish Community Centers Association v. State Tax Commission, 520 S.W.2d 23 (Mo. 1975); Order Minor Conventuals v. Lee, 409 N.Y.S.2d 667 (1978); Gospel Volunteers, Inc. v. Village of Speculator, 324 N.Y.S.2d 412 (1971); Greater New York Corporation of Seventh-Day Adventists v. Town of Dover, 288 N.Y.S.2d 334 (1968), appeal dismissed, 295 N.Y.S.2d 932 (1968); Appeal of Laymen's Weekend Retreat League, 343 A.2d 714 (Pa. 1975).

[247]Davies v. Meyer, 541 S.W.2d 827 (Tex. 1976) (a chapel and a minister's residence located on the property were deemed exempt).

[248]Mount Tremper Lutheran Camp, Inc. v. Board of Assessors, 417 N.Y.S.2d 796 (1979).

[249]Alton Bay Camp Meeting Association v. Town of Alton, 242 A.2d 80 (N.H. 1968).

[250]Lake Louise Christian Community v. Township of Hudson, 159 N.W.2d 849 (Mich. 1968).

essentially religious purposes is exempt under statutes that exempt property used exclusively for religious purposes. Thus the following printing operations have been held to be exempt from tax: a printing facility owned by a religious denomination and which printed religious periodicals and Sunday school materials for affiliated churches;[251] a printing facility that promoted religion;[252] a printing facility that published two magazines devoted to religious purposes with no diversion to commercial or secular uses, even though the magazines contained some political and economic views;[253] and a church-owned printing facility that published a weekly newspaper informing members of the work of the church.[254] However, one court denied exemption to a Bible society that printed and distributed Bibles but that was not affiliated with any particular religion or denomination.[255] It is unlikely that a church-owned printing facility would qualify for an exemption in those states that exempt only buildings and property used exclusively for religious worship.

The courts have held that the regional and national administrative offices of a religious denomination are exempt under a statute exempting property used exclusively for religious purposes.[256] However, where a statute exempts only buildings used for religious worship, the exemption is not available.[257]

Religious bookstores[258] and church-operated retirement homes[259] have been denied exemption under statutes exempting only buildings used for religious

[251]Himes v. Free Methodist Publishing House, 251 N.E.2d 486 (Ind. 1969); Christian Reformed Church in North America v. City of Grand Rapids, 303 N.W.2d 913 (Mich. 1981) (press sold all products at cost and operated at a loss).

[252]State Board of Tax Commissioners v. Warner Press, Inc., 248 N.E.2d 405 (Ind. 1969), modified, 258 N.E.2d 621 (Ind. 1970).

[253]America Press, Inc. v. Lewisohn, 345 N.Y.S.2d 396 (1973), aff'd, 372 N.Y.S.2d 194 (1975).

[254]Archdiocese of Portland v. Department of Revenue, 513 P.2d 1137 (Ore. 1973).

[255]American Bible Society v. Lewisohn, 369 N.Y.S.2d 725 (1975), aff'd, 386 N.Y.S.2d 49 (1976).

[256]Kansas City District Advisory Board, Church of the Nazarene v. Board of County Commissioners, 620 P.2d 344 (Kan. 1980) (an adjoining camp that was not used exclusively for religious purposes and a caretaker's residence were not exempted); Board of Trustees of the Kansas East Conference of the United Methodist Church v. Cogswell, 473 P.2d 1 (Kan. 1970).

[257]Leggett v. Macon Baptist Association, Inc., 205 S.E.2d 197 (Ga. 1974).

[258]Swearingen v. City of Texarkana, 596 S.W.2d 157 (Tex. 1979).

[259]Retirement Ranch, Inc. v. Curry County Valuation Protest Board, 546 P.2d 1199 (N.M. 1976), cert. denied, 549 P.2d 284 (N.M. 1976).

worship. Parochial schools,[260] credit unions,[261] recreational facilities,[262] bookstores,[263] and retirement homes[264] have been denied exemption under statutes exempting property used exclusively for religious purposes.

Many statutes exempt property "used exclusively" for religious purposes. An *exclusive use* generally is construed to mean a primary, inherent, or principal use in contrast to secondary or incidental uses.[265] It has been held that the term *exclusively* does not necessarily mean "directly" or "immediately,"[266] that a use that is incidental and reasonably necessary to an exempt use is properly exempted from tax,[267] and that the exemption of property used exclusively for exempt purposes does not require constant activity or vigorous or obvious activity but rather requires that the property be devoted to no other use than that which warrants the exemption.[268] If part of church-owned property is used for commercial purposes, it cannot be deemed "used exclusively" for religious purposes.[269] And, if a church rents out a portion of its property, the property rented does not qualify for exemption.[270]

Many jurisdictions recognize the "partial exemption" doctrine. Under this doctrine, property that is used in part for exclusively religious purposes is entitled to a partial exemption based upon the percentage of use or occupancy that is devoted to an exempt use.[271] To illustrate, where one substantial part

[260]Immaculate Heart of Mary High School, Inc. v. Anderson, 526 P.2d 831 (Idaho 1974); Seventh-Day Adventist Kansas Conference Association v. Board of County Commissioners, 508 P.2d 911 (Kan. 1973).

[261]Central Credit Union v. Comptroller of the Treasury, 220 A.2d 568 (Md. 1966).

[262]Peninsula Covenant Church v. County of San Mateo, 156 Cal. Rptr. 431 (1979) (swimming pool, five tennis courts, and locker rooms).

[263]Berean Fundamental Church Council, Inc. v. Board of Equalization, 183 N.W.2d 750 (Neb. 1971).

[264]Evangelical Lutheran Good Samaritan Society v. County of Gage, 151 N.W.2d 446 (Neb. 1967).

[265]Pentecostal Church of God of America v. Hughlett, 601 S.W.2d 666 (Mo. 1980); Order Minor Conventuals v. Lee, 409 N.Y.S.2d 667 (1978).

[266]Seventh-Day Adventist Kansas Conference Association v. Board of County Commissioners, 508 P.2d 911 (Kan. 1973).

[267]San Francisco Boys' Club, Inc. v. County of Mendocino, 62 Cal. Rptr. 294 (Cal. 1967).

[268]Wildlife Preserves, Inc. v. Scopelliti, 321 N.Y.S.2d 1004 (1971).

[269]Greater Anchorage Area Borough v. Sisters of Charity, 553 P.2d 467 (Alaska 1976).

[270]Tusculum College v. State Board of Equalization, 600 S.W.2d 739 (Tenn. 1980).

[271]Burgess v. Four States Memorial Hospital, 465 S.W.2d 693 (Ark. 1971); Fraternal Order of Eagles v. Holland, 226 N.W.2d 22 (Iowa 1975); Ruston Hospital, Inc. v. Riser, 191 So.2d 665 (La. 1966); Nebraska Conference Association of Seventh-Day Adventists v. Board of Equalization, 211 N.W.2d 613 (Neb. 1973); Town of Swanzey v. City of Keene, 339 A.2d 25 (N.H. 1975); Independent Church of the Realization of the Word of God, Inc. v. Board of Assessors, 437 N.Y.S.2d 435 (1981).

of a building was used by a religious organization and another substantial part
was used for commercial purposes, the building was taxable on a pro-rata
basis.[272] Some courts hold that if any part of a building is used for commercial
purposes, then the entire facility is subject to tax.[273]

A number of courts have stated that a liberal and not a harsh or restrictive
construction is to be given to the term *religious* in the exemption provisions
of property tax statutes.[274] Nevertheless, religious organizations that in reality
are tax-evading shams will not benefit from property tax exemptions. Thus,
one court held that a purported religious organization that was organized primarily for tax avoidance purposes; that had no sacraments, rituals, educational
classes, religious meetings, or trained clergy; and that did not require any belief
in a supreme being was not entitled to exemption.[275]

It is important to emphasize that most exemptions are based on the use to
which property is put. Courts often observe that use rather than ownership of
property determines the availability of an exemption.[276] It is also commonly
held that the objects or purposes of an organization are not controlling in
determining the availability of a property tax exemption. Again, it is the actual
use to which property is put that is controlling.[277]

Finally, the exemption of property used exclusively for religious purposes
or for religious worship has been challenged on a number of occasions on the
ground that such exemptions violate the First Amendment's nonestablishment
of religion clause. The Supreme Court historically viewed such challenges as
frivolous.[278] In 1970, the Court agreed to hear a challenge to the constitutionality
of New York's statute that exempted from taxation all property used exclusively
for religious purposes. With only one dissenting vote, the Court upheld the
constitutionality of this exemption provision.[279]

---

[272]Sisters of Charity v. County of Bernalillo, 596 P.2d 255 (N.M. 1979).

[273]Greater Anchorage Area Borough v. Sisters of Charity, 553 P.2d 467 (Alaska 1976).

[274]Lutheran Campus Council v. Board of County Commissioners, 174 N.W.2d 362
(N.D. 1970).

[275]Ideal Life Church v. County of Washington, 304 N.W.2d 308 (Minn. 1981).

[276]United Presbyterian Association v. Board of County Commissioners, 448 P.2d 967
(Colo. 1968).

[277]Southside Church of Christ v. Des Moines Board of Review, 243 N.W.2d 650 (Iowa
1976).

[278]Walz v. Tax Commission, 397 U.S. 664, 686 n.6 (1970).

[279]For a detailed discussion of the *Walz* case, see chapter 15, *infra*.

# Part Three

---

# Church and State

# 15

# A SUMMARY OF CONSTITUTIONAL HISTORY

Congress shall make no law respecting an establishment of religion, or prohibiting the free exercise thereof . . . .[1]

The First Amendment religion clauses were the product of the egalitarian and individualistic fervor of the fledgling Republic. The federal government— "Congress"— would never be able to commit the sin of certain of the colonies: establishment of an official religion. Correlatively, the right of each citizen to "freely exercise" his religion was protected from federal encroachment. Justice Stewart, dissenting in the *Schempp* case, observed:

As a matter of history, the First Amendment was adopted solely as a limitation upon the newly created National Government. The events leading to its adoption strongly suggest that the Establishment Clause was primarily an attempt to insure that Congress not only would be powerless to establish a national church, but would also be unable to interfere with existing state establishments.[2]

Justice Reed, dissenting in the *McCollum* case,[3] observed:

[1]U.S. CONST. amend. I (1791).

[2]School District of Abington v. Schempp, 374 U.S. 203, 309-10 (1963). *See also* Jaffree v. Board of School Commissioners, 554 F. Supp. 1104 (S.D. Ala. 1983) (extensive historical analysis), *stay granted,* ___ U.S. ___ (1983); R. CORD, SEPARATION OF CHURCH AND STATE: HISTORICAL FACT AND CURRENT FICTION (1982); McClellan, *The Making and the Unmaking of the Establishment Clause,* in A BLUEPRINT FOR JUDICIAL REFORM (P. McGuigan & R. Rader eds. 1982).

[3]People of State of Illinois ex rel. McCollum v. Board of Education, 333 U.S. 203, 244 (1948).

The phrase "an establishment of religion" may have been intended by Congress to be aimed only at a state church. When the First Amendment was pending in Congress in substantially its present form, "Mr. Madison said, he apprehended the meaning of the words to be, that Congress should not establish a religion, and enforce the legal observation of it by law, nor compel men to worship God in any manner contrary to their conscience." Passing years, however, have brought about acceptance of a broader meaning . . . .[4]

Justice Story, writing early in our nation's history, noted that "the real object of the [first] amendment was . . . to prevent any national ecclesiastical establishment, which would give to an hierarchy the exclusive patronage of the national government."[5]

This construction of the intent of the framers of the religion clauses is supported by the absence of judicial opinions interpreting these clauses for the first one and a half centuries following their enactment. Prayers, Bible readings, and religious instruction in the public schools; rental of public facilities by church groups; religious symbols on public property; tax exemptions for religious organizations; and state assistance to religious education were seldom if ever challenged since such practices were plainly far from the congressional establishment of a national religion prohibited by the First Amendment. In a related context, the Supreme Court has observed that "[i]f a thing has been practiced for two hundred years by common consent, it will need a strong case for the Constitution to affect it."[6]

Other judges, however, have interpreted the historical precedent as supporting a much broader interpretation of the establishment clause.[7] Many would concur with Justice Brennan's conclusion that a too literal quest for the advice of the Founding Fathers upon these issues is futile and misdirected since "the historical record is at best ambiguous, and statements can readily be found to support either side of the proposition."[8] Nevertheless, Justice Brennan con-

---

[4]Justice Douglas, concurring in Engel v. Vitale, 370 U.S. 421, 442 (1962), remarked: "I cannot say that to authorize this prayer is to establish a religion in the strictly historic meaning of those words. A religion is not established in the usual sense merely by letting those who choose to do so say the prayer that the public school teacher leads."

[5]J. STORY, COMMENTARIES ON THE CONSTITUTION 728 (1833).

[6]Jackman v. Rosenbaum Co., 260 U.S. 22, 31 (1922). See also Coler v. Corn Exchange Bank, 250 N.Y. 136, 138 (1928) (Cardozo, J.) ("Not lightly vacated is the verdict of quiescent years.").

[7]Everson v. Board of Education, 330 U.S. 1, 31 (1947) (Rutledge, J., dissenting); People of State of Illinois ex rel. McCollum v. Board of Education, 333 U.S. 203, 212 (Frankfurter, J., concurring).

[8]School District of Abington v. Schempp, 374 U.S. 203, 237 (Brennan, J., concurring).

ceded that the framers of the First Amendment were "preoccupied" with the "imminent question of established churches."[9]

Three factors have considerably broadened the meaning and effect of the First Amendment's religion clauses, and particularly the establishment clause. The first occurred in 1803 when the United States Supreme Court ruled that "an act of the legislature, repugnant to the Constitution, is void," and that the federal judiciary was to be the ultimate interpreter of the Constitution.[10] Thereafter, federal judges had the power—nowhere given in the Constitution itself— to invalidate national or state legislation that they deemed inconsistent with the Constitution. A law that established a religion, violated an individual's right to freely exercise his religion, or contravened any other provision of the Constitution could be invalidated by a federal court. The nature of the American polity had been redefined.

The second factor that considerably extended the scope of the First Amendment was the judge-made doctrine of "incorporation," expressed in 1937 in the landmark case of *Palko v. Connecticut*.[11] The Supreme Court ruled in *Palko* that those provisions of the Bill of Rights—the first ten amendments to the federal Constitution—that were "implicit in the concept of ordered liberty" were incorporated into the Fourteenth Amendment's due process clause and thus became applicable to the states.[12] This decision was of fundamental significance, for the framers of the Bill of Rights never intended these amendments to apply to the states. Chief Justice Marshall himself, the author of *Marbury v. Madison*,[13] observed over a century prior to *Palko* that the Bill of Rights "contain no expression indicating an intention to apply them to the state governments. This court cannot so apply them."[14] Marshall's admonition was ig-

---

[9]*Id.*

[10]Marbury v. Madison, 1 Cranch 137 (1803).

[11]302 U.S. 319 (1937).

[12]The Fourteenth Amendment provides in part: "[N]or shall any State deprive any person of life, liberty, or property, without due process of law . . . ." It is important to note that the Fourteenth Amendment is a limitation on the power of "States." By comparison, the Bill of Rights, including the First Amendment, was intended to be a limitation solely upon the power of Congress.

[13]*See* note 10, *supra*, and accompanying test.

[14]Barron v. Mayor and City Council, 32 U.S. (7 Pet.) 243 (1833). *See also* Adamson v. California, 332 U.S. 46 (1947), in which Justice Frankfurter observed:
    Those reading the English language with the meaning which it ordinarily conveys, those conversant with the political and legal history of the concept of due process, those sensitive to the relations of the States to the central government as well as the relation of some of the provisions of the Bill of Rights to the process of justice, would hardly recognize the Fourteenth Amendment as a cover for the various explicit provisions of the first eight amendments. . . . The notion that the Fourteenth Amendment was a covert way of imposing upon the States all the rules

nored by a majority of the Supreme Court in *Palko*. In 1940, the Court concluded that the religion clauses of the First Amendment were "implicit in the concept of ordered liberty," and accordingly concluded that they were limitations upon state as well as federal action.[15] Thus, since 1940, no state "can make a law respecting the establishment of religion or prohibiting the free exercise thereof . . . ." And, significantly, the term *state* has been construed to mean any subdivision or agency of a state. The First Amendment thereby applies to cities, counties, boards of education, and every other level, department, office, or agency of government.

A third factor that has extended the reach of the First Amendment's establishment clause is the willingness of the federal courts, since 1948, to liberalize the concept of "establishment" to such a degree as to prohibit conduct that had been deemed consistent with the First Amendment for over a century and a half.

But the establishment clause is not the only religion clause contained in the First Amendment. There is another: "Congress shall make no law . . . prohibiting the free exercise [of religion]." This latter clause—the "free exercise clause"—is fundamentally incompatible with the philosophy of disestablishment contained in the establishment clause: disestablishment necessarily restricts the free exercise of religion. Thus, the recent judicial emphasis upon disestablishment has at times collided with free exercise interests and with other express and implied rights (speech, assembly, association) contained in the First Amendment. Chief Justice Burger, in *Walz v. Tax Commission*,[16] noted this underlying tension: "The Court has struggled to find a neutral course between the two Religion Clauses, both of which are cast in absolute terms, and either of which, if expanded to a logical extreme, would tend to clash with the other." Similarly, Justice Stewart, dissenting in *Schempp*,[17] observed: "[T]here are areas in which a doctrinaire reading of the Establishment Clause leads to irreconcilable conflict with the Free Exercise Clause." The Supreme Court has attempted to synthesize the religion clauses by emphasizing the concepts of "neutrality" and "accommodation." Thus, the Court has observed:

> The general principle deductible from the First Amendment and all that has been said by the Court is this: that we will not tolerate either governmentally established religion or governmental interference with religion. Short of those expressly pro-

---

which it seemed important to Eighteenth Century statesmen to write into the Federal Amendments, was rejected by judges who were themselves witnesses of the process by which the Fourteenth Amendment became part of the Constitution. *Id.* at 63-4.

[15]Cantwell v. Connecticut, 310 U.S. 296 (1940).

[16]397 U.S. 664, 668-69 (1970).

[17]*See* note 8, *supra,* at 309.

scribed governmental acts there is room for play in the joints productive of a benevolent neutrality which will permit religious exercise to exist without sponsorship and without interference.[18]

The Court has also stated:

[T]his Court repeatedly has recognized that tension inevitably exists between the Free Exercise and the Establishment Clauses . . . and that it may often not be possible to promote the former without offending the latter. As a result of this tension, our cases require the State to maintain an attitude of "neutrality," neither "advancing" nor "inhibiting" religion.[19]

In *Zorach v. Clauson*,[20] the Court spoke of the need of "accommodating" the religious needs of the people.

Notwithstanding the emphasis upon "neutrality" and "accommodation," there is a marked judicial preference of the establishment clause over the free exercise clause. Justice Rehnquist has observed:

The Court apparently believes that the Establishment Clause of the First Amendment not only mandates religious neutrality on the part of government but also requires that this Court go further and throw its weight on the side of those who believe that our society as a whole should be a purely secular one. Nothing in the First Amendment or in the cases interpreting it requires such an extreme approach to this difficult question, and "any interpretation of the Establishment Clause and constitutional values it serves must also take account of the free exercise clause and the values it serves."[21]

Chief Justice Burger has observed: "One can only hope that, at some future date, the Court will come to a more enlightened and tolerant view of the First Amendment's guarantee of free exercise of religion . . . ."[22]

Ironically, the Supreme Court, in the same decision that invalidated voluntary, school-sponsored Bible readings as violative of the establishment clause, acknowledged that "the State may not establish a 'religion of secularism' in the sense of affirmatively opposing or showing hostility to religion, thus 'preferring those who believe in no religion over those who do believe.' "[23]

[18]Walz v. Tax Commission, 397 U.S. 664, 669 (1970).
[19]Committee for Public Education & Religious Liberty v. Nyquist, 413 U.S. 756, 788 (1973).
[20]343 U.S. 306 (1952).
[21]Meek v. Pittinger, 421 U.S. 349, 395 (1975) (Rehnquist, J., dissenting).
[22]Meek v. Pittinger, 421 U.S. 349, 387 (1975) (Burger, C.J., dissenting).
[23]School District of Abington v. Schempp, 374 U.S. 203, 225 (1963).

# 16

# LANDMARK SUPREME COURT DECISIONS INTERPRETING THE RELIGION CLAUSES

The United State Supreme Court in *Marbury v. Madison*[1] held that the United States Constitution is the "paramount" or supreme law of the land, and that "[i]t is emphatically the province and duty" of the federal courts to construe the Constitution. Federal courts thus have the ultimate authority to construe provisions in the Constitution.[2] Since the United States Supreme Court is the highest court in the federal judicial system, its interpretations of the Constitution are entitled to the greatest deference. An interpretation of a constitutional provision by the Supreme Court in effect becomes the supreme law of the land, and must be followed by all state and lower federal courts until the Supreme Court reverses itself and overrules the earlier decision, or until the Court's ruling is invalidated by ratification of an amendment to the Constitution. The importance of Supreme Court interpretations of the First Amendment's "religion clauses"[3] should thus be apparent.

The Supreme Court seldom discussed the religion clauses in the first century and a half following their enactment. Since 1947, however, the Court has construed the religion clauses on a number of occasions. Some of the more significant of these decisions will be summarized in this chapter.

---

[1] 1 Cranch 137 (1803). *See* chapter 15, note 8, and accompanying text.

[2] "We are under a Constitution, but the Constitution is what the judges say it is." Charles Evans Hughes, Speech, May 3, 1907.

[3] The First Amendment provides that "Congress shall make no law respecting an establishment of religion or prohibiting the free exercise thereof . . . ." The first phrase of the amendment—"Congress shall make no law respecting an establishment of religion"—is referred to as the *establishment clause.* The second phrase—"or prohibit the free exercise thereof"—is referred to as the *free exercise clause.*

## §A. Everson v. Board of Education[4]

A New Jersey statute authorized local school districts to make arrangements for the transportation of children to and from schools. One township board of education, acting pursuant to this statute, adopted a resolution authorizing reimbursement to parents of money expended by them for the bus transportation of their children on buses operated by the public transportation system. Part of this money was for the payment of transportation of some children in the community to Catholic parochial schools. A taxpayer filed suit against the board of education, alleging that the state law and board of education resolution constituted a violation of the First Amendment to the United States Constitution insofar as they forced taxpayers to pay for the transportation of children to Catholic schools.

The New Jersey Court of Errors and Appeals concluded that the statute and resolution did not violate the First Amendment, and the taxpayer appealed directly to the United States Supreme Court. In upholding the statute and school board resolution, the Supreme Court rendered the first modern interpretation of the First Amendment's "establishment clause." After briefly describing the colonial experience of established religions and persecution of religious dissenters that "found expression in the First Amendment," the Court observed:

> The "establishment of religion" clause of the First Amendment means at least this: Neither a state nor the Federal Government can set up a church. Neither can pass laws which aid one religion, aid all religions, or prefer one religion over another. Neither can force nor influence a person to go or to remain away from church against his will or force him to profess a belief or disbelief in any religion. No person can be punished for entertaining or professing religious beliefs or disbeliefs, for church attendance or nonattendance. No tax in any amount, large or small, can be levied to support any religious activities or institutions, whatever they may be called, or whatever form they may adopt to teach or practice religion. Neither a state nor the Federal Government can, openly or secretly, participate in the affairs of any religious organizations or groups and vice versa. In the words of Jefferson, the clause against establishment of religion by law was intended to erect "a wall of separation between church and state."[5]

Measuring by this standard, the Court concluded that the First Amendment did not prohibit New Jersey from spending tax revenues to pay the bus fares of parochial school pupils as a part of a general program under which it paid the fares of pupils attending public and other schools. "We must be careful,"

[4]330 U.S. 1 (1947).
[5]*Id.* at 15-16.

observed the Court, "in protecting the citizens of New Jersey against state-established churches, to be sure that we do not inadvertently prohibit New Jersey from extending its general state law benefits to all its citizens without regard to their religious beliefs."[6] The Court acknowledged that payment of the bus fares of parochial school students as well as the protection of parochial school pupils by means of state-paid policemen and firemen and the use of public streets and sidewalks by parochial school pupils did provide some assistance to such pupils, but the Court insisted that

> cutting off church-schools from these services, so separate and so indisputably marked off from the religious function, would make it far more difficult for the schools to operate. But such is obviously not the purpose of the First Amendment. That Amendment requires the state to be a neutral in its relations with groups of religious believers and non-believers; it does not require the state to be their adversary. State power is no more to be used so as to handicap religions, than it is to favor them.[7]

Finally, the Court held that the free exercise of religion, also protected by the First Amendment, would be abridged by a state law excluding certain citizens on the basis of their religion from receiving the benefits of public welfare legislation.

§B. People of State of Illinois ex rel. McCollum v. Board of Education[8]

In 1940, interested members of the Jewish, Roman Catholic, and a few of the Protestant faiths formed a voluntary association in Champaign, Illinois, called the Champaign Council on Religious Education. The council obtained permission from the local board of education to offer classes in religious instruction to public school pupils in grades four to nine inclusive. Classes were made up of pupils whose parents signed printed cards requesting that their children be permitted to attend. Classes were held weekly, thirty minutes for the lower grades and forty-five minutes for the higher. The council employed the religious teachers at no expense to the school authorities, but the instructors were subject to the approval and supervision of the superintendent of schools. The classes were taught in three separate groups by Protestant teachers, Catholic priests, and a Jewish rabbi. Classes were conducted in the regular classrooms of the school building. Students who did not choose to take the religious instruction were not released from public school duties; they were required to

[6]Id. at 16.
[7]Id. at 18.
[8]333 U.S. 203 (1948).

leave their classrooms and go to some other place in the school building for the pursuit of their secular studies. Students who were released from secular study for the religious instruction were required to be present at the religious classes.

The constitutionality of this "released time" program was challenged by the parent of a public school student on the ground that it violated the First Amendment's prohibition of the establishment of a religion. The state courts of Illinois upheld the constitutionality of the program, and the case was appealed directly to the United States Supreme Court. The Supreme Court struck down the released time program on the ground that it was "beyond all question a utilization of the tax-established and tax-supported public school system to aid religious groups to spread their faith" and thus "falls squarely under the ban of the First Amendment."[9] The Court noted in particular that the state's tax-supported public school buildings were used for the dissemination of religious doctrine, and that the state materially aided religious groups by providing pupils for their religious classes through use of the state's compulsory school machinery. "This is not separation of Church and State," the Court concluded.

The Court rejected the argument that the First Amendment was intended to forbid only governmental preference of one religion over another, and not impartial governmental assistance of all religions. The Court also rejected the contention that forbidding the use of public school property to aid all religious faiths in the dissemination of their doctrine constituted an impermissible governmental hostility to religion. A manifestation of governmental hostility to religion would be impermissible, the Court agreed, but it found no such hostility under the facts of this case. The Court concluded:

> [T]he First Amendment rests upon the premise that both religion and government can best work to achieve their lofty aims if each is left free from the other within its respective sphere. . . . [T]he First Amendment has erected a wall between Church and State which must be kept high and impregnable.[10]

Justice Jackson, in a concurring opinion, cautioned that it may be unnecessary if not impossible to cast out of secular education all that some people may reasonably regard as religious instruction:

> Music without sacred music, architecture minus the cathedral, or painting without the scriptural themes would be eccentric and incomplete, even from a secular point of view. Yet the inspirational appeal of religion in these guises is often stronger than in forthright sermon. Even such a "science" as biology raises the

[9]*Id.* at 210.
[10]*Id.* at 212.

issue between evolution and creation as an explanation of our presence on this planet. Certainly a course in English literature that omitted the Bible and other powerful uses of our mother tongue for religious ends would be pretty barren. And I should suppose it is a proper, if not an indispensable, part of preparation for a worldly life to know the roles that religions have played in the tragic story of mankind. The fact is that, for good or ill, nearly everything in our culture worth transmitting, everything which gives meaning to life, is saturated with religious influences, derived from paganism, Judaism, Christianity—both Catholic and Protestant—and other faiths accepted by a large part of the world's peoples. One can hardly respect a system of education that would leave the student wholly ignorant of the currents of religious thought that move the world society for a part in which he is being prepared.[11]

In a dissenting opinion, Justice Reed insisted that the First Amendment was never intended to prohibit religious instruction of public school children during school hours. He agreed that government cannot "aid" all or any religions, but he construed the word *aid* to mean purposeful assistance directly to a church or religious organization itself. Justice Reed recounted many examples of government accommodation of religious practices, and observed:

The prohibition of enactments respecting the establishment of religion do not bar every friendly gesture between church and state. It is not an absolute prohibition against every conceivable situation where the two may work together any more than the other provisions of the First Amendment—free speech, free press—are absolutes.[12]

Justice Reed concluded that "[t]his Court cannot be too cautious in upsetting practices embedded in our society by many years of experience" and that devotion to the great principle of religious liberty "should not lead us into a rigid interpretation of the constitutional guarantee that conflicts with accepted habits of our people."[13]

### §C. Zorach v. Clauson[14]

Shortly after deciding that released time programs allowing public school students to receive religious instruction on school property were unconstitutional, the Supreme Court was faced with the task of deciding the constitu-

[11]*Id.* at 236.
[12]*Id.* at 255-56.
[13]*Id.* at 256.
[14]343 U.S. 306 (1952).

tionality of released time programs that permitted public school children to leave school property to receive religious instruction.

New York City developed a program that permitted its public schools to release students during the school day so that they could leave the school buildings and grounds and go to religious centers for religious instruction or devotional exercises. Students were released upon written request of their parents. Those not released stayed at school. The churches and other religious centers made weekly reports to the schools. All costs of the program were paid by religious organizations.

A group of parents challenged the constitutionality of the program. In particular, the parents argued that the program constituted an establishment of religion in violation of the First Amendment since the weight and influence of the school was put behind a program of religious instruction; public school teachers policed the program, keeping track of students who had been released; and classroom activities came to a halt while students who had been released were on leave.

The Court rejected the parents' challenge. While acknowledging that "there cannot be the slightest doubt that the First Amendment reflects the philosophy that Church and State should be separated," the Court held that the First Amendment "does not say that in every and all respects there shall be a separation of Church and State."[15] A strict separation, observed the Court, would cause the state and religion to be aliens—hostile, suspicious, and even unfriendly. Municipalities would not be permitted to render police or fire protection to religious groups; policemen who helped parishioners to their places of worship would violate the Constitution; and prayers in the nation's legislative halls, the proclamations making Thanksgiving Day a holiday, and "so help me God" in courtroom oaths—these and all other references to the Almighty that run through our laws and ceremonies would flout the First Amendment.

In one of its most eloquent descriptions of the meaning of *establishment,* the Court observed:

> We are a religious people whose institutions presuppose a Supreme Being. We guarantee the freedom of worship as one chooses. We make room for as wide a variety of beliefs and creeds as the spiritual needs of man deem necessary. We sponsor an attitude on the part of government that shows no partiality to any one group and that lets each flourish according to the zeal of its adherents and the appeal of its dogma. When the state encourages religious instruction or cooperates with religious authorities by adjusting the schedule of public events to sectarian needs, it follows the best of our traditions. For it then respects the religious nature

[15]*Id.* at 312.

of our people and accommodates the public service to their spiritual needs. To hold that it may not would be to find in the Constitution a requirement that the government show a callous indifference to religious groups. That would be preferring those who believe in no religion over those who do believe. Government may not finance religious groups nor undertake religious instruction nor blend secular and sectarian education nor use secular institutions to force one or some religion on any person. But we find no constitutional requirement which makes it necessary for government to be hostile to religion and throw its weight against efforts to widen the effective scope of religious influence. The government must be neutral when it comes to competition between sects. It may not thrust any sect on any person. It may not make a religious observance compulsory. It may not coerce anyone to attend church, to observe a religious holiday, or to take religious instruction. But it can close its doors or suspend its operations as to those who want to repair to their religious sanctuary for worship or instruction. No more than that is undertaken here.

The released time program of New York City was found to be valid under this test. The Court distinguished *McCollum* on the ground that classrooms were used in that case for religious instruction and the force of the public school was used to promote that instruction. In the present case, the public schools did no more than accommodate their schedules to a program of outside religious instruction. "We follow the *McCollum* case," concluded the Court, "[b]ut we cannot expand it to cover the present released time program unless separation of Church and State means that public institutions can make no adjustments of their schedules to accommodate the religious needs of the people. We cannot read into the Bill of Rights such a philosophy of hostility to religion."[16]

## §D. Engel v. Vitale[17]

The New York Board of Regents, a governmental agency having broad supervisory power over the state's public schools, recommended that the following nondenominational prayer be recited in each public school at the start of every school day: "Almighty God, we acknowledge our dependence upon Thee, and we beg Thy blessings upon us, our parents, our teachers, and our country."

A group of parents whose children attended a public school in which the "Regents' prayer" was recited challenged the constitutionality of the practice in state court. The New York state courts upheld the constitutionality of the practice on the condition that no child be compelled to join in the prayer over his own or his parents' objection. The parents appealed to the United States

[16]*Id.* at 313-14.
[17]370 U.S. 421 (1962).

Supreme Court, which ruled that the practice constituted an establishment of religion in violation of the First Amendment:

> [W]e think that the constitutional prohibition against laws respecting an estab-
> lishment of religion must at least mean that in this country it is no part of the
> business of government to compose official prayers for any group of the American
> people to recite as a part of a religious program carried on by government.[18]

The Court rejected the contention that the prayer was permissible because it was nondenominational and voluntary, since the establishment clause "does not depend upon any showing of direct governmental compulsion and is violated by the enactment of laws which establish an official religion whether those laws operate directly to coerce nonobserving individuals or not."[19] Furthermore, the Court refused to concede that the Regents' prayer was in fact "voluntary" since when the power and prestige of government is placed behind a particular religious belief "the indirect coercive pressure upon religious minorities to conform to the prevailing officially approved religion is plain."[20]

In rejecting the contention that its decision evidenced a hostility toward religion which itself contravened the First Amendment, the Court observed:

> [T]here grew up a sentiment that caused men to leave the cross-currents of
> officially established state religions and religious persecution in Europe and come
> to this country filled with that hope that they could find a place in which they
> could pray when they pleased to the God of their faith in the language they chose.
> And there were men of this same faith . . . who led the fight for adoption of our
> Constitution and also for our Bill of Rights with the very guarantees of religious
> freedom that forbid the sort of governmental activity which New York has at-
> tempted here.[21]

The Court acknowledged that governmental endorsement of the Regents' prayer was insignificant in comparison to the encroachments upon religion which were uppermost in the minds of those who ratified the First Amendment, but it reasoned that "it is proper to take alarm at the first experiment with our liberties" in order to preclude more substantial violations.

In dissent, Justice Stewart traced the many spiritual traditions of our nation, including the recitation of prayer before legislative and judicial sessions, the references to God in the Pledge of Allegiance and the national anthem, pres-

[18]*Id.* at 425.
[19]*Id.* at 430.
[20]*Id.* at 431.
[21]*Id.* at 434-35.

idential proclamations of national days of prayer, the provision of military and institutional chaplains at government expense, and imprinting the words "In God We Trust" on coins and currency, and concluded that it was arbitrary to deny school children the right to share in this spiritual heritage by forbidding them to voluntarily recite a prayer at the start of each school day.

## §E. School District of Abington v. Schempp[22]

The State of Pennsylvania enacted a law that stipulated: "At least ten verses from the Holy Bible shall be read, without comment, at the opening of each public school on each school day. Any child shall be excused from such Bible reading, or attending such Bible reading, upon the written request of his parent or guardian."

A family having two children in the public schools filed suit to halt enforcement of the Pennsylvania law on the ground that it constituted an impermissible establishment of religion in violation of the First Amendment. A federal district court agreed that the law violated the establishment clause, and the State appealed directly to the United States Supreme Court. The Supreme Court, in affirming the lower court ruling, stated that "to withstand the strictures of the Establishment Clause there must be a secular legislative purpose and a primary effect that neither advances nor inhibits religion."[23] The Court concluded that the reading of the Bible at the start of each school day was indisputably a religious practice and as such it violated the First Amendment. It did not matter that participation in the readings was voluntary, or that the readings themselves were relatively minor encroachments on the First Amendment, since "[t]he breach of neutrality that is today a trickling stream may all too soon become a raging torrent."[24]

The Court agreed that the State "may not establish a 'religion of secularism' in the sense of affirmatively opposing or showing hostility to religion," but it did not believe that its decision in any sense had that effect.[25] The Court also acknowledged that

> one's education is not complete without a study of comparative religion or the history of religion and its relationship to the advancement of civilization. It certainly may be said that the Bible is worthy of study for its literary and historic qualities. Nothing we have said here indicates that such study of the Bible or of

[22]374 U.S. 203 (1963).

[23]*Id.* at 222.

[24]*Id.* at 225.

[25]*Id.*

religion, when presented objectively as part of a secular program of education, may not be effected consistently with the First Amendment.[26]

Finally, the Court rejected the contention that its decision collided with the majority's right to the free exercise of their religion:

> The very purpose of a Bill of Rights was to withdraw certain subjects from the vicissitudes of political controversy, to place them beyond the reach of majorities and officials and to establish them as legal principles to be applied by the courts. One's right to . . . freedom of worship . . . and other fundamental rights may not be submitted to vote; they depend on the outcome of no elections.[27]

Justice Stewart, in dissent, argued that the neutrality mandated by the First Amendment required that school children be permitted, on a voluntary basis, to start their day with Bible reading since "a refusal to permit religious exercises is thus seen, not as the realization of state neutrality, but rather as the establishment of a religion of secularism, or at the least, as government support of the beliefs of those who think that religious exercises should be conducted only in private."[28] Justice Stewart also maintained that readings from the Bible unaccompanied by comments and addressed only to those children who chose to be present did not represent the type of support of religion barred by the establishment clause.

### §F. Walz v. Tax Commission[29]

The New York legislature enacted a property tax law that exempted real property owned by nonprofit corporations and associations that were organized exclusively for religious, charitable, benevolent, educational, scientific, or literary purposes. A taxpayer filed suit in the New York state courts to prevent the New York City Tax Commission from granting property tax exemptions to religious organizations for properties used solely for religious worship on the ground that such exemptions required the government to make "contributions" to religious organizations in violation of the principle of separation of church and state embodied in the First Amendment. The New York state courts upheld the constitutionality of the exemption and the case was appealed to the United States Supreme Court.

The Supreme Court, with only one dissenting vote, affirmed the constitu-

---

[26]*Id.*

[27]*Id.* at 226.

[28]*Id.* at 313.

[29]397 U.S. 664 (1970).

tionality of the New York law. After noting that the purpose of the establishment clause is the prevention of "sponsorship, financial support, and active involvement of the sovereign in religious activity,"[30] the Court concluded that the exemption of properties used exclusively for religious purposes did not constitute sponsorship or financial support of religious organizations by the state. "The grant of a tax exemption is not sponsorship," noted the Court, "since the government does not transfer part of its revenue to churches but simply abstains from demanding that the church support the state."[31] In addition, property used for religious purposes was but one of a wide variety of classifications of property that were exempted from tax. The state had not singled out church-owned property for the exemption, but rather it had included such property in a long list of other exempted properties owned by organizations whose activities the state had decided were socially desirable and deserving of protection through exemption from tax.

Finally, the Court emphasized that any practice that leads to an excessive governmental entanglement with religion is prohibited by the establishment clause. It acknowledged that either taxation of churches or exemption occasioned some governmental involvement with religion. However, it concluded that elimination of the exemption would lead to a greater entanglement "by giving rise to tax valuation of church property, tax liens, tax foreclosures, and the direct confrontations and conflicts that follow in the train of those legal processes."[32] On the other hand, the exemption "creates only a minimal and remote involvement between church and state and far less than taxation of churches."[33] The Court also stressed that "an unbroken practice of according the exemption to churches, openly and by affirmative state action, not covertly or by state inaction, is not something to be lightly cast aside,"[34] and it quoted Justice Holmes' earlier observation that "[i]f a thing has been practiced for two hundred years by common consent, it will need a strong case for the [Constitution] to affect it."[35]

### §G. Wisconsin v. Yoder[36]

The *Yoder* case involved the constitutionality of applying a state compulsory attendance law to Old Order Amish children who had completed the eighth

[30] *Id.* at 668.
[31] *Id.* at 675.
[32] *Id.* at 674.
[33] *Id.* at 676.
[34] *Id.* at 678.
[35] *Id.*
[36] 406 U.S. 205 (1972).

grade.[37] The principal significance of the decision lies in the Court's construction of the "free exercise clause" of the First Amendment. After emphasizing that "only those interests of the highest order and those not otherwise served can overbalance legitimate claims to the free exercise of religion,"[38] the Court enunciated a three-pronged test for assessing the constitutionality of governmental action under the free exercise clause:

1. Is the activity interfered with by the state motivated by and rooted in legitimate and sincerely held religious belief?
2. Is the activity interfered with by the state unduly and substantially burdened to the extent of affecting religious practice?
3. Does the state have a compelling interest in limiting or restricting the religiously motivated activity that cannot be accomplished through less restrictive means?

This test is the current means of assessing the constitutionality of governmental limitations of religiously motivated activity under the free exercise clause.

### §H. Committee for Public Education and Religious Liberty v. Nyquist[39]

In striking down various provisions of New York Law authorizing tuition reimbursement grants and tax credits for parents with children in private schools, the Court articulated a three-pronged test for evaluating the constitutionality of government action under the establishment clause: "To pass muster under the Establishment Clause the law in question, first, must reflect a clearly secular purpose, second, must have a primary effect that neither advances nor inhibits religion, and, third, must avoid excessive government entanglement with religion."[40] The Court observed that the concept of "entanglement" connoted not only involvements between church and state, but also, in a broader sense, any degree of government involvement in religious life that is apt to lead to potentially divisive political strife.

[37]See chapter 13, § H, supra.
[38]406 U.S. at 215.
[39]413 U.S. 756 (1973).
[40]Id. at 773 (citations omitted).

# 17

# THE PRESENT MEANING OF THE FIRST AMENDMENT RELIGION CLAUSES

## §A. The Establishment Clause

In the *Nyquist*[1] case, the Supreme Court enunciated the current test for determining the constitutional validity of governmental action under the establishment clause.[2] To be consistent with the establishment clause, a law or government-sanctioned practice must satisfy each part of a three-pronged test:

1. a clearly secular purpose
2. a primary effect that neither advances nor inhibits religion
3. no excessive entanglement between government and religion

This three-pronged test has been applied in many contexts since its first articulation in *Nyquist*. Several of the more notable cases will be summarized in the table that follows.

SELECTED LAWS AND GOVERNMENTAL
PRACTICES CHALLENGED IN THE FEDERAL
COURTS UNDER THE ESTABLISHMENT CLAUSE SINCE 1970

| | Constitutional | Unconstitutional |
|---|---|---|
| 1. State law gave churches the power to block the issuance of liquor permits within a 500-foot radius. Larkin v. Grendel's Den, Inc. 103 S. Ct. 505 (1982) | | X |

[1]Committee for Public Education and Religious Liberty v. Nyquist, 413 U.S. 756 (1973). The *Nyquist* case was discussed in chapter 15, *supra*.

[2]The First Amendment religion clauses, like all of the other provisions of the Bill of Rights, are limitations upon the power of government. Thus, they generally have no application to private individuals and organizations.

| | Constitutional | Unconstitutional |
|---|---|---|
| 2. State law required posting of Ten Commandments in each public school classroom. *Stone v. Graham*, 449 U.S. 39 (1980) | | X |
| 3. State monies used to reimburse both church-operated and public schools for performing various testing and reporting services mandated by state law. *Committee for Public Education and Religious Liberty v. Regan*, 444 U.S. 646 (1980). | X | |
| 4. Loaning of state-approved secular textbooks to pupils attending church-related schools. *Wolman v. Walter*, 433 U.S. 229 (1977) | X | |
| 5. State monies used to supply students in church-related schools with same standardized tests and scoring as used in public schools. *Wolman v. Walter*, 433 U.S. 229 (1977) | X | |
| 6. State monies used to supply students in church-related schools with speech, hearing, and psychological diagnostic services. *Wolman v. Walter*, 433 U.S. 229 (1977) | X | |
| 7. State monies used to supply students in church-related schools with therapeutic guidance and remedial services. *Wolman v. Walter*, 433 U.S. 229 (1977) | X | |
| 8. State monies used to supply students in church-related schools with field trip transportation. *Wolman v. Walter*, 433 U.S. 229 (1977) | | X |
| 9. State monies used to supply students in church-related schools with guidance counseling. *Wolman v. Walter*, 433 U.S. 229 (1977) | | X |
| 10. Payments to colleges that were characterized as "sectarian" but not "pervasively sectarian" under state law providing for annual grants to eligible colleges and universities. *Roemer v. Board of Public Works*, 426 U.S. 736 (1976) | X | |

|  | Constitutional | Unconstitutional |
|---|---|---|
| 11. Reimbursements to parents for costs of nonpublic school tuition, *Sloan v. Lemon,* 413 U.S. 825 (1973) |  | X |
| 12. State appropriations for maintenance and repair of church-related schools. *Committee for Public Education v. Nyquist,* 413 U.S. 756 (1973) |  | X |
| 13. State law authorizing tuition reimbursement and tuition tax credits to parents having children in nonpublic schools. *Committee for Public Education v. Nyquist,* 413 U.S. 756 (1973) |  | X |
| 14. Direct federal and state grants to church-affiliated colleges for the purpose of constructing buildings in which only secular courses would be taught. *Tilton v. Richardson,* 403 U.S. 672 (1971) |  | X |
| 15. State aid to nonpublic school teachers teaching secular subjects. *Lemon v. Kurtzman,* 403 U.S. 602 (1971) | X |  |
| 16. Military Selective Service exemption from conscription requirements for those conscientiously opposed to participation in war on grounds of religious training and belief. *Negre v. Larson,* 410 U.S. 437 (1971) | X |  |
| 17. Construction and maintenance of a cross on public property in a state park. *American Civil Liberties Union v. Rabun County Chamber of Commerce, Inc.,* 678 F.2d 1379 (11th Cir. 1982) |  | X |
| 18. State legislature for sixteen consecutive years selected and paid one minister, representing one denomination, as its chaplain to open each session with prayer. *Chambers v. Marsh,* 675 F.2d 228 (8th Cir. 1982) |  | X |
| 19. Public school district permitted students to gather at school with supervision either before or after regular school hours to participate in religious exercises. *Lubbock Civil Liberties Union v. Lubbock Independent School District,* 669 F.2d 1038 (5th Cir. 1982) |  | X |

| | Constitutional | Unconstitutional |
|---|:---:|:---:|
| 20. Public school district program permitted students to be released from school during regular hours to obtain religious instruction off of school property. *Lanner v. Wimmer,* 662 F.2d 1349 (10th Cir. 1981) | X | |
| 21. North Carolina Department of Transportation printed a "motorists' prayer" on state maps that it distributed. *Hall v. Bradshaw,* 630 F.2d 1018 (4th Cir. 1980) | | X |
| 22. School district permitted observance of holidays having both a religious and secular basis. *Florey v. Sioux Falls School District,* 619 F.2d 1311 (8th Cir. 1980) | X | |
| 23. County board meetings began with a prayer recited by a local clergyman. *Bogen v. Doty,* 598 F.2d 1110 (8th Cir. 1979) | X | |
| 24. Public high schools offered an elective course in transcendental meditation. *Malnak v. Yogi,* 592 F.2d 197 (2nd Cir. 1979) | | X |
| 25. Distribution of Gideon Bibles to public school students. *Meltzer v. Board of Public Instruction,* 548 F.2d 559 (4th Cir. 1977) | | X |
| 26. Federal government financially supported the Christmas Pageant of Peace on federal park land adjacent to the White House. *Allen v. Morton,* 495 F.2d 65 (D.C. Cir. 1973) | X | |
| 27. Maintenance of a lighted granite monument containing the Ten Commandments on government property. *Anderson v. Salt Lake City Corporation,* 475 F.2d 29 (9th Cir. 1973) | X | |
| 28. Mandatory chapel attendance for students at federal military academies. *Anderson v. Laird,* 466 F.2d 283 (D.C. Cir. 1972) | | X |
| 29. Printing of national motto "In God We Trust" on all United States currency. *Aronow v. United States,* 432 F.2d 242 (9th Cir. 1970) | X | |

|  | Constitutional | Unconstitutional |
|---|---|---|
| 30. State law exempted church-operated day-care centers from licensing requirements. *Forest Hills Early Learning Center, Inc. v. Lukhard*, 540 F. Supp. 1046 (D. Va. 1982) | X | |
| 31. State law required public schools to give a balanced treatment to both evolutionary and Biblical theories of creation. *McLean v. Arkansas Board of Education*, 529 F. Supp. 1255 (D. Ark. 1982) | | X |
| 32. Bible classes taught in public schools, emphasizing the secular, literary, and historical worth of the Bible, and omitting all religious emphasis. *Wiley v. Franklin*, 474 F. Supp. 525 (E.D. Tenn. 1979) | X | |
| 33. Tax exemption for religious organizations. *Haring v. Blumenthal*, 471 F. Supp. 1172 (D.C.D.C. 1979) | X | |
| 34. Government scholarships awarded to all needy college students, regardless of whether they attended a public or private school. *Americans United for Separation of Church and State v. Blanton*, 433 F. Supp. 97 (M.D. Tenn. 1977) | X | |
| 35. Public school baccalaureate service conducted in high school auditorium for graduating seniors, with a local clergyman delivering a message. *Goodwin v. Cross County School District*, 394 F. Supp. 417 (E.D. Ark. 1973) | X | |

## §B. The Free Exercise Clause

The present construction of the free exercise clause may be summarized as follows:

1. Government may never interfere with an individual's right to believe whatever he wants.
2. In determining whether the government may interfere with or restrict religiously motivated conduct, the courts must consider (a) whether the activity

was motivated by and rooted in legitimate and sincerely held religious belief, (b) whether the activity was unduly and substantially burdened by the government's action, and (c) whether the government has a compelling interest in limiting the religious activity that cannot be accomplished by less restrictive means.[3]

Two things must be noted about the free exercise clause. First, the concept of free exercise is fundamentally incompatible with the philosophy of disestablishment contained in the establishment clause.[4] This tension has been aggravated in the past few decades by judicial emphasis upon disestablishment. Chief Justice Burger, in the *Walz* decision, commented on this underlying tension: "The Court has struggled to find a neutral course between the two Religion Clauses, both of which are cast in absolute terms, and either of which, if expanded to a logical extreme, would tend to clash with the other."[5] Similarly, Justice Stewart, dissenting in *Schempp,* observed: "[T]here are areas in which a doctrinaire reading of the Establishment Clause leads to irreconcilable conflict with the Free Exercise Clause."[6] The Supreme Court in more recent years has attempted to synthesize the religion clauses by emphasizing the concept of neutrality:

> The general principle deducible from the First Amendment and all that has been said by the Court is this: that we will not tolerate either governmentally established religion or governmental interference with religion. Short of those expressly proscribed governmental acts there is room for play in the joints productive of a benevolent neutrality which will permit religious exercise to exist without sponsorship and without interference.[7]

Second, the notion that religiously motivated conduct is subordinate to *compelling* governmental interests involves an intrinsically subjective test. When is a governmental interest "compelling"? The answer in each case ultimately depends upon a judge's convictions about the proper extent and content of religious practice. The following cases, which represent significant interpretations of the free exercise clause by the federal courts, should shed some light on the current substance and application of this clause.

[3]Wisconsin v. Yoder, 406 U.S. 205 (1972).

[4]*See generally* chapter 15, *supra.*

[5]Walz v. Tax Commission, 397 U.S. 664, 669 (1970).

[6]School District of Abington v. Schempp, 374 U.S. 203, 309 (1963).

[7]Walz v. Tax Commission, 397 U.S. 664, 669 (1970).

SELECTED LAWS AND GOVERNMENTAL
PRACTICES CHALLENGED IN THE FEDERAL
COURTS UNDER THE FREE EXERCISE CLAUSE SINCE 1970

| | Constitutional | Unconstitutional |
|---|---|---|
| 1. IRS revoked religious university's tax-exempt status because of its rule prohibiting interracial dating and marriage. *Bob Jones University v. United States*, ___ S. Ct. ___ (1983) | | X |
| 2. State university refused to permit Christian students to use vacant classrooms on a regular basis for religious exercises. *Widmar v. Vincent*, 102 S. Ct. 269 (1981) | | X |
| 3. Tennessee constitution forbade clergymen from running for state legislature. *McDaniel v. Paty*, 435 U.S. 618 (1978) | | X |
| 4. State law requiring all children to attend school until age sixteen challenged by Amish sect that refused to send children to school past the eighth grade. *Wisconsin v. Yoder*, 406 U.S. 205 (1972) | | X |
| 5. State terminated welfare assistance to a child for lack of a social security number despite parents' claim that they were opposed to social security numbers on religious grounds. *Callahan v. Woods*, 658 F.2d 679 (9th Cir. 1981) | | X |
| 6. Government charged defendant with counterfeiting currency notwithstanding his belief that he was justified in his actions because of his objection, based on religious grounds, to the currency system established by the Federal Reserve Act. *United States v. Grismore*, 564 F.2d 929 (9th Cir. 1977) | X | |
| 7. Police department grooming regulations opposed on the ground that they violated the free exercise of religion. *Marshall v. District of Columbia*, 559 F.2d 726 (D.C. Cir. 1977) | X | |

|    |                                                                                                                                                                                                                                                  | *Constitutional* | *Unconstitutional* |
|----|--------------------------------------------------------------------------------------------------------------------------------------------------------------------------------------------------------------------------------------------------|:----------------:|:------------------:|
| 8. | Pacifist Quakers compelled by the IRS to pay full income tax without deduction for governmental military spending. *Graves v. Commissioner,* 529 F.2d 392 (6th Cir. 1978)                                                                          | X                |                    |
| 9. | The federal government charged an Indian with violation of the Bald Eagle Protection Act notwithstanding his claim that his sale of eagle parts and feathers constituted the free exercise of his religion. *United States v. Top Sky,* 547 F.2d 486 (9th Cir. 1976) | X |            |
| 10.| Court ruled defendant to be in contempt for his refusal, allegedly based on religious grounds, to stand when the judge and jury entered the courtroom. *In re Chase,* 468 F.2d 128 (7th Cir. 1972)                                                 | X                |                    |
| 11.| Black Muslim convicted of smuggling heroin despite defense that usage of drugs was sanctioned by his religion. *United States v. Spears,* 443 F.2d 895 (5th Cir. 1971)                                                                             | X                |                    |
| 12.| City ordinance banned solicitation of funds for religious purposes and the distribution of religious literature without a city-issued permit. *Cherris v. Amundson,* 460 F. Supp. 326 (E.D. La. 1978)                                             |                  | X                  |
| 13.| City ordinance forbade all religious proselytizing without first listing as references two owners of city business property who would attest to the good moral character and reputation for honesty of the applicant. *Levers v. City of Tullahoma,* 446 F. Supp. 884 (E.D. Tenn. 1978) |  | X |
| 14.| City ordinance forbade the distribution of religious materials from door to door. *Murdock v. City of Jacksonville,* 361 F. Supp. 1083 (M.D. Fla. 1973)                                                                                           |                  | X                  |

## §C. Procedure for First Amendment Analysis

When confronted with the task of assessing the permissibility of a particular religious exercise, the following methodology may be helpful in reaching a tentative solution. It is based on well-established judicial precedent.

1. Does a particular law or government-sanctioned practice benefit, promote, or advance religion?

a. If so, the government action will constitute an impermissible "establishment of religion" unless it satisfies all of the following three criteria: (1) a clearly secular purpose, (2) a primary effect that neither advances nor inhibits religion, and (3) the action does not involve an excessive entanglement between government and religion.

In applying these criteria, the following principles should be borne in mind: (1) government action that benefits all persons equally and only incidentally advances religion will generally be upheld; (2) since an emphasis on the establishment clause often collides with the right to freely exercise one's religion, application of the above-listed criteria should be done in such a way as to facilitate "benevolent neutrality" of the government toward religion and "accommodation" of religious interests.

b. If a particular law or government-sanctioned practice does not benefit, promote, or advance religion, there is no violation of the establishment clause.

2. Does a particular law or government-sanctioned practice limit, prohibit, or impede (actually or potentially) religious belief?

a. If so, the government action, without exception, will constitute an impermissible violation of the constitutional right to the free exercise of religion.

b. If not, there is no violation of the free exercise clause.

3. Does a particular law or government-sanctioned practice limit, prohibit, or impede (actually or potentially) religiously motivated conduct?

a. If so, the government action will constitute an impermissible violation of the free exercise clause if all of the following conditions are satisfied: (1) the conduct interfered with by the government is motivated by and rooted in sincerely held religious beliefs; (2) the government's action unduly and substantially burdens a religious practice; and (3) the government does not have a compelling interest in limiting the religiously motivated conduct, or if a compelling interest does exist, the government has not used the least restrictive means of accomplishing it.

b. If a particular law or government-sanctioned practice does not limit, prohibit, or impede religiously motivated conduct, there is no violation of the free exercise clause.

4. Do not use step 2 or 3 if the government is taking action that allegedly benefits, promotes, or advances religion. In such a case, step 1 must be employed. Step 1 takes account of free exercise interests, yet it applies in the context of affirmative governmental aid to religion. Steps 2 and 3 apply only in contexts involving no affirmative governmental aid to or support of religion.

# 18

# SIGNIFICANT FIRST AMENDMENT
# ISSUES

## §A. The Right to Witness

### 1. DOOR-TO-DOOR WITNESSING

The Supreme Court has repeatedly affirmed the right of persons to solicit religious contributions, sell religious books and merchandise, and disseminate religious doctrine on a "door-to-door" basis.[1] Thus, municipal ordinances that condition the exercise of such a right upon the prior acquisition of a permit or license or upon the payment of a "tax" or fee have generally been held unconstitutional. Illustratively, the Supreme Court has struck down a city licensing scheme used by city officials to ban Jehovah's Witnesses from going door-to-door in heavily Catholic neighborhoods and playing a phonograph record that attacked the Roman Catholic Church as an "enemy" and the church of the devil.[2] Similarly, the Court has invalidated a municipal "license tax" that was imposed upon the door-to-door solicitation and evangelistic activities of Jehovah's Witnesses.[3] The Court observed: "Those who can tax the privilege of engaging in this form of missionary evangelism can close its doors to all those who do not have a full purse. Spreading religious beliefs in this ancient and honorable manner would thus be denied the needy. Those who can deprive religious groups of their colporteurs can take from them a part of the vital power of the press which has survived from the Reformation."[4] Finally, the Court has

---

[1]Murdock v. Pennsylvania, 319 U.S. 105 (1943); Largent v. Texas, 318 U.S. 418 (1943); Jamison v. Texas, 318 U.S. 413 (1943); Cantwell v. Connecticut, 310 U.S. 296 (1940).

[2]Cantwell v. Connecticut, 310 U.S. 296 (1940).

[3]Murdock v. Pennsylvania, 319 U.S. 105 (1943).

[4]*Id.* at 112.

invalidated a municipal ordinance that prohibited anyone engaged in distributing literature to summon the occupants of a home to the door.[5]

The Court has noted that a city may protect its citizens from fraud, as by requiring a stranger in the community to establish his identity and demonstrate his authority to represent the cause he espouses. Cities may also limit door-to-door proselytizing and solicitation where necessary to preserve public safety, health, order, and convenience. Strict safeguards, however, must attend any such limitations.[6]

Numerous lower federal court decisions have similarly protected the rights of persons to engage in door-to-door religious activities.[7]

## 2. IN PUBLIC PLACES

The Supreme Court likewise has zealously protected the right to disseminate religious doctrine in public places. Thus, the Court has struck down a city ordinance that prohibited the distribution of handbills on city streets as applied to Jehovah's Witnesses who distributed religious handbills to pedestrians in a downtown area.[8] The Court has also invalidated a city ordinance under which a Baptist minister was convicted for holding a religious meeting on city streets without a permit.[9] In striking down the ordinance, the Court held that no ordinance that gives city officials discretionary authority, in advance, to allow or refuse individuals the right to speak publicly on religious matters could ever be constitutionally valid. The Court did emphasize, however, that a carefully worded ordinance that conditioned the right to hold public religious meetings in public places on the prior receipt of a municipal permit or license could be constitutionally valid if it (1) removed all discretion on the part of city officials by listing the specific preconditions for issuance of a license, and (2) the specified preconditions were constitutionally permissible, such as the preservation of public peace and order. In another decision[10] the Court upheld the conviction of five Jehovah's Witnesses who paraded through a city carrying a sign stating "Religion is a Snare and a Racket," in violation of an ordinance that prohibited "a parade or procession" on a city street without a license. The Court observed that the city officials had no discretion to grant or deny a license, since the

---

[5]Martin v. City of Struthers, 319 U.S. 141 (1943).

[6]See the discussion under § A.2., *infra*.

[7]Weissman v. City of Alamogordo, 472 F. Supp. 425 (D.N.M. 1979); McMurdie v. Doutt, 468 F. Supp. 766 (N.D. Ohio 1979); Murdock v. City of Jacksonville, 361 F. Supp. 1083 (M.D. Fla. 1973).

[8]Jamison v. Texas, 318 U.S. 413 (1943).

[9]Kunz v. New York, 340 U.S. 290 (1951).

[10]Cox v. New Hampshire, 312 U.S. 569 (1941).

prerequisites for obtaining a license were specifically and clearly set forth in the ordinance. Also, the stated purpose of the ordinance and its various preconditions were permissible: preserving the public safety, convenience, peace, and order by preventing conflicts in scheduling; controlling the time, place, and manner of each use of the public streets; and enabling the police to oversee each use and thus minimize the risk of disorder.

In conclusion, the following principles should be noted:

1. No law or regulation that gives government officials unbridled discretion to permit or disallow a religious meeting or service or any other religious activity on public property can be consistent with the First Amendment guarantee of free exercise of religion.

2. A law or regulation that requires a license or permit before a religious meeting or activity may be held on public property can be constitutionally valid if

   a. specific guidelines exist for determining whether to grant or disallow a license or permit, which remove all discretion from those officials who must pass on applications
   b. guidelines only ensure public order, peace, health, safety, or convenience
   c. no less restrictive public remedies to protect the peace and order of the community are appropriate or available

3. A permit or licensing scheme is unconstitutional unless it (1) provides for a ruling on an application within a specified brief period of time, (2) places the burden on the government of showing that the law's guidelines are not satisfied, and (3) makes available prompt, final, judicial resolution of the issue.[11]

Numerous lower federal court decisions have similarly protected the rights of persons to engage in religious activities on public property.[12]

## §B. Prayer on Public Property

The Supreme Court ruled in 1962 that the First Amendment would be violated by official encouragement of voluntary group prayer in the public schools.[13] Since 1962, it has been impermissible for a state, a state agency, or a public school representative to encourage public school students to engage

---

[11]Freedman v. Maryland, 432 U.S. 43 (1977); Walker v. Wegner, 477 F. Supp. 648 (D.S.D. 1979).

[12]International Society for Krishna Consciousness v. Eaves, 601 F.2d 809 (5th Cir. 1979); International Society for Krishna Consciousness v. Bowen, 600 F.2d 667 (7th Cir. 1979); International Society for Krishna Consciousness v. Rochford, 585 F.2d 263 (7th Cir. 1978).

[13]Engel v. Vitale, 370 U.S. 421 (1962).

in the recitation of prayer on public school property, even on a purely voluntary basis.

Several other courts in recent years have applied the Supreme Court's ruling in a variety of circumstances. The Court's specific holding in *Engel* that no officially prescribed religious exercise can take place on public school property has been affirmed by a number of courts.[14] Thus, state laws and school board regulations that have encouraged the voluntary recitation of the Lord's Prayer have been invalidated on First Amendment grounds.[15] One court has prohibited the voluntary recitation of the following prayer before morning refreshments in public kindergarten classrooms: "We thank you for the flowers so sweet; we thank you for the food we eat; we thank you for the birds that sing; we thank you, God, for everything."[16] Another court prohibited the voluntary recitation of a prayer by public school kindergarten students, even though it contained no direct reference to a deity.[17]

Other courts have prohibited the use of public school facilities for prayer and religious exercises prior to or following regular school hours.[18]

The courts have been more tolerant of religious exercises on public university property. To illustrate, the Supreme Court of Delaware has invalidated an absolute ban by the University of Delaware on all religious activities in school buildings.[19] The university's ban was applied so as to prohibit Christian students from meeting periodically in the "commons" rooms of campus dormitories for religious worship. The Court concluded that

> the University cannot support its absolute ban of all religious worship on the theory that, without such a ban, University policy allowing all student groups, including religious groups, free access to dormitory common areas would necessarily violate the Establishment Clause. The Establishment cases decided by the United States Supreme Court indicate that neutrality is the safe harbor in which to avoid First Amendment violation: neutral "accommodation" of religion

[14]Karen B. v. Treen, 653 F.2d 897 (5th Cir. 1981); Johnson v. Huntington Beach Union High School District, 137 Cal. Rptr. 43 (1977).

[15]Opinion of the Justices, 307 A.2d 558 (N.H. 1973); American Civil Liberties Union v. Albert Gallatin Area School District, 307 F. Supp. 637 (W.D. Pa. 1969).

[16]Stein v. Oshinsky, 348 F.2d 999 (2nd Cir. 1965).

[17]De Spain v. De Kalb County Community School District, 384 F.2d 836 (7th Cir. 1967).

[18]Lubbock Civil Liberties Union v. Lubbock Independent School District, 669 F.2d 1038 (5th Cir. 1982); Brandon v. Board of Education, 635 F.2d 971 (2nd Cir. 1980); Hunt v. Board of Education, 321 F. Supp. 1263 (S.D. W.Va. 1971); Commissioner of Education v. School Committee of Leyden, 267 N.E.2d 226 (Mass. 1971); State Board of Education v. Board of Education of Netcong, 262 A.2d 21 (N.J. 1970); Trietley v. Board of Education, 409 N.Y.S.2d 912 (1978).

[19]Keegan v. University of Delaware, 349 A.2d 18 (Del. 1975).

is permitted, while "promotion" and "advancement" of religion are not. University policy without the worship ban could be neutral toward religion and could have the primary effect of advancing education by allowing students to meet together in the commons rooms of their dormitory to exchange ideas and share mutual interests. If any religious group or religion is accommodated or benefited thereby, such accommodation or benefit is purely incidental, and would not, in our judgment, violate the Establishment Clause.[20]

The court distinguished decisions prohibiting religious exercise by public primary and secondary school students on the ground that such decisions did not, like the present case, involve "activity by adult residents of a living complex in common areas generally set aside for the benefit of such residents."[21]

In a similar case, the United States Supreme Court struck down a policy of the University of Missouri at Kansas City that made university facilities available generally to all student groups except those wanting to meet for religious worship and religious teaching.[22] The Court stressed that where a university regulation excludes any group from meeting solely on the basis of the content of the group's speech, the university must show that the regulation is necessary to serve a compelling state interest and that it is narrowly drawn to achieve that end. In rejecting the university's claim that the maintenance of a strict separation of church and state constituted a sufficiently "compelling" interest to justify the abridgment of religious expression, the Court observed:

Our cases have required the most exacting scrutiny in cases in which a State undertakes to regulate speech on the basis of content. On the other hand, the State interest asserted here—in achieving greater separation than is already ensured under the Establishment Clause of the Federal Constitution—is limited by the Free Exercise Clause and in this case by the Free Speech Clause as well. In this constitutional context, we are unable to recognize the State's interest as sufficiently "compelling" to justify the content-based discrimination against students' religious speech.[23]

The Court emphasized that a university can impose reasonable regulations affecting the time and place of group meetings, and can exclude any group that violates reasonable campus rules or substantially interferes with the opportunity of other students to obtain an education. It also held that if a school does not make its facilities available to any student group, it is not required to make them available to religious groups.

[20]*Id.* at 16 (citations omitted).
[21]*Id.* at 18.
[22]Widmar v. Vincent, 102 S. Ct. 269 (1981).
[23]*Id.* at 277 (citations omitted).

A federal court has upheld the constitutionality of a Massachusetts law that stated:

At the commencement of the first class of each day in all grades in all public schools the teacher in charge of the room in which each such class is held shall announce that a period of silence not to exceed one minute in duration shall be observed for meditation or prayer, and during any such period silence shall be maintained and no activities engaged in.[24]

Finally, it has been held that the practice of opening county board meetings with prayer did not violate the First Amendment if no law or regulation required the prayer, if presence during the prayer was voluntary, if no expenditures of public funds were involved, and if the primary effect and purpose of the prayer was public decorum and solemnity at county board meetings.[25]

### §C. Display of Religious Symbols on Public Property

Several courts have ruled on the constitutionality of displaying religious symbols on public property. Many courts have concluded that the maintenance of crosses on public property constitutes an impermissible establishment of religion.[26] One court has observed:

The employment of publicly owned and publicly maintained property for a highly visible display of the character of the cross in this case necessarily creates an inference of official endorsement of the general religious beliefs which underlie that symbol. Accordingly, persons who do not share those beliefs may feel that their own beliefs are stigmatized or officially deemed less worthy than those awarded the appearance of the city's endorsement . . . . The government has no business placing its power, prestige, or property at the disposal of private persons or groups either to aid or oppose any religion.[27]

Other courts have approved of the maintenance of crosses on public property.[28] In one such case, the court emphasized that the cross was maintained

---

[24]Gaines v. Anderson, 421 F. Supp. 337 (D. Mass. 1976).

[25]Bogen v. Doty, 598 F.2d 1110 (8th Cir. 1979).

[26]American Civil Liberties Union v. Rabun County Chamber of Commerce, Inc., 678 F.2d 1379 (11th Cir. 1982); Fox v. City of Los Angeles, 587 P.2d 663 (Cal. 1978); Eugene Sand and Gravel, Inc. v. City of Eugene, 558 P.2d 338 (Ore. 1976); Lowe v. City of Eugene, 463 P.2d 360 (Ore. 1969).

[27]Lowe v. City of Eugene, 463 P.2d 360, 363 (Ore. 1969).

[28]Paul v. Dade County, 202 So.2d 833 (Fla. 1967); Meyer v. Oklahoma City, 496 P.2d 789 (Okla. 1972).

"to decorate streets and attract holiday shoppers to downtown, rather than establish or create a religious symbol or to promote or establish a religion."[29]

One court has held that it is constitutionally permissible for public schools to temporarily display children's artwork in school rooms and halls, even though some of the artwork is religious.[30] The court reasoned:

> Are school children to be forbidden from expressing their natural artistic talents through media including religious themes? Or, are the results of their efforts to be excluded from display and recognition merely because they choose to adopt a religious, rather than a secular subject? The answer should be obvious. To impose such a restriction would more nearly approach a restraint upon the exercise of religion than does the present practice of the school board in permitting such displays.[31]

The Supreme Court of New Hampshire has upheld a state law requiring that all public school classrooms contain a sign stating "In God We Trust."[32] The court observed that such words "appear on all coins and currency, on public buildings, and in our national anthem, and the appearance of these words as a motto on plaques in the public school need not offend the Establishment Clause . . . ."[33]

Nativity scenes on public property during the Christmas season have been upheld on the ground that they have a secular purpose, a primary effect that neither advances nor inhibits religion, and do not lead to an excessive entanglement between church and state.[34] Other courts have ruled that nativity scenes on public property constitute an impermissible establishment of religion.[35]

A federal appeals court has approved the maintenance of a granite monolith bearing the Ten Commandments on public property.[36] The court reasoned that in applying the three-part establishment clause test

> we must strike a balance between that which is primarily religious and that which is primarily secular albeit embodying some religious impact. A tempered approach

[29]Paul v. Dade County, 202 So.2d 833-835 (Fla. 1967).

[30]Chamberlin v. Dade County, 143 So.2d 21 (Fla. 1962).

[31]*Id.* at 35-6.

[32]Opinion of the Justices, 228 A.2d 161 (N.H. 1967).

[33]*Id.* at 164.

[34]Citizens Concerned for Separation of Church and State v. City of Denver, 526 F. Supp. 1310 (D. Colo. 1981); Lawrence v. Buchmueller, 243 N.Y.S.2d 87 (1963).

[35]Donnelly v. Lynch, 525 F. Supp. 1150 (D.R.I. 1981). The United States Supreme Court has agreed to review this decision. A ruling is expected in 1983.

[36]Anderson v. Salt Lake City Corp., 475 F.2d 29 (10th Cir. 1973).

obviates the absurdity of striking down insubstantial and widely accepted references to the Deity in circumstances such as courtroom ceremonies, oaths of public office, and on national currency and coin . . . . Overzealous rigidity may diminish or ultimately destroy the bulwark we have erected against governmental interferences in matters of religion.[37]

The court concluded:

It does not seem reasonable to require removal of a passive monument involving no compulsion, because its accepted precepts, as a foundation for law, reflect the religious nature of an ancient era . . . . The wholesome neutrality guaranteed by the Establishment and Free Exercise Clauses does not dictate obliteration of all our religious traditions . . . . We cannot say that the monument, as it stands, is more than a depiction of a historically important monolith with both secular and sectarian effects.[38]

One court has held that the Smithsonian Institution's physical illustration of the theory of evolution did not constitute the establishment of a "religion of secular humanism."[39] On the contrary, the court concluded that a ban on all references to evolutionary theory in a public museum would itself constitute a violation of the establishment clause.

Use of a county seal depicting a cross, some sheep, and the motto "Con Esta Vencemos" ("With this we conquer") was upheld against the claim that it constituted an impermissible establishment of religion.[40] The court concluded that the purpose of the seal was to authenticate documents and to commemorate the Christian, Spanish, and sheepherding heritage of the county; that the seal had only a benign reference to religion and thus did not have a primary effect of advancing religion; and that use of the seal resulted in no entanglements between church and state.

Finally, use of the national motto "In God We Trust" on all United States coins and currency has been upheld on the ground that such use "has nothing whatsoever to do with the establishment of religion" since its use "is of a patriotic or ceremonial character and bears no true resemblance to a governmental sponsorship of a religious exercise."[41]

[37]*Id.* at 33.

[38]*Id.* at 34.

[39]Crowley v. Smithsonian Institution, 462 F. Supp. 725 (D.C.D.C. 1978), aff'd, 636 F.2d 738 (D.C. Cir. 1980).

[40]Johnson v. Board of County Commissioners, 528 F. Supp. 919 (D.N.M. 1981).

[41]Aronow v. United States, 432 F.2d 242, 243 (9th Cir. 1970).

## §D. Use of Public Property for Religious Services

May public property ever be utilized for religious services? In a leading decision, the New Jersey Supreme Court held that "religious groups who fully reimburse school boards for related out-of-pocket expenses may use school facilities on a temporary basis for religious services as well as educational classes."[42] The court observed that "there was a secular purpose in leasing the school facilities. That purpose was to enhance public use of these properties for the common benefit of the residents of East Brunswick."[43] The court also noted that the "primary effect" of the rental arrangement was not the advancement of religion:

> While we would be naive in refusing to note the obvious advantages to young congregations in the temporary use of school premises, to hold that this scheme primarily benefits religion would be absurd. The community as a whole is benefited when nonprofit organizations of interest to its members prosper.[44]

Finally, the court could find no "excessive entanglement" between church and state:

> [N]o significant administrative function is involved. The processing of an application by a clerk is hardly an act of excessive entanglement. Moreover, inasmuch as no use of school premises is made during regular school hours, there is no need for supervision to insure that no religion seeps into secular institutions. The danger of political fragmentation is miniscule, as appropriations are not involved. The mere fact that some persons in the community oppose the use of the schools by sectarian groups should not prevent these groups from enjoying the benefits of premises which the tax dollars of many of their members helped to construct.[45]

The court cautioned that "truly prolonged use of school facilities by a congregation without evidence of immediate intent to construct or purchase its own building would be impermissible."[46]

Similarly, another court has held that the rental of a state university stadium to an evangelist for religious services did not constitute the establishment of a religion:

[42]Resnick v. East Brunswick Township Board of Education, 389 A.2d 944, 960 (N.J. 1978).

[43]*Id.* at 954.

[44]*Id.* at 955.

[45]*Id.* at 958.

[46]*Id.*

We do not believe that leasing Sun Devil Stadium for an occasional religious service at a fair rental value is an appropriation or application of public property for religious purposes . . . . The twin keys to the use of the stadium are fair rental value and the occasional nature of the use. The lease to a religious group, on a permanent basis, of property on the University campus, for example, would be an entirely different matter because by the permanency of the arrangement, the prestige of the State would be placed behind a particular religion or religion generally. Also, the lease of campus facilities for occasional use, but not for fair rental value, would violate the provision of our Constitution [*i.e.,* of the State of Arizona] as being an appropriation or application of State property for religious purposes.[47]

## §E. Sunday Closing Laws

The Supreme Court has upheld the validity of Sunday closing laws against the claim that they constitute the establishment of the Christian religion.[48] The Court has observed:

[T]he "establishment" clause does not ban federal or state regulation of conduct whose reason or effect merely happens to coincide or harmonize with the tenets of some or all religions.
. . . .
Sunday is a day apart from all others. The cause is irrelevant; the fact exists. It would seem unrealistic for enforcement purposes and perhaps detrimental to the general welfare to require a State to choose a common day of rest other than that which most persons would select of their own accord.[49]

Numerous state and lower federal court rulings have upheld the validity of Sunday closing laws against the contentions that such laws (1) are unconstitutionally vague and uncertain in describing the activities that are either forbidden or allowed,[50] (2) unconstitutionally discriminate against religions that do not observe a Sunday sabbath,[51] (3) "establish" a religion,[52] (4) constitute an im-

[47]Pratt v. Arizona Board of Regents, 520 P.2d 514, 517 (Ariz. 1974).

[48]Braunfeld v. Brown, 366 U.S. 599 (1961); McGowan v. Maryland, 366 U.S. 420 (1961).

[49]McGowan v. Maryland, 366 U.S. 420, 442, 452 (1961).

[50]*See, e.g.,* Hechinger Co. v. State's Attorney, 326 A.2d 742 (Md. 1974); Voronado, Inc. v. Hyland, 390 A.2d 606 (N.J. 1978), *appeal dismissed,* 439 U.S. 1123 (1978); Charles Stores Co. v. Tucker 140 S.E.2d 370 (N.C. 1965).

[51]Raleigh Mobile Home Sales, Inc. v. Tomlinson, 174 S.E.2d 542 (N.C. 1970); State v. Giant of St. Albans, Inc., 268 A.2d 739 (Vt. 1970).

[52]Discount Records, Inc. v. City of North Little Rock, 671 F.2d 1220 (8th Cir. 1982); Epstein v. Maddox, 277 F. Supp. 613 (N.D. Ga. 1967), *aff'd,* 401 F.2d 777 (1967); Mandel v. Hodges, 127 Cal. Rptr. 244 (Cal. 1976); People v. Acme Markets, Inc., 372 N.Y.S.2d 590 (1975).

permissible exercise of the police power,[53] (5) arbitrarily discriminate between those commodities that may be sold and those that may not,[54] and (6) deny the equal protection of the laws.[55]

In a related matter, one court has held that the establishment clause was violated by an order of the governor of California granting state employees paid time off on Good Friday,[56] although the same court a year later approved the validity of a Good Friday holiday for public school employees.[57] Another court struck down a state law prohibiting the sale of alcoholic liquor on Good Friday on the ground that the law constituted an impermissible establishment of a religion.[58]

## §F. The Right to Refuse Medical Treatment

Several cases in recent years have dealt with the right of an individual to refuse medical treatment on religious grounds. Such cases often involve treatment that is apparently necessary to save the diseased or injured person's life. In a majority of cases, courts have upheld the right of an adult to refuse potentially life-saving medical treatment on religious grounds, unless the individual is (1) mentally incompetent, (2) the parent and sole provider of young children, or (3) a pregnant woman. The majority rule was well-summarized by a New York court:

> As a general rule, every human being of adult years and sound mind has a right to determine what shall be done with his own body and cannot be subjected to medical treatment without his consent. Specifically, where there is no compelling state interest which justifies overriding an adult patient's decision not to receive blood transfusions because of religious beliefs, such transfusions should not be ordered. Such an order would constitute a violation of the First Amendment's freedom of exercise clause.
>
> However, judicial power to order compulsory medical treatment over an adult patient's objection exists in some situations. It may be the duty of the court to assume the responsibility of guardianship for a patient who is not compos mentis

[53]Lockwood v. State, 462 S.W.2d 465 (Ark. 1971); State v. Underwood, 195 S.E.2d 489 (N.C. 1973).

[54]Zayre v. City of Atlanta, 276 F. Supp. 892 (N.D. Ga. 1967); Genesco, Inc. v. J. C. Penney Co., Inc., 313 So.2d 20 (Miss. 1975); State v. K Mart, 359 A.2d 492 (N.J. 1976).

[55]Hames Mobile Homes, Inc. v. Sellers, 343 F. Supp. 12 (N.D. Iowa 1972); Southway Discount Center, Inc. v. Moore, 315 F. Supp. 617 (N.D. Ala. 1970); Supermarkets General Corp. v. State, 409 A.2d 250 (Md. 1979).

[56]Mandel v. Hodges, 127 Cal. Rptr. 244 (1976).

[57]California School Employees Association v. Sequoia Union High School District, 136 Cal. Rptr. 594 (1977).

[58]Griswold Inn, Inc. v. State, 441 A.2d 16 (Conn. 1981).

[mentally competent] to the extent of authorizing treatment necessary to save his life even though the medical treatment authorized may be contrary to the patient's religious beliefs. Furthermore, the state's interest, as parens patriae [*i.e.*, protector of its citizens], in the welfare of children may justify compulsory medical care where necessary to save the life of the mother of young children or of a pregnant woman.[59]

The courts have uniformly held that life-saving medical treatment can be administered to a minor child despite his or her parents' refusal to consent to such treatment on religious grounds, unless the treatment itself poses a significant danger to the child. One court has held:

[P]arents . . . have a perfect right to worship as they please and believe what they please. They enjoy complete freedom of religion. The parents also have the right to use all lawful means to vindicate this right.
. . . .
But this right of theirs ends where somebody else's right begins. Their child is a human being in his own right with a soul and body of his own. He has rights of his own—the right to live and grow up and live without disfigurement.

The child is a citizen of the State. While he "belongs" to his parents, he belongs also to his State. Their rights in him entail many duties. Likewise, the fact the child belongs to the State imposes upon the State many duties. Chief among them is the duty to protect his right to live and to grow up with a sound mind in a sound body . . . .

When a religious doctrine espoused by the parents threatens to defeat or curtail such a right of their child, the State's duty to step in and preserve the child's right is immediately operative.[60]

Another court has observed that "it does not follow that parents who wish to be martyrs for their religious beliefs have a right to impose such martyrdom upon their offspring . . . ."[61] When a minor child's life is not in danger, some courts have permitted the child's parents to refuse consent to medical treatment on religious grounds. The Supreme Court of Pennsylvania has held: "We are of the opinion that as between a parent and the state, the state does not have an interest of sufficient magnitude outweighing a parent's religious beliefs when

[59]In re Melidio, 390 N.Y.S.2d 523, 524 (1976). *Accord* Holmes v. Silver Cross Hospital, 340 F. Supp. 125 (N.D. Ill. 1972); Montgomery v. Board of Retirement, 109 Cal. Rptr. 181 (1973); In re Osborne, 294 A.2d 372 (D.C. App. 1972); People v. Duncan, 205 N.E.2d 443 (Ill. 1965).

[60]In re Clark, 185 N.E.2d 128, 132 (Ill. 1962). *Accord* In re Karwath, 199 N.W.2d 147 (Iowa 1972); Muhlenberg Hospital v. Patterson, 320 A.2d 518 (N.J. 1974); In re Sampson, 317 N.Y.S.2d 641 (1970).

[61]Muhlenberg Hospital v. Patterson, 320 A.2d 518, 521 (N.J. 1974).

the child's life is *not immediately imperiled* by his physical condition."[62] Other courts have reached the opposite conclusion.[63]

## §G.  Definition of "Religion" and "Religious"

Occasionally it is important to know how the courts have defined the term *religion*. The First Amendment expressly prohibits the establishment of "religion" and protects its free exercise; the Civil Rights Act of 1964 prohibits discrimination by employers on the basis of an employee's religion; the Internal Revenue Code and several state tax laws exempt religious organizations from taxation; and many other federal, state, and local laws and regulations use the term.

The Supreme Court has noted that "religions" need not be based on a belief in the existence of God: "[N]either [a state nor the federal government] can constitutionally pass laws or impose requirements which aid all religions as against nonbelievers, and neither can aid those religions based on a belief in the existence of God as against those religions founded on different beliefs."[64] The Court added that "among religions in this country which do not teach what would generally be considered as a belief in the existence of God are Buddhism, Taoism, Ethical Culture, Secular Humanism and others."[65]

The Supreme Court has also equated purely moral or ethical convictions with "religious" belief:

Most of the great religions of today and of the past have embodied the idea of a Supreme Being or a Supreme Reality—a God—who communicates to man in some way a consciousness of what is right and should be done, of what is wrong and therefore should be shunned. If an individual deeply and sincerely holds beliefs that are purely ethical or moral in source and content but that nevertheless impose upon him a duty of conscience to refrain from participating in any war at any time, those beliefs certainly occupy in the life of that individual "a place parallel to that filled by . . . God" in traditionally religious persons. Because his beliefs function as a religion in his life, such an individual is as much entitled to a "religious" conscientious objector exemption . . . as is someone who derives his conscientious opposition to war from traditional religious convictions.[66]

One federal appeals court judge, in seeking to ascertain whether a Christian day school's policy of refusing to admit black students constituted a valid ex-

---

[62]In re Green, 292 A.2d 387, 392 (Pa. 1972).
[63]In re Sampson, 317 N.Y.S.2d 641 (1970).
[64]Torasco v. Watkins, 367 U.S. 488, 495 (1961).
[65]*Id.* at 495 n.11.
[66]Welsh v. United States, 398 U.S. 333, 340 (1970).

ercise of the Christian religion, concluded that religious belief depends upon whether the belief is based on either a theory of "man's nature or his place in the Universe," has an institutional quality about it, and is sincere.[67]

Another court, in concluding that the Science of Creative Intelligence (Transcendental Meditation) is a religion, observed that "[c]oncepts concerning God or a supreme being do not shed their religiosity merely because they are presented as a philosophy or a science."[68] The court also observed that such elements as "clergy, places of worship or explicit moral code" need not be present for a practice or belief to constitute a religion.[69] The court concluded that "a belief in the existence of a pure, perfect, infinite, and unmanifest field of life" constitutes a religious belief.[70]

The courts have held that the following beliefs and practices are not religious: a federal law that prohibits the use of federal funds for nontherapeutic abortions;[71] beliefs and practices that tend to mock established institutions and that are obviously shams and absurdities and whose members are patently devoid of religious sincerity;[72] refusal to accept a social security number as a precondition to the receipt of government aid;[73] the use of marijuana by an individual who claimed that marijuana "was the fire with which baptisms were conducted by John the Baptist";[74] the consumption of marijuana by an individual who claimed that it extended and intensified his "ability to engage in meditative communication with the Supreme Being, to attain spiritual peace through union with God the Father and to search out the ultimate meaning of life and nature";[75] the consumption of Kozy Kitten cat food by an individual who claimed that the

---

[67]Brown v. Dade Christian Schools, Inc., 556 F.2d 310, 324 (5th Cir. 1977) (dissenting opinion).

[68]Malnak v. Yogi, 440 F. Supp. 1284, 1322 (D.N.J. 1977).

[69]Id. at 1326. See also Stevens v. Berger, 428 F. Supp. 896, 900 (E.D.N.Y. 1977) ("neither trappings of robes, nor temples of stone, nor a fixed liturgy, nor an extensive literature or history is required to meet the test of beliefs cognizable under the Constitution as religious, and one person's religious beliefs held for one day are presumptively entitled to the same protection as views of millions which have been shared for thousands of years").

[70]Id. at 1324.

[71]Woe v. Califano, 460 F. Supp. 234 (D.C. Ohio 1978).

[72]Theriault v. Silber, 495 F.2d 390 (5th Cir. 1974).

[73]Callahan v. Woods, 479 F. Supp. 621 (D.C. Cal. 1979). But cf. Stevens v. Berger, 428 F. Supp. 896 (S.D.N.Y. 1977).

[74]State v. Brashear, 593 P.2d 63 (N.M. 1979). But cf. People v. Woody, 40 Cal. Rptr. 69 (1964) (use of peyote by members of the Native American Church held to be a "religious" practice).

[75]People v. Collins, 78 Cal. Rptr. 151 (1969).

food was "contributing significantly to [his] state of well-being";[76] the sale of golden eagle feathers by an Indian in violation of the Bald Eagle Protection Act;[77] deeply rooted convictions of Indian heritage;[78] and the promotion of a homosexual life-style.[79]

[76]Brown v. Pena, 441 F. Supp. 1382 (D.C. Fla. 1977).

[77]United States v. Top Sky, 547 F.2d 486 (9th Cir. 1976).

[78]Matter of McMillan, 226 S.E.2d 693 (N.C. 1976).

[79]Church of the Chosen People v. United States, 548 F. Supp. 1247 (D.C. Minn. 1982).

# Appendix

# SELECTED TREASURY DEPARTMENT FORMS

| Form | Title | Purpose |
|------|-------|---------|
| SS-4 | Application for Employer Identification Number | To obtain employer identification number from the IRS for purposes of social security, withholding, and federal income tax returns. Churches with nonministerial employees generally must have an employer identification number. |
| SS-8 | Information for Use in Determining Whether a Worker Is an Employee for Purposes of Federal Employment Taxes and Income Tax Withholding | To obtain an IRS ruling on whether a worker is an employee or self-employed. Ministers and church employees may find this form helpful in clarifying their status. |
| SS-15 | Certificate Electing Social Security Coverage | To waive exemption from FICA taxes. This form is obsolete after 1983. |
| SS-15a | List to Accompany Certificate on Form SS-15 Waiving Exemption from Taxes Under the Federal Insurance Contributions Act | To list employees covered by employer's waiver of FICA taxes. This form is obsolete after 1983. |
| W-2 | Wage and Tax Statement | For employer to report annual income and withheld income and FICA taxes to employees. The IRS maintains that churches must issue this form to every employee. |
| W-3 | Transmittal of Income and Tax Statements | For employers to transmit employee W-2 forms to the Social Security Administration. |
| W-4 | Employee's Withholding Allowance Certificate | For employees to report withholding allowances to assist their employer in determining the amount of taxes to be withheld. |

(Continued on next page)

| Form | Title | Purpose |
|------|-------|---------|
| | | Ministers' wages are exempt from withholding, but ministers can elect voluntary withholding by filing this form with their employing church. Nonministerial church employees should complete this form. |
| 940 | Employer's Annual Federal Unemployment Tax Return | For employers to compute and report unemployment taxes. It is not required of churches. |
| 941 | Employer's Quarterly Federal Tax Return | For employers to report federal income and FICA taxes withheld from employee wages. Due quarterly. Churches must file this return if they are required to withhold federal income or FICA taxes from the wages of any nonministerial employee. Employers reporting only withheld federal income taxes use Form 941E. |
| 941E | Quarterly Return of Withheld Federal Income Tax | For employers to report federal income taxes withheld from employee wages. Employers who withhold both federal income and FICA taxes must use Form 941. After 1983, churches will no longer use Form 941E since they will no longer be exempt from FICA taxes. |
| 990 | Return of Organizations Exempt from Income Tax | For exempt organizations to annually report revenue, expenses, assets, liabilities, disbursements for exempt services, and compensation paid to officers and directors. Not required of churches. |
| 990 Schedule A | Organizations Exempt Under 501(c)(3) | Supplement to Form 990 for organizations exempt under section 501(c)(3) of the Internal Revenue Code. Not required of churches. |
| 990-T | Exempt Organization Business Income Tax Return | Tax return of exempt organizations, including churches, engaged in an unrelated trade or business. |
| 1023 | Application for Recognition of Exemption | To apply for an IRS ruling or determination letter on an organization's exempt status under section 501(c)(3) of the Internal Revenue Code. Churches are automatically exempt from federal income taxes, but may voluntarily file this form in order to obtain written confirmation of their exempt status. |
| 1040 | U.S. Individual Income Tax Return | To compute and report federal income taxes. Used by taxpayers who itemize deductions. Ministers generally must use this form. |

(Continued on next page)

| Form | Title | Purpose |
|------|-------|---------|
| 1040 Schedule A | Itemized Deductions | To report itemized deductions such as large uninsured medical expenses, state and local taxes, interest payments, charitable contributions, and major uninsured casualty losses. |
| 1040 Schedule C | Profit or Loss from Business or Profession | To compute and report self-employment income and related deductions. Ministers who do not satisfy the common law definition of an employee report income on this form. |
| 1040 Schedule SE | Computation of Social Security Self-Employment Tax | To compute and report social security taxes on self-employment earnings. This form is used by ministers who have not elected exemption from social security coverage. |
| 1040A | U.S. Individual Income Tax Return | To compute and report federal income taxes. Used by taxpayers who do not itemize deductions. This form cannot be used by taxpayers who pay estimated taxes, such as most ministers. |
| 1040-ES | Estimated Tax for Individuals | To compute and pay estimated federal income and social security taxes. This form contains four payment-vouchers that ordinarily must be filed quarterly (April 15, June 15, September 15, and January 15) with one-fourth of a taxpayer's estimated federal income and social security taxes, unless he chooses to pay his entire estimated taxes with the first payment-voucher. This form is used by taxpayers whose wages are not subject to tax withholding, such as most ministers. |
| 1040EZ | Income Tax Return for Single Filers with No Dependents | To compute and report federal income taxes. This form is available only to single taxpayers claiming no exemptions for age or blindness, claiming no dependents, and having taxable income of less than a prescribed amount. |
| 1096 | Annual Summary and Transmittal of U.S. Information Returns | To summarize for the IRS all Forms 1099 issued by an organization paying compensation to nonemployees. A church that issues Form 1099 to its minister or any other person must transmit copies of all such forms to the IRS with a Form 1096. |

(Continued on next page)

| Form | Title | Purpose |
|------|-------|---------|
| 1099-INT | Statement for Recipients of Interest Income | To report payment of interest in excess of $10 to recipients. Churches paying interest in excess of $10 to any individual must provide him with this form on or before January 31 of the following year. |
| 1099-NEC | Statement for Recipient of Nonemployee Compensation | To report payment of nonemployee compensation of $600 or more to any individual in any year. Churches use this form to report compensation in excess of $600 paid to ministers who are deemed self-employed, to guest speakers, to evangelists, and to other nonemployees. |
| 2031 | Waiver Certificate to Elect Social Security Coverage for Use by Ministers, Certain Members of Religious Orders, and Christian Science Practitioners | To waive a minister's exemption from social security coverage. Obsolete after 1967. |
| 2106 | Employee Business Expenses | To report travel and transportation expenses incurred in connection with an employer's business. |
| 4361 | Application for Exemption from Self-Employment Tax for Use by Ministers, Members of Religious Orders, and Christian Science Practitioners | To apply for exemption from social security taxes. Available to ordained, commissioned, and licensed ministers who are opposed to social security on the basis of religious convictions. The form must be timely filed. |

# INDEX